Mousa to Mackintosh

Mousa to Mackintosh

The Scottishness of Scottish Architecture

Frank Arneil Walker

in memory of

Jasna

a lifetime love

Published in 2023 by
Historic Environment Scotland
Enterprises Limited SC510997

Historic Environment Scotland
Longmore House
Salisbury Place
Edinburgh EH9 1SH

Historic Environment Scotland
Scottish Charity SC045925

British Library Cataloguing-in-Publication Data.
A catalogue record for this book is available from
the British Library.

ISBN 978 1 84917 328 5

Text Copyright – Frank Arneil Walker 2023

Introduction Text Copyright – Fiona Watson 2023

Copyright – Historic Environment Scotland 2023

All rights reserved. No part of this publication
may be reproduced, stored in or introduced into a
retrieval system, or transmitted, in any form, or by
any means (electronic, mechanical, photocopying,
recording or otherwise) without the prior written
permission of Historic Environment Scotland.

Typeset in Garamond, Brunel and Gill Sans
Printed and bound in Italy by L.E.G.O. S.p.A.

Cover

Mousa Broch and finial from Charles Rennie Mackintosh's
Glasgow School of Art

Contents

	Introduction	9
	Preface	19
1	**National and International** The Ambivalence of Architectural Identity	23
2	**Myths, Brochs and the Geography of Art** Cave to Cashel	49
3	Castles, Palaces and Country Houses Kildrummy to Drumlanrig	75
4	The Palladian Paradigm and the Castle Style Classical Kinross to Castellar Culzean	79
5	Temples, Towers and Turrets Classicism to Romanticism	101
6	The Recovery of Scottishness Abbotsford *Bricolage* to Baronial *Bravura*	125
7	Documentation, Restoration and Revival Anderson and Lorimer	151
8	'that deep and filial affection' Charles Rennie Mackintosh and the way ahead	171
9	National Tradition and the International Style The Scottish Thirties	193
10	Scottishness at the Millennium Modern to Post-Modern	217
11	Envoi	247
	Writings on Scottish Architecture	249
	Glossary	254
	Notes	261
	Bibliography	269
	Acknowledgements	277
	Index	278

Introduction

Fiona Watson

Most European 'nations' are mongrels, a product of the comings and goings, to-ings and fro-ings involved in trade, conquest, colonisation or dynastic horse-trading over centuries and millennia. Scotland is no different. What we call 'Scottishness' is no more than a set of circumstances where people have interacted and continue to interact with their environment and with one another to produce an evolving and developing culture. The search for an essential 'Scottishness' has often been politically motivated, but if the search for the 'purely' Scottish is a can of worms, it is nevertheless possible to identify qualities that reflect a particular response to the experience of living at what has been called 'the utmost ends of the earth' with its own underlying topography and unique history.[1]

And then, of course, there is the Scottish climate, which has evolved like everywhere else to provide periods of more or less warmth and rainfall. Climate change has, for example, affected forest cover, though human activity has played its part, particularly in the lowlands, so that by the later Middle Ages there was a shortage of timber so pressing the Scottish parliament had to intervene.[2] With timber often unavailable for large-scale projects and low-status timber dwellings having disappeared, the survival of stone structures gives a particular impression of building culture.

Woden Law Hill Fort
HES Canmore SC677288

However, architects, especially in more recent times, *did* look back for inspiration and what they saw was monumental stone building. Stone was also plentiful, increasingly transportable and necessary to create the pattern of dense urbanisation with its tall, multi-use buildings.

Of course, what denotes 'Scottish' at any given time is also a thorny issue and it is fascinating to trace the ascendancy of regional aspects of Scotland's culture to become standard-bearers of the 'national' experience. The most obvious example over the last millennium has been the eclipsing of lowland culture as representative of Scotland by aspects of highland history and culture. The relationship between the built environment and the national story is necessarily complex as well as revealing of economic, social, political and cultural circumstances, not to mention the aspirations of those with wealth and opportunity.

It also reflects the very particular, not to mention often fraught, relationship with Scotland's nearest neighbour. England was one of Europe's wealthiest and most precocious medieval kingdoms before transforming itself into a successful colonial power even before the creation of Great Britain. Though the move to a shared Protestantism after 1560 finally brought the two countries closer together, the Scots were previously known as 'the antidote to the English',[3] allying particularly with the French but maintaining close economic ties with many other European nations, including the prosperous Low Countries. From crow-stepped gables to Renaissance palaces, Europe's influence on Scotland is long-standing and pervasive, if usually adapted to Scottish needs and desires or incorporated into older structures or complexes.

But since 1603 (when the Scottish king became king of England too), and particularly, 1707 (when the separate English and Scottish parliaments were dissolved and a new parliament of Great Britain instituted at Westminster), Scotland has been bound politically, economically and often culturally with the more powerful nation south of its border. For over two hundred years, many Scots were eager players in the global imperial project, accruing wealth, industrialising, basking in the potent image of Britain around the world. If they did not deal directly in slaves, then some Scots were certainly slave owners and the trade that set Glasgow on its path to becoming a major city of empire certainly depended on the misery of unfree labour. But if Scotland's inhabitants came to be found across the earth – as colonial administrators, soldiers, missionaries – Scotland itself was transformed by the global forces unleashed by industrialisation and colonialism in a process that is still evolving.

Scotland is renowned for the grandeur of its mountainous landscapes, and more than 50% of the Scottish landmass is indeed upland or moorland. Over 80% of the land is used for agricultural purposes, but only a tiny fraction – around 8% – is planted with arable crops. The dominance of upland landscapes also helps to explain the surprising fact that only around 2.5% of the land is currently urban, mostly located in the Central Belt lying between the Southern Uplands and the Highlands.[4] Scotland is one of the most urbanised countries in the world but its strong romantic affection for its scenic beauty has had a very powerful and enduring cultural effect.

It was very different in the past. For a start, most people lived in the countryside. They were also distributed fairly evenly around the country, reaching a peak of around 1 million by the end of the thirteenth century, compared to 5.4 million today. Given that England's population has risen, albeit not evenly, from around 4.7 million to an estimated 56.5 million over the same period, it should be clear that Scotland's topography and physical attributes such as soil quality have proved a formidable barrier to economic activity and urban development in the more recent past.[5]

Scotland's history begins 10,000 years ago, with the end of the last Ice Age and the arrival of hunter gatherers from Europe. But it was the advent of techniques and ideas associated with the domestication of wild grasses and animals – otherwise known as agriculture – around 6,000 years ago that began to radically transform the landscape. As families began to settle in one place, they became far more attached – literally and metaphorically – to their land, a phenomenon that, while far from unique to Scotland, would eventually facilitate peculiarly Scottish responses to the need to house and protect people and animals, especially once individuals had managed to elevate themselves into chiefly positions. The desire and the means to create visual expressions of power over the landscape were now in place.[6]

The arrival of the Romans in Scotland in the AD 70s lifts the lid a little in terms of written descriptions of the people living largely beyond the limits of the Roman Empire but still connected to it, whether through warfare or trade. But it was Christianity that proved the Empire's greatest legacy, influencing both the belief systems of those espousing the new religion and the physical expressions of the Church's growing power over coming centuries. Certainly, these physical expressions owed much to the common experience of Christianity across western Europe. But they were also a product of the resources available in the northern part of the island of Britain and more immediate cultural influences, particularly Ireland in the early Christian centuries.[7]

The permanent withdrawal of the Romans in AD 414 affected most of what would become Scotland rather less than those parts of Britain which had been more thoroughly Romanised. But there were legacies, both positive and negative. Hill forts – often abandoned before the arrival of the legions, thanks to the increasing stability provided by more powerful chiefs – came back into use after the Roman withdrawal. Over time, smaller forts were superseded by larger, more complex edifices that carefully controlled the space inside to delineate the status of those entering, as at Dundurn in Strathearn and Dunadd in Argyll. But this was not the whole story, as recent excavations of low-lying and extensive palace complexes at Rhynie in Aberdeenshire and Forteviot in Perthshire make clear.[8]

Such developments are surely connected to the first mention of kings – a Christian concept promoting divinely sanctioned hierarchy and authority – from the sixth century. There had clearly been a consolidation of power by certain identifiable groups, including the Picts who had fought against the Romans; the Scots (Irish) who had come across the Irish Sea to help them and subsequently decided to settle in the north-west and the Hebrides; as well as the Anglo-Saxons who arrived in the south of England from Europe in the fifth century, pushed out the Britons already living there to the western edges, before reaching the north of England by the late sixth century. They tried to push further north too but were defeated by the Pictish king of Fortriu at Nechtansmere in AD 685. From then on, the Fortriu kings not only dominated the other Pictish kingdoms but also put client kings into Dal Riata from the 720s.[9] They were also masters of 'designed landscapes', using architecture and elaborate sculpture to make statements about power relationships. Across the various kingdoms in what would become Scotland, this period witnessed a revived interest in building for the dead, with Christian elements incorporated into older ritual landscapes.[10] Such ancestor worship reinforced dynastic continuity so that notions of 'lineage' blended into material culture.

But at the end of the eighth century, a new race – a new threat – arrived in the terrifying form of Norse longships. Though initially focused on hit and run raids on the treasures kept in the various monasteries around the coasts, the Scandinavians soon began to take territory across Britain and Ireland; in 839 they inflicted a terrible defeat on the kings of Fortriu and Dal Riata. Out of this catastrophe arose the kingdom of Scotland – Alba – which officially comes on record in AD 900, though its arrival, never mind its survival, was very far from inevitable.

The new kingdom of Alba (the Gaelic word for Britain, or at least the northern part of it) was essentially a rebranding by the grandson of a king of Dal Riata who had escaped east out of the way of the Norse and assumed the Pictish kingship too. It was a Gaelic-speaking kingdom and remained so for over four hundred years, with new forms of organisation replacing Pictish structures, partly out of the need to combat the Norse. Alba's rulers were warriors, rotating the kingship between two branches of the royal family to ensure an adult male sat on the throne, an Irish system known as tanistry. Raiding south – the only real option – into Anglo-Saxon Northumbria was a tried and tested method of keeping the king's men happy, bringing back slaves, cattle and other booty on a good day; or running into English armies and usually coming off worst on a bad one.

There is little cultural activity to provide evidence for the desires and aspirations of early Scottish society. Hill forts and crannogs were still being used but the low-lying Pictish palaces soon fell into disuse. Now kings needed castles for protection but also to project power and authority through what we would now call 'architecture'[11] – like the brochs of prehistory,[12] castles became lasting dynastic emblems that could outlast a particular king and allow for multi-generational continuity. At the same time, the Scottish Church – rooted in Ireland but long reconciled to the authority of the bishop of Rome – had more than a dozen monastic communities scattered around eastern Scotland, as well as abbeys and churches. Senior churchmen played a key role in Scottish politics and ceremonial events, just as they had under the kings of the Picts.

By the end of the tenth century, the kings of Scotland had succeeded in pushing the border down through Anglo-Saxon territory to the River Tweed, as well as making inroads into the British kingdom of Strathclyde in the south-west. Militarily, they were usually overcome by English armies trying to stop this expansion, but just as often proved useful to English kings seeking to see off their own Norse threat and take or recover territory. At the same time, bloodfeuds within the royal family provided a degree of instability that ultimately primogeniture – inheritance through eldest sons – helped to solve.[13]

As with much of western Europe, modernisation from the later eleventh century was a process of adaptation rather than revolution, in Scotland's case creating an embryonic state out of a loose confederation of various peoples acknowledging the king of Scots as their lord. England was the exception thanks to the Norman conquest of 1066, which saw both Normans and their well-organised ways of doing things transplanted almost wholesale. King David I (1124–53) did much to aid this transformation in Scotland, transplanting Norman friends from England into the south-east particularly, formalising the administration of Scottish towns in return for the payment of customs to the Crown, and speeding up the introduction of the reformed continental monastic orders which were extremely adept at exploiting their growing portfolio of agricultural land and other natural resources, dyking and draining terrain that had previously been unproductive. The runrig system – operated by means of an annual ballot of the strips of land belonging to each community – became ubiquitous in lowland Scotland, spreading many centuries later to the highlands with which it is now associated. Animals were taken up to summer pastures where they were tended from a temporary residential base of timber and stone 'shielings' on higher ground well away from growing crops, another medieval innovation that was instituted first in the lowlands and migrated to the highlands.[14]

But it was animal husbandry that underpinned Scotland's wealth in the later Middle Ages, with sheep replacing cattle as the barometer of affluence, certainly in the lowlands. The cloth manufacturers of the Low Countries bought up Scottish wool often years in advance, and Berwick, on the border with England, became a port of international significance attracting a permanent German and Flemish presence. In the twelfth century, architecturally advanced new abbeys and monasteries were built, presumably on the back of the wool trade. In the following century, state-of-the-art castles sprang up in many different styles, including the shield-like Caerlaverock near the western border with England, the enormous edifice at Bothwell on the River Clyde and noble Kildrummy in Aberdeenshire. Advances in the technology of monumental stone construction would filter down to less prestigious buildings thereby consolidating a skilled workforce that included at least one female engineer in 1302.[15] The human population was increasing too, thanks to the comparatively warm climate, prompting the expansion of towns like Perth, Dundee and Aberdeen.[16]

The next catalyst for change was far more dramatic, though broader economic and climatic changes also played their part from the fourteenth century. In 1296, after decades of peace and prosperity, Scotland and England went to war. Even before a blow was struck, Edward I of England's undermining of Scottish independence had pushed the Scots into a formal alliance with France – England's enemy – a relationship that would endure, for good and ill, for almost three centuries. Throughout his attempted conquest, King Edward attempted to upgrade a few Scottish castles by encircling them with palisades and/or upgrading gatehouses. But this was not Wales, which had few places of strength to occupy. In Scotland, by contrast, there was already a plethora of castles in which to house English garrisons. Indeed, the ubiquity of these garrisons prompted the Scottish King Robert Bruce (1306–29) to deliberately slight the kingdom's fortifications. However, after his death the elites resumed their reliance on well-fortified strongholds, and architecture in general entered a new defensive phase because of the war.[17]

The changing climate, characterised by colder, wetter conditions that brought failed harvests and the outbreak of various animal diseases, made life difficult even before the arrival of the Black Death in 1349. But the wool trade was still buoyant, reaching a peak in the 1370s, until that too began to decline thanks to disruptions in Europe, post-Black Death collapses in population and the desire for higher quality wool in cloth manufacture. But many of Scotland's economic difficulties were replicated across the continent. Nor was it all doom and gloom. New export markets opened to Scotland's raw materials, and fourteenth century inflation seems to have been demand-based and therefore a symptom of economic growth.[18]

There is certainly evidence for wealth spreading across a wider social spectrum between the fourteenth and sixteenth centuries as the population plummeted as a result of the Black Death.[19] As elsewhere in Europe, attempts were made by the country's legislators to stop those of lower status from wearing the silks and furs, pearls and embroidery that supposedly should grace only the persons of richer folk,[20] though the repetition of such legislation suggests it was a losing battle. There was enough money – or credit – too for impressive building works, from royal palaces to cathedrals, baronial tower-houses to bridges. Elite residences also began to reflect new ideas about privacy; kings and nobles no longer wanted to spend most of their time in their great halls along with their retainers but withdrew to private chambers *en famille*.[21]

The fifteenth and sixteenth centuries marked further important developments as the Scottish state increased its reach, instituting a central college of justice in Edinburgh in 1532, for example. This made Scottish kings less reliant on their senior nobility to police the kingdom's constituent parts even if the latter wielded considerable power over their own estates. The choice of Edinburgh for this national seat of justice was no accident either: 'by the 1470s more than half of Scotland's overseas trade passed through its port of Leith; and by the 1530s more than two-thirds did'.[22]

Edinburgh had become Scotland's capital, with the prestige architecture, and, soon enough, overcrowding in the medieval city, to go with it.

By now, too, the kingdom was no longer the Gaelic-speaking, Irish-rooted entity it had been 250 years earlier; the original language of Alba was in retreat from 1300 as Anglo-Saxon Scots made headway, and from 1513 its kings no longer spoke the language of their forebears. The division of the kingdom between highlanders and lowlanders, noted from as early as the thirteenth century, became a gulf that grew increasingly wide. Gaelic culture was no longer mainstream, retreating far from the heart of government, while the outlook and priorities of its chiefs, with some exceptions, were no longer understood and often deemed detrimental to law and order.[23]

This was a time of confidence, the projection of Scotland as a proud, ancient and ambitious kingdom whose independence had been fought for and successfully won against a much stronger neighbour. Not everyone was entirely convinced, of course – the papal ambassador who attended an extravagant hunt involving the construction of a wooden palace complete with glass and innumerable soft furnishings near Blair Atholl in the 1530s marvelled 'that such a thing could be in Scotland, considering that it was named The Arse of the World'.[24]

As further proof of Scotland's status, at least in the eyes of its own rulers, it is certainly true that, while fourteenth century kings had tended to marry local girls, their successors were powerful enough to wade into the European marriage market, with all the costs and benefits that entailed.[25] The marriage of James III with Margaret, daughter of the king of Denmark, in 1469, for example, ultimately brought the islands of Orkney and Shetland to the Scottish crown, expanding the kingdom to its current, and fullest, geographical extent. This diplomatic upgrade culminated in the sixteenth century with the marriage of James V to, firstly, the king of France's daughter, Madeleine, and secondly, to Marie, member of the powerful French de Guise family, who had also been on Henry VIII of England's hit list. Contact with Europe went both ways, too, whether it was the presence of Scottish merchants at the staple ports of Bruges, in modern-day Belgium, then Veere in the Netherlands, or Scottish soldiers serving across the continent but particularly in France.[26]

However, Europe's diplomatic alignments were about to suffer severe upheaval as Protestantism began to find favour with some rulers after the publication of the German priest Martin Luther's *Ninety-Five Theses*, which listed abuses and what he deemed non-doctrinal practices within the Church. While Scotland initially took advantage of the desire of major Catholic powers to keep the northern kingdom in the fold (hence James V's lucrative French marriages), the accession to the throne of his tiny daughter, Mary, Queen of Scots, acted as a catalyst for Scotland's own major break with the past. Unhappy with the French influence exerted by Mary's mother and regent, Marie de Guise, many Scottish lords began to seek support, not to mention lucrative pensions, from Elizabeth I's Protestant England. Then, in 1560, shortly after Marie's death, the Scottish parliament outlawed the mass and approved a Reformed confession of faith, despite its queen remaining Catholic and soon to return to her native land from France.[27]

Overnight, the great Scottish pilgrimage centres – Tain, Whithorn, St Andrews and the royal saint Margaret's tomb at Dunfermline – lost their *raison d'être*. It is true that some Scottish churches suffered at the hands of urban mobs galvanised by the Protestant lords as a prelude to the Reformation. But the extent of the damage was probably limited. Neglect, thanks to the siphoning off by Crown and nobility of a large percentage of ecclesiastical revenues that had once belonged to the Catholic Church, as well as the finishing touches provided by Oliver Cromwell's occupying armies in the 1650s, meant that so many of Scotland's magnificent medieval abbeys and cathedrals are now romantic ruins.[28]

The influence of the Reformation and Protestantism on Scotland has a long and complex history. The avowed intention of the Reformers of 1560 to put a school in every parish was a progressive one, albeit often stymied for lack of sufficient funds, but Scotland's literacy rates soon began to rise. The Highlands were not neglected either, though the lack of Gaelic-speaking ministers proved a hindrance to the advance of the new religion. On the other hand, the Presbyterian version of Protestantism espoused by the Reformers brought them into conflict with their monarchs, whilst giving local male worthies (called elders of the church) unprecedented power over the moral lives of their neighbours. Enforced penitence for all sorts of sins was something the poet Robert Burns was to experience personally two centuries later, but it was those accused of witchcraft who bore the brunt of the Church's desire to regulate lives here on earth.[29]

Queen Mary's son James was at least brought up as Protestant, though he far preferred the hierarchical certainties of Episcopalianism over the egalitarian sympathies of Presbyterianism. An expert on witchcraft, he was also intent on succeeding his childless cousin Elizabeth on England's throne, a distinct possibility now that both kingdoms were Protestant. When that moment finally arrived in 1603 with the Union of the Crowns, King James decamped from Edinburgh in haste, promising to return regularly to his native land. He came back once, in 1617.[30]

Though James desperately wished to unite his two kingdoms, they remained separate, and Scotland was largely governed through parliament and the king's Privy Council. With the royal court no longer in residence, Edinburgh suffered economically, and it is a moot point how much the lack of royal expenditure on both day-to-day consumption and prestige projects impacted on Scotland as a whole. Nevertheless, both Scotland's nobility and Scotland's merchants jumped at the opportunity to move in English circles. Some became extremely rich in this period, while others felt the squeeze.[31]

At the same time, James VI and I was eager to exploit his northern kingdom's natural resources, granting monopolies in, for example, iron smelting (requiring the use of nearby woodlands) to both English and home-grown entrepreneurs, particularly in the Highlands which the king was eager to 'civilise' and exploit. However, it was often major Highland families such as the Campbells of Argyll and the Mackenzies of Kintail – with a long record of advancement through Crown service – who profited most.[32]

Though born in Dunfermline, James's son Charles I knew little about his northern kingdom and, with his Catholic sympathies, was even less able to tolerate Presbyterianism. His increased authoritarianism was offensive in England too, but it was Scotland that boiled over first, beginning a civil war that ultimately raged across the three kingdoms (Ireland too) from 1639 to 1650. Charles lost his head, a Commonwealth was set up under Oliver Cromwell, and Scotland was invaded and held by English troops between 1650 and 1660. This did considerable damage to Scottish pride in their ability to see off the English, as they had done in previous conflicts; now the best Scottish soldiers were deemed to be highlanders, whose bloodcurdling charges led by Alasdair MacColla on the Royalist side under the command of the Marquis of Montrose had resulted in several remarkable victories before Montrose's capture in 1650.[33]

These wars, combined with a further deterioration in the climate, certainly took their toll. But with the restoration of the Stuarts in the person of Charles II in 1660, the Scots chafed at their inability to access the colonial markets the English had been making their own since the beginning of the century. Many leading Scots pressed for an economic union with England, but there was no interest in such an arrangement south of the border. Now the limitations of the union of the Crowns of England and Scotland became clear; if English commercial interests, particularly those of the East India Company (formed in 1600), might in any way be threatened by Scottish commercial activity, the king would not countenance it.[34]

This became even more debilitating during the reign of William III and II (1689–1702), who had been chosen as ruler by both the Scots and the English in place of Charles II's brother, the authoritarian and Catholic James VII and II, by virtue of being Protestant and married to James's daughter. As Prince of Orange in the Netherlands, William had the interests of the Dutch East India Company to further, as well as the English one. Despite the atrocious conditions of the 1690s where famine followed on from bad harvests, the Scots – thoroughly frustrated – took a huge gamble with the hard cash of investors across the country to try to found a colony of their own in the isthmus of Panama in South America. The result was a disaster that wiped out many a fortune.

This played its part in encouraging Scotland's leaders to negotiate an incorporating Union with England in 1707. Though many had misgivings, for those who would profit most from those opportunities, the choice seemed either obvious or unavoidable. Scotland's parliament was subsumed into the one at Westminster, followed in 1708 by the dissolution of the Privy Council, dealing yet another blow to Edinburgh's status as a functioning capital.[35]

The benefits of union took two generations to become unequivocal. In the meantime, dissatisfaction with the new royal dynasty in London – distant descendants of James VI and I from the duchy of Hanover – provoked three rebellions – mostly, but not exclusively, focused on Scotland – aimed at restoring the exiled Stuarts to their British thrones. The last, launched in 1745, had come close to success, but in the end English Jacobites did not rise in sufficient numbers to see off the Hanoverians. However, the brutal aftermath of the Jacobite defeat at Culloden in 1746 highlighted the huge internal divide between lowland Scots, generally Presbyterian and content to be part of the British state, and highland Scots, often Episcopal or Catholic, for whom the Union did not seem to sufficiently represent their interests.[36]

By then, major structural change was already underway as wealth flowed into Scotland from the colonies and revolutionary scientific ideas began to translate into new industrial processes. Glasgow – originally a burgh belonging to its bishop and a comparatively small medieval town – began to expand. Much of this was due to the activities of its tobacco lords, who made vast amounts of money on the backs of slaves working on Caribbean plantations, coming to dominate the European tobacco trade from the 1740s. Their mansions – kitted out with the best materials from around the world – lay in what is now the Merchant City in the heart of Glasgow but what was then the western edge of the town. Later, some Glasgow merchants would buy estates in the surrounding countryside, a habit that was replicated across Scotland as those of comparatively modest backgrounds returned home from the colonies with the wherewithal to join the aristocracy.[37]

However, every part of Scottish society benefited from slavery, including 'weavers of "slave cloth" for the West Indies; fishermen who exported dried fish to feed the slaves; workers in the mills who processed the raw cotton harvested by slave labour; the crews of the vessels who sailed across the Atlantic; and the officials, lawyers and clergymen who administered the slave colonies and the spiritual needs of their owners'.[38] Scotland was not unique in enjoying the economic benefits that accrued from this terrible trade. But nor was it exempt.

There were plenty of domestic developments too. The modernisation of agriculture – begun in England as early as the sixteenth century – began to have an impact on lowland Scotland. Here the old communal runrig system was abolished in a piecemeal fashion when leases came up for renewal in favour of individual tenants who would have every incentive now to invest in new equipment and technologies. Those who found themselves without land drifted into the towns to work in the new factories springing up, a process less dramatic but just as socially disruptive as the more famous Highland clearances.[39]

In the Highlands themselves, many a rebellious Jacobite found himself transformed into a respectable fighting man as part of the British army. But it was also fashionable for young highlanders of both genders to find work for some of the year (perhaps the quieter winter months) in the lowlands, returning home with a smattering of English with which to bemuse their elders. Money had also been poured into infrastructural innovations such as roads and bridges in the Highlands since the early eighteenth century, in the hope of rendering the area more amenable to government control.[40]

The demand for infrastructural investment was not restricted to the north and west, however. Roads began to reach even more remote parts, followed by railways and steamboats, bringing new commercial opportunities to those who had once been unable to take advantage of them. It was not all plain sailing: women in Inveraray, for example, were unable to work in a woollen manufactory set up at Loch Lomond around 1800 because they spent so many backbreaking months of the summer digging peats;[41] others found it impossible to make improvements because landlords would immediately raise rents. But slowly wetlands and peat bogs were drained, rivers contained behind dykes, houses and agricultural buildings built out of stone and slate rather than timber and turf, crowded medieval urban cores abandoned by the wealthy in favour of sweeping new and elegant parts of towns. The classical architectural triumphs built for Scotland's nobility – no doubt competing with the imperial nouveau riche – sometimes required the removal of ancient towns and villages out of sight, as at Inveraray, Hamilton and Scone where the principal residences displayed a new level of sophistication in design and layout.[42] Whether the inhabitants breathed a sigh of relief that their new houses were better built probably depended on how easy it was to heat them.

Scotland rode the imperial wave long and hard, reaping the benefits of access to global resources and international markets while labour at home and abroad remained comparatively cheap (or effectively free, in the case of enslaved people). There was a revolution, too, in how North Britain – as some then called it – was perceived beyond its borders. The well-to-do began to flock north, particularly to the Highlands, now it had been 'rehabilitated'. They were keen to experience its sublime landscapes or the hunting, shooting, fishing and lavish hospitality that Highland estates now offered; from the nineteenth century deer or other game took centre stage rather than the sheep that had replaced the people and cattle in the eighteenth century. This process of rehabilitation, begun with James Macpherson's Ossian, was given an official stamp of approval by the triumphant arrival of King George IV, resplendent in tartan (partially banned by the British government after Culloden) in Edinburgh in 1822, an event presided over by the Border sheriff-cum-novelist Walter Scott. It reached its apogee with Queen Victoria's purchase of her own Highland estate at Balmoral, whereafter the annual pilgrimage north in the autumn became de rigueur for a British aristocracy inclined to feel at home almost anywhere.[43] 'Romantic Scotland', with its misty mountains, its glens and its castles was well and truly born, spawning an enduring legacy that has been both positive and negative. As we shall see, Scotland became one of the world's most industrialised countries; yet its international image remained – indeed remains – resolutely romantic.

Demographic change also brought about transformation. No longer was the population overwhelmingly rural. Towns grew into cities, and villages became towns. By 1900 50% of the population lived in urban centres over 10,000 strong, compared with 17% a century earlier.[44] No longer was the population evenly distributed across the country; it was instead focused along the Forth–Clyde line and up the east coast. Now too large swathes, particularly in the Highlands, were almost empty of people, the transition to what was deemed by those instituting it as improvement much more dramatic than it had been in the south a century earlier. In a culture that prized the oral over the written, the ties of clan over the formal mechanisms of the state, most Highland tenants did not have written rental agreements and so could be removed all at once instead of piecemeal when leases came up for renewal. Initially, they were sent to less productive areas around the coasts but eventually emigration – which had once been the preserve of the wealthy – became a mechanism for change, though many went to the industrial cities of the south as well as the imperial diaspora.[45]

But as with the Black Death, those who made it through did manage to win better conditions for themselves, this time by direct political action. The Crofting Act of 1886 brought security of tenure to Highland smallholders and set up a mechanism to ensure fair rents.[46] Meanwhile, urban poverty, exacerbated by overcrowding and poor-quality housing, led to outbreaks of disease, but violent protest was ruthlessly dealt with.[47]

In many ways, Scotland was a conservative country dominated by landed and industrial interests and the sway of the kirk. But the growing middle classes began to challenge the status quo, finding a focus on the iniquity of landowners presenting their own candidates as local church ministers. This was the key issue of the Disruption of 1843, which saw over four hundred ministers leave the established Church to form the Free Church. With extraordinary commitment and energy, it soon had its own schools, places of worship and even a new college (at Edinburgh University) to train ministers, finally rejoining the Church of Scotland only in 1929.[48]

Much of this made little difference to the urban poor, struggling with overcrowding, inadequate sanitation and long working hours. Disease had long been rife in such communities, but cholera – which did not respect class boundaries – led finally to the construction of public water supplies, beginning with the huge Loch Katrine scheme which brought fresh water and the romance of the Highlands to Glasgow from 1859.[49]

The twentieth century brought the pace of change to even giddier speeds. Whilst deindustrialisation has happened across much of Europe, Scotland – which so closely identified with its great heavy industries from shipbuilding to coal – seemed to experience a crisis of confidence with their demise. The loss of Empire, too, brought the costs and benefits of the Union into closer focus and the issue of independence to be raised, though as yet mostly among a minority of literary folk, who began to explore what defined Scottishness. Scotland had asserted itself culturally from the middle of the nineteenth century, rejecting its place as 'North Britain' but now the focus was on political change and, following the path of Ireland, a move towards 'Home Rule'.[50] By 1885, the UK had responded with the creation of the Scottish Office, a department of government which handled Scottish administrative affairs until 1999, the year when Scotland became a devolved country within the UK with its own directly elected government.

Yet, for others, Scotland represented an escape from the challenges of modernity, a place to seek solace in an idealised rural past that fossilised the 'natural' order of things in favour of traditional elites, as typified by the writing of men like J M Barrie and John Buchan. Such a nostalgic view found correspondence in the mock baronial style of stately-pile-building which allowed those with sufficient cash to recreate that idealised past (albeit with mod cons such as electricity and indoor plumbing essential to civilised living). But this was not the only way of looking at the world through a Scottish lens. Architects like Charles Rennie Mackintosh and painters like Samuel Peploe, Helen Paxton Brown and J D Fergusson embraced the light, at home and abroad, challenging conventional hierarchies and looking to the future.[51]

Conservative Scotland was dealt a severe blow by the First World War, not least by the consequent stagnation of the 1920s, which produced the biggest exodus of the nation's young people in its history, to England and further afield. This, together with the terrible numbers of war dead, placed bargaining power once again – as at the time of the Black Death – in the hands of the workers, rather than the owners of production. Union activity – comparatively unusual before the war – led to mass rent strikes and other collective activity, prompting a battle between police and strikers in the heart of Glasgow in 1916. But the biggest winner was the Labour Party (founded in 1900), which ultimately experienced a rise in support at the expense of the Liberal Party. However, recognition of a particularly Scottish slant on contemporary issues soon found expression in the foundation of the Scottish National Party in 1934.[52]

Rural Scotland was not immune to change either, not least as mechanisation began to make further inroads into the numbers of people employed on the land from at least the 1930s, a trend that rapidly increased in the aftermath of the Second World War with a new drive to make the country self-sufficient. The population decline in the Highlands continued apace, as jobs contracted and the attractions of the bigger cities enticed its young people away, a problem that successive governments and other civic bodies have struggled to deal with, though there are some grounds for optimism in the recent past.[53]

Post-war governments also succeeded in making conditions better. The New Towns constructed across central Scotland from the 1950s were a genuine attempt to deal with overcrowding in the big cities with much thought given to the health and wellbeing of those who would live and work there. At the same time, the effects of globalisation eventually dealt a terminal blow to many of the remaining manufacturing industries that it was intended the inhabitants of these New Towns should work in.[54]

Every era, new technology, trend, or government intervention produces its winners and losers, unintended consequences for good and/or ill. Scotland itself, born in difficult times out of the replacement of the Pictish language and culture with a Gaelic one, has witnessed many convulsions in its sense of self, its valued occupations and ways of life, its projection of itself to the outer world. That Scotland will endure is not at issue. But what form its architecture will take is another question entirely. This book addresses a question about the nature of architecture in Scotland and, as we shall see, how its building culture was shaped and styled over thousands of years by internal conditions and external forces.

Preface

'Scottish architects' attempts to find the holy grail of Scottishness [have] *kept architecture in a state of high anxiety for 500 years'*
Ranald MacInnes *et al, Building a Nation: The Story of Sotland's Architecture*[1]

To attempt to identify the recurring presence of 'Scottishness' in the architecture of Scotland may seem to some daunting while perhaps to others of questionable necessity. And yet it is irresistible. The search is not, of course, new, though it is surely an exaggeration to claim, as some have done, that Scottish architects and architectural historians have engaged in some sort of quasi-spiritual quest for half a millennium. Such a contention has its picaresque attraction but it is not so much this but rather the boldness of the claim which merits attention. For it is its very exaggeration which, paradoxically, does justice to the elusiveness of the quarry and the seductive, if not necessarily neurotic, allure of the search. What is certainly true is that throughout the development of architecture in Scotland – at any rate since the sixteenth century – there have been those architects, and those who commissioned them, who have tried to set their buildings in an intellectual context which, while responsive to continental winds of change, still earthed its radical stability in indigenous culture. This quality of austere stability, as literal as it is metaphorical, in so far as Scottishness has largely been a matter of mass and masonry, can be seen recurring in the country's architecture from the Iron Age drystone walling of Mousa Broch to the smooth ashlar planes of the Museum of Scotland built on Chambers Street, Edinburgh, some two thousand years later.

Mousa Broch and the National Museum of Scotland
HES Canmore DP347523, SC1377175

The chapters that follow attempt to disclose those recurring formal qualities which seem to identify a distinct national characteristic of Scottishness. For some, the word 'national' may have what has been called 'an obscurely disreputable ring';[2] interpreted in its narrow, provincial sense, it may offend. Yet it should not be forgotten that the very idea of nationalism, cultural or political, is of semantic necessity a premise of *inter*-nationalism. The architecture of Scotland, however distinctive it may from time to time appear, is, was, and always will be, a sub-set of European and indeed global architecture. Every history of architecture is the story of the recurrent interaction between national (regional) and international (global) culture. The pendulum may swing one way then the other but the dialectic is continuous.

But this is not, strictly speaking, a history of architecture – at least not in any detailed examination of the social, economic or technological aspects of architecture. What matters here are the formal qualities of architecture, the forms and formal relationships, that seem to identify a distinct characteristic of Scottishness. That this identity is distinct does not mean that it is in every respect unique and exclusive, or that it is always and everywhere to be approved or applied. It is, after all, the privilege of architects to be selective, or indeed to have *any* dealings with whatever may be deemed local culture. Moreover, while affecting different countries or regions in different ways, the great movements in the history of art and architecture nevertheless impose common cultural disciplines across continents; to a very great extent, forms and formal systems are shared. Nor, for a variety of reasons, which may have something to do with local conditions or with the specific emphases of these external influences, are particular national nuances continuously evident. None the less, it is clearly the case that from time to time national and regional variants of the historical styles do exist, and indeed that these variants may themselves in turn act as influences. We readily refer, for example, to Normandy Gothic, Tuscan Renaissance, Bohemian baroque, Belgian Art Nouveau. This does not mean, of course, that we may also speak of, say, Normandy baroque, though we might well talk of Bohemian Gothic. But in such a case, does the adjective 'Bohemian' connote more than the merely locational? Is there perhaps what has been called a national mode of vision 'which asserts itself, always the same in all centuries'?[3] This may be doubted, if only in terms of its constancy. Be that as it may, it is the contention of this book that there *is* a recurring recognisable Scottishness in the architecture of Scotland, aspects of which appear to be present in the country's architecture at different historical moments in different architectural styles.

Scotland has always been open to outside influence. But in this it is neither exceptional nor, surely, outstanding. What makes the country simply 'different' is, to some considerable extent, its geography, namely its particular locational, climatic and geological position on the Atlantic edge, and, to a much greater extent, its history, with its particular accumulation, assimilation and interpretation of cultural ideas. But while geography remains by and large the same, history is forever in flux.

A good deal of what I have to say in the pages that follow is drawn from various publications which I have written or to which I have contributed over the years, from conference papers I have delivered at home and abroad, but predominantly from lectures I have given, particularly those to my students in what was then the Department of Architecture and Building Science in the University of Strathclyde in Glasgow. Conscious at the time I was teaching at Strathclyde that the students I was working with (by far the majority of whom were Scots) knew little or nothing of the architecture of their own country, I introduced a course for third and fourth year students which attempted to give a synoptic view of the historical development of architecture in Scotland from prehistoric times to the work of Charles Rennie Mackintosh. In this I was assisted by some Strathclyde colleagues and several invited academics from other institutions who brought their own specialist knowledge to the subject to the great benefit of my students and me. No contribution was more intellectually stimulating or more enthusiastically delivered than that made by Charles McKean, then Secretary and Treasurer of the Royal Incorporation of Architects in Scotland and later Professor of Scottish Architectural History at the University of Dundee. Charles died while I was beginning to write this book and although I knew he had been seriously ill I had not expected, and was much saddened by, his death. My subject here is one to which he had devoted much time, wedding wide-ranging historical research to polemical advocacy. The phrase 'The Scottishness of Scottish Architecture' was first used, I believe, by Charles as the title of a short essay he prepared in late 1983 to coincide with the Festival of Architecture held in the following year to mark the 150th anniversary of the founding of the Royal Institute of British Architects. Was there, he asked, a 'Scotstyle'? In a letter he wrote to me at the time, enclosing a draft of the essay and asking for my comments, he pointed out that 'the purpose of this essay is not so much to answer the question, as to legitimise the fact that the question itself is a valid one and may be asked'. Bearing in mind the cultural shadow which for long had hung over Scotland from the south, there was a certain irony in the fact that the very phrase 'the Scottishness of Scottish Architecture' was an adaptation of the title Nikolaus Pevsner had given to the Reith Lectures he delivered in 1954 – 'The Englishness of English Art'. For the rest of his life Charles continued to pose the question and provide answers. Like many others I am indebted to his stimulation and erudition. Many of Charles's ideas and insights are to be found in the pages that follow. He would have written this book better than I.

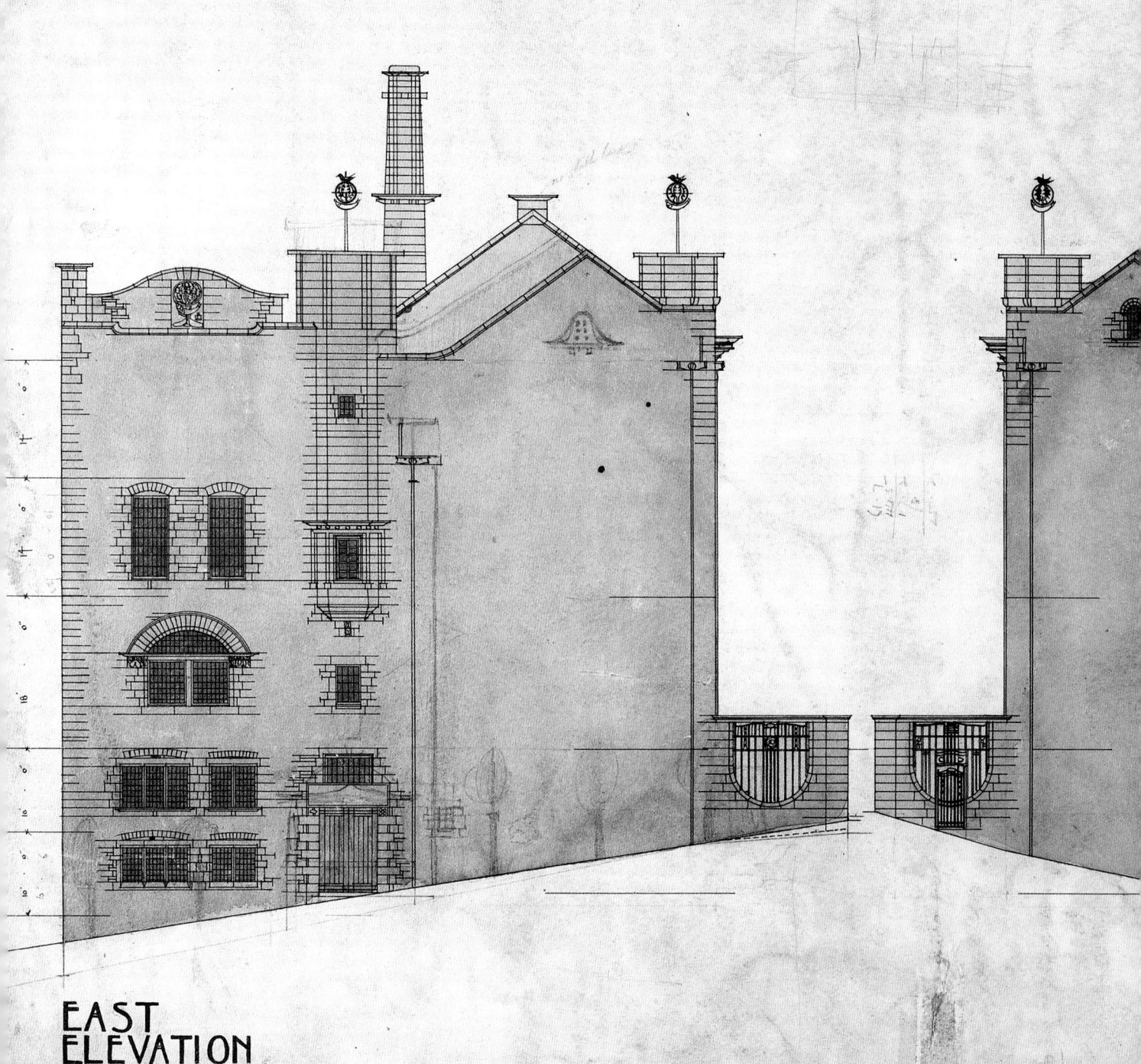

Chapter 1
National and International
The Ambivalence of Architectural Identity

'Architecture is the work of nations'[1]

Charles Rennie Mackintosh

If Mackintosh, an architect who might well be regarded as the most renowned his country has produced, can ascribe the making of his art not to individual genius but to national culture, it is perhaps surprising that attempts to investigate this 'Scottishness of Scottish architecture' have been rare. If, indeed, 'modes of vision are refracted by nationality'[2] – to paraphrase Mackintosh's meaning in the grander language of a renowned art historian – then one may well wonder why it is that, in those synoptic studies of the history of Scottish architecture which do exist, the delineation of recurring national characteristics and qualities is so tentative. Is there a fear of succumbing on the one hand to parochialism or on the other to nationalist arrogance? Moreover, what makes the absence of any detailed exploration of the Scottishness of Scottish architecture all the more strange are the references scattered throughout the texts of these histories to borrowings 'heavily derivative of Continental and English patterns'.[3] Of course, the development of architecture in Scotland has at different moments been influenced by the stylistic forms and building procedures of other cultures – English, French, Italian, Irish, Dutch, German and Baltic architecture among them. If this Englishness, Frenchness or Italianness, for example, can be so readily recognised, why not Scottishness?

But perhaps it is uncharitable to criticise architectural historians for not arriving at a more refined interpretation of Scottishness. After all, despite the time limits applied by some authors, the task entailed in such studies – collating vast amounts of research material and making chronological and stylistic sense out of the historical evidence – is considerable. This is a demanding procedure, and a necessary one, for it is only on the basis of the knowledge accumulated through inventories, gazetteers, lists, typological and biographical studies, and the structured and insightful organisation of this evidence by writers such as Dunbar, Glendinning, MacInnes and MacKechnie[4] that a coherent historical perspective can be framed. But is there not more to the picture than perspective? From the achievements of such historians might it not be possible to begin to induce some understanding of what it is that makes the picture sometimes, in some sense, distinctly Scottish? And might it not also be possible to observe a certain Scottishness at work as a creative propensity on a wider cultural front and from this infer the nature of its impact on architecture? In one context or the other – and here attention is focused on the former – what

Glasgow School of Art
East elevation by Charles Rennie Mackintosh 1897
The Glasgow School of Art

is in question is the character and composition[5] of Scotland's architectural identity.

The most obvious and least controversial response to the question, as those historians I have cited above are well aware, is to adduce geography. What makes Scottish architecture Scottish is that it exists in Scotland. Or, as another writer somewhat naively puts it: 'Scottish architecture, whether it be of churches, castles or houses … is nearly always peculiarly Scottish'.[6] Such assertions, however, like the reduction of Darwinian theory to the trite 'survival of the fittest' dictum, may be true but they are little more than tautology. Even so, it is worth pausing to elaborate the particular implications of the geographical argument.

Since its emergence as a nation over a millennium ago, Scotland's boundaries have remained more or less constant. Lying on the edge of Europe, it is a country all but surrounded by sea having only a relatively short, if sometimes disputed, land frontier with its single neighbour, England. This is hardly a unique condition but it is decidedly not the experience of the majority of countries who may or may not have a coastline and whose land boundaries, often co-terminous with *several* other countries, may have a far from stable history. The permanence and relative inviolability of Scotland's 'long-settled borders'[7] make the locational definition unequivocal. But the relevance of the country's geography to its architecture is not confined to determining territorial limitations. Other factors such as geology and climate are implicit in the geographical argument. Scotland is a land of stone, a fact evident in the walls and roofs of its built structures for several thousand years. If once it was also a land of forests, there is little evidence to suggest that even its medieval builders ever employed 'sophisticated techniques of timber construction such as are known to have been developed in … England and Norway'.[8] Scotland, as Charles McKean, former Professor of Architectural History at the University of Dundee, has observed, has the relatively rare distinction of having no strong surviving tradition of framed timber building.[9] Stone, ashlar or snecked, rubble-built or harled, has always provided the hard shell of Scottish architecture. Scotland is also a land of clouded skies, rain in all its forms and gusting winds, and these climatic concomitants of Scotland's geography have for centuries played their part in shaping the country's architecture. Steeply pitched roofs, austere walls, gaunt gables and small deeply-set windows; these have been the traditional responses to the challenge of the Scottish weather. But to draw attention to these factors is merely to enunciate the particular expression of a general principle. It is no more than reasonable to expect that the architecture of a particular place should be found to be constructed of indigenous materials, be built to answer the environmental demands of the local climate and that such responses should vary from place to place – a Hebridean black house is not the same as an adobe dwelling in Upper Egypt. As historians of architecture have long observed, the evidence clearly suggests that differences in architectural form result from the differing interactions of these geological and meteorological variables. What is more, these architectural responses become, as it were, 'emblematically embedded'[10] in local or national culture.

But is it invariably the case that architectural forms emerge as responses to local environmental conditions? Certainly, for centuries, by far the majority of buildings have been built predominantly from local materials, their forms, formal arrangement and constructional detail adapted to cope with the local weather. Since the early nineteenth century, however, improvements in transportation have made it possible to convey building materials across increasingly vast distances with an ease and frequency previously impossible to contemplate. Today, for example, even at the smallest scale of construction, a family house erected on a Scottish Hebridean island may well incorporate a timber-frame structure from Germany, Spanish slates and windows manufactured in Sweden. Not only that, but the development of new structural materials and methods over the same period of time – steel, laminated timber and, particularly, reinforced concrete – has exploded the spatial and economic options for architects and designers. There is, for example, every likelihood that a simple dwelling in the desert suburbs of Cairo will be a reinforced concrete box, often a box in a high-rise crate of similar boxes. As for the challenge of weather, hot or cold, humid or dry, continued advances in heating, ventilation and air-conditioning coupled with the sophistication of modern building technology in glass and plastics have made almost anything possible. If the current sustainability movement has succeeded in re-orientating designers towards local resources, this has been largely a matter of the generation and conservation of energy. In short, though the sustainability argument may well predicate a return to traditional materials and forms, architecture is no longer necessarily circumscribed by geographical limitations.

And, in any case, geology and climate are not the only factors in play. Design is not merely a matter of ensuring that the building stands up and keeps the wind and rain out. Other questions arise, both functional and formal. Every building has, explicitly or implicitly, a set of functional demands it is shaped to satisfy. These, concerned with the activities and processes to be housed, will be the particular requirements of the individual or body commissioning the building, an agenda worked out by the client with or without the co-operation of the designer engaged. These functional briefs, engendering different building types, will clearly vary over time. If they do reflect the special and possibly unique needs, attitudes, customs and even beliefs of a particular people in a particular place, this is likely to be a relationship of diminishing specificity. National or localised requirements may persist for some building types in some contexts – a Scottish Presbyterian kirk will neither function as, nor look the same as, a Turkish mosque or even a Coptic church – but in today's globalised society such distinctions are perhaps peripheral (one might say parochial) when set against those metropolitan forces which make urban residential and commercial architecture much the same the world over. In effect, the needs of activity and process which may shape a building brief are more and more detached from localised custom and increasingly bound by more objective international criteria. Common functional expectations mean that contemporary buildings – administrative offices, urban hotels, suburban supermarkets, hospitals – look remarkably similar, whether they are built in London, Cape Town, Dubai, Shanghai, Sydney, Buenos Aires or Seattle. While some activities and processes may still call for place-specific solutions, architecture seems everywhere more and more the same.

This might be held to throw the whole question of Scottishness in architecture, indeed all 'attempts to form "national" definitions of architecture'[11] in doubt, but it would be a mistake to misinterpret the trend toward the impersonal and deracinated in this way. However much contingent geographical or functional factors cease to be of significance in shaping architectural form, or, indeed, however impressive advances in computer science applied to the methodology of architectural design may be, every building has, whether acknowledged as such or not, an individual, living and breathing designer or design team. 'National architectural identity, like national identity overall, *is created* rather than dictated by the soil' (my italics).[12] Moreover, as the philosopher Alain de Botton continues, 'It is the privilege of architects to be selective about which aspects of the local spirit they want to throw into relief.'[13] These designers carry their own cultural baggage, exercising their will on the particular problem in hand as a matter of conviction, predilection or simply whim – at least to the extent that client control, technical limitations or economic exigencies permit. This may entail the application of preferences, priorities, or emphases in the ordering of the functional requirements of the brief and the determining of structural, constructional and environmental proposals. Such attitudes may spring from education and from experience, perhaps as much from innate predisposition as from conscious commitment. There are psychological and sociological dimensions to Scottishness. And just as one designer may exhibit an allegiance to the philosophy and formal language of a particular hero-architect and another espouse the traditional values of, say, classicism, so a third may impart a national 'gloss' to architectural identity. This last may be no more than the unconscious emanation of national character or it may be a deliberate effort to express (for example) Scottishness. It has been argued that 'no building of distinction in the past or present has been created by a conscious attempt to imbue architecture with a national characteristic'.[14] But this is far from convincing. Designers may seldom be so confessional or so comprehensively didactic, yet they do, nevertheless, design in a certain way because they enjoy and have an affection for a particular 'style' and a desire to practise it. In any exploration of Scottishness in Scottish architecture, there can be no more pertinent exemplar than Charles Rennie Mackintosh who wrote explicitly of his love and affection for the buildings of his native land – it was, he owned, 'dear to my heart and entwined among my inmost thoughts'.[15] There can be little doubt that, as a consequence, he intended to imbue his work 'with a national characteristic'. And surely he succeeded.

The suggestion that a particular building can be recognisably 'Scottish' (with or without the conscious intention of its designer) implies several things. First, there must be something in the forms or formal arrangement of the building to prompt that recognition. Secondly, there must be something in the make-up of the designer, some legacy of cultural inheritance, to promote, whether consciously or unconsciously, the creation of such forms or relationships of forms. Thirdly, there must be a corresponding element of cultural knowledge and awareness within the observer enabling the inherent Scottishness to be recognised. Where the designer's conscious strategy is strictly revivalist and the Scottish forms and formal relationships of the past are correctly recaptured, albeit while satisfying contemporary criteria of safety, convenience and comfort, these three conditions are readily seen to apply. But is this comparison valid? For example, the orders and details of classicism, are, after all, universally recognised, their provenance and incidence in the past studied and acknowledged: the forms and the rules for their relationships are codified and known, even though these may from time to time be deliberately toyed with or abused. It may make plausible sense to assume that there exist architectural forms and formal relationships which can be classified as 'Scottish'. But what *are* these forms? Can they be recognised in the architecture of the past? And if so, besides the possibility of their slavish revival, is there an alternative present-day transformative reinterpretation possible?

But wait! The elucidation of Scottishness in the buildings of the past may be a perfectly legitimate pursuit for the architectural historian (and a modest attempt will be made to achieve that here), but is the perpetuation and calculated infusion of this Scottishness into contemporary architectural design equally defensible? Commending the latter has its dangers because the infusion can, on the one hand, be weak and, on the other, overcooked. Formal allusions can be insipid and banal or they can be exaggerated and absurd; the intellectual commitment of the designer can be superficial, flirtatious or naive, or it can be pious, self-indulgent, even alarmingly chauvinistic. Some may take a quasi-moral line believing that at a time when Scotland as a political entity is acquiring an increasing measure of self-confidence and self-government there is a parallel need to know and understand our tradition and to express our growing cultural self-knowledge in some contemporary way. It is difficult to take exception to such an attitude, whether or not it is prompted by a political agenda – certainly there is every reason to welcome the study of all aspects of Scotland's history, a subject long neglected in education policy – but it would be unwise to justify the pursuit of Scottishness, whatever that may turn out to mean, on self-righteous moral grounds. That it is *our* tradition may be an *added* reason for an interest in, and enthusiasm for, such Scottishness but, as art historian E H Gombrich writes, 'Without first liking a game, a style, a genre, or a medium we are hardly able to absorb its conventions well enough to discriminate and understand.'[16] Perhaps it is just as well that, in the struggle to identify and come to creative terms with this Scottishness, 'our inclination to enjoy … precedes any attempt to rationalise or defend that enjoyment'.[17] And (it may be wise to acknowledge here) this is no less true for the architectural historian than it is for the designer. But the questions remain. What are these forms that interest and delight us? What do we mean when we speak of a Scottish architectural identity?

Identity is an intriguing concept and not without a certain ambivalence. It has been well described as a 'situational construct':[18] an awareness of separateness, individual distinction, even uniqueness, but also, paradoxically, a sense of sameness, common or shared values and attitudes. Any person may be said to have his or her own specific and unique identity, but that same person will also share identity in varying group contexts, often in layered relationships. Any nation will have its own identity, the agreed common identity of a diversity of 'lesser' identities, which will in turn be subsumed in a 'greater' regional or continental identity. In one case, the identity is established by exclusion, in the other, by inclusion. There are countless areas at countless levels in which such inclusive or group identity may be apprehended – left-handed people, Gaelic speakers, golfers, Presbyterians, and so on – in all of which the apperception has both an internal and an external aspect. The fact that as a result of upbringing, education or employment a person may identify himself or herself as 'working class' or 'middle class' does not diminish his or her unique exclusive identity as an individual, though it may of course qualify thought and action. Such identity effects, at any particular time, an implicit contract between the given and the received, between nature and nurture, between the values, attitudes and skills. of the individual and those of the group. Identities can develop, change or cease, but every identity, constant or ephemeral, subsists within this kind of dialectic, that is to say, where oppositions, contraries, polarities meet. To reiterate, identity is *ambi*-valent.

Cultural identities are no different. For culture, as the literary scholar Cairns Craig has observed, 'is the site of a dialogue, it is a dialectic, a dialect'[19] and this 'condition of "being between" is not the degeneration of a culture but the essential means of its generation'.[20] What then of architectural identity? Here, too, identity is shaped by a continual interplay *between*, on the one hand, as has been stressed above, 'the geography of art',[21] the influence of the place, its landscape, geology, climate and, not least, the consequent 'national character', *and*, on the other, the changing modifications of time evident in the unfolding history of art and architecture. There are many examples: Brunelleschi shaping a specifically Tuscan Renaissance in which the proto-Renaissance of the Florentine past was melded with new ideas drawn from the Roman Antique; the Dientzenhofers, *père et fils*, creating a uniquely Bohemian baroque which combined strong local traditions of Gothic with new forms and formal relationships emanating from seventeenth century Italy; or Robert Adam linking the romantic skylines of baronial Scotland with the ordered symmetries of international country-house classicism to evolve his own Castle Style (see Chapter 4). Whatever else architecture may be about, it is about place (space) and time. It is a dialogue between place (space) and time, whether we speak of architecture in terms of its theoretical conception as idea, or its physical manifestation as building, or its perceptible apprehension as experience. In different places and at different times, architecture is always attempting to resolve the dialectical claims made by the history of art and the geography of art. The tide of ideas, of ideological and formal changes in architecture time and again shifts the sands on many different shores.

Scotland's shores are very much 'at the edge'. Life clings to the fringed verge of Europe; beyond is the vast ocean. Remote on the rim, far from the fecund ease of the warm south, the Scot's experience has often been hard and raw, the table frugal, the labour austere, the 'walk as a thinker … not by the meadows and wheatfields, and the green lanes, and the ivy-clad parish churches, where all is gentle and antique and fertile, but by the bleak sea-shore which parts the certain from the limitless, where there is doubt in the sea-mew's shriek, and where it is well if, in the advancing tide, he can find a footing on the rock'.[22] Written in the middle of the nineteenth century, this description of the thinking Scot with its haunting evocation of a landscape at once physical and intellectual may paint a picture too romantic for twenty-first century taste but, in its contrasting imagery, it points up the significance of life at the existential edge. Scotland's peripheral position and perspective have affected its cultural experience. The tidal surges in cultural history, the great movements in European art and architecture, often taking longer to reach Scotland's shores, have at times become diluted, diffused or discontinuous in their impact. While the globalisation of the modern world may have altered our perspectives on time and space, remoteness from the centre has in the past made our culture now provincial, now distinctly unique.

This is not, of course, to imply that one culture is superior to another or to suggest that the periphery is abjectly submissive to the cultural imperialism of what might be called the core. It is true that Scotland, invariably engaged with its immediate and more powerful neighbour, England, has at times been forced to, or has chosen to, accommodate itself to differing forms of cultural colonialism – the widespread linguistic suppression of Lallans and Gaelic by English is perhaps the most pervasive and permanent example of this. It is also true that there have been other cultural influences at work in Scotland (an edge is, after all, as American urban planner Kevin Lynch has pointed out,[23] also a path) and that these have often been welcomed as counterbalancing forces. Scots have followed several paths, some English, some Irish, some French, some Norse, and some from the Netherlands and Germany. The search for Scottishness is not a search for some wholly exclusive identity but rather an attempt to determine those qualities of material, building technique and, above all, *form* that appear to be characteristic of the architecture built in that geographical area we know today as Scotland. Many of these qualities will be shared in a common stylistic identity; some may not.

There are two comments to be made here. The first is a general one, a reiteration of the importance of the give-and-take of cultural exchange, something already mentioned and again best expressed in Cairns Craig's words.

> the terms in which we analyse culture have to operate within the dialectic not simply of history but of geography: culture *takes place* and a place exists only because it has boundaries that have to be crossed entering and leaving it, and it has histories and archaeologies inscribed in it. Culture is a place of dialogue [24]

The second observation is more specific, namely that it is as a consequence of this dialogue that no art or architecture can be solely national. There is no Scottish architecture that is not, or was not, in some way international, ie *inter*-national, that was not to some degree imported from, or influenced by, the architecture of another place or other places.

> The architecture of Scotland is chiefly of foreign origin. But the richly turreted chateau and the church of flamboyant Gothic, when transported from France to our own rugged shores and sterile moorland, adapted themselves … and under-went a series of … changes which suited better to the available materials, to the climate, and to the tastes and habits and wants of the people of Scotland.[25]

But this is perhaps to overstate a case that might have been more persuasively made by putting the adverb 'chiefly' in italics – 'The architecture of Scotland is *chiefly* of foreign origin'. For, while it must be acknowledged that nothing is built in a cultural vacuum, there is surely an argument to be made for the stand-alone validity of some vernacular architecture. Such buildings are thirled to place and are, as it were, out of time. It is true that even in prehistoric time there may be a degree of interaction between place and place. It may even be the case that some ancient 'will to form' is even then imperceptibly at work in man's mind. But, in so far as the nature of the place remains largely unchanged (a condition now scarcely imaginable), vernacular architecture remains more or less the same. It preserves its appearance, its physiognomy is unchanged – at least until it may be obliged to adjust in some way to exposure to the modern world. Even then, by virtue of its timeless age, an expression may linger, and the vernacular impart a continuing if elusive nuance to national architectural identity, like the persistent if enigmatic grin of the Cheshire cat.

In the introduction to his seminal study of *The Historic Architecture of Scotland*, John Dunbar has suggested that 'Not until a particular framework of historical events was imposed upon the foundations of geography … did a distinctive national style of architecture begin to emerge'[26] in Scotland. But though this view, shared no doubt by many, might seem blind to the archaeological past, it fully acknowledges the importance of the interplay of history and geography in the making of a national culture. Furthermore, it can be argued that in the context of what may, by way of distinguishing it from the rude conventions of vernacular building, be called polite or self-aware architecture – the kind of architecture Dunbar clearly has in mind – what begins under foreign tutelage may by adaptation and over time become, to all appearances and interpretations, an indigenous *national* tradition. Such a tradition may, in the continuing dialogue between the geography of art and developments in the history of art, be subjected to the challenge of immigrating ideas as a result of which further assimilation and adaptation may take place *or* the old order may succumb or accommodate itself to the lineaments of the new. In the shaping of architectural identity, there are continuities and discontinuities to be observed.

Architectural continuities over time, the continuities that occur in the history of art, are those forms and formal relationships that architectural historians and critics categorise and recognise as the 'styles' – in the western tradition, Egyptian, Classical, Byzantine, Romanesque, Gothic, Renaissance, Mannerist, baroque, Rococo, Neoclassical. Such classification is, of course, imperfect – circumscribing and debilitating the individual work of art – but it is a necessary and useful tool with which to order perception and thought. Architectural continuities that occur in the geography of art, the qualities that characterise the enduring face of a place, such as the Scottishness which is the subject of this book, are more multiplied and much more controversial. The Swiss art historian Heinrich Wölfflin referred to them as those 'national physiognomies which cannot quite be effaced even by imported styles'.[27] Indeed it may be that the spirit of certain places may have an affinity with certain historical styles – and vice versa. If Wölfflin is right to conclude that the Italians have 'a plastic talent' which found its finest expression in the sixteenth century or that the Germanic north's 'painterly faculty' flourished in the baroque period, it does not seem unreasonable to infer that Scottishness, too, may have its more fulfilled moments.

The continuities invoked here are continuities of form: those forms and formal relationships of a national character or tradition, those of a supra-national invasive nature (the styles) and those evolved in the recurring dialectic between the two which perpetuate a *trans*formed indigenous tradition. Form articulates the practical demands of the programme from drawing board to building site; form mediates architecture from conception to perception; and, not the least significant aspect of this investigation, it is form that can carry a residual symbolic charge long after its original functional *raison d'être* has ceased to apply. In the repeated cultural confrontations which occur between the geography of art and the history of art, national character – Scottishness – may at times persist, imparting a distinct cast to imported norms and forms; at other times it may be barely or equivocally evident; while at still other times it may be overwhelmed, as persuasive external forces provoke a crisis or discontinuity in architectural identity. But the question remains. What are these putative 'Scottish' forms and formal relationships?

Chapter 2
Myths, Brochs and the Geography of Art
Cave to Cashel

'Mythology is what never was, but always is …'
Stephen of Byzantium, sixth century AD

Early in the opening chapter of Nikolaus Pevsner's *The Englishness of English Art*, the published version of his 1955 Reith Lectures, the writer pauses to consider whether his investigation of 'a national point of view … in appreciating works of art and architecture' is a justifiable pursuit.[1] No doubt this seemingly hesitant approach to his subject was much conditioned by the noxious influence fascist nationalism had had on the world over the previous 20 years, a tragedy of which he, as a German émigré, was well aware. But the argument he chooses is a much less emotive one: 'in an age of such rapid communications as ours, with such an international force as science in command, with daily press and illustrated journals, with wireless and film and television keeping everyone all the time in touch with all other parts of the world',[2] there is little reason, he writes, to present a case that in any way 'glorifies' nationality. The dangers of the 1930s and 40s may now have been largely (if not totally) consigned to history, but in today's globalised world the same appeal for internationalism might well be made, and

Ossian's Stone, Sma' Glen
Photograph by Rev James Bannatyne Mackenzie c1870
HES Canmore DP157063

made in spades. Pevsner, however, dismissing his misgivings, quickly rejects these objections to his thesis, arguing that the study of what he prefers to call 'the geography of art' is not to be understood as narrowly and exclusively nationalistic; on the contrary, it can only succeed in widening our appreciation and understanding.

In a comparable sense it could be suggested that to speak of 'a national point of view' or 'national character' in a pre-historic[3] context, or even in a pre-medieval age when the first hesitant historical chronicles were being painstakingly penned in some monastery scriptorium, is to intrude a wholly alien and anachronistic concept. Tribal, ethnic or religious frontiers may well have existed then but there was no *national* entity and no *national* consciousness. There was no country called Scotland, while those people to whom the name Scots has been given were no less Irish. Nevertheless, because in those distant days life was fundamentally bound to place, the impact of local geography on local culture was direct, intense and ineluctable. Early Scotland (to continue the anachronism) may not have experienced any unifying political structure or understood the concept of nationhood, but it was, geographically, geologically and environmentally, essentially the same place it is today. There is good reason then to look for the built beginnings of Scottishness in those place-defining structures that have survived from the Neolithic, Iron and so-called Dark Ages. And in this search there are two related avenues of investigation. There is first the poetic route, exploring the evidence of myth and legend, mysterious, sometimes absurd, often illuminating and provocative, and, secondly, that more scientifically mapped track through the past that leads along the stone-strewn road of archaeology. If the 'idiom of legend'[4] appears fanciful in its assertions, then the statements of archaeology are often so hedged about with caveats and equivocation that it sometimes seems that myth may be as near to the truth as the prosaic resolutions of science. Imagination, after all, precedes corroboration.

In forging[5] a claim for an ancient Scottish culture, no myth was more powerful than that of Ossian. The work of this third century Celtic bard was first collated in *Fragments of Ancient Poetry, collected in the Highlands of Scotland, and translated from the Gaelic, or Erse Language* by the Inverness-shire schoolmaster and tutor James Macpherson in 1760. Within a few years came more of the same in the form of the six books of *Fingal, an Ancient Epic Poem* (1762) and the eight books of *Temora* (1763), both epic poems written by Ossian and translated by Macpherson. Then, in 1765, *The Works of Ossian* appeared. More wraith-like than real, as subsequent controversy was to reveal, blind patriarchal Ossian nevertheless seemed to speak for a people whose confrontation with the forces of nature was raw and immediate, his verses a chronicle of the heroic and tragic events of a pre-Christian Caledonia. Whether his life and work had any verifiable historical substance scarcely seemed to matter. Macpherson's claim to have rescued these 'lost' works from the obscurity of a centuries-old oral tradition which, until then undefiled and unremarked, had preserved the folk-memories of an all but forgotten past on the periphery of Europe, was not without foundation. He had travelled throughout the Scottish Highlands and Islands transcribing line upon line of the Gaelic verse he heard there. If he was never able satisfactorily to demonstrate the provenance of his published verse,[6] the simple almost biblical cadence of his 'translations', their rhythmic description and narrative cast in heroic, melancholic vein against a background of wild nature, chimed with a contemporary passion for the sublime and convinced many of their authenticity.

Macpherson's 'translated' verses were soon themselves translated into several European languages. In Germany, Herder, Goethe and Schiller were smitten; Herder dreamed of visiting Scotland to 'hear the living songs of a living people'.[7] Napoleon was never without a copy of Ossian. The American polymath Thomas Jefferson thought 'this rude bard of the North the greatest poet that has ever existed'[8] and planned to learn Gaelic in order to read the original texts. In Scotland, Robert Burns, who had read and admired the work of 'Ossian, prince of poets',[9] made a pilgrimage to the bard's reputed grave at Glen Almond near Crieff. And Walter Scott, more than sceptical that Ossian had ever sung, praised Macpherson for 'giving a new tone to poetry throughout all Europe'.[10] Perhaps paradoxically, some of the earliest seeds of European Romanticism were gathered from stony Scottish soil.

In terms of literary scholarship, all this – or at best most of it – might be, and was, deemed a fraud. But it was more than mere deception, it was myth, albeit (to what degree is still disputed) manufactured myth. As would happen with Teutonic legend, the Scandinavian and Icelandic sagas, and the epic *Kalevala* of the Finns, a lost legacy of story and song had been resurrected: Macpherson had 'heard the voice of the north'[11] and given English words to it.

Moreover, Macpherson had done this at a time when the cultural fortunes of Scotland ran at a low ebb, flushed away in a tide of Anglicisation that had begun with the Union of 1707, swelled in the aftermath of two disastrous rebellions and had culminated in a wave of cultural imperialism flooding across what had become North Britain. Against this background he had contrived to re-establish a specifically Scottish culture within a European context. He had conflated nature and nation in myth in the precociously romantic recognition that 'nature creates nations',[12] that in the experience of so-called primitive people the fundamentals of the human condition were most keenly felt and most powerfully expressed. As one commentator on the Ossian controversy has written, 'the philosophical, as opposed to the antiquarian, justification of the poems is to be found in the doctrine of the Noble Savage'.[13]

To look for the roots of 'Scottishness' in architecture in the mythic world of Ossian may seem at best fanciful, at worst absurd. It is surely compounding deceit to search through writing which must be regarded as substantially an eighteenth century fabrication in order to construct even the mistiest of pictures of third century building. Yet, at a time long before the advent of scholarly scientific archaeology, there were many whose fascination with the 'noble savage' led them to speculate wildly on the shelters and dwellings built in the natural landscape and even some who, persuaded that the 'arts have their infancy as well as man',[14] drew from these imaginative excursions into the past an explanation for the origin of the architectural styles. Throughout the eighteenth century 'Adam's house in Paradise'[15] appeared in many forms, from the temple-tainted primitive hut believed to be the timber-framed progenitor of all classical architecture (for, after all, as the philosopher Herder had proclaimed, 'the Greeks, too ... were savage'),[16] to the bent timber shelter interwoven with branches and foliated forms hypothesised as the prototype of Gothic.[17] More fundamental still, and decidedly less tendentious, was the increasing evidence that the first homes made by human hands were no more than holes in the ground or caves in the rock. It is impossible to know what, if any, references or clues Macpherson may have gleaned from the fragments of genuine Gaelic verse which he collected and studied; all that can be said is that whatever allusions are made in the poems to the built shelters of Ossian's time must reflect how he and many of his contemporaries imagined their forebears had lived.

It is, of course, raw nature which predominates in the settings of Ossian's tales – the sea-girt, river-riven, rock-hard landscape of Scotland's mountains, moors and forests. Here, survival is a struggle. In this hostile world, shelter is found from the elements and from the enemy 'in the cave of the rock'[18] and in those tribal redoubts where 'the people gather to the hall',[19] where fires burn, warriors feast and the 'bards advance, and sing, by turns, the praise of Ossian'.[20] This is a spare and gaunt architecture of 'echoing halls', lofty and bare, of mossy towers rising from massive walls, of fortified enclosures and bleak but sheltering courtyards. But, as the historian Hugh Trevor-Roper has comprehensively exposed, it is an architecture of dreams, an anachronistic fantasy of 'late medieval ideas of knight-errantry, halls, towers, palaces'.[21] As a highlander, Macpherson would have been familiar with the legacy of medieval castle and tower-house building so evident in the Scottish landscape and doubtless his romantic imagination imbued his verses with this imagery. And there is, too, corroboration of Iron Age precedent: the evidence of aerial photography enables the archaeologist Anna Ritchie to speak of 'the large timber halls that we assume Pictish chiefs

Ossian's Stone, Sma' Glen
Sketch and plan by James Skene 1832
HES Canmore DP353461

lived in'.²² Aerial photography has also revealed the post-hole traces of large Neolithic hall structures at Balbridie in Aberdeenshire and Claish near Callander, sub-rectangular in plan with rounded ends, the former astonishingly dated to between 3600 BC and 3250 BC.

There are also vague hints in the Ossian texts of another architecture, an architecture of death, where man is laid to rest 'in the narrow house'²³ – a reference perhaps to the long-stalled burial chambers common across Scotland and the north-western seaboard of Europe. There is every likelihood that Macpherson, whose Ossianic verses frequently advert to tombs of 'heaped-up earth'²⁴ and grey gravemarkers 'half sunk in the ground',²⁵ was also familiar with those mysterious standing stones and burial cairns that were to be found scattered across the Scottish landscape and in particular in those areas of the Highlands and Western Isles he had trawled for Gaelic verse. Nor was he the first to set them in mythical context.

In *A Description of the Western Isles of Scotland*, which appeared in 1703,²⁶ almost 60 years before Macpherson introduced Ossian to the literary world, Martin Martin had documented and commented on these same enigmatic stone monuments. His is no poetic epic filled with 'chronological absurdities'²⁷ but a dispassionate account prepared at the instigation of some influential members of the Royal Society in London: he recounts what he saw, his descriptions objective, sometimes even augmented by dimensional information. Nevertheless, though plausible reasons for many of the ancient stones and structures he observes can be inferred from funerary procedures, defensive needs or the requirements of Christian worship, much remains a mystery to him, a mystery whose only explanation seems to lie in the mythical beliefs held by the local population. Of high standing stones on Lewis, for example, he records that 'Some of the ignorant vulgar say, they were men by enchantment turned into stones; and others say, they are monuments of persons of note killed in battle'.²⁸ Of the huge rock-cut chamber on the Orkney island of Hoy known as the Dwarfie Stone, 'The common tradition is that a giant and his wife made this their place of retreat.'²⁹ Such, too, is the nature of the legends that Macpherson would plunder. Less fabulous perhaps are local convictions that, for example, stone circles were 'Places design'd to offer Sacrifice in time of Pagan Idolatry' when the sun or the moon was worshipped.³⁰ Whatever cannot be satisfactorily explained is consigned, if reluctantly, to legend or else attributed to foreign influences. Martin's highlanders and islanders speak 'Irish' (meaning Gaelic – Martin, born in Skye, was himself a Gaelic speaker), a genuine affinity which, though he does not elaborate, extended well beyond the linguistic to encompass the full cultural spectrum. On Skye and Mull he visits many forts 'erected on the coast … and supposed to have been built by the Danes. They are called by the name of *dun*, from *dain*, which in the ancient language signified a fort.'³¹ While the text might be interpreted to suggest that Martin may have doubted the attribution to the Danes, it should be stressed that these few speculative attempts to construct a historical socio-cultural context for the antiquities he encountered are little more than asides. Alongside his other discussions of topography, climate, flora and fauna, husbandry, food and drink, and diseases and their cures, Martin is concerned to comment on the *built* environment and, while what he has to say on this subject can hardly be considered to be archaeology, he does assemble and to some extent categorise a considerable amount of evidence. Caves, cairns, standing stones, stone circles, brochs, forts, castles, crosses, chapels and houses (both under ground and above ground): he identifies and describes each. It is scarcely an exaggeration to say that, while dimensional data are minimal, attempts at dating wisely eschewed and interpretations sometimes dependent on popular myth, Martin's are the first documented steps along the archaeological road.

Those sparse 'architectural' references which are to be found in Macpherson's Ossianic writings are, of course, entirely tangential to his wider poetic concerns. Brief and infrequent as they are, however, they invoke a picture of rugged unsophisticated structures utterly in thrall to the Scottish landscape and climate. No delineation of the precise form these primitive buildings may have taken emerges from the texts, other than – and this is not insignificant – a marked sense of enclosure circumscribed somewhat imprecisely by high towered walls. Natural man is portrayed as a 'lonely dweller of the rock'³² who, when he builds, perpetuates the sheltering function of the cave to create an architecture which is materially at one with its environment but in which the worlds of outside and inside are distinct and separated by stark walls of stone. There is no suggestion of trabeation or of the open-framed 'primitive hut' with its intimations of gridded coextensive classicism. This omission was, in a fortuitous way, apposite, for Macpherson's romantic literary allegiance to the mythic heritage of the nation had its contemporary parallel in the world of architecture where, 'in the second half of the eighteenth century, the concept of "national" slowly came to mean "other than classical"'.[33]

Martin's 'architectural' comments (if his descriptions of the man-made structures he found on his travels can be so termed) are altogether different to those few references to be found in Macpherson's Ossianic writings, devoid of any poetic intent, brief and, it seems reasonable to assume, reliable. There are stops on his itinerary where his observations seem almost to anticipate something of Macpherson's imagery. On Barra, for example, he remarks on the high stone wall of Kisimul Castle noting that 'within the wall there is an old tower and a hall',[34] elements that in fact do repeatedly figure in Ossian's tales. Kisimul may date from as early as the eleventh or twelfth century but is much more likely to have been built in the fifteenth; in either case something like a millennium, give or take a century or two, separates it from the time of Ossian. The few other castles and the various stone crosses, chapels and churches which Martin mentions are similarly distant from pagan times. But he does identify a number of distinct built forms and structures from the pre-Christian era which can serve here as a crude, limited, but convenient typological basis for a more matter-of-fact investigation in search of the first signs of built Scottishness, an examination in which these prehistoric remains are neither impenetrable enigmas nor the stimuli to flights of fancy but instead viewed in the light of contemporary knowledge, albeit at a very superficial archaeological level. The search is not for scientific revelation but for architectural intimation. The built 'types' are stone circles, burial cairns, forts, duns and brochs.

Calanais, Isle of Lewis
Historic Environment Scotland

On Tiree Martin found 'several great and small circles of stone'.³⁵ At Calanais on Lewis (Martin calls the village 'Classerniss'), he marvelled at the magnificent stone circle and pillared avenue set out with the 'most remarkable stones for number, bigness, and order'.³⁶ These lines and rings of standing stones, and their timber predecessors, which were erected across the Scottish mainland and islands from the end of the third millennium BC until the beginning of the first millennium BC, appear to have served some socio-religious need associated with astronomical orientation, astrological interpretation or burial rites (or perhaps a combination of these beliefs). In many cases, burial cists or low settings of stones containing cremated remains have been found within the rings. Martin regarded the Lewis circles as places 'appointed for worship'.³⁷ On Orkney he saw the Ring of Brodgar, grandest of all Scotland's stone circles with a diameter of 103 metres, and thought it a place designed perhaps 'to offer sacrifice'.³⁸ Almost nothing, however, is certain; imagination may make a poetic leap to construct some plausible scenario but it remains the case that 'we are dealing with functions that can probably never be recovered by archaeological means'.³⁹ But if we do not know what took place in terms of function, we know unequivocally what *took place* in terms of form. Stone circles may not qualify to be considered architecture in any generally accepted sense of the word but they clearly do as architecture does: they define place. This definition, this curving enclosure, this earliest conceptual echo of speleological space, remains a fundamental formal gambit in architecture.

If the enclosing geometry of standing circles seems to recall, however notionally, the circumscribed dwelling space of the cave, cairns may be said to recreate that space to house the dead. Neolithic cairns were noted by Martin on Lewis and Skye. Though he was not, of course, in the business of field research, his suggestion that these 'heaps of stones', as he also described them, were associated with funerary rites and burial was percipient. Circular or oval in plan, these masonry mounds conceal single or many-chambered tombs. Access passages, lined and roofed in stone slabs, lead to inner spaces planned in the form of a circle, square or elongated rectangle. Several distinct types, classified by plan arrangement and location, have been found. The most spectacular example is the burial cairn at

Ring of Brodgar, Orkney
HES Canmore DP069234

Ring of Brodgar
Drawing by Waller Hugh Paton 1873
HES Canmore DP069234

Maeshowe, a site Martin could not have known when he made his visit to Orkney as the tomb was not opened until 1861. Here the built hillock, circular in plan and shaped as a shallow dome, is some 35 metres across and rises more than 7 metres. Housed within, at the heart of the mound, is a 4.6 metre square space, the burial chamber, reached by a 9 metre-long passage. The chamber is walled in stone, with standing stone buttresses at each corner and a 'vaulted' roof formed by long horizontal stone slabs corbelled inwards from each of the four walls. Constructed around 2800 BC (before the Egyptian pyramids), Maeshowe is exceptional in the scale and detail of its interior chamber and it is this that makes it 'one of the finest buildings of prehistoric Europe'.[40] In its external form, however, it does not depart from the norm. As mounds of heaped random masonry rising low in the landscape, cairns assume a shape deriving directly from their construction, their circular plan form often clearly defined by stone kerbing. This highly visible circumferential edge may be further reinforced by a ditch and in some cases, known as 'ring cairns', by a ring of standing stakes or stones. In many cairns the opening to the access passageway has been blocked and masked so that the purity of the rubble-built form is unimpaired. Covered in turf, these cairns might well be the mouldering 'green mounds' and 'green tombs' that appear from time to time in Ossian's verse. In others, however, the entrance is to some extent dramatised by placing it at the centre of a concave wall cut across the edge of the mound,[41] perhaps the first instance of a designed facade in the architecture of Scotland.

In Martin's text the words 'fort' and 'dun' appear to be interchangeable; indeed in his commentary on the island of Lewis he refers to 'several natural and artificial forts … which are called *dun*'[42] and on Mull to 'some old forts here called *duns*'.[43] Furthermore, in certain passages the structures he describes would, in contemporary terminology, be considered 'brochs', a term Martin does not use. The distinctions are best clarified in archaeologist Graham Ritchie's definition:

> Duns are small drystone forts, which share some of the structural features of brochs – checked entrances, guard-cells and mural features – but do not have the all-round hollow-wall construction or the height of the latter.[44]

It is clear that in describing a fort on Lewis as 'composed of large stones … of a round form, made taperwise towards the top, and … three stories high: [where] the wall is double, and hath several doors and stairs, so that one may go round within the wall',[45] Martin is speaking of a broch. Similarly, several forts on Skye – 'they are round in form, and they have a Passage all round within the Wall'[46] – must also be regarded as brochs. On the other hand, his remarks on a fort on Bernera, 'having a vacuity around the walls, divided in little Apartments',[47] may be more likely to refer to a dun. From the point of view of the professional archaeologist the fact that Iron Age brochs appear to be a development from earlier duns and that duns themselves perhaps overlie earlier forts may be matters of protracted concern and controversy. In the architectural perspective these fine distinctions of date and detail are of lesser interest than the built form which is evolving. In this respect it is the broch that commands attention. Surprisingly, in a brief description of the islands of Orkney and Shetland, Martin does not mention perhaps the finest of all surviving brochs at Mousa.

Brochs are by no means as old as cairns or stone circles or other field monuments from Neolithic times. Unique to Scotland, they are generally thought to have been built during a period stretching from the beginning of the first century BC to the end of the first century AD and perhaps beyond. It might be reasoned, then, that given the permanence of their masonry structure and their relatively dense incidence in western and northern Scotland, they might have been familiar elements in the fabricated third century landscape of Ossian and his contemporaries. But this is not so. Macpherson makes no mention of brochs, nor do his verses describe anything that might be construed as such. And this is all the more surprising as on his tour through the Highlands and Western Isles in search of literary fragments for his patriotic project he must surely have encountered these ruinous inscrutable towers. At Glenelg, for example, where he collected a variety of poetic passages from the local minister, could he have missed the brochs of Dun Trodden

Maeshowe, Orkney
Section and plan copied from James Farrer monograph 1875
HES Canmore DP149336

Fig. 2.

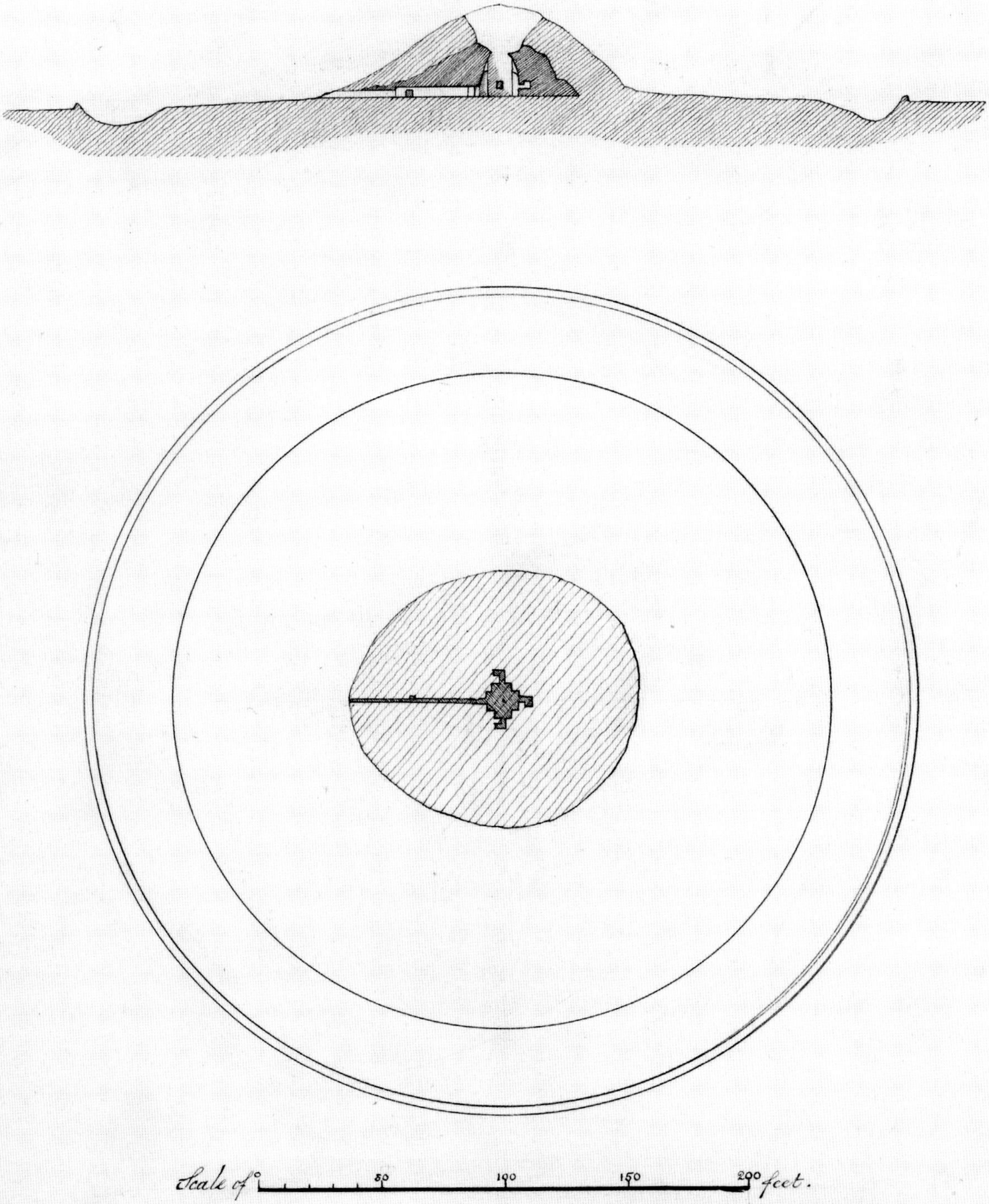

Scale of 50 100 150 200 feet.

Plan and Section of Maeshowe.

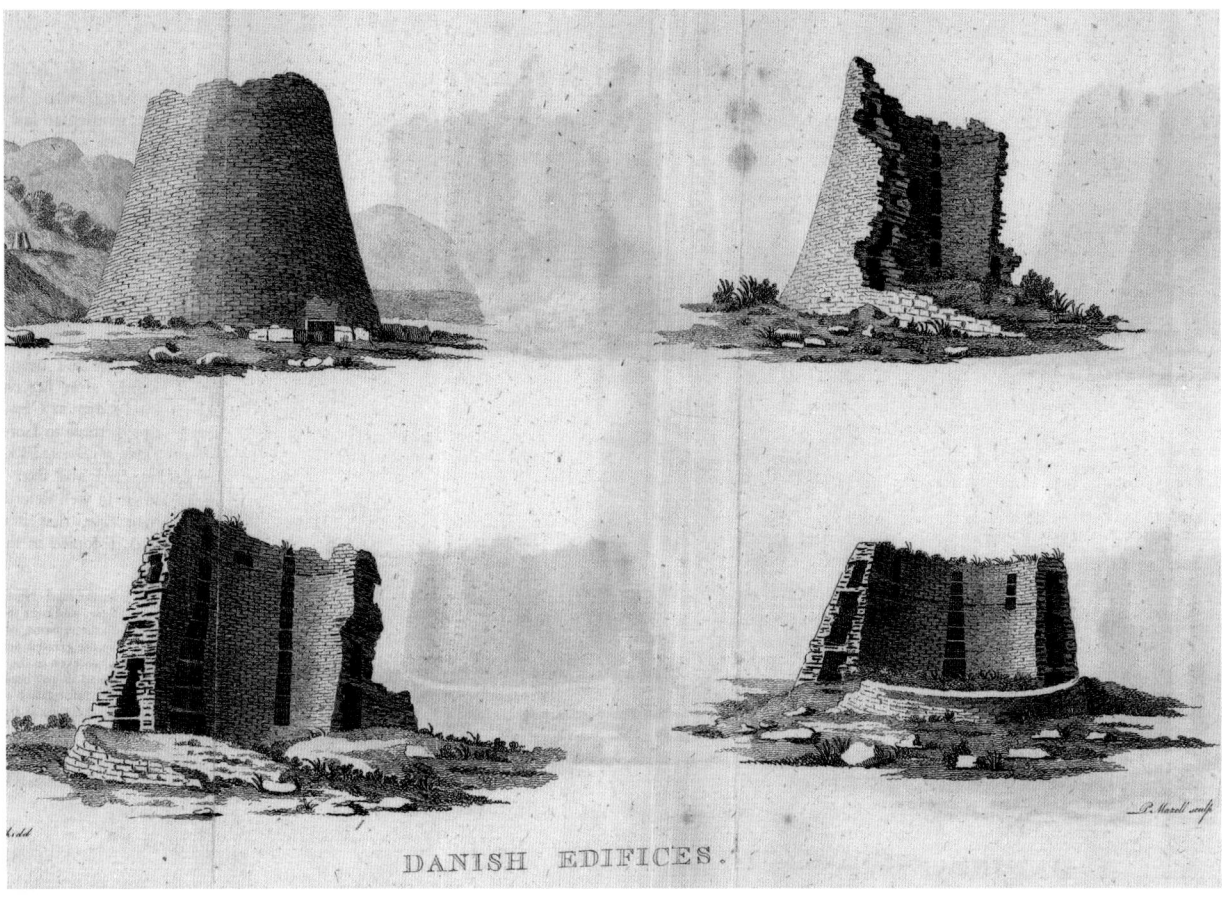

Dun Telve and Dun Troddan, Glenelg
Engravings from *A Tour in Scotland and Voyage to the Hebrides* 1772
HES Canmore SC1009604

and Dun Telve? Or continuing to Skye, did he not pass by the mighty masonry wall of the Dun Beag broch? Other travellers were stopped in their tracks by these strange sights, compelled to contemplate their sculptural power and speculate on the kind of people who built them. And just as Martin Martin had noted such things, in 1772 Thomas Pennant was struck by these same monumental ruins to such an extent that the descriptive passages in Volume 2 of his *A Tour in Scotland and Voyage to the Hebrides* were accompanied by no less than four illustrations drawn by the artist and engraver Moses Griffith. It is hard to believe that Macpherson did not know of these unique structures and difficult to understand why he did not adduce their puzzling and evocative forms to his myth-making purpose.

Moses Griffith's engravings of the great broch of Dun Telve at Glenelg portray the ruined tower's facing masonry, both inside and out, as what appears to be dressed freestone laid in regular courses. This is a falsification of the reality for the broch's stonework is random in size and coursing, but it is an aesthetic strategy which, by its simplification and regularisation of overall texture, does not diminish the lithic mass and indeed tends to intensify the tapering cylindrical form of the structure. Here again is that circle found in the stone rings and cairns, now drawn up into three dimensions, the palpable earth-bound solidity of the broch emphasised by the batter of the walls and the absence of any openings. Here again is the sheltering sense of enclosure from elements and enemy. Here, too, is the almost tactile presence of stone. It is the sheer austere power of this form, uninterrupted externally by any penetration or void other than the low entrance doorway, which dignifies the broch and which makes

Dun Beag, Skye
Engravings from *A Tour in Scotland and Voyage to the Hebrides* 1772
HES Canmore SC1009584

it the first and perhaps even the most memorable carrier of an essentially architectural Scottishness. Nor is it only the clarity of the broch's stony form that embodies this 'national' character. The walls that rise to shape the tower are in fact hollow, the outer and inner skins of masonry separated by a more or less continuous gap within which curving stair flights ascended to the upper storeys and, presumably, the roof, and which must also have afforded some measure of protection from wet and windy weather. It is true that at the lowest level of what are known as *solid-based* brochs there was no such cavity but there, too, the wall was often penetrated by short passages leading to mural cells. This double-skinned or hollowed-out wall, sometimes referred to as an 'inhabited wall', would persist as a recurring feature in Scottish building. And we might add a further form, though its existence is to be inferred rather than seen: the conic form of the rush-covered timber roof that must have risen from the broch parapet. In short, by the beginning of the Christian era, there already existed a handful of simple but distinct formal devices evolved through what, paraphrasing Pevsner, we might call the 'geography of architecture' that have remained intermittently recognisable throughout the historical development of architecture in Scotland.

To the standing circles, cairns, duns and brochs identified by Martin more than three hundred years ago, modern archaeological research has, from its beginnings in the late nineteenth century, added a succession of roundhouse dwelling types stretching across prehistoric time from the Neolithic period through the Bronze and Iron Ages well into the first millennium AD. At Skara Brae on Orkney, where the building of sheltered space seems to have begun

around 3000 BC, the earliest excavated houses are circular in plan. Later, more remarkable built remains to be seen there have squarish rooms with rounded internal corners. The drystone walls of the settlement's compacted cluster of dwelling spaces and passages are embedded to the wallhead in packed midden material which forms turf-covered banks and mounds reminiscent of the curving flanks of burial cairns. At Jarlshof, an agglomeration of circular dwelling units of greatly differing dates abut and overlie one another in a similar palimpsest of rounded cellular spaces. Among these various remains are Bronze Age houses, dating from around 800 BC; circular or oval in plan, they have peripheral cells formed by drystone buttressing extending into the central space. Nearby are later Iron Age dwellings, again circular but without any internal buttressing. The diameter of such roundhouses, whether constructed in stone or timber, varies across the country from 5 metres to more than 15 metres. In some examples, developing skills in timber construction may have made a more open plan possible or an inner ring of wooden posts may have helped support the structure of a thatched or turfed roof, as happened in those parts of the country where timber was more plentiful and the outer walls of the roundhouse instead of being built in stone were framed and laced with wattle-and-daub. The ruinous vestiges of a broch which may have risen as high as 13 metres are also to be found at Jarlshof. Constructed in part from the stone quarried from the ruins of the broch are four Pictish wheelhouses from the first millennium AD. These later roundhouses, which are confined to the Outer Hebrides and Shetland, have stone piers radiating inwards from the perimeter wall like the spokes of a wheel, some of the recesses formed being semi-domed. Again, no doubt this is the masonry version of a timber prototype.

Vestigial evidence of prehistoric timber construction is widespread across Scotland, though the cropmark discoveries at Balbride and Claish already mentioned are exceptional in date. Post holes, rain ditches and the occasional survival of worked timbers buried in boggy ground have contributed to archaeologists' knowledge, particularly of those roundhouse dwellings that were common in pre-Roman times. If the Neolithic dating of Balbridie and Claish is correct then there is little question that the inhabitants of Bronze and Iron Age Scotland were 'capable of building large circular wooden houses'.[48] The hundreds of crannogs to be found in Scotland are part of this legacy. Safely surrounded by the water of a river or an inland loch, these artificial or adapted islands were also dwelling structures built to a circular plan. In some examples timber piling driven into the river or loch bed supported a framed platform on which the dwelling could be constructed. In other cases, where timber was scarce, underwater mounds or cairns, some natural, some man-made, might be revetted with wooden piles to form a secure foundation. The completed dwelling was the familiar roundhouse with its circumferential wall and conic roof of thatch or turf.

Given the repeated application of the circle in the planning of prehistoric structures, it is not surprising that some archaeologists should speak of a 'generalized "roundhouse" type'.[49] Perhaps some sense of the enclosing security of the cave lingered in these dark dwellings. Perhaps over the centuries the very process of building was ritualised in some way that would have honoured this and other folk memories. But practicalities must have been crucial. Nothing could have been more conducive to the continuity of the roundhouse type than the ease with which a circular structure could be set out on site – all that was needed was a tethered cord drawn tight as a moving radius – while the adoption of the circle ensured the most economic relationship of materials used to dwelling space achieved. This ubiquitous model persisted well into the first millennium AD. During the Roman occupation, close to the time of the second invasion north around AD 140, several broch towers were still being built in areas of the country far from the concentrations of earlier brochs, though by whom and for what reason is a matter of controversy. A particularly marked development of the time was 'the emergence of circular stone houses to replace timber prototypes',[50] among them the distinctive wheelhouses already mentioned. But while the roundhouse model survived, a change was underway.

The relatively brief Roman presence in Scotland, from AD 80 until the early years of the third century, was exploratory and punitive, always

Skara Brae, Orkney
HES Canmore DP273476

essentially military. Occupation did not mean settlement. No significant civil buildings were erected. It is a peculiarly paradoxical fact that the only Roman 'temple' to be built in Scotland was neither unequivocally a temple nor built along orthogonal classical lines. Located near the Antonine Wall at Camelon, 'The old Temple upon the Bank of the River Carron', as the English antiquarian and clergyman William Stukeley described it in 1720,[51] was a beehive-shaped structure constructed in dressed freestone, almost certainly the work of legionary masons. A single round-arch entrance opened to a *circular* chamber, 8.5 metres in outside diameter, under a domed vault which was open at the top at a height of 6.7 metres. Known as 'Arthur's O'on' (Arthur's Oven), its purpose remains unknown. Stukeley suggested it may have been used by soldiers in their devotions while others have proposed that it was some form of triumphal monument commemorating a Roman commander and his victory. In 1743 it was demolished to provide stones for a new weir being built nearby, a loss which so upset Sir John Clerk of Penicuik that in 1760 he had a replica built as a doocot over the pedimented entry to the stables block at Penicuik House.

This small enigmatic structure, built on a circular plan like the houses of the tribes the Romans were attempting to subdue, stood alone. No other civic or religious monument has survived. But the legions did leave their mark on the landscape. The Antonine Wall, a defensive earthen barrier, was raised across the country from coast to coast, numerous forts were built to house the legionary forces, lines of watch

Arthur's O'on, Stenhouse
Drawing from *Itinerarium septentrionale* 1726
HES Canmore DP266263

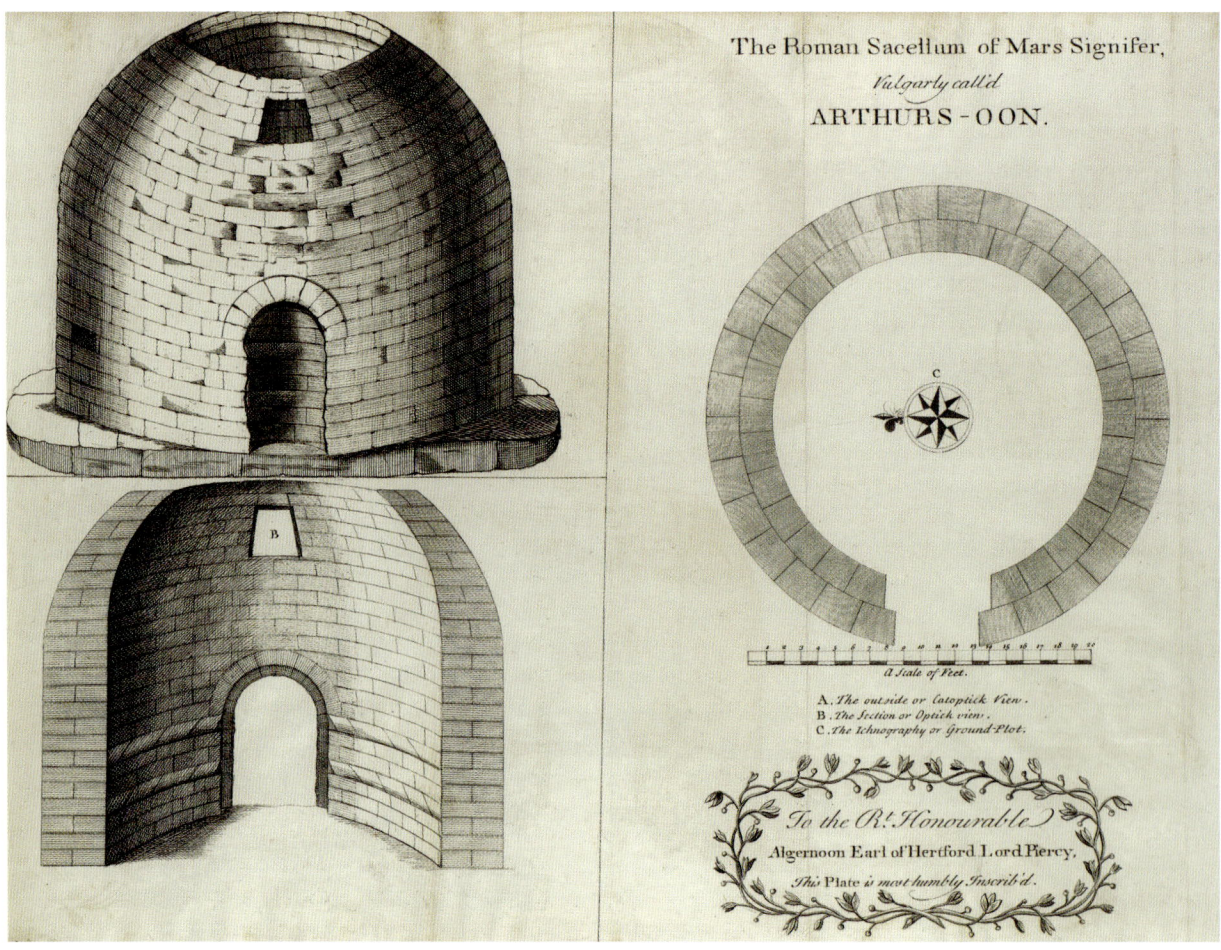

towers sprang up, but no permanent settlement was established and no significant civic buildings erected. Nevertheless, the indigenous population must have been awed and impressed, not only by the extent of the Antonine Wall and the organising power that lay behind such an intrusion on the natural landscape but also by the implacable rectilineal geometries of the military camps. It is possible that some of the native Caledonii, whether as prisoners or labourers, may have observed the strange rites followed by the Roman surveyors in establishing the main ordinates of the precise orthogonal geometry that governed the internal dispositions of their forts. These were complex procedures sanctified by tradition and, as the renowned architectural historian Joseph Rykwert has elaborated,[52] carried out with all the compelling rigour of ritual. It is much more likely, however, that in the immediate aftermath of the occupation, the local tribes would have wandered over the forts and camps, some of which had been destroyed, some of which had been abandoned, marvelling at the walls, ramparts, barracks, bath-houses, workshops and granaries and above all the unfamiliar strict formal order that determined both the shape of these individual buildings *and* their spatial inter-relationship.

Rectangular or sub-rectangular buildings were not, of course, unknown in pre-Roman Scotland. Few examples survive in stone but it is probable that many others were constructed in timber, the evidence for which has in most cases long disappeared. But nothing was built with the invaders' precision, a precision that was both geometrical and technological. Once the Romans had gone, however, this legacy may have begun to influence indigenous building. South of Hadrian's Wall, where the occupation was longer, more pervasive and more settled and the built evidence of Roman construction more apparent, the number of rectangular-plan structures greatly increased, though the building of circular or oval enclosures still continued.[53] North of the border things happened more slowly; there the change 'from round to rectangular seems to have taken place sometime in the middle of the first millennium AD'.[54] Though slow, the change proved permanent and the evidence sufficiently widespread and convincing to lead some archaeologists to conclude that the impact of orthogonal planning had wrought nothing less than the 'wholesale reorganization of domestic space'.[55] However unconscious its assimilation, however

hesitant and protracted in its effect, in setting the challenge of new, historically developed ideas against the old geographical conventions of place, the cultural impact of the Roman invasion had, for the first significant time in the Scottish context, provoked architectural change.

From those Dark Age centuries between the departure of the Romans and the Norse invasions, the architectural evidence remains scant. In the west, where the kingdom of the Scots, Dál Riata (Dalriada), united Argyll and Lochaber with Antrim, the old ways of building continued in the eremitic and monastic landfalls established by Christian missionaries from Ireland. On Eileach an Naoimh in the Firth of Lorne a small group of ruinous stone buildings survives from the sixth century, 'the finest example in Scotland of a Celtic island sanctuary'.[56] Among the remains are a circular grave enclosure, a burial cairn and a once-domed double-beehive drystone structure. Of the settlement founded by Columba on Iona, also in the sixth century, only the enclosing *vallum*, three stone standing crosses from the eighth century and perhaps vestiges of the small stone cell fancifully known as 'St Columba's Shrine' remain from the first millennium AD. The early monastic timber structures, 'rectangular or circular in plan',[57] were superseded by later medieval stone building. Similar ditches and cashel walls, generally demarcating a circular or approximately circular enclosure or fort, appear elsewhere in Scotland at this time. North of the central lowlands, Pictish settlement also continued pre-occupation patterns of building in stone and timber – circular burial cairns, hill forts, roundhouses, wheelhouses, crannogs and long sub-rectangular halls. By the eighth century, however, as Christianity spread across Scotland from Iona in the west and Northumbria in the south, the need for places of worship and retreat ushered in a new stone architecture influenced by those contemporary continental models favoured by a church increasingly orientated towards Rome. In 711 the Pictish king Nechtan wrote to abbot Ceolfrid in Northumbria requesting 'architects [masons] who might build a stone church in the Roman manner'.[58] What if anything resulted from this plea is unknown. Though some fragmentary architectural evidence of religious building from the eighth or ninth centuries does survive, it is not until the late tenth century, by which time the kingships of the

Picts and Scots had fused under Cineád mac Alpin (Kenneth MacAlpin) and the state of Scotland had begun to take shape, that the simple Romanesque form of these early churches begins to become clear. This could be seen both in the Irish-influenced chapels of the west and north and the more Anglicised churches of the east and south. A simple architecture indeed – at first, little more than a prismatic gabled cell; later, with a smaller cellular chancel in the east; later still, perhaps, with a round or square stone tower in the west – but an architecture of stone whose very simplicity, as with the standing circle, as with the broch, attested the power of fundamental form. To this raw aesthetic of Scottishness architecture would return.

Beehive Structure, Eileach an Naoimh
Historic Environment Scotland

Chapter 3

Castles, Palaces and Country Houses

Kildrummy to Drumlanrig

'With all their local and regional variations … towers had emerged and developed from the fourteenth century onwards in ways that … constitute a castellar heritage that is distinctly Scottish'
Geoffrey Stell in A Dakin *et al* (eds) *Scotland's Castle Culture*

If the native tribes of second century Scotland were impressed and perhaps also bemused by the sophisticated order of the camps, forts and long miles of cross-country earthworks constructed by the Roman legions, their descendants must have looked with utter amazement at the soaring walls and towers of the great Romanesque abbeys and churches rising among them a thousand years later. A second imperial power, papal, peaceable, but no less colonial than the first, had reached the very edge of Europe, bringing with it its own latter-day Roman architecture. Thanks to the perspicacity and promotion of the Canmore dynasty, who, from the accession of Malcolm III in the eleventh century, succeeded in consolidating royal power in a unified Scotland, the country found itself 'in the full floodstream of European ecclesiastical activity'[1] as the various orders of the Roman Church established themselves north of the border. Stone piled on stone, round arch on round arch, as the walls at Kelso, Jedburgh, Dunfermline, St Andrews and Kirkwall abbeys rose to unimaginable heights, testimony to the skills of medieval master builders and the cross-border reach of monastic polity. This was an international architecture. What survives of it remains, even today, immensely impressive. The great broad-buttressed gable of the north transept at Kelso rising in five stages to a temple top flanked by truncated bulwark-like towers; steep gable pediments at skyline and porch, round arches – three over two over two over one – a high circular window echoed in the oculus at the apex: it still stands implacable, fortress-like, like some city gate opening to the principal north–south street of a Roman town. The nave at Dunfermline, robust and rugged, flat-walled triforium and clearstorey carried on a round-arched arcade of massive cushion-capped cylindrical piers cut with jagged chevrons. And at St Magnus in Kirkwall, the same majestic Durham-derived simplicity. If there is any Scottishness in all this it is at best elusive: the

Kelso Abbey
North transept of Kelso Abbey by R W Billings c1845
HES Canmore DP312448

Castle Sween, Rothesay Castle and Bothwell Castle
HES Canmore SC366683, DP252739, Historic Environment Scotland

patent geometries of circle and triangle, walls threaded with mural passages, austere monumentality.

Contemporary castellar architecture was no less in debt to influences drawn from abroad. It seems likely that the designers of the earliest defensive redoubts of the western seaboard and northern isles were Gaels or Norse, as local as the stone they built with. The high coursed rubble mass of Castle Sween could scarcely be ruder in conception and execution; quadrilateral in plan, its walls are featureless but for minimal buttressing at the corners and a single round arch doorway to the south. Similar planar or curving mural stands survive at Skipness, where the layout was also quadrilateral, at Rothesay, where the plan was oval, and at the polygonal castles of Dunstaffnage, Tioram, Mingary, Dunvegan and Kisimul. Not surprisingly perhaps, in all this there is something of the impregnability, if not the formal elegance, of the broch.

Later castles do, however, attest a more tutored approach. At Inverlochy, for example, built in the third quarter of the thirteenth century, the plan is almost square, the four corners marked by round towers, each with its curving mural stair. Four circular towers were added to the oval curtain wall at Rothesay at much the same time as Inverlochy was under construction. By the end of the thirteenth century, probably under the direct or indirect influence of Edward I of England's masons, whose architectural skills were 'to be numbered among the most accomplished in Europe',[2] this general pattern was much employed, though the plan of the enclosing walls might be quadrangular, polygonal, or even triangular, and the number of towers might vary. At Bothwell, Kildrummy and Dirleton a single drum tower or *donjon* dominated the other peripheral towers, a feature whose French provenance has been sourced to the great fortress of Coucy built in the second quarter of the century. At Bothwell, Kildrummy and Caerlaverock, towers were coupled to create a fortified gatehouse whose twinned cylindrical bulwarks flanking the entrance made a bold and intimidating advance from the castle walls, a defensive strategy probably also French in derivation.[3] Outliving its military *raison d'être*, the single

Mousa to Mackintosh 51

cylindrical tower, whatever its origin, would long continue as a formal feature of Scottish architecture. Paired towers, too – generally round but occasionally square – would recur. This may have had as much to do with the persistent attraction of simple solid geometry as it did with defence or symbolic allusion, and was perhaps as much grounded in predisposition as chosen by rational preference.

Following the social and economic upheaval wrought by the protracted Wars of Independence the grand feudal fortresses of thirteenth century Scotland were superseded by a model altogether more compacted in function and form. A few large curtain wall castles with massive gatehouses continued to be built, as at Doune and Tantallon, but it was the more economic, more tightly packaged tower-house which became what architect and former Inspector of Ancient Monuments in Scotland Stewart Cruden has called 'the universal standard type'.[4] Probably foremost among the 'key progenitors'[5] of this model was the tower raised at Edinburgh Castle by David II in the second half of the fourteenth century. By virtue of its height, dominant location and royal patronage, it must have exercised a profound influence on the architectural aspirations of the country's landowning nobility. Whether square or oblong in plan,[6] the dimensions of these new tower-houses were limited by the span of a stone vault. Chamber stacked over chamber, a tower-house might be three, four or sometimes five storeys high, the walls thick enough to counteract the thrust of the flooring or vaulting at the upper levels and be stable over such height. With its spare scatter of small window openings, the tower rose in sheer planes to a corbelled parapet behind which might be a crowstep-gabled caphouse. This deceptively primitive masonry box could, in certain respects, be said to have had its formal antecedents in the Scottish past: its blocky mass a distant descendant of the country's early rudimentary stone structures; its gaunt verticality rising to a defensible wallhead a reincarnation of the broch. In another respect, this was 'the traditional medieval hall up-ended'.[7] In still another, the degree to which the thick masonry walls of the towers were hollowed out to create seating embrasures, garderobes, recesses, mural stairs and passages makes it impossible not to think of the dark tunnelled chambers of the Iron Age dun, broch or roundhouse. However much such faint echoes were (or are) acknowledged, the tower-house became a distinctively Scottish building type and remained so for almost three hundred years.

Such links with the past may not have been entirely fortuitous – as always, material resources, climatic conditions and recurring needs play their part – but it would be extremely tendentious to suggest that they were regularly or deliberately contrived. Nevertheless, the self-conscious cultivation of Scottishness, essentially the need to command national respect in the European context, was certainly embodied in the policy of 'cultural assertion'[8] pursued by the Stuart kings during the fifteenth century. As in many contemporary nations historians laboured to create a convincing national lineage suitably ancient and respectable. In his *Chronica Gentis Scotorum* written towards the end of the fourteenth century, the priest John of Fordun had provided chapter and verse for the origin and development of the Scottish nation. The Scots it seemed had, like the Israelites, come out of Egypt, though they had travelled in a different direction, arriving in their remote promised land by way of Spain and Ireland! In 1440, another priest, Walter Bower, abbot at Inchcolm, elaborated the story, adding myth to myth, in his sixteen-book *Scotichronicon* which incorporated Fordun's earlier work. A century later Hector Boece, first principal of Aberdeen University, drew on these and other sources to produce a further *Historia Gentis Scotorum*. In a preface addressed to James V, he wrote, 'I have attempted to write the history of our nation, by far the most ancient of them all'.[9] However chauvinistic such claims, however absurd some of the genealogies and chronologies advanced may seem to us now, these texts contributed significantly to the Stuart monarchy's national confidence, a confidence expressed in the court's patronage of the arts, not the least remarkable example of which was an ambitious programme of building which managed to embrace both an openness to the latest European fashions and a patriotic desire to stress the dynasty's continuity with a Scottish past.

Something of this wish to establish continuity with the past was evident in the ecclesiastical architecture of the fifteenth century. A number of scholars have drawn attention to the revival of those Romanesque forms that had characterised Scottish architecture in

Caerlaverock Castle
Historic Environment Scotland

the twelfth century.[10] The re-appearance of cylindrical piers and round arches has been noted at Dunkeld Cathedral, St Machar's Cathedral in Aberdeen, the Church of the Holy Rude in Stirling, St Mary's, Haddington, and in the reconstruction of the choir of the Abbey on Iona. This fifteenth century reversion to a twelfth century historical precedent has been judged both negatively – condemned as 'an inferior architecture, the fag-end of the international medieval tradition'[11] – and positively as a reflection of 'a mood of Scottish national self-awareness and confidence',[12] which simultaneously encouraged the importation of new architectural ideas from continental Europe. Was this recapitulation of the past simply a lazy patriotism or did it perhaps betray a tentative affinity with new Renaissance forms?

Whatever the divergence in evaluation, there is no disagreement over the view that this was 'a totally Scottish architecture'.[13] What made it so was the conscious act of revival and reform. Forms that were in the twelfth century freshly assimilated from the historical development of English and European architecture had, with the passage of time, become part of the built heritage of Scotland, their 'second-hand' Scottishness an example of the kind of amalgamation that emerges in the recurring dialogue between the history of art and the geography of art. That this was more than the mere consequence of unscholarly provincial interpretation and incorporated an indigenous affection and aptitude for the austere does not advance the specification of the resulting structures much beyond the calculated deployment of simple geometries and heavy monumental form. On the other hand, vague as this speculation may be, the physical manifestation in both ecclesiastical and castellar architecture is clear. And perhaps nowhere is this more so than in St Machar's Cathedral, Aberdeen. Here in the nave, completed in the second quarter of the fifteenth century, is an almost Romanesque simplicity. Superimposed at the centre of the west front is a heavily moulded round-arch doorway and seven elongated round-arch windows. Flanking these are two machicolated, square towers 'of military not ecclesiastical provenance' now surmounted by octagonal spires constructed in the early sixteenth century but originally carrying crowstep-gabled caphouses.[14] Defensive or allusive, or perhaps both, this invocation of the Scottish tower-house form is surely an act of architectural affirmation.

Whereas, during the twelfth century, the Canmore dynasty had greatly fostered the building of abbey churches, priories and monasteries, the Stuart monarchy wished rather to consolidate and ensure the dominance of royal power regarding ecclesiastical polity. This policy found some expression in the building of such burgh churches as St Giles, Edinburgh, St Michael's, Linlithgow, and King's College Chapel, Aberdeen, and the tolbooths at Linlithgow and Glasgow, all of which were surmounted by a crown spire, 'a symbol understood across Europe [to convey] the new, untrammelled sovereignty claimed by kings within their realms'.[15] But it was the succession of great palaces intermittently constructed throughout the fifteenth and sixteenth centuries that sealed the Stuarts' power at home and bolstered their reputation abroad.

St Machar's Cathedral, Aberdeen
HES Canmore SC536304

St Giles Cathedral, Edinburgh
Historic Environment Scotland

The first of these palaces, and the most compact in conception, was Linlithgow. Begun with the east range in the 1420s by James I, by the end of the century its square courtyard plan, with high ranges on all four sides, square towers rising at each corner and turnpike stair towers in each of the internal angles of the court, had been clearly delineated and partially built. During James IV's reign this ambitious conception was largely realised, making Linlithgow 'probably the most advanced Renaissance palace north of the Alps'.[16] In the 1530s James V, abandoning the original entrance to the palace at the centre of the east range, created a new axial approach from the south, building a porch with flanking rounds and, at the head of the Kirkgait, an 'outer entrie' mini-gatehouse with twinned semi-octagonal 'rounds'. Subsequent construction, the last period of building extending into the early 1600s, completed the work. Consciously Italian in its general concept, the palace was inevitably stylistically heterogeneous in execution. Long in the building, it exhibited features identifiable as Romanesque, Gothic, Renaissance and Tudor, their provenance French, Italian, English and Scottish. Yet everything is mastered by the sheer power of the overriding architectural idea of a *palatium ad modum castri* (a palace in the shape of a military camp)[17] and the severity with which this has been interpreted. As the architectural historian Colin McWilliam has rightly observed, 'The block-like compactness of the exterior is perhaps [Linlithgow's] most memorable quality, for individually the outer fronts are severe almost to the point of blankness.'[18] Without in any way invalidating its European aspiration and derivation, this assessment alone might justify an argument for Linlithgow's Scottishness. And there are other, specifically castellar, factors to support such a case – the vaulted passages, turnpike stairs, recesses and garderobes that penetrate the walls of the east range, the 'outer entrie' and south porch with their gatehouse-like form and, perhaps, the east barbican or so-called 'Utter Gret Bulwerk'.

The impressive gateway created by James IV at Stirling Castle in the first decade of the sixteenth century, part of an extensive programme of works which transformed that ancient stronghold into

Linlithgow Palace
National Art Survey of Scotland photograph c1900
HES Canmore SC853745

another royal residence of European stature, may well have been the prototype for the Linlithgow Forework. Now much reduced, the original grandeur of Stirling's frontispiece can only be imagined. On each side of the castle gateway stood two cylindrical towers machicolated and castellated, themselves flanked by similar recessed towers. All four were roofed with slated cones and linked by a wall walk. Richard Fawcett's comment that the forework 'was perhaps more reminiscent of painted castles in French illuminated manuscripts than of a functional artillery fortification'[19] may reveal something of the Stuarts' cultural aspirations, point to design provenance and hint that what now mattered most in architectural terms was as much formal or symbolic delight as practical necessity. But it should also be acknowledged that the cone-capped, twin-drum gatehouse structure, 'French-inspired fashion'[20] though it might be, was a form already assimilated into Scottish architecture.

Beyond the Stirling Forework an outer close leads to the Great Hall. Also constructed during James IV's reinvigorating building campaign at the start of the sixteenth century, it was built to a rectangular plan of dimensions without precedent in Scotland. High walls rise to corbelled machicolation supporting a castellated parapet with false cannon; set back behind, crowstep gables terminate the roof. Tall bay windows, English Tudor in character, light the south end of the lateral walls, but even this spectacular intrusion cannot quite diminish the hall's reiteration of the forework's fortified Scottish theme. Not so the Royal Palace located nearby on the west side of the castle's outer close. Commissioned by James V in the late 1530s, its plan is quadrangular like Linlithgow, with the royal lodgings for king and queen arranged around an inner courtyard. Unlike Linlithgow, however, the palace's completion within the relatively short time span of two decades ensured that the building possessed a distinct architectural integrity and that this coherence expressed James's enlightened pan-European outlook. As a result, the building incorporated new Renaissance ideas both in the organisation and detail of its design – one of the earliest in Britain and Ireland to do so.[21] The facades to the north, east and south are ordered in bays in which high segmental-arched recesses alternate with windowed panels; below the arches sculpted figures

Stirling Castle

Historic Environment Scotland

stand on single two-stage, baluster-like columns. This unusual arrangement may be a reflection of provincial architectural skills. On the other hand, while the provenance of the elevational design remains unclear, continental sources – Italian, Netherlandish, German, and particularly French – have been proposed for some of its detail features and there can be little doubt that in investing his palace with the lineaments of classical architecture James wished to align his kingdom with mainstream European culture. And yet, above the Renaissance facades rose crenellated battlements and bare gables with crowstepped skews which, though they too had continental roots in the Low Countries or Baltic, were and would remain 'architectural emblems of Scotland even up to the present day'.[22]

While the Stirling Forework and Great Hall were under construction, James IV was also engaged in the rebuilding of the royal palace in the capital, Edinburgh. Like Linlithgow, the plan of his Holyrood Palace (Holyroodhouse) was quadrangular and it remains so, though the appearance of the enclosing ranges was later substantially recast. What does survive from the second quarter of the sixteenth century is the tower begun by James IV and completed by James V at the north-west corner of the palace's courtyard plan. Though this is not strictly speaking a gatehouse, its form is 'still very defensive'[23] and an unmistakable echo of the forework at Stirling. The principal west front of this tower is itself a twinned tower. Two cylindrical drums flanking a central bay rise through four storeys to machicolated battlements behind which short inner drums carry bellcast conical roofs originally capped by imperial crowns. It was James V's intention to mirror this powerful and recognisably Scottish structure by building a corresponding tower at the south-west corner of the palace plan in order to frame the west facade, a project later realised in the extensive restoration work carried out in the 1670s for James VI when 'the old Scottish Castle Style … found a new, propagandist value, underlining Stuart entitlement to reign'.[24]

The first years of the sixteenth century saw construction begin on yet another Stuart palace, this time at the royal hunting lodge at Falkland in Fife. There, before his death at Flodden in 1513, James IV established once more the familiar quadrangular plan and completed some of the flanking ranges. It is not this achievement, however, but rather the later continuation of the work by his son which survives as

Holyrood Palace
Historic Environment Scotland

the more remarkable legacy. Remarkable yet puzzling. For James V's contribution to the development of the palace took the form of two contemporary yet stylistically contrasting projects. Between 1537 and 1542 he reconstructed the courtyard facades of the east and south ranges, creating what have been described as 'the most sophisticated architectural works of that date in Britain'.[25] As at Stirling the facades are designed in regular bays. Here, however, where they are defined by pilaster buttresses fronted by Corinthian columns on high pedestals, there is a finer classical aplomb. Between the columned buttresses are lintelled windows, the taller mullion-and-transom lights of the upper storey flanked by roundels carved with portrait reliefs. All this was elegant, up to date and fashionably French. Meanwhile, however, at the west end of the south range, James was building a massive gatehouse on much more familiar traditional lines. On each side of the arched entrance to the palace rose two swelling drum towers over which conically roofed inner drums emerged from behind corbelled battlemented parapets; the similarity to the north-west tower at Holyrood and the forework at Stirling was striking. In the symbolism of its mock-military bearing, even more in the impact of its bulging forceful form, imperial and imperious, all this was solidly Scottish.

It is true, as John Dunbar has asserted, that the Renaissance facades of the Stuart royal palaces 'had no successors and exerted no general influence'.[26] But there were certainly other aspects of these buildings that did. The courtyard plan with its inbuilt potential to favour horizontal living continued to be adopted, though as yet with none of the ordered or arcaded elegance of continental models. The Earl's Palace at Birsay, Orkney, built in the last quarter of the sixteenth century, had towers at the corners of its quadrangular plan. At Tolquhon, Aberdeenshire, there were two towers diagonally sited across the courtyard, one cylindrical, the other 'Auld Tour' square in plan. Tolquhon also incorporated an identifiably Scottish element which had featured repeatedly in the Stuart palaces. The twin-towered gatehouse or *châtelet* here, however, had a symbolic role, having neither the masonry thickness nor scale to function as a soundly defensive structure. Much more impressive must

Falkland Palace
Historic Environment Scotland

have been the gatehouse at the Palace of Boyne in Banffshire. Also built to a courtyard plan, Boyne was one of the strangest residences to be constructed during this late sixteenth century period, in several respects decidedly unusual in design. Unlike most of the 'castles' being erected at this time, which were enlargements or alterations of existing houses, it was an entirely new structure replacing an older building nearby. With its high curtain walls and corner towers, it could easily have been mistaken for a thirteenth century stronghold. Moreover, in layout it was rigorously, almost classically, symmetrical with a foursquare plan, identical circular towers at the four corners, and an axial approach leading to the gatehouse located precisely at the centre of the south front. Several other drum-flanked portals, similar in form but varying in size and 'defensive' conviction, appeared elsewhere before the end of the century: at the obliquely set twin-towered entry to Seton; in 'pantomime scale'[27] at Rowallan in Ayrshire; and with grandiloquent panache at Fyvie (see below). Just how fashionable this mock-fortified feature had become is perhaps best judged by its appearance at Mar's Wark in Stirling (1570–2) where octagonal towers, reminiscent of the 'entries' James V had built at Linlithgow (perhaps even of the castle forework only a short distance uphill), flanked the entrance to the regent's palace.

In each of their four grand palaces – and nowhere more explicitly than at Falkland – the Stuarts declared their identity to be both national and international. While clearly anxious to espouse the systematic order and formal details of a Renaissance architecture already evident in France and Italy, the dynasty's builders appear to have been equally determined to indulge an indigenous addiction to the formal delights of solid geometry. How else to explain the uneasy contemporary conjunction of regularly bayed facades enlivened by classical columns and ornament with quasi-fortified castellar gatehouses whose harled drum towers have their formal antecedents in a medieval and perhaps even more distant past? If only because it had little or no tradition of partitive spatial organisation predicated

Mar's Wark, Stirling
Drawing by R W Billings, engraved by J H Le Keux 1852
HES Canmore DP344257

on framed timber construction, Scottish architecture's historical liking for more starkly sculptural form was as understandable as its desire to be up-to-date with the latest continental vogue. Moreover, frequently complementing this affection in the minds of those Scottish landowners who, following the example of the monarchy, sought to upgrade their properties in the latest Renaissance fashion, was an innate thrift born of limited resources which made them eschew building anew in favour of alteration, adaptation and accretion. If the consequence of this canniness meant, as has been argued, that such houses of the later sixteenth and early seventeenth centuries 'lack the easily comprehensible shapes of Azay le Rideau or of Chambord',[28] it also ensured that the relatively austere walls of the tower-house continued to dominate the Scottish countryside, albeit accentuated by a contrasting skyline flourish of faux-fortified fun. As the seventeenth century began, the great houses of Scotland, or *châteaux* as Charles McKean has called them,[29] did not yet put on the full formal dress of symmetrical classicism. Instead, in the dialectical encounter between traditional Scottish ways of building and imported international ideas, a new and unique synthesis was achieved. Old familiar forms survived: the high bare walls of the square or oblong tower-house with windows located according to contingent need; the addition of a second and sometimes a third tower forming an L-plan or so-called Z-plan arrangement; the grafting on of a fat drum tower; perhaps the addition of a 'fortified'

Rowallan Castle
Historic Environment Scotland

twin-cylinder gateway, the elevated vestigial memory of corner towers in corbelled rounds and bartizans; the 'defensive' wallhead; crowstep gables; conic roofs. But new Renaissance forms now also appeared: pilasters, cornices, strapwork, aedicules, arcading, balustrading; windows increased in size, their disposition grouped and tiered; pediments replaced gablets over doorways, windows and dormers; in calculated contrast to the plain harled walls, dressed stone was adopted for quoins, skews, margins and other decorative details.

Nowhere was this more exuberantly displayed than in those 'castle-wise'[30] mansions built in Aberdeenshire and the North-East in an astonishing burst of building activity beginning in the last quarter of the sixteenth century and stretching well into the seventeenth. Notably at Huntly, Castle Fraser, Crathes, Midmar, Craigievar and Fyvie, but evident too in many other local houses, the essential formal elements of what has become known as the Scots Baronial style emerged. In most cases some pre-existent structure was altered or enlarged, an old tower heightened, a new tower or towers built; the native tradition of building was maintained and the resulting structures perhaps best understood as 'products of a precocious, first-phase castle revival'.[31] And just as these respectfully retrospective transformations were directed by design (a number of mason–architect families are known to have been engaged) so, too, the fashionable signs of Renaissance organisation, ornament and detail were sometimes designed in, grafted on to – at Huntly literally superimposed on – the solid stock of Scottish form. This was no abject parochial revivalism of the past. Nor was there any wholehearted acceptance of the canonic ideas of classicism. What was achieved was something fresh, a distinct Scottishness seen, as Nikolaus Pevsner memorably described it, in 'the

Fyvie Castle
Andreas Karnholz / Alamy Stock Photo

extreme contrast of soaring sheer walls and the most unexpected crustaceous projections on top'.[32]

Pevsner, concerned with *The Englishness of English Art*, does not give much attention to artistic matters north of the border but he does acknowledge the distinct autonomy of Scottish culture[33] and considers that 'extreme contrast' seen in the mature tower-house as 'the best introduction possible' to what he calls 'the Scottish polarity'.[34] In so far as he elaborates the nature of this polarity (and he has little to say on the matter) Pevsner's insight has an intriguing attraction. On the one hand, he highlights a predilection for formal austerity, the 'delight in sheer height of a *block* of a building' (my italics). On the other, there is what seems to him to be a Celtic fascination for the intricate, the daedal, that 'delight in the fantastical' seen in the agitated skyline.

This vertical solidity or *blockiness* is fundamental in both a constructional and formal sense. As if intent on preserving a planar integrity no matter how high it rises, the tower-house eschews the Gothic strategy of external buttressing. Instead it prefers to maintain structural stability by thickening the lower stages of the walling internally and, in many cases, by the additional buttressing effect inherent in various L- or Z-plan arrangements common to many tower-houses. This way of doing things does not generally result in any marked increase in the size of openings at the upper levels where the structural loading is less (as, for example, it does in the bell towers of Romanesque churches). Again, it is as if there is some innate predilection for building mass, for the dominance of solid over void. Naturally this solidity is most evident – whether as a result of structural, defensive or quasi-defensive demands – at the lower levels of the building, the openings there being confined to small doorways, gunloops, and so on. Above, where windows must be allowed to break through the surface planes of harl or rubble, their size never threatens to impair the dominance of the wall. Openings occur in response to the internal requirements of the plan and much less frequently as a consequence of any self-conscious

Huntly Castle
Historic Environment Scotland

elevational design. Though all are relatively small, they may be varied in size. Moreover, the limited plan area and vertical nature of the building ensures that there is little opportunity to develop much horizontal alignment of windows at each floor level, while any axial placing of lights one above the other is often disturbed by a change in window size or detail or by offset openings effecting, as it were, a stutter in fenestration. Overall, a distinct pleasure is taken in asymmetry, not only in the arrangement of openings penetrating the walls but in the building mass itself, evident in the solid geometries of abutting jambs, stair towers, gables and roof planes.

Yet, paradoxically, part of the aesthetic delight of many *later* tower-house examples, and certainly of the Aberdeenshire Castles of Mar, is the assimilation, however tentative, of some aspects of classical order and detail into the asymmetric matrix of tower-house form. Most spectacularly at Huntly, a horizontal range of three regularly spaced, oriel windows, clearly of French Renaissance provenance, stretches across the uppermost level of the 'palace' facade. At Craigievar, the balustrading which fences the viewing platform on the castle's high square tower is classical in form while two tall turrets are roofed with ogee helmets in contrast with the traditional slated cones which cap the bartizans.[35] Castle Fraser, too, has ogee-domed turrets and classical balustrading. More significant here, however, is the fenestration: windows are repeatedly aligned vertically while on the four-bay south front the entire wall plane is treated symmetrically with superimposed openings and a clear central axis marked by an arched doorway. But it is at Fyvie that this newly fashionable addiction is most

Castle Fraser
Historic Environment Scotland

comprehensively indulged, extending beyond planar elevational design to the massing of the building as a whole. Here, the south front of the castle, refashioned to a quadrangular plan, was transformed by the introduction of a tall 'gatehouse' centrepiece with twin drums linked at high level by a gabled triumphal arch, set between a late fourteenth century tower to the east and a mid fifteenth century tower to the west: the result, a monumental symmetrical facade. But this compositional closure is exceptional and Fyvie, like all the great houses of the North-East, retains its baronial tower-house character, its tall stark walls surmounted by a restless skyline of corbelled cone-capped bartizans, gabletted eaves dormers and chimneyed gables – its Scottishness never in doubt. For, like the native propensity to build austerely and to build high, this hard agitated crust of 'projections on top' has its roots in the same past, in the corbelled battlements, parapets, machicolations, caphouses, turrets and brattishing at the wallhead of castle and tower-house.

Nonetheless, Fyvie was an intimation of change. It seems highly probable that its intended 'Linlithgow-like' plan,[36] quadrangular with four corner towers, was to some degree French-inspired, based on the plan of the chateau of Ancy-le-Franc and thus, through the latter's émigré architect, Sebastiano Serlio, indirectly influenced by the new architecture of the Italian Renaissance. And though two quarters of the plan remained unbuilt, the cleverly aggregated south front responded to the same guiding principles of external symmetry and balance. At the centre of this facade, Fyvie's Seton Tower, so strongly evocative of the traditional castellar gatehouse (though not perhaps entirely without some French precedent), had its

Craigievar Castle
HES Canmore SC357706

own separate, direct and immediate impact. At nearby Craigston, a similar high, quasi-triumphal arch links tall (not quite identical) twinned towers. The towers, square in plan rather than round, are gabled, the connecting central gable at Fyvie replaced by a recessed square tower rising to a fashionable balustraded viewing platform. Corner corbellings on the gable flanks indicate an intention to build square turrets which would have further animated an already 'riotous' roofscape.[37] A building still eminently Scottish in its various individual forms, it is clear that, despite the differing widths of its twin towers, the desired aim is classical symmetry, making Craigston 'the most obviously modern'[38] of these castles in the North-East. Thus, whether in the form of Fyvie's putative plan, the arrangement of its south front, with its dominant centre and flanking wings, or in the balanced tripartite U-plan composition of Craigston, in both plan and elevation new design parameters had been set. Asymmetry was increasingly abandoned. Even so, some of the recognisably Scottish forms of the tower-house tradition would, for a time, persist.

In the first few decades of the seventeenth century a series of houses, built mainly in the eastern Lowlands, conformed to Craigston's model, though not on the same scale – McKean counts 'at least twenty' such buildings, calling them villas 'rather than great country seats'.[39] Baberton (Kilbaberton) near Edinburgh was archetypal (before its transformation in 1765), its two-storey-and-attic form firmly symmetrical with short matching jambs advancing from the main block to form a double-L- or U-plan. Windows, pedimented and pilastered, were aligned vertically. Replacing bartizans, finials accented the skews. Two turnpike stairs, tucked in the re-entrant angles of an open forecourt barely wider than the gables, were capped with leaded ogee helmets rather

Craigston Castle
HES Canmore DP151471

Mousa to Mackintosh 67

Baberton House
Sketch by Charles McKean
Courtesy of Margaret McKean

than slated cones. Yet however classical Baberton aspires to be in overall design disposition and ornamental detail, the vertical emphasis of the house's chimneyed gables, the clasped turnpikes, the harled walls, the steep skews and roof planes, and the asymmetrical placing of the main entrance doorway ensure it retains a distinct measure of Scottishness. The same is true of the refashioning of Pitreavie in Fife, indeed perhaps more so. Although four storeys high and constructed in coursed stone, the architecture is almost identical: chimneyed gabled wings forming a U-plan, steep roofs, corbelled turnpikes in the re-entrants, windows aligned and arranged symmetrically, an off-centre entrance. Here, however, there are neither finials nor bartizans at the skews, the turnpikes have traditional slated cones and the walls are all but devoid of classical ornament or detail making Pitreavie 'an architecture of pure mass'[40] and thus identifiably Scottish. Other houses to adopt what has been called the 'peculiarly Scots U-plan',[41] though not always with a rigid adherence to symmetry, included Winton in East Lothian, Wrychtishousis in Edinburgh and Argyll's Lodging in Stirling, all of which combined an increasingly evident preference for Renaissance ornament and detail, both outside and in, with a continued affection for more baronial, 'castle-wise' form.

Pitreavie
Photograph by John Fleming c1890
HES Canmore SC1106518

Argyll's Lodging
Photograph 1889
HES Canmore SC1167080

This renewed creative tension between the classical and the castellar was perhaps first most successfully resolved not in any rural residence but in a major urban building constructed in the nation's capital from the late 1620s. To propose, as one writer on the history of architecture in Scotland has done, that George Heriot's Hospital (School), Edinburgh, was 'the first fully Renaissance building in Scotland'[42] is perhaps to push critical judgement too far, but it was certainly a portentous achievement. Civic and public in impact rather than aristocratic and private, its architectural provenance was, nonetheless, royal and palatial. Quadrangular in plan with corner turrets, it adopted a model already evident at Linlithgow and increasingly familiar from French and Italian pattern books, which provided exemplars of architectural composition and detail. Unlike Linlithgow and the only partially realised palace at Fyvie, however, its symmetries and details were complete and completed. Set on a low balustraded podium, the building's four elevational ranges, flanked by slightly advancing square towers, were identical in their compositional strategy, though varied in the treatment of the central axes. A square steeple topped by a domed octagon stood at the middle of the principal facade, the three other ranges accented by central ogee-capped turrets rising above the eaves. Windows, framed in aedicules or surmounted by pediments and strapwork, were aligned both vertically and horizontally. Continuous string courses marked sill or floor lines. A magnificent arched portal flanked by coupled columns 'encrusted with detailing drawn from pattern-books' marked the entrance below the steeple.[43] All this was classical and doubtless internationally aspirational even if it was not yet 'fully Renaissance'. For allusions to a tradition of indigenous forms were not absent. Corner towers, the steepled frontispiece and exceptionally tall chimney stacks exerted a powerful vertical thrust on what was otherwise an essentially horizontal building. Rising above the ridge line of the ranges, the four four-storey flanking towers had corbelled parapets with ogee-capped bartizans, turning them in effect into 'corner "tower-houses"'.[44] In each angle of the inner courtyard, turnpike stairs recall those at Linlithgow, Baberton, Pitreavie and elsewhere, though here they are not cylindrical but take the form of embedded octagons similar to the courtyard staircase constructed at the centre of Linlithgow's north range only ten years before. These stairs, too, have ogee-helmets which, rising well above the roof like the domed steeple, tower bartizans and tall chimneys, add to the serrated Scottish skyline.

Further fusions of Renaissance ideas with the native forms and formal predilections of Scottish architecture continued, especially in the later decades of the century. At Holyrood, the duplication of the tower built for James V, 'necessitated by the modernist, classicist demand for symmetry',[45] contributed to the creation of a new west front screening the courtyard ranges behind. Between the two twin-towered towers stretched a severely plain eleven-bay facade, corniced and balustraded and dramatised at the centre by a grandly Doric portico and frontispiece (see below). The palatial scale of the quadrangular plan might be rarely repeated, but the tower-flanked facade found frequent favour. In the 1660s and 70s a number of country houses successively exploited its elevational potential. At Panmure in Angus and the enlarged house of Balcaskie in Fife (see below), wide three-storey facades, with regularised fenestration (not quite symmetrical at Balcaskie), were framed by book-end square towers, topped in one case by ogee roofs and in the other by slated pyramids. In the reconstruction of Methven Castle in Perthshire, essentially a filled U-plan where the composition was tighter and much more vertical, the flanking towers were round and bell-capped. Reflected about the central axis of the composition of all three of these facades, frontal gables with apex stacks rose from the wall plane adjacent to the towers – an echo perhaps of the twinned U-plan gables at Baberton and Pitreavie, a strategy repeated at Bannockburn, Philipstoun and Careston. Among other facades with flanking turrets or facade gables or a combination of both were Hatton, Leslie, Kinneil, Gallery and Marlefield. In all of these, bilateral symmetry was dominant, the use of Renaissance detail to enrich door and window surrounds was restrained and, despite the implacable compositional rigour, there was as yet no recourse to the classical orders to articulate the facade. Roofscapes retained their visual significance: slated slopes remained steep, skews were crowstepped, chimneys rose from eaves and ridge.

George Heriot's Hospital, Edinburgh
North elevation c1830, second-floor plan c1843
HES Canmore DP155596, DP055033

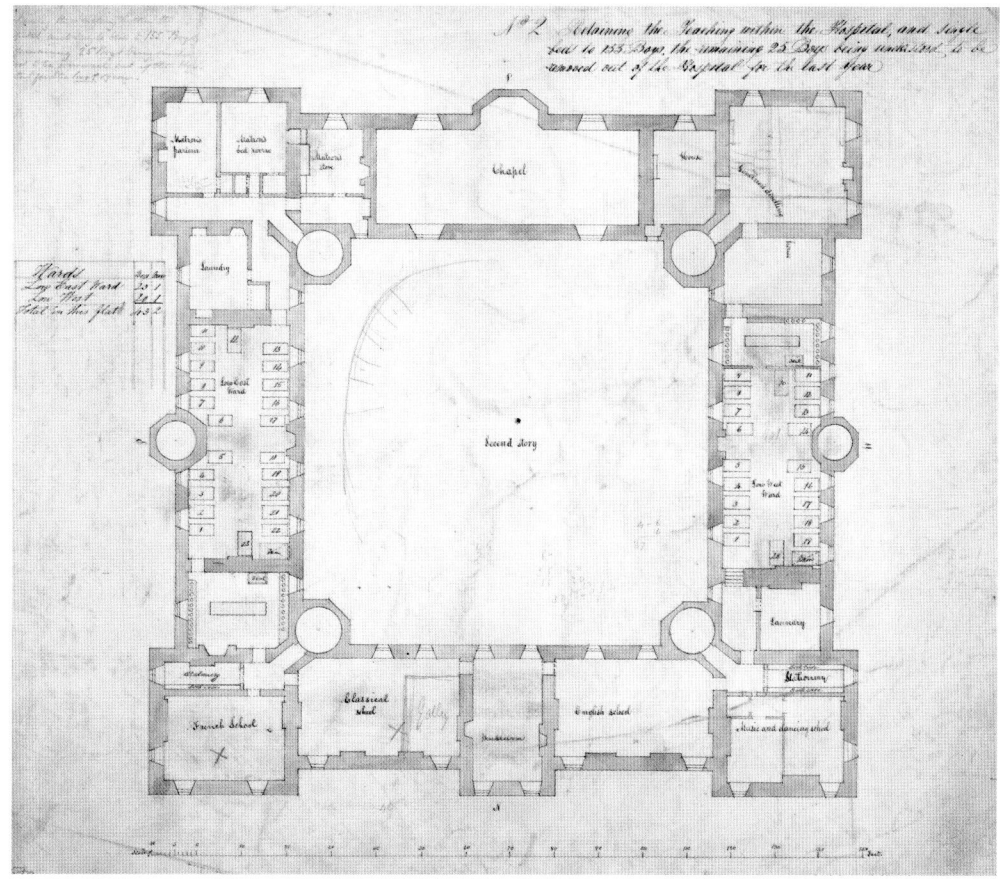

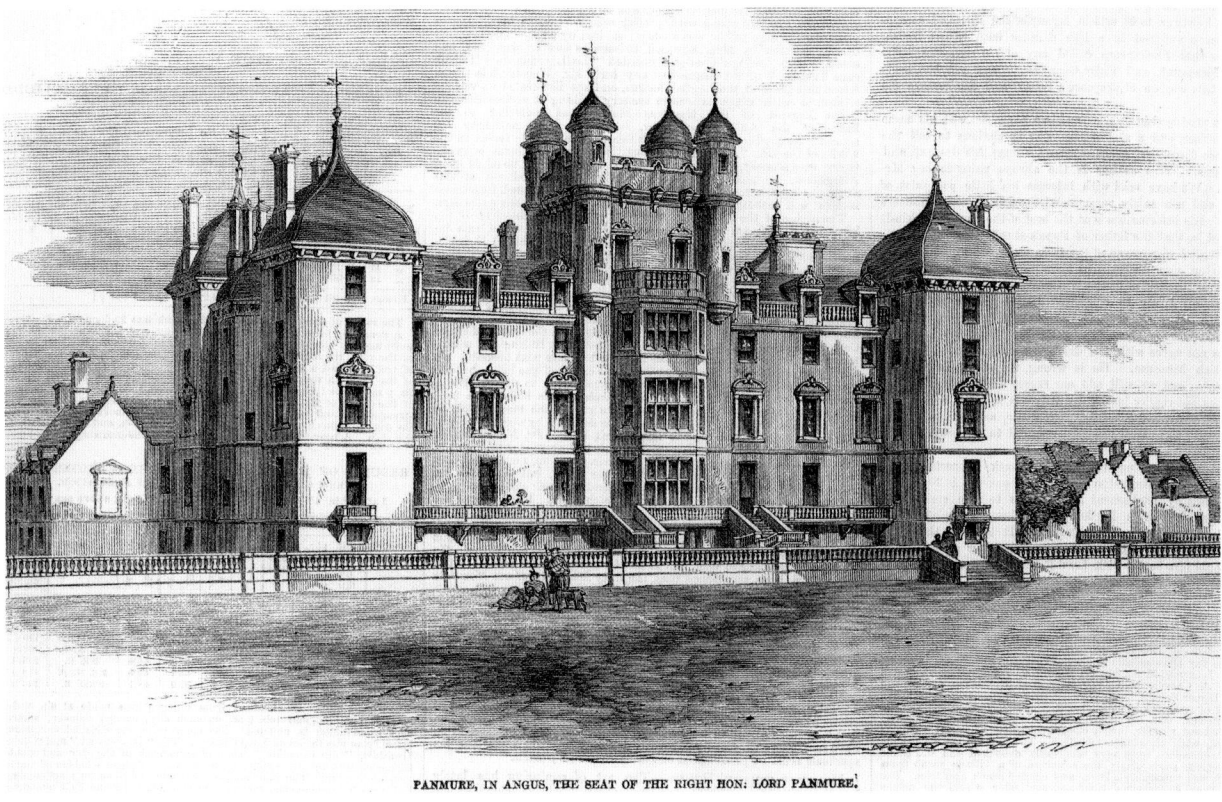

Panmure
Etching c1860
HES Canmore SC1422215

It has been argued that 'symmetry cannot have been the objective' of the architects and masons who built these seventeenth century houses.[46] It is true that the great majority of castles, tower-houses and 'castle-wise' mansions which had been built in Scotland were asymmetrical in form and whether this was a consequence of the often agglutinative growth of buildings over time, or the result of ad hoc responses to contingent need, or conceivably the expression of some inherent aesthetic preference, it undoubtedly constituted a strong and persistent tradition. It is true, too, that all is not always as it seems and that on close examination the bilateral symmetry of many of the houses mentioned above turns out to be in some way incomplete or flawed either in plan or elevation or both. But it is surely unreasonable to ascribe these imperfections to anything other than functional convenience or the adaptation of the new to the necessarily retained old. There is an attractive piquancy in the suggestion that aesthetic predilection might have intervened to thwart the predictable perfections of symmetrical design but such an argument is too subtly nuanced to be credible. Moreover, it is difficult to deny the cumulative persuasion of the evidence. As the century drew to a close, more and more properties had been transformed, deliberately recast in symmetrical discipline and classical detail, their Scottish qualities creatively, if sometimes inadvertently, incorporated into the mix. Nowhere was this trend clearer than in the evolving career of the most prominent Scottish architect of the late seventeenth century and early eighteenth century, Sir William Bruce.

In 1665, Bruce purchased Balcaskie in Fife, a late sixteenth century L-plan house, and from 1668 he began to enlarge and remodel it. A new three-storey, north front with crowstepped gables, balanced, but not identical, on each side of the facade, was flanked by pyramid-roofed advancing towers. In resolving the old with the new, compromise was inevitable in terms of gable widths, floor heights and

Balcaskie
HES Canmore DP158112

fenestration, but it is clear that Bruce was striving for bilateral symmetry in the composition of the elevation. The same ambition, modified by a respect for traditional forms or simply tempered by the constraints of existing building or the limitations of his client's purse, characterised his work at Thirlestane, Selkirkshire, a few years later. Here the west end of the great castle was reconstructed with a new entrance, marked by a high-level pediment and a pilastered and pedimented doorpiece, both set between its existing circular towers. Lower ogee-roofed pavilions were introduced advancing from the towers on the flanks. Ascending to the raised balustraded forecourt which linked the pavilions, a broad flight of steps further dramatised the axial approach. In his transformation of Holyroodhouse in the 1670s, Bruce was no less committed to bilateral symmetry, even if here this was most publicly, paradoxically and conservatively expressed in the reflection of the early sixteenth century twin-towered tower. At the same time, he was more outspoken in his detailed deployment of the new classical language of architecture elsewhere at Holyrood, notably in the cupola-topped Doric aedicule which marked the palace entrance at the centre of the west range and in the disciplining grid of superimposed orders applied to the courtyard elevations. At Drumlanrig Castle, Dumfriesshire, Bruce may also have injected a significant classical, even baroque, influence on the design, though from 1686 work on site advanced under the direction of James Smith. The concept is palatial and familiar – 'the general model for the house is George Heriot's Hospital'[47] – a quadrangular plan with square corner towers and ogee-domed circular stair towers in the internal angles of the courtyard. The principal north front, two storeys high rising to three and four storeys in the outer towers, is raised on a balustraded terrace not dissimilar to the elevated approach at Thirlestane. Here, however, the terrace is carried on a vaulted arched loggia and the ascent made by a magnificent horseshoe-shaped perron staircase. The five-bay facade between the

Kinross House
Engraving 1685
HES Canmore SC891901

towers is defined by giant order fluted Corinthian pilasters carrying a balustraded entablature. Its central entrance bay is treated as an elongated aedicule, the semi-circular pediment of which breaks through the balustraded eaves. Above, recalling Holyrood, rises an octagonal clock tower with coroneted dome. On each side of the facade, inner balustraded towers step up to the outer towers which are balustraded between corner bartizans. Bruce's command of classical organisation and proportion (if indeed the built design can be ascribed to him) is considerable, yet despite the grand axial drama of the approach to the castle, the uncompromised symmetry and the theatrical bluster of this principal facade, there are still flaws: the Corinthian pilasters are uncomfortably attenuated, especially in the central aedicule; the window pediments of the upper floor trespass on the eaves entablature; the outer bays of the five-bay front overlap the inner towers *on the same plane*. On the other hand, the very verticality of pilasters and aedicule, of the corner towers, stair towers, bell tower and chimney stacks, asserts an unmistakable Scottishness. Perhaps, too, that same aesthetic inheres in the unpretentious disciplined severity of the castle's east, west and south elevations with their tall windows and 'thrusting roof line'[48] of turreted towers and high chimneys.

Confronting this apparent dichotomy, this delight in 'the juxtaposition of old and new, Scottish and continental', Charles McKean has invoked what he calls 'the Scottish architectural anti-syzygy',[49] a formal contrariness described in Scottish culture in the twentieth century by Hugh MacDiarmid which, as will be evident, is repeatedly present in this investigation of Scottishness in architecture. But at Kinross House, built by Bruce for himself in the 1680s and generally regarded to be his masterpiece, it is difficult to detect this delight. Raised on a basement of channelled rustication, the two-storey ashlar facade is eleven bays wide, the outer three bays on each

Kinross House
HES Canmore SC1029102

side advancing slightly between fluted Corinthian pilaster quoins. Several continuous string courses, an entablature with modillion cornice, a low attic and piended roof planes emphasise the building's classical horizontality. Gone are the frontal gables; gone the steep roofs. Gone, too, are the flanking towers (if we ignore the low detached ogee-roofed pavilions which sit apart on each side linked to the principal west elevation by low concave walls). Gone are any architectural allusions to the Scottish past. Completed in the last decade of the century this is surely the first fully classical building in Scotland. If its Scottish location lends it a national distinction, it is one borrowed on the basis of international assets. To some it must have seemed to mark the dawn of a new age: writing in 1717, Sir John Clerk of Penicuik, 'Scotland's chief arbiter of taste in matters architectural in the second quarter of the eighteenth century',[50]

deemed Bruce the very 'introducer of Architecture in this country'.[51] Few would have disagreed, but some, perhaps less enamoured of the recent union with England, might have begun to wonder if classicism could have a Scottish face beyond the dour physiognomy of Kinross.

Recent research[52] has suggested that the architectural expression of Scottishness was not, in fact, so comprehensively repressed as historiography has hitherto maintained. By focusing on the aspirations of patronage Charles Wemyss pointed to a 'clear division' of intent between the *noblesse de robe* whose acquired nobility as tenants-in-chief of the Crown derived from land purchased with 'new' money and the *noblesse d'épée* whose aristocratic status was determined by their possession of long-established hereditary estates. While the former built new classical country seats for themselves, in much the same way as the diversifying merchant class of Venice had a century earlier built their Veneto mansions in the latest Palladian fashion, the latter 'reformed their dynastic seats without losing the traditional military

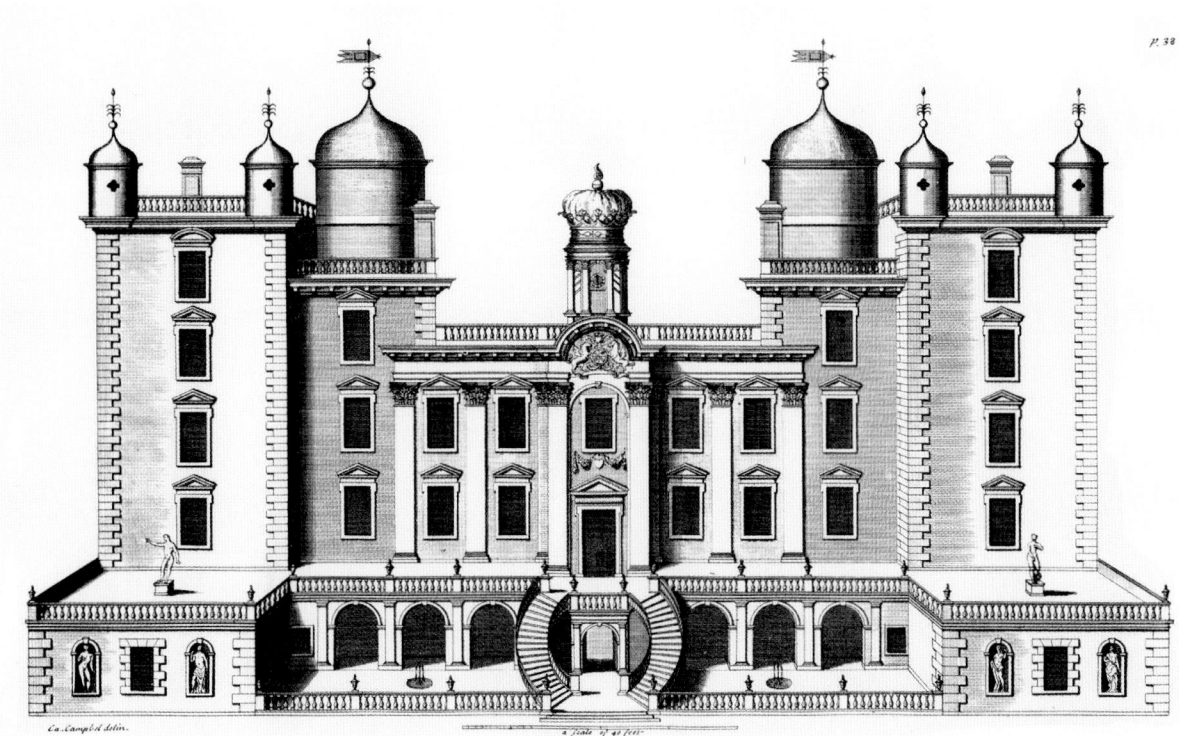

Drumlanrig Castle
Drawing of main front from Vitruvius Scoticus 1810
HES Canmore SC704832

symbols of nobility' so that 'their houses projected an aura of history rather than wealth'.[53] At Kinross, Bruce, whose personal wealth was not inherited but 'closely associated with the administration of the Scottish Treasury'[54] where he had served as collector of foreign excise, built solely for himself and did so in strict classical style. At Thirlestane, Drumlanrig and Holyrood, on the other hand, where he was obliged to respond to the contingent limitations of existing buildings and to the aspirations of his aristocratic and royal clients, he played a more inclusive game melding the new with the old, classical with castellar. As architectural historian Aonghus MacKechnie has argued,

by celebrating his own national tradition Bruce showed that the languages of castellated national antiquity and of [international] classicism could coexist, and that castles could be enjoyed as the architecture both of the past and of the present[55]

Perhaps even at Kinross Bruce was uneasy. Developing the gardens and landscaping at Kinross in strictly formal sequence with 'quadrant links and courts in the Palladio manner'[56] he extended the grand central axis of the layout out across Loch Leven to terminate in Lochleven Castle, the ruined fourteenth century tower-house where Mary, Queen of Scots, had been imprisoned. Was this no more than a respectful but valedictory gesture to the past or was it perhaps an arm's-length acknowledgement of a lingering national nostalgia?

Kinross House and Lochleven Castle
HES Canmore SC704832

Chapter 4

The Palladian Paradigm and the Castle Style
Classical Kinross to Castellar Culzean

'the most original creations of eighteenth century European architecture'

Alistair Rowan, *Designs for Castles and Country Villas by Robert & James Adam*

By the early years of the eighteenth century the innovations of Sir William Bruce and his near contemporary, James Smith, whom the architect Colen Campbell, 'propagandist of the Palladian movement in British architecture',[1] believed to be 'the most experience'd Architect'[2] in Scotland, had effected 'a complete and irreversible revolution in Scottish architecture'.[3] Both men had held the important position of Surveyor or Overseer of the Royal Works in Scotland and both were well aware of the most recent European developments in the history of architecture not only through the filter of English practice but also in terms of their direct personal experience on continental Europe. Both had travelled and studied abroad: Bruce in the Low Countries and in France; Smith in Italy. Both were familiar with the latest pattern books and treatises, not least, particularly in

Hopetoun House
Detail of elevation drawing from *Vitruvius Britannicus* 1714
HES Canmore DP064041

Smith's case, with the ideas of the sixteenth century Italian architect Andrea Palladio whose Veneto mansions and more particularly his *I quattro libri dell'architettura* (*The Four Books of Architecture*) would have a profound influence across Europe and beyond. By exemplifying their accumulating knowledge of classical architecture in increasingly sophisticated projects, Bruce and Smith largely succeeded in loosening, though not wholly detaching, Scottish architecture from its native roots. The coincidence of this transformation with the 1707 Union of the Parliaments and the corresponding collapse of an independent *Scottish* strategy in political, economic and cultural matters – a loss later intensified by post-Jacobite repressions – resonates with both positive and negative significance. Perspicacious or perverse, as the century progressed, Scottish architecture increasingly acquired what many regarded as a new respectability.

Bruce's proposals for Hopetoun House, West Lothian, his last major work, built from 1699 to 1703, are clearly sourced from continental precedent. The exceptional bi-axial plan of the house itself, a Greek

Hopetoun House

Elevation drawing and plan from *Vitruvius Britannicus* 1714

HES Canmore DP064041, Hendrik Hulsbergh; after Sir William Bruce Plate 75 from Colen Campbell's *Vitruvius Britannicus*, 'The Plan of Hopetoun House' National Galleries of Scotland. Purchased by the Patrons of the National Galleries of Scotland 1997

cross set within a square, appears to derive from the Villa Rotonda via the Château de Marly, while the overall layout with flanking service wings linked to the house by colonnaded quadrants – in this case, convex – is also Palladian. Externally, too, the impact was 'Palladian with an easy horizontality'[4] that was far removed from the thrusting towers, chimneys and ogee-helmeted turrets of Drumlanrig. At Hamilton Palace, Lanarkshire, the remodelling of which began a few years earlier under James Smith's direction but was not completed until 1701, the same calm horizontality characterised the building's extended elevations. Although the palace was constructed on an 'old-fashioned' U-plan, the duke and his architect shared a familiarity with the latest developments in England and the continent, which ensured that the design was uncompromisingly classical, its most innovative and impressive feature a splendid tetrastyle portico set at the centre of the principal facade. Aspects of the planning and elevational design of these two buildings would recur in many of the country houses built in Scotland during the eighteenth century.

The precisely balanced symmetries of Bruce's bi-axial plan at Hopetoun did not survive unscathed by the radical alterations and enlargement of the house which William Adam began in 1721. Bruce's Palladian sophistication was, in any case, a somewhat precious concept with almost no parallel in Scottish architecture. But it is perhaps worth noting that evidence of the same continental sources that Bruce had drawn on for this centralised plan did appear in a series of speculative designs for 'royal palaces' prepared by the Jacobite émigré John Erskine, earl of Mar. A number of drawings show bi-axial plans developed around central domed spaces, refinements of the Palladio-derived concept which Jules Hardouin-Mansart had realised at the Château de Marly and which Mar knew from his time in France. Exiled for his part in the unsuccessful rebellion of 1715–16, Mar spent the remainder of his life on the continent where, when not involved in political intrigue, he passed his time conceiving a variety of ambitious architectural schemes, many vast in scale, all informed by scholarly knowledge but almost all never to be realised. It has been suggested that, in pursuing this enforced career, Mar's intention was not simply to update and internationalise Scottish architecture by emulating French or Italian precedent but to transform these classical sources in order 'to create a Scottish Jacobite architectural style'.[5] If this is so, it is difficult to judge from his work what the formal lineaments of this style might be. A few drawings prepared in Paris in 1723 show plans and elevations of a relatively small house near Brechin for Mar's cousin Lord Dun. Entirely classical in its detail, the house's narrow principal south facade of three bays defined by giant-order Ionic pilasters has a vertical emphasis that might just be construed as Scottish. Mar's design was never built but the facade did reappear as a portico at the centre of William Adam's seven-bay north front of the House of Dun, completed in 1742, but in such modified form as to be all but unrecognisable. More convincing than the elevations for the house near Brechin are the accompanying plans and sections which reveal

Design for a house near Brechin
Unexecuted elevation drawing by William Adam 1723
National Records of Scotland

Design for a house near Brechin
Unexecuted section drawing by William Adam 1723
National Records of Scotland

'a six-storeyed building with a half-mezzanine floor (providing a Pipers' Gallery in each Hall), with access to every floor by three staircases of which two are of the traditional newel type, set in the thickness of the exterior walls at the corners'[6] and which thus seem to have adapted the traditional tower-house, stripping it of 'baronial excrescences and encasing the remaining mediaeval structure in Roman fancy dress'.[7] Much earlier, long before his banishment, Mar had done exactly this, regularising the old tower-house at his estate at Alloa because, as he later wrote, there was 'something in the old Tower, especially if made conforme to the new designe, wch. is very venerable for its antiquity and makes not a bad appearance'.[8] But, however intriguing, this is scant evidence with which to substantiate a significant or pervasive Scottishness. In any event Mar's exile ensured his influence on architectural events in Scotland remained considerably less than it might otherwise have been.

While the cross-in-square perfection of Hopetoun's original plan was compromised by the later changes made by William Adam, Bruce's Palladian conceit of a wide forecourt with colonnaded quadrants leading to flanking pavilions remained, though not without some changes being made. The most obvious of these was the reversal of the colonnade curves from convex to concave. But there were others. While Adam suppressed Bruce's stress on the central axis of the building by the removal of the stone cupola which rose high over the central staircase behind the facade, he widened the pavilions which flanked the forecourt, adding a central pediment and tall cupola to each. Seen in the distant perspective of the grand axial approach, each cupola effects a vertical thrust flanking the horizontal attic storey of the main house – the faintest echo perhaps of the corner-towered castellar compositions of the previous century. A more positive evocation of this tradition seems to have been present in Adam's near-contemporary design for Floors Castle in Roxburghshire where the starkly plain house, an oblong box three-storeys-and-basement high, was accented at all four corners by square towers.[9] Yet here, too, though there was little in the way of classical detail or ornament beyond the pedimented towers, the overall layout was expansively symmetrical and Palladian, the tower-flanked eleven-bay north front linked by cranked arcades to U-plan service pavilions opposed across a wide forecourt. Indeed, this idea of the country house conceived as a 'Palladian assemblage'[10] evident in Bruce's Hopetoun plans, proved to be a recurring theme of Scottish architecture throughout the eighteenth century and beyond. Plans varied from those with a grand axial approach and spacious forecourt in which the flanking pavilions were linked to the estate mansion by quadrant colonnades or arcades to those where identical lower wings were simply extended on each side of the main facade plane.

By mid century, forecourt plans had been projected at many country houses both new and recast, among them Blairdrummond, Donibristle House, Hopetoun House, Floors Castle, Mavisbank, Haddo House, Taymouth Castle and Duff House.[11] Many of the more prestigious commissions made a competent display of the classical orders and ornament, particularly in always-more-ambitious early design proposals. Such elevational schemes were often focused on a facade

Floors Castle
Drawing of north elevation by William Adam c1723
HES Canmore SC1025745

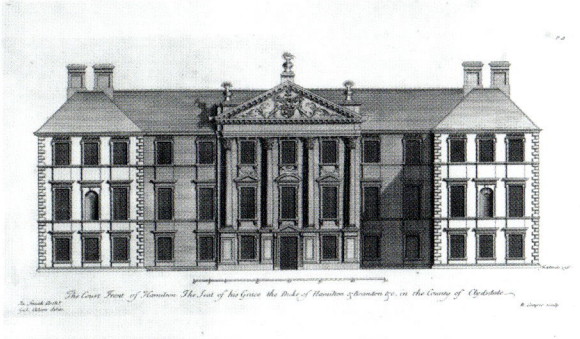

Hamilton Palace
Drawing showing elevation of the south front c1730 by William Adam, photograph of the north front c1880
HES Canmore SC750229, DP091509

portico similar to that first seen at Hamilton Palace.¹² This pedimented tetrastyle model, derived like the grand forecourt plan from Palladian precedent (in the case of Hamilton probably from the church of San Giorgio Maggiore in Venice with its pedimented giant order Corinthian columns raised on panelled socles)¹³ would also become a recurring feature of country house design in eighteenth century Scotland. Among those houses where by mid century the strategy was apparent were Dalkeith House, Hopetoun House (portico not built), Yester House, Newliston House (unbuilt) and Duff House. For a hundred years, from Sir William Bruce to Robert Adam, so successful did the Palladian paradigm prove that it is difficult to discern any inherent Scottishness in Scottish architecture beyond perhaps a persistent sense of stern reserve which, whether for aesthetic or merely economic reasons, was increasingly preferred to the temptations of the baroque. Built in mid century, Dumfries House, Ayrshire, its facade pedimented but lacking a portico, is perhaps the best – and the dullest – example of this particular trait. Less austere, however, and much more endearing is its charming neighbour, Auchinleck House, which does have a portico, typically engaged or 'pressed in' on the facade, as at Hamilton. Far from displaying any chance or gratuitous Scottishness, Auchinleck, delicate and decorous, is patently European, international in derivation and aspiration. Indeed (and here lies paradox), so evidently Palladian is Auchinleck that it is easy to imagine this delightful house poised in the sleepy afternoon heat on the bank of some sluggish Veneto canal.

There is, however, one house which, for all its Palladian affinities, yet succeeds in affirming an unmistakably national identity. When first projected by William Adam, Duff House (1735–40), Banff, was conceived in the grandest terms, the house linked by nine-bay colonnaded quadrants to U-plan service wings which were topped off with domed cupolas reminiscent of those at Hopetoun. The plan of the house itself was also fundamentally Palladian, based on tripartite division and cross-axial symmetry. The elevations were no less classical, the principal facade richly detailed, with an engaged portico of finely wrought fluted Corinthian pilasters. But Adam, not content to provide his client, Lord Braco, with a standard design solution of respectable European provenance, effected some daring departures from prevailing classical orthodoxy, both in terms of plan and elevation. It is these which give Duff House its special quality of Scottishness.[14]

At Hopetoun Adam had retained something of the Palladian house plan which Bruce had introduced, albeit with some modification. Now at Banff he made more radical interventions by adding a projecting square tower at each corner of the plan, a move he had already made at Floors Castle and surely, despite antecedents south of the border and in a variety of French and Italian treatises, a deliberate evocation

Duff House
Historic Environment Scotland

of the Scottish past. An ingenious arrangement of accommodation at these corner apartments entailed the introduction of service 'mezzaninos' and spiral service stairs positioned in such a way at the internal angle of each tower as to suggest a dim memory of the turnpikes locked in the internal angles of the courtyards at Linlithgow, Heriot's Hospital and Drumlanrig.

Besides these planning innovations the towers had, of course, corresponding elevational consequences. Raised on a rusticated ground storey, the house's two principal storeys were articulated by giant order fluted Corinthian pilasters which defined engaged three-bay porticos on the south and north facades and flanked the eight exposed faces of all four corner towers. This unusually lavish architectural treatment, surmounted on all four facades by a fine entablature with a continuous modillion cornice rising to pediments south and north, was further enhanced by curving flights of stairs reflected symmetrically on each side of the south portico terrace and, more remarkably, by the building of a balustraded attic storey. At each corner of this attic, a pilastered and corniced tower rose to a dome with composite chimney stacks gathered in an octagonal pinnacle at its apex. Adam had already introduced attic storeys at Hopetoun and Newliston (his design for the latter house unbuilt) and had recommended a similar effect at Mavisbank, though there he had been over-ruled. This fate had almost befallen his design for Duff House when Lord Braco had wanted to abandon the extra storey, believing that this would make the building 'less exposed to Storms'.[15] Much later, in the 1760s, 'an ambitious idea to remove the entire attic storey'[16] was envisaged when proposals (which proved abortive) were advanced to build flanking service wings. While Lord Braco's climatic objection seems more likely to conceal a desire to make savings, the aesthetic argument would be more convincing *if* – but only if – the overriding architectural aim were to hold to the principles of Palladian orthodoxy. But was this Adam's intention? Duff House is a building of international stature,

Dumfries House
HES Canmore DP033628

it is unequivocally classical, the architectural detail and execution outstanding, yet it is a building which re-asserts a national tradition. The compressed vertical thrust of the pilastered main building, the tall domed towers advancing at the corners, the chimneys, even the urns of 'Adam's elaborate skyline',[17] all contribute to the building's Scottishness. Indeed, in this regard it might be argued that the absence of quadrant links and outer pavilions, whether as Adam planned or as later architects proposed, has meant that the building rises from its parkland landscape with all the stark abruptness of the tower-house.

This failure to realise the full Palladian conceit, so intensifying whatever nostalgia for the 'castle-wise' buildings of Scotland's past William Adam may have vested in his towered design for Duff House, was, of course, unintended and entirely fortuitous. Elsewhere, however, castellar ambition was more deliberate. About the time that Adam was raising an action in the courts against his client, Lord Braco, for non-payment of fees for his work at Duff House, the 3rd Duke of Argyll was about to come to a decision regarding the architectural form and character of a new castle to take the place of the Campbells' 'ruinous and almost uninhabitable'[18] tower-house at Inveraray on Loch Fyne. A varied sequence of proposals had preceded the final design adopted at Inveraray, the earliest of which appears to have been a scheme thought to have been prepared by Vanbrugh, architect of Blenheim Palace, for the 2nd Duke in the early 1720s. This sketch proposal, showing a square courtyard plan with round corner towers, was conceived in a castellar idiom, the walls battlemented, the towers rising to corbelled parapets circling conic roofs. If not yet quite 'Gothick' in character, it was certainly medieval in evocation and bore striking affinities with the completed castle. Further proposals of unknown date, probably obtained from another English architect, Roger Morris, who had also worked for the 2nd Duke, took a different approach. These later plans were still square but with a central staircase hall taking the place of the courtyard in Vanbrugh's scheme and with square towers rather than round engaged at the corners. Externally, as Lindsay and Cosh have pointed out in their wonderfully exhaustive study *Inveraray and the Dukes of Argyll* (1973), this speculative design, which Morris had conceived in a distinct but muted classical character, was not without some similarities to Adam's Duff House: besides the square towers, a 'base

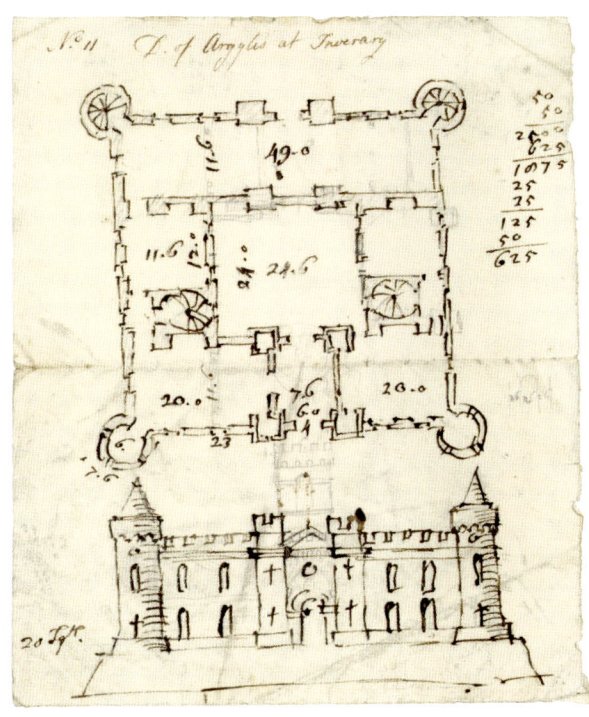

storey above ground, double stair to a round-headed first-floor entrance, and cornice running the length of the front between second and third storeys'.[19] But this resemblance (if that is not too strong a word) is surely no more than coincidental; nor can it be said to be significant beyond the fact that corner towers, albeit no longer square, remained an important element in the final Inveraray design. A third set of drawings, c1743–5, obtained from the military engineer Dugal Campbell, envisaged a vastly inflated 'House for the Duke of Argyll at Inverarey' [sic], geometrically inventive in plan and section, again castellar in its architectural forms, but outrageously ambitious in scale. Campbell held an important position in the Civil Branch of the Ordnance and was a kinsman of the 3rd Duke, but it is difficult to imagine that this proposal could have been taken seriously. In the event, in 1744 the commission was given to Roger Morris.

In his final proposals for Inveraray, Morris refined the symmetrical rigour of his earlier plans while at the same time assimilating the medieval conceit which, some two decades before, had been championed by Vanbrugh and which evidently still figured prominently in the architectural fancy of the 3rd Duke. On the one hand, the inner courtyard of Vanbrugh's scheme was rejected in favour of a central

Inveraray Castle, Argyll and Bute

Sketch plan and elevation by Sir John Vanbrugh c1720
© Victoria and Albert Museum, London.

Roger Morris plans and elevations c1744
HES Canmore

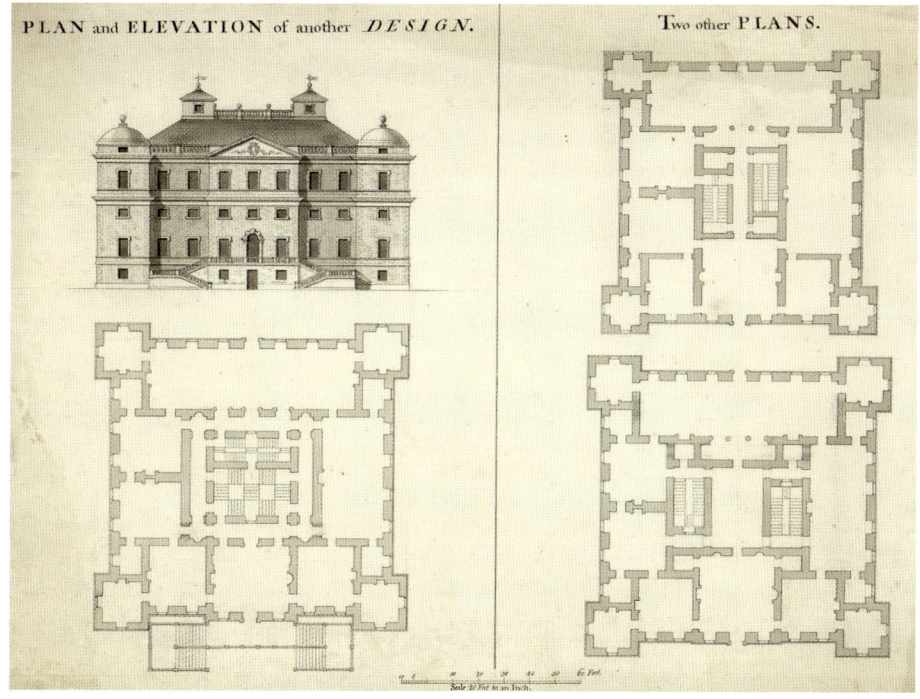

hall with parallel flanking staircases over which rose a high lantern tower; on the other, Vanbrugh's proposal for a gallery extending along the entire north side of the castle, his battlemented walls and his round corner towers[20] were incorporated in an architecture made even more Gothick by the introduction of hooded pointed-arch windows at every level. The decision to build a fosse or dry moat around the castle, first proposed in Dugal Campbell's drawings, added a further anachronistic element.

Work began in 1745. With Morris located in London, the appointment of an executive architect less remotely based was deemed necessary. This task fell to William Adam, who from 1730 held the position of Mason to the Board of Ordnance in Scotland and was considered to be 'the ablest man we have in Scotland for Carrying on so great a Design'.[21] Not surprisingly perhaps, Adam 'found the Gothic style adopted by Morris somewhat embarrassing'[22] but, beyond seeking guidance on the precise geometry of the pointed-arch window openings, he deferred properly to the Englishman's design. Within a few years, however, both Adam and Morris were dead and the supervision of the work became the responsibility of Adam's son John assisted by his younger brother Robert. Robert's involvement was brief and of little immediate consequence at Inveraray itself, yet it would in time prove to have been of some significance in the evolution of his unique and evocatively Scottish 'Castle Style'.

But just how Scottish was the castle at Inveraray? (Indeed, how Scottish was Robert Adam's 'Castle Style'? – but of this more later.) It has been rightly observed that Morris's plan, square and symmetrical, with its central space surrounded by other rooms, is essentially Palladian and 'stems ultimately from Serlio'.[23] The 3rd Duke certainly held copies of both Serlio and Palladio in his library but the more immediate precedents were English. Central hall spaces lit from above had appeared at Mereworth (1722–25), designed by the Duke's kinsman Colen Campbell and illustrated in his *Vitruvius Britannicus*, which Argyll also possessed, and at the self-consciously Palladian Chiswick House, begun 1725, by Lord Burlington and William Kent. For examples of a central hall with double stairs, however, Morris must have turned to Vanbrugh, to Castle Howard (1699–1712), Blenheim (1705–24), and especially to the now demolished Eastbury Park, Dorset, begun in 1718, which, with its 'clearstorey enclosing both central hall and double main stairs in exactly the same way as Inveraray',[24] he himself had completed in the 1730s. Several earlier English buildings have also been suggested as possible influences on the design of Inveraray. Notable among these is Wollaton Hall, in Nottinghamshire, completed in 1588 with a central hall rising to a high clearstorey, staircases on each side of the hall and advancing square towers at each corner of a square plan. Similar developments of the late medieval fortified house with its battlemented walls and corner towers include Michelgrove in Sussex (c1536), Lulworth Castle in Dorset (begun 1588), and Ruperra in Glamorganshire (1626). At Michelgrove the turrets were octagonal but at both Lulworth and Ruperra they were round and almost detached from the square plan, a very 'un-Scottish feature, for the towers and turrets of sixteenth- and seventeenth-century [Scottish] castles were always subtly integrated',[25] but one which was, nonetheless, adopted at Inveraray. Indeed, setting aside the building's distant Italian antecedents, it is clear that in terms of its plan and section Inveraray drew not on Scottish but on English precedent.

This was even more so – and more visibly so – in the Gothick elevational treatment of the castle. 'Gothick', that is to say that unscholarly recovery of medieval Gothic forms which had begun to exercise an aberrant romantic appeal on the eighteenth century's otherwise classical taste, was entirely an English vogue. Why then should Argyll and his architect, Roger Morris, whose previous experience as a designer had given him 'little understanding of Gothic detail',[26] have adopted this approach? Why should an English fashion find its first significant architectural expression by the shore of a remote sea loch in western Scotland?

The results of the tentative engagement with revived Gothic forms already evident in English architecture prior to the 1740s were often whimsical, their design and execution carrying little archaeological conviction. Vanbrugh, for example, had toyed with the emerging fashion and his c1720 sketch proposal for Inveraray, with its battlemented and turreted invocation of a medieval past, had caught the imagination of the 3rd Duke. Indeed the Duke, as Earl of Islay, had already built a Gothick tower at Whitton Place, Middlesex, in the 1730s. An awareness of the castellar architecture of Lulworth and Ruperra,[27] towered, crenellated and lit by hooded pointed-arch windows, must also have sharpened the Duke's enthusiasm. The publication in 1742 of Batty Langley's *Ancient Architecture, Restored, and Improved, by a Great variety of Grand and Usefull Designs, Entirely New in the Gothick Mode for the Ornamenting of Buildings and Gardens* may have provided Morris, who seems to have been involved in the building of the Whitton Place tower, with further practical exemplars of Gothick detail and perhaps with some theoretical basis on which to ground the new (or revived) style. The architectural historian James Macaulay has suggested that since the Duke of Argyll was chief of the ancient Campbell clan and since 'In Scotland the castle was the accepted and understood symbol of a landowner's suzerainty',[28] it should come as no surprise that when the Duke built his new castle he 'chose the Gothic mode'.[29] The grounds for this assertion are slight and unconvincing. He cites little more than Scotland's long tradition of castle building and while it might be argued that this establishes a continuity of medieval forms such as towers, turrets and corbelling, it does not offer a persuasive provenance for the pointed-arch windows, hood mouldings and tracery which are such characteristic and repetitive features at Inveraray. No doubt a certain castellar medievalism had survived in Scottish architecture although it is difficult to accept Macaulay's contention that, for example, 'the full-blooded spirit of Gothicism persists in Drumlanrig Castle'.[30] The style of Inveraray is indeed, as Macaulay rightly says, 'emblematic'. But emblematic of what? Certainly not of a specifically Scottish past.

In fact, that the 2nd Duke of Argyll should have been among the patrons of Langley's book that celebrated and advocated Gothick for its national (English) origins, not only points to an interest in the architectural style. It also hints at the degree to which the Campbells of Inveraray looked to London and aligned themselves with Hanoverian power. The 3rd Duke's political affiliations were no less unionist – he had in fact been a commissioner active in the negotiations leading to the 1707 Treaty of Union – and his new castle at Inveraray was clearly intended as a statement both of clan power and Campbell loyalty to the Crown in London. In mid eighteenth century Scotland, a too-ardent Scottishness could be dangerous. In the very year when Prince Charles Edward Stewart raised his standard at Glenfinnan on Loch Shiel, foundations were being laid at Inveraray for a building whose Englishness would, in the repressive aftermath of the rebellion, assert the emergence of a new cultural reality. As Aonghus MacKechnie has so cogently argued, the Duke's castle signified 'an absolute commitment to the recently made and more recently threatened state that was

Protestant Britain, the alignment with English culture and the myth of a single "national" history which this demanded.'[31]

In this new Britain, eighteenth century Scotland, shorn of sovereignty, played a conflicted role. On the one hand, the country experienced both Improvement, with all the pain and disruption of the Clearances, and the intellectual liberation of the Enlightenment. In a climate of increasing commercial and agricultural prosperity, an urban culture focused on the universities of Edinburgh, Glasgow, Aberdeen and St Andrews released an astonishingly creative surge in intellectual activity. Suddenly Scotland excelled in philosophy, the sciences, medicine, history, social theory, political economy and the arts. Rejecting the term 'North Britain' (used after the 1707 Act of Union in an attempt to play down any idea of a separate Scottish identity), the Scottish literati identified with similar liberating movements elsewhere: 'Their orientation was cosmopolitan.'[32] The philosopher David Hume, not content to be Scottish or even British, chose to consider himself 'a citizen of the world'. Thus, although thirled to London in terms of politics and patronage, this burgeoning culture – rational, tolerant and literate – aspired to and attained an *international* distinction which transcended the limitations and tensions of the compromised *national* status which, albeit as a result of economic *force majeure*, had been inflicted upon the country. While it was, paradoxically, true that the new dominance of the English language at the expense of Scots and Gaelic undoubtedly enabled those who had embraced it to reach a wider audience, whether directly or in translation, for the men of the Scottish Enlightenment the 'British myth', which continued after the Jacobite defeat at Culloden, remained a remained a narrow and inadequate concept. But Scottish culture also had its more genuinely popular side, more often rural rather than urban, romantic rather than rational, introspective rather than outward-looking. A wealth of poetry written in both the Scots and Gaelic languages was without parallel in the sophisticated anglicised literary world of Edinburgh. In lowland Scotland Robert Fergusson and Robert Burns, writing *Poems Chiefly in the Scottish Dialect*, celebrated the events and characters of everyday life in town and country, not without the sharp cutting edge of satire. At the same time, the poems of Alasdair Mac Mhaighstir Alasdair, Rob Donn and Dugald Buchanan constituted 'a period of renewed Gaelic awareness' in the north.[33] No poetic content had, however, a more immediate appeal (more in English translation than in the original Gaelic), than the imagined raw reality of a distant all-but-forgotten Scotland starkly revealed in the Ossianic verses which James Macpherson had collected, compiled and, it seems, in very large measure composed (see Chapter 2). Despite the controversy which arose over their authenticity when published in the 1760s, so successful were these *Fragments of Ancient Poetry Collected in the Highlands of Scotland* on the *international* literary stage that for a time they became in effect the sacred text of a compensatory *national* myth capable of preserving a Scottish consciousness in the face of an increasingly aggressive Britishness. Thus, by two reciprocal routes, the cultural Unionism imposed on post-Jacobite Britain was, though not subverted, at least called in question.

Ambitious and shrewd enough to sense the architectural ambiguities – and opportunities – implicit in this new British culture, Robert Adam hedged his bets. Turning at times to Gothick, most often to the more ordered and more marketable norms of international classicism, and latterly also to the unique ambivalence of his own Castle Style, he proved to be the outstanding Scottish architect of the second half of the eighteenth century.

As a young man skilled in drawing and 'building things',[34] Robert's passions were – and remained – painting and architecture. Some early drawings survive not only of classical houses, which were, after all, the stock-in-trade of the family's flourishing building business (to assist in which Robert had been obliged in 1745 to quit his university studies in Edinburgh) but also of picturesque landscapes and, more surprisingly perhaps, of medieval, frequently castellar, buildings, both observed and fancied. These architectural flirtations must surely have been stimulated by his experience at Inveraray assisting first his father and then his brother John in the realisation of Roger Morris's design. A number of sketch proposals from the years before he departed for Italy in 1754 depict what are best called 'Rococo Gothick' caprices.[35] In several, the governing compositional principle was 'of a small central building joined by screen walls to a pair of flanking pavilions',[36] a strategy ironically classical, not to say Palladian, which Robert would no doubt have begun to assimilate as a young apprentice in the family firm. But, apart from the Gothick facade applied to the medieval chapel at Yester House in 1753, these *folies* remained on paper, no more than exploratory fancies. In fact, in his entire career Robert realised only one completely new structure in the Gothick style and that not until the late 1770s when, as part of a series of both exterior and interior design proposals for the Earl of Northumberland's medievalising renovation of Alnwick Castle, he was commissioned to build Brislee Tower. For the moment, however, in the day-to-day business of serving his apprenticeship and earning a living, Robert was still his father's son and when, after William's death, he and his brothers undertook their first independent commissions, they maintained the family firm's long established commitment to classical architecture. Begun in 1754, Dumfries House near Cumnock, on which all three brothers, John, Robert and James, appear to have worked, was a staid exercise in Palladian classicism; 'competent and acceptable' is one scholar's reserved assessment.[37] This plainness may be as much the result of the economies made by the client, the Earl of Dumfries, as it is the product of its young designers' still evolving skills. A two-storey-and-basement, nine-bay mansion, pedimented over the central three bays with a pediment-wide flight of steps leading to the entrance and arcuated quadrants linking the house to lower two-storey pavilion wings, it nevertheless convincingly demonstrated the brothers' classical credentials, if only in a somewhat bleak and austere way. The design had none of their father's more robust ebullience nor as yet any of the suave proportional elegance and inventiveness which Robert would later develop. Even so, a fascination with Gothick remained. Only three years later, John and James began the building of Douglas Castle, an outrageously aggrandised version of Gothick Inveraray never to be completed. But by then Robert was in Dalmatia (present day Croatia) in search of the Antique.

Robert Adam arrived in Genoa in January 1755 in company with the Hon. Charles Hope, brother of the Earl of Hopetoun, for whom the Adam brothers had completed the building of Hopetoun House. His Grand Tour, which was to transform his life, would last until January 1758: it would bring him face to face with the classical buildings of Renaissance Italy, from Brunelleschi's Florence, to the Rome which Giovanni Battista Piranesi had pictured in his many etchings, to the Veneto of Palladio; it would provide him with a perspective on the history of art and architecture stretching back to the great monuments of the Antique world. Just as important if he were to realise his declared ambition to be 'the remover of taste from Italy to *England*'[38](my italics), the tour would introduce him to a cultivated circle of aristocratic fellow travellers whose acquaintance would in due course pay dividends in terms of social acceptance and patronage. But first he had much to learn. Just how much is clear from a comment made by the French architect and draughtsman, Charles-Louis Clérisseau, who, following their meeting in Florence, had been persuaded by Robert to become his companion and tutor for the remainder of the tour, sharing his 'utmost knowledge of architecture, of perspective, and of designing and colouring'.[39] Adam was, wrote Clérisseau, 'very ignorant of architecture when he came to me, except the Gothic',[40] an assessment which, if Clérisseau is to be believed, while it singled out a particular stylistic propensity, was probably more fundamentally intended as a broader verdict on the Scotsman's provincial untutored taste. In any event, Clérisseau set about giving his new pupil and friend 'some taste for the antique'. Adam was an eager student. In Rome, the days were too short: there was so much to see and draw. He found himself accepted in *émigré* society; he encountered fellow architects, among them William Chambers and Robert Wood, intent as he was in coming to creative terms with classicism. He met the painters Allan Ramsay, Raphael Mengs and Pompeo Batoni, was on friendly terms with Cardinal Albani, then the foremost collector of antique sculpture and he bought up 'all the books of architecture'[41] he could find. All the while his collection of measured drawings, perspective views and sketches of Rome's buildings, ancient and modern – his prized investment for a prosperous future – was growing and growing. So overwhelming were these experiences that he declared himself 'antique mad'. So marked was his progress under the discipline of Clérisseau's tutelage that he could maintain, with a characteristic lack of modesty, that his friendship with Giovanni Piranesi was based on the Roman's enthusiastic commendation that 'I have more genius for the true noble architecture than any Englishman ever was in Italy'.[42]

This 'true noble architecture' was the classical architecture of the Antique world, an architecture which, though at times weakened or abused, had persisted throughout the history of art, an architecture which, it seemed, made little or no concession to the geography of art. It was Piranesi who weaned Adam from the limiting rule-governed austerities of neo-Palladianism, encouraging him to develop a freer nobler interpretation of the past. The architect, he wrote, 'must not content himself with copying faithfully the ancients but studying their works he ought to shew himself an inventive … creative Genius … he ought to open himself a road to the finding out of new ornaments and new manners'.[43] The spirit of the Antique transcended time and place: it was the architect's task to grasp and revivify this spirit. Adam's search for 'new ornaments and new manners' was insatiable. Everywhere the fecundity of Roman architecture, ancient and modern, impressed and enthused him. From Rome to Florence, Bologna, Padua and Venice; from Venice to Split (Spalatro) in Dalmatia. There in five weeks of intensive measuring and sketching he, Clérisseau and two draughtsmen recorded the remains of Diocletian's Palace, later to be collated in a splendidly produced publication he would dedicate to no less a person than the Hanoverian king.

Such was the extent of Adam's ambition. Back in Britain with a whetted taste for the polite society of 'an English life'[44] and a cool eye cast on the market, he set up practice in London in 1758. No longer the raw novice at remote Inveraray or Fort George, he was now at the centre of things; no more the provincial Scot, he was now, as his letters from Italy had boasted, 'my dearest Mother's British boy'.[45] His brothers James and William joined him. Commissions poured in and, with its sophisticated and inventive interpretation of classical sources, the Adam style prospered, most notably in the field of domestic architecture, both urban and rural. The overall schema adopted for the country house remained broadly Palladian – a central block with flanking wings or pavilions – but now a freer, more eclectic, often more decorative approach applied. No less elegant in proportion than the earlier houses of Lord Burlington and William Kent with their pedimented temple fronts and Venetian windows, the architecture of these urbane residences drew on a yet richer range of classical forms – relieving arches featured frequently, Diocletian windows appeared both large and small, columns and pilasters were often subtly elongated, bowed projections advanced at the centre of some facades, at Luton Park (1761–74) and Gosford (1790–2) a dome rose behind the portico, at Kedleston (c1760–8) a triumphal arch motif dominated the south front.

Yet there was also a more restless romantic side to Adam's creativity which, however much reinforced by the experiences of the Grand Tour, owed its origin to his upbringing and apprenticeship in Scotland. Landscape, picturesque landscape, sublime landscape, the wild craggy landscape of 'the mountain and the flood',[46] fascinated him to such an extent that throughout his life he continually drew and painted such scenes. From childhood, Caledonia proved a 'meet nurse' to Adam's creative spirit. He produced well over a thousand, perhaps thousands, of these compositions both topographical and imaginary. In almost all of them small figures featured in the foreground serving to increase the scale and drama of the scene while in the middle distance, perched above wooded slopes on a cliff-buttressed eminence, rose a towered and crenellated castle. As with landscape, this obsession with castles may also have begun in childhood: in 1740 William Adam had extended the family estate of Blair Adam near Kinross, incorporating the small fifteenth century tower-house of Dowhill, a roofless ruin whose hilltop location and crumbling masonry must have fired young Robert's imagination as he played in and around its walls. Later experience as an apprentice architect brought hands-on practical knowledge of such buildings as well as a growing awareness of the national tradition of castellar architecture; not only had William Adam worked with his sons on the fortified barracks at Fort George, Fort Augustus and Fort William but the family firm had also carried out repairs and adaptations on several historic Scottish castles – Edinburgh, Stirling, Blackness, Dumbarton, Duart, Braemar and Corgarff among them. Nor were his emerging conceits of fancy, those countless drawings he produced, without stimulation. At Fort George he encountered a kindred spirit in the artist Paul Sandby whose topographical drawings and watercolours, so congenial in sensibility, influenced and validated Robert's vision. But that the castle might be more than a mere relic of the past to be respected, repaired and perhaps even restored, and more, too, than the indulged delight of his romantic imagination, must soon have become clear. No doubt, 'inspired by the curtain and gatehouse towers on [those] medieval buildings'[47] he had encountered, he must have felt this enthusiasm vindicated by the work of Sir John Vanbrugh, whose castellar buildings at Blackheath and elsewhere were known to the Adams – 'rough jewels of inestimable value' Robert later called them.[48] If not because of the example set by Vanbrugh, then certainly as a result of his own involvement at Inveraray, the feasibility of conceiving and building a *contemporary* castle must have begun to lodge in Robert's mind. This early tentative conviction with its architectural amalgam of romantic caprice, historical knowledge and constructional *nous*, the experience of the Grand Tour could only intensify. The towered silhouettes of Italian hill towns and Rhenish castles, the powerful three-dimensional geometries of Roman and Venetian fortifications, not least the theatrical drama of Piranesi's *concetti*, these, too, are surely among the formal forces that shaped Robert Adam's unique Castle Style.

Adam's reasons for developing this distinctive style were essentially architectural, that is to say his motivation was formal, prompted by the possibilities implicit in his ever-increasing portfolio of romantic castle-crested landscapes. At the same time he was shrewd enough to realise that were he to bring a buildable order to his dreams such a product would find a market. And so it proved. For there were those, particularly among his circle of estate-owning acquaintances, who saw in this novel Castle Style both an opportunity to indulge in the increasingly fashionable picturesque and a means of overtly asserting familial associations with a medieval past which, rendered politically innocuous by the success of the unifying British myth, could still exercise its nostalgic appeal. In mid century, in the immediate wake of the second Jacobite uprising, it had been tactless, not to say dangerous, to espouse any kind of architectural agenda, castellar or otherwise, that might have been construed to have a measure of Scottish content. By the latter decades of the century, however, the cultural climate of Britishness was sufficiently well established and secure enough to countenance a growing desire on the part of those commissioning country houses to build an *ersatz* 'ready-made antiquity' as an expression of historical continuity, genuine or fabricated. Powerful as the built declaration of lineage might be, the allusive potential of this sentimentally satisfying architecture carried no symbolic threat to the status quo, social, cultural or political. That the Castle Style could prove significantly cheaper than the classical alternative because of its less refined materials and detailing doubtless added to its attraction.

Mellerstain House
HES Canmore DP265894

For whatever reason or combination of reasons, the Castle Style proved successful. But it accounted for little more than 10% of the Adam practice output. Moreover, it is important to stress that Adam's allegiance to the fundamental formal disciplines of classical architecture remained constant. It was a commitment evident in virtually his entire work. Just as his few dalliances with Gothic detail might be explored within Palladian schema, so, too, the compositional design of his castles submitted to a similar overarching order of symmetry. But not in any sense to the framed order implicit in classicism. The architecture of Adam's Castle Style is an architecture of *mass*. His earliest 'castles' were simple tripartite blocks crenellated along the parapets and lit by hood-moulded lintelled windows. At Ugbrooke in Devon (c1763–8) and Whitehaven in Cumbria (c1769), pavilions advanced and rose at the ends of the battlemented building. At Mellerstain, Berwickshire (c1770–78), a similar formula was adopted but with the additional emphasis of a raised centre. This strategy was repeated and elaborated in the principal west front of Wedderburn, also in Berwickshire (c1768–71), where the outer 'pavilions', reduced to room-sized turrets, were octagonal in plan and the modelling and fenestration of the central pavilion more developed. Here, too, at the centre of the south facade, a bowed projection was created. This last feature had earlier appeared in the small chapel block at Ugbrooke, as had relieving arch forms framing the ground-floor windows. Both elements would become increasingly evident as Adam's Castle Style matured. Bowed projections, semi-circular or segmental, were incorporated into the design of Culzean, Ayrshire (1777–90), Oxenfoord, Midlothian (1770–2), Dalquharran, Ayrshire (1782–90), Seton, East Lothian (1789–91), Airthrey, Stirlingshire (1790–1), Mauldsley, Lanarkshire (1791–2) and Stobs, Roxburghshire (1792–3). Relieving arches were just as frequently employed. At Caldwell in Renfrewshire (1771–3), for example, the tripartite composition of the north front of the three-storey house was enlivened by relieving arches, high in the centre, lower on the flanks (perhaps the vestigial imprint of the triumphal arch), while at Culzean the feature appeared on every elevation. Culzean was perhaps Adam's most castle-wise castle. Incorporating an ancient tower-house, it yet remained

Caldwell House
Photograph by T and R Annan and Sons c1889
HES Canmore DP247795

essentially classical in its composition and in much of its architectural detail. Seen from the south, its central four-storey block had a parapet of corbelled battlements accented at the corners by small bartizans (a distinctly Scottish element which Adam had adopted at Caldwell) while lower wings, abutting and slightly overlapping the higher centre with rounded turrets at their corners, were similarly crenellated. It was, however, the later north facade which best captured the essence of the Castle Style, in part because of its architectural movement – bulging at the centre of the facade, more than a semicircle in plan, was a massive drum-like projection flanked by narrower wings battlemented and bartizaned – but most convincingly because of its maritime landscape setting, the whole composition poised on the cliffs above the sea, a dramatic realisation of Adam's romantic sketches.

Can Adam's Castle Style be termed a 'Scottish' style? A case can certainly be made, even though only a relatively small proportion of the practice's output comprised castle commissions. The majority of these were built in Scotland where the new style 'seemed to find a particularly receptive audience'.[49] Their design engrossed a range of forms – curved and octagonal projections, battlemented parapets, towers and turrets, conic-roofed bartizans, crow-stepped gables – which could be understood to convey a sense of Scottishness. Their cumulative massing and irregular silhouettes, particularly when seen in distant oblique perspective as Adam had pictured his dream castles in drawings and watercolours, evoked picturesque affinities with the tower-houses and castles of the Scottish past. On the other hand, several Castle Style designs were projected, and some built, in England,[50] and then with no variation in style from those built in Scotland. Moreover, many of the forms adduced to the Castle Style were unquestionably classical – semi-circular relieving arches, round-arch windows, Venetian windows, pilasters – while the symmetrical order of plan and elevation adopted in Adam's castles, however creatively deployed, was fundamentally derived from the traits of international classicism. Seton, the most inventively three-dimensional of all the castles, even had a quasi-Palladian forecourt with concave quadrant links to extensive offices. The Scottishness of Adam's Castle Style is far from clear-cut; there is, indeed, something of that same dual architectural identity, national and international, which characterised the palaces of the Stuart kings.

Seton House
HES Canmore DP033413, SC1380670

In terms of detecting any inherent national Scottish agenda, assessments are inevitably ambivalent. However, it would be difficult to deny the view that the Castle Style can be regarded, to some considerable degree, as an architectural response to the Ossianic fervour of the latter half of the eighteenth century. One writer has gone so far as to suggest that Adam's castles were 'a living reminder of the Ossianic age',[51] though this is surely an unsupportable contention imputing as it does an anachronistic level of architectural sophistication to the mythical past. Moreover, when towards the end of his life Adam was engaged to design a house on the slopes rising above the Spey near Kingussie in Badenoch for Ossian's translator (or creator) James Macpherson, the result was a symmetrical mansion of almost Regency elegance, cool and reserved in detail. And in this there is the greatest irony, for if there is any aspect of the Castle Style which seems to bind it to Scotland it is the relationship of architecture and landscape implicit in the architect's creative imagination.[52] Adam's central theoretical concept of architectural 'movement', something he was careful to point to and explain on the very first page of the first volume of *The Works in Architecture of Robert and James Adam*, which he had published between 1773 and 1778, precisely elaborates that relationship.

> *Movement* is meant to express, the rise and fall, the advance and recess, with other diversity of form, in the different parts of a building, so as to add greatly to the picturesque of the composition. For the rising and falling, advancing and receding, with the convexity and concavity, and other forms of the great parts, have the same effect in architecture, that hill and dale, foreground and distance, swelling and sinking have in landscape: That is, they serve to produce an agreeable and diversified contour, that groups and contrasts like a picture, and creates a variety of light and shade, which gives great spirit, beauty and effect to the composition.[53]

Mauldslie Castle
Perspective view by David Bryce 1860
HES Canmore DP255361

The argument is clear: the forms of architecture should conform to and resonate with those of the natural landscape. But what type of natural landscape? Again the answer is necessarily ambivalent. The descriptive terms Adam employs – 'hill and dale' – imply a gentle, soft countryside and indeed this is entirely appropriate to what he calls 'the picturesque of the composition'. Many of Adam's watercolour sketches are reminiscent of the landscape paintings of Claude Lorraine, conveying an image of pleasant undulating countryside with wooded slopes, lakes and rivers perhaps more Italianate than Scottish. But there are others picturing precipitous cliffs and tumbling waterfalls which evoke a wilder northern landscape more in accord with 'the romantic aestheticization of the Highland landscape'[54] which followed in the wake of Ossian's verses. The battlemented towers and bastions of the castles and ruins, real or imagined, which rise on the skyline of these views, cohere in irregular masses shaped in light and shade, rising and falling, advancing and receding, their 'agreeable and diversified contour' an abstracted response to the natural world around them. As Adam's Castle Style evolved from the toy-fort simplicity of Ugbrooke or Mellerstain to the more three-dimensional complexity of Culzean, Seton or Mauldslie, the impact of this architectural 'movement' became more patent and more powerful. So, too, where the context of the castle became more savage and sublime, as in the cliff-top case of Culzean rising abruptly from the rock, nature seemed to demand a more radical response.

This was more than the perspective aggregation of battlemented towers and turrets. Now the symmetrical organisation of plan and elevation seemed to be called in question. Encouraged by his patron, the 10th Earl of Cassilis, 'to indulge to the utmost his romantic and fruitful genius',[55] Adam's willingness to add differing asymmetrical wings flanking the central symmetry of

Culzean Castle
Drawing by Robert Adam c1777
© Sir John Soane's Museum, London. Photograph by Ardon Bar-Hama

Culzean's north elevation (kitchen accommodation to the east, brewery and other offices on the west) may be an indication of a tentative change in architectural sensibilities, though the core of the building with its powerful round tower remained uncompromisingly symmetrical. Did Adam feel the wild drama of 'the seaward aspect of Culzean'[56] demanded some correspondingly 'unregulated' response? Perhaps – though it has to be acknowledged that in certain drawings prepared to show the effect of the great house rising over the cliffs below, the drama of the setting seems deliberately understated, rendered picturesque rather than sublime. It may be argued, too, that the asymmetry which the castle presents to the north would never have been seen, except from the sea, and that rarely. It was, as it were, a safe risk to take. Perhaps. But there is other evidence to substantiate the architect's readiness to escape from the straitjacket of symmetry at Culzean. Whatever architectural response the Culzean cliffs might have suggested, whatever constraining conditions the rest of the site might have dictated, Adam contrived to relate house, stables, farm and other offices in a layout quite unlike the symmetrical solutions he adopted, for example, at Seton, Airthrey and Stobs. There, conventional axiality and rigorously reflected forms applied; at Culzean, the building was placed in a freer asymmetrical context. The most readily perceptible sense of this asymmetry characterises the route the visitor must take approaching Culzean from the south-east, for the principal entrance is not aligned with the main north–south axis of the plan but is positioned on the shorter east side of the house – a location 'dictated by the planning exigencies of adding to an existing [tower-house] core'.[57] Gradually, as he or she passes through a 'ruined' arch with asymmetrical towers, along a 'serpentine viaduct'[58] which crosses a cleft in the landscape, and on through a second archway opening

to the forecourt carriage ring, the castle is revealed in romantic perspective. Elsewhere, too, apart from the terraces to the south of the house, the estate's avenues and pathways eschew any axial formality – though, of course, it is difficult to assess the part Adam may have played, directly or indirectly, in the delineation of these lesser routes. Nevertheless, Adam's tentative engagement with asymmetry at Culzean is clear enough. It is this proclivity, wedded to the nationally evocative forms of his Castle Style, which, in decades to come, would lead to the rebirth of Scottishness in much of Scottish architecture.

Culzean Castle
HES Canmore DP058610

Chapter 5
Temples, Towers and Turrets
Classicism to Romanticism

'the architecture of Scottish national identity would mutate frequently'
Miles Glendinning and Aonghus MacKechnie, *Scotch Baronial*

The stylistic flexibility of the Adam office nicely expressed the architectural legacy of the latter years of the eighteenth century, a legacy whose differing stylistic alternatives reflected a confusing ambivalence of cultural identity. By far the majority of Adam designs were built or rebuilt in a classical idiom that was broadly Palladian, or at any rate Italianate, in derivation – country houses, estate buildings, bridges, town houses, civic buildings and 'street schemes'. This was an architecture rational in its ethos, *international* in inspiration and aspiration, and thoroughly consonant with the spirit of the Enlightenment. But also on offer was the practice's distinctive Castle Style. Identifiably Scottish, though not exclusively so either in patronage or location, it catered for a market much more restricted in terms of clientele and building type – almost exclusively country house 'castles' for landed patrons with only a few rare applications to more civic commissions.[1] This was an architecture which, while in the main no less rational in the symmetrical logic of its planning, affected a restlessness in massing and skyline attuned to the 'movement' of picturesque and sublime landscape. Mildly inebriated too with the burgeoning allusive spirit of Romanticism, it was an architecture *national* in inspiration and aspiration, if not yet unequivocally Scottish. Both approaches had their progeny.

In Scotland, the Adam family, though the dominant practitioners in the eighteenth century, had not, of course, been the only architects to espouse and develop classical design. Others committed to the same ends and at work in Scotland included Sir John Clerk of Penicuik, Allan Dreghorn, John Douglas and John Baxter, all four of whom were responsible for the design of country houses in classical style.[2] More significantly, in England. in the earlier years of the century, two Scots, Colen Campbell and James Gibbs, had figured prominently in the practice and in the advocacy of classical architecture. Both had come to the study of architecture when in Italy. Before returning to practise in England, Campbell imbibed

Bridewell Prison
Edinburgh from the Calton Hill by Alexander Nasmyth 1820
Museums & Galleries Edinburgh – City of Edinburgh

the same Palladian disciplines that had impressed themselves upon Inigo Jones a hundred years before. Gibbs, in the studio of Carlo Fontana, inclined to an approach more akin to the English baroque of Christopher Wren. Between 1715 and 1725 Campbell had published *Vitruvius Britannicus*, three volumes of plates illustrating a range of architectural designs in the classical style, many of them his own. Intended to promote 'a specific national architectural taste',[3] that is to say a *British* style, its inclusion of a range of works influenced by 'the Renowned Palladio', an architect who had, in the words of the book's introduction, 'arrived to a *Ne plus ultra* of his art',[4] was enough to give Campbell access to the influential circle of Lord Burlington and place him, for a time, at the centre of the English Palladian movement. A few years later in 1728, *A Book of Architecture*, 'expressly intended as a pattern book for gentlemen in remoter areas of the country',[5] had appeared. Compiled by James Gibbs, this too was a self-publicising venture full of the architect's own designs, both built and unrealised; yet so practical was it as a catalogue of ideas that it proved to be 'probably the most widely used architectural book of the century'.[6] It was this same profitable strategy of travel, study and publication which Robert Adam would follow later in the century.

Others, too, contemporaries of Adam, undertook the Grand Tour as the springboard to a successful career. A number of 'London Scots' – William Chambers, Robert Mylne, Charles Cameron and James Playfair among them – also travelled and studied in continental Europe, where they had 'made it their business to engage with the most advanced tendencies of continental neo-classicism'.[7] Subsequently, all four established themselves in London. Only Chambers, however, published a treatise comparable in its influence to the folios of Campbell, Gibbs and Adam. Of the four, only Playfair established a practice with a predominantly Scottish clientele. But, with the exception of Cameron, who may never have crossed the border and ultimately pursued a career as court architect in imperial Russia, all carried out commissions north of the border.

Some of these projects prefigured an increasingly austere trend in Scottish classicism. Duddingston House (1763–8) by Chambers, a five-bay block with balustraded eaves fronted by a freestanding pedimented tetrastyle portico, exploited a simple but compelling compositional formula, already used by

Duddingston House
Photograph c1955
HES Canmore SC536653

John Adam at Paxton House (1758) and ultimately deriving from the precedent of Palladio's Villa Rotonda at Vicenza. Pedimented, too, but lacking a portico, Mylne's contemporary Cally House (1763–5) was larger with flanking wings, Palladian in conception like Paxton; but for its unusual six-bay facade it might well have emerged from the Adam office. At Cairness House (1788, 1791–7), however, Playfair rejected Italianate models, all but dispensing with conventional classical detail in favour of a stark stripped-down geometry drawn, it seems most likely, from the French neoclassicists Boullée and Ledoux whose work he had encountered on a visit to France in 1787. Such astylar extremes were not, however, to be pursued in Scotland and from the beginning of the nineteenth century, while decorative excess in the exterior of buildings would generally be eschewed, whether by choice or financial necessity, it was those more classically orthodox forms and themes evident in the work of the Adam brothers and that of the majority of their contemporaries and successors, which would prevail. Porticos and pediments would proliferate.

For many the classical temple was seen as the embodiment of good taste. And just as Palladio had imagined a direct formal relationship between the antique temple and the country house so, in the first few decades of the new century, and particularly in the 1820s, this affinity was expanded to embrace virtually the entire range of contemporary building types. Moreover, stimulated by publications such as Stuart and Revett's *Antiquities of Athens*, which appeared in successive volumes in 1767, 1789, 1795 and 1816, architects increasingly looked beyond Rome and Italy seeking to emulate the 'calm grandeur and noble simplicity' of Greek precedent. The Greek temple became the model of architectural excellence. The popularity of peristylar architecture soared, although despite one notably national attempt (see below) the temple template was rarely realised in Scotland in

Cairness House
Photograph 1963
HES Canmore SC1550147

Mousa to Mackintosh

its precise peripteral form.⁸ Some few monuments, fully peristylar in form, *were* built, such as the Burns Monument, Ayr (1817–23) and the Dugald Stewart Monument on Calton Hill, Edinburgh (1831). But columned porticoes, Doric, Ionic or Corinthian, hitherto largely confined to estate mansions and churches, appeared in abundance. They continued to be seen in numerous country houses and in churches, but now, along the new streets and squares being laid out and developed in Scotland's cities and towns, the same formal strategy was ubiquitous: the portico pattern was repeated in museums, galleries, halls and institutional buildings in Glasgow, Edinburgh, Aberdeen and Perth, in courthouses in Glasgow,⁹ Perth and Ayr; in custom houses in Leith and Greenock; and in schools at Dollar, Edinburgh, Inverness and Dundee. Among those architects in thrall to this country-wide classicising fashion were David Hamilton, William Stark, Robert Reid, Thomas Hamilton, William Burn, Archibald Simpson and William Henry Playfair. Unlike the previous generation, few in this group had travelled abroad and none had made a serious study of the antique classical architecture *in situ*, yet all affected, for a time at least, an informed allegiance to what would later be called the 'Hellenic Vision'.¹⁰

The fact that this enthusiasm for the pediments, porticos and peristyles of the Greek Revival was no less ardent elsewhere throughout Europe, and indeed across the Atlantic in the new American nation, did not diminish Scottish fervour. But neither, paradoxically, did the *international* nature of neoclassicism preclude its conscription to *national* ends. Therefore when, in 1817, in the triumphant afterglow of the Napoleonic Wars, the proposal was first promulgated that a National Monument should be raised in Scotland to honour the fallen, the suggestion was quickly advanced in a letter to *The Times* that the Parthenon was by far the most appropriate architectural model for such a project. What can be more worthy of a nation, the writer's effusive advocacy went, than to recreate 'a building which was the boast of a country … from which we derive all our philosophy, all our morals, all our taste, all our love of liberty, all our eloquence, all our poetry; in short, all that is good'?¹¹ Greek classicism, it seemed to some, was imbued with every possible virtue. Was not the Parthenon after all the unimpeachable canon of refined good taste? Did it not forever stand as an icon of high culture? Were its ranks of identical columns not the citizen symbols of enlightened democratic polity? And besides being in tune with what was acknowledged to be a 'national predilection for Greek geometry',¹² were not its 'austere profiles'¹³ the very aesthetic expression of all that was rational, even puritanical, in the Scottish psyche?

In 1820, a correspondent to the *Scots Magazine*¹⁴ rehearsed the reasons why the Committee on the National Monument should undertake the 'Restoration of the Parthenon'. No building could be regarded as a finer paradigm of architectural excellence. Since detailed measured information already existed, built reproduction was entirely feasible. There were scenic similarities between Athens and Edinburgh, the 'Athens of the North', which strongly favoured the choice of Calton Hill as the setting for the Monument. Nor was a suitable building material lacking; Pentelic marble might not be to hand but Edinburgh freestone was surely every bit as good (here, amid all the abject eulogising of everything Greek, was just a hint of national, or at least local, self-confidence). Finally, with a no-less-Scottish concern for financial caution, the writer suggested that, with the limited budget available, 'it would be hopeless to aim at distinction in any other known style of architecture'¹⁵ than the austere Greek Doric. It was a claim which the passage of time would soon render ironic.

A final decision to go ahead was taken in 1822 when a sub-committee of the General Committee of subscribers 'unanimously resolved to restore the Parthenon of Athens on the Calton Hill'.¹⁶ Supportive commentary recounted several aspects of the case that had already been made: the prominence and drama of the chosen site, the availability of good sandstone for building, the existence of a work-force of skilled masons already practised in the building of the streets and squares of Edinburgh's New Town. The decision was also argued on the grounds that, since the Parthenon was already ruinous and likely to be further damaged in 'the first struggles of Grecian freedom', its reconstituted manifestation at the opposite end of Europe was entirely justified. Indeed, by rebuilding the Parthenon, Scotland would not only save what was by common

Burns Monument, Ayr
Engraving by Thomas Hamilton c1816
HES Canmore DP006988

consent agreed to be the finest example of classical architecture but in doing so would 'give the greatest impulse to the *National Genius*' and lay 'the surest foundation for our own future eminence in the arts of *original design*'.[17] Here was an argument which not only appeared to uphold architectural reproduction as a respectable endeavour but in its perverse earnestness seemed to associate the Parthenon, the apotheosis of Mediterranean classical architecture, with the spirit of northern Scottish culture.

In 1823 the General Committee, which included such Scottish luminaries as Sir Walter Scott, Lord Elgin, Henry Cockburn and Francis Jeffrey, put the English architect C R Cockerell in charge of the project, with W H Playfair named as resident architect the following year. Cockerell had spent several years studying in Greece, Turkey and Italy and as a consequence was regarded as the leading archaeological and aesthetic authority on Greek architecture; there could hardly have been a more respected choice. He began by preparing a brief memorandum in which he, too, justified the choice of the Parthenon as model. It might have been expected that the case he advanced would have been based on refined connoisseurship and scholarship. But instead, perhaps because he was aware of the need for some compatibility between historical concept and geographical context to counter the opposition of those who found the idea of the transfer of a Greek temple from the sun-scorched summit of the Athens acropolis to the cloudy brow of Calton Hill culturally illogical if not frankly absurd, he defended the decision with an argument which was more romantic in its thesis than rational. Each country or region, he wrote, had evolved its own architectural forms in response to the local climate, materials, and so forth. He noted how these forms, in his view, generally contrasted with the nature of the dominant landscape. In countries where the land was low and flat 'an elevated or perpendicular architecture has always been adopted' – Egyptian pyramids, Assyrian ziggurats, Flemish cloth halls, Fenland cathedrals. On the other hand, in mountainous countries a low, horizontal architecture in which the 'unbroken line, the order, the symetry [*sic*], contrasted admirably with the wild irregularity of the scene' was the rule. Thus, as

National Monument, Calton Hill, Edinburgh
Historic Environment Scotland

in Greece, so in Scotland; the classical style was to be preferred. Inasmuch as this was a contention focused on form and specifically on the relationship of built form to its physical location, it was not unrelated to Robert Adam's earlier expressed view that architecture should in some sense be shaped to complement what he called the 'movement' of the surrounding landscape. It was not, however, necessarily an argument for classical architecture *per se* but rather, at a deeper level, for the relativity of cultural forms. Had Cockerell not been content with adducing the picturesque to the argument, he might more logically have inferred that Scottish architecture should find its roots in Scottish conditions. Such a conclusion would not, however, be long delayed.

Meantime building on Calton Hill began. Cockerell's drawings precisely replicated the dimensions of the Parthenon. The work, executed in 'finest Craigleith stone', went ahead under the supervision of Playfair. But by 1829, with only the west end of the temple built – no more than the stylobate, twelve columns and architrave stones – the money had run out. Scotland had proved unwilling to fund its National Monument. Playfair wrote to Cockerell: 'Our Parthenon is come to a dead halt, and is, I am afraid, likely to stand up a striking proof of the pride and poverty of us Scots'.[18] Opponents of the project had forecast as much. As early as 1822 a writer to the *Quarterly Review*, clear-sighted enough to see that the Parthenon was inescapably a Greek national monument 'and not a monument of Scotland', had warned that the whole venture would end badly as 'a perpetual and painful solecism'.[19] And so it proved. National dignity lay both literally and metaphorically in ruins. Any idea that this putative epitome of a distinctly Scottish neoclassicism might somehow have been symbolically imbued with the democratic aspiration, civic consciousness or cultural distinction of ancient Greece could be seen to be pie … on the skyline. It could scarcely have been a surprise. If the international character of neoclassicism was capable of carrying any national meaning it was at the British level and not the Scottish. Already in the capital's New Town, the rational order of the street plan, won in competition by the young architect James Craig, had been realised as 'an ideogram of the United Kingdom of England and Scotland',[20] two squares named for the countries' patron saints, George and Andrew,[21] linked by a broad avenue bearing the name of the Hanoverian king. Whatever Scottishness remained vested in the incomplete peristyle on Calton Hill was an embarrassment and, in the words of one of Scotland's finest writers, 'a very suitable monument to certain national characteristics'.[22] In making this judgement many years later might Robert Louis Stevenson have had in mind not merely parsimony but also that political pusillanimity that has so often made Scotland 'almost afraid to know itself'?[23] Perhaps.

And yet, whatever the embarrassment, whatever the shame, it would be hard to deny the sheer picturesque delight of the Monument's ruinous open peristyle seen at the end of Edinburgh's Princes Street, perched high on the hill, above and between the twinned pressed-in porticos of Waterloo Place. Had Robert Adam encountered such a view in Rome he would surely have recorded it in one of his sketches or *capricci*. Romantic classicism indeed.

Adam's romantic classicism, born in the pen and wash sketches he made of the crumbling ruins of the Roman Forum, reached its maturity in his classicising take on the medieval castle. The Castle Style was uniquely his, though several of his contemporaries and successors attempted to match its anachronistic stylistic fusion. There were those, too, patrons and architects alike, whose fascination with the battlemented towers and turrets of the past led them to develop castellar architecture in new directions. In one case at least, where this entailed no more than a respectful reiteration of the forms and formal relationships of late medieval building, the result would in time be seen as a precocious realisation of a Scottishness to come.

Sometime in the last quarter of the eighteenth century, probably in the late 1770s, the Honourable William Gordon began to contemplate making alterations and additions to the family seat at Fyvie in Aberdeenshire. Earlier in the century, William Adam had been engaged by Gordon's father, the 2nd Earl of Aberdeen, to upgrade the condition of the castle but, although the buildings were surveyed and design proposals prepared, 'it may be doubted whether any major work was in fact carried out'.[24] At the time, 1732–5, Adam was building nearby Haddo House, a fine exercise in fashionable Palladian style and it is probable that his proposals for Fyvie may have entailed some measure of adaptation to classical norms. It is just possible that, around half a century later, William Gordon also consulted the Adam office. A single pen and wash drawing, now in Sir John Soane's Museum in London and speculatively dated c1789, may have been prepared by Robert or James Adam or some other hand in their office. It shows the south range at Fyvie: the facade's four-storey height has been maintained as has the high gatehouse archway in the central Seton Tower, but all three towers have been stripped of gabletted eaves dormers and corbelled cone-roofed rounds. Bartizaned parapets survive while a pedimented panel fronts the gable over the central arch. Far from following this vaguely Castle Style idiom, however, the work commissioned by Gordon and carried out in the early 1790s respected and indeed repeated Fyvie's *existing* architectural character. This quality, invested in the extensive rebuilding of the south and west ranges at the beginning of the seventeenth century, was unequivocally that of the Scottish Baronial style. As MacGibbon and Ross would later assert in their unsurpassed documentation of Scotland's castellated architecture, Fyvie had

> all the distinguishing features of the style – plain walls below the parapet and exuberance of enrichment above; corbelling freely used where the central round towers change to the square as well as to support the angle turrets; sharp-roofed turrets perched on every corner; dormer windows raised on top of the parapet; gables finished with crow-steps, and plain chimney heads; minor details all equally Scottish, including the small corbel ornaments under the turrets, the cable and billet patterns, and the whole form and application of the mouldings.[25]

Gordon's changes lowered the south range from four to three storeys but left the three turreted towers with their 'exuberant enrichment' unimpaired. Moreover, the form of the outer Meldrum and Preston Towers was faithfully recreated in the new Gordon Tower which he added at the north end of the castle's west wing. That he should have honoured the past is hardly surprising for he had, like countless other young men of means, made the Grand Tour, imbibing the fashionable visual and literary heritage of the classical world, but that he should have honoured the Scottish past rather than that of Antique Rome sets Gordon apart. Even in Rome, in 1766, he had made his fealty clear in the portrait he commissioned from Pompeo Batoni. In sartorial terms this was that

Fyvie Castle
Historic Environment Scotland

same provocative conjunction of the national and the international that Robert Adam had confronted and expressed in his Castle Style architecture. But here, albeit in the putatively flattering landscape of the Antique in which Batoni has placed his sitter, the confrontation is perhaps less ambivalent: the senatorial toga has become a tartan kilt and plaid, the architectural glory that was Rome is now fragmentary and ruinous, and Gordon has drawn his sword as if to challenge the cultural hegemony of classicism with the blade of romantic nationalism. How different from Batoni's staid portrait of James Adam painted only a few years before. Gordon's pose may be stagily contrived, even faintly ludicrous, and there is almost certainly no serious political edge to his determined stance (though as a Catholic he may still have nurtured a nostalgia for the Stuart cause), but there is, nevertheless, a serious intent to be inferred in this vainglorious painting. In the history of art, it is a sign of the changing times, a sign that cultural identity now discovers itself in the geography of art.[26] No wonder then that the new work at Fyvie should re-assert the Scottishness of Scottish architecture. In its 'determined and largely successful attempt to repeat the old work', it is 'even for a date in the 1790s, an astonishingly early essay in the Baronial Revival'.[27] Yet the Gordon Tower is, in its ambition and execution, no more than a straightforward reiteration of the forms and formal arrangements established at Fyvie and across Aberdeenshire some two hundred years earlier. A further half century would pass before the revival had fully refined its unique and creative take on the Scottish tradition of baronial building.

Some ten years before William Gordon gave a first thought to the changes at Fyvie, another Gordon, Alexander, 4th Duke of Gordon, engaged the architect John Baxter to rebuild Gordon Castle near Fochabers. Baxter, who had studied in Italy from 1761 until 1767, designed a vast new mansion, its 174-metre-long south facade organised in a straight-line Palladian composition with a high central block linked to flanking pavilions, its continuous crenellated parapets set on corbels and machicolations of 'Italian detail … unique in Scotland in its day'.[28]

Mousa to Mackintosh 109

These endless battlemented parapets, the high central tower, incorporating the original fifteenth century tower-house, and the four bayed projections which marked the corners of the main block imparted a 'faintly medieval air'[29] to the design. On the other hand, the architectural detail below the parapets was wholly classical, the project's colossal scale and all but implacable symmetry far from Gothic. Affinities with the evolving Adam Castle Style were clear.

Similar tendencies, though not the same overblown ambition, were evident in a number of other castellated country houses built before the turn of the century. Palladian disciplines generally prevailed, though not without the introduction of some medieval detail. More villa than castle, petite where Gordon Castle was gross, the Hermitage of Braid, Edinburgh, (c1785) by Robert Burn, though essentially classical in its symmetrical organisation, with a pavilion roof and tripartite elevations lit by Venetian windows, flirted with Gothic allusion in short battlemented eaves punctuated at the corners with tiny bartizans. More expansive in elevation but without Gordon's 'gigantism',[30] Melville Castle, Midlothian (1786–91), and Lanrick, Perthshire (from 1791), were similarly symmetrical with a dominant central block and outer wings diminishing in height. They, too, were castellated at the eaves, though only Lanrick had bartizans. At Melville, the four-bay, three-storey centre was flanked by taller round towers lit by pointed-arch windows; at Lanrick the smaller outer towers were similarly lit: an evident debt to the Gothic pretensions of Inveraray and Douglas and one which would be repeatedly paid in a succession of country houses built over the next 30 years or so. Round corner towers recurred at Monzie, Perthshire (c1795–1800), and at Eglinton, Ayrshire (1798–1803), where the composition was dominated by a larger tower rising at the centre of the plan, circular in plan rather than square as at Inveraray. Parapets were castellated and some windows hooded but, unlike Inveraray, there were no pointed arches. Both buildings were designed by John Paterson, who had worked with Robert Adam and whose practice continued the Castle Style tradition. If Paterson's work lacked the inventiveness and subtleties of 'movement' in the best

Monzie Castle
Scottish Colorfoto c1920
HES Canmore SC1209184

of Adam's castles, the unsophisticated austerity of form seen at Monzie and Eglinton nevertheless packed a powerful neoclassical punch. A lighter, altogether more charming, neoclassicism was evident at Rossie Castle, Angus (1790–1800), where a central tripartite block was connected by short linking bays to square towers, themselves linked by low arcading to small square gazebo-like outer pavilions. Classical in its compositional symmetries, round-arch windows, arcades and relieving arches; medieval in its corbelled crenellation, bartizans and occasional hood mouldings, the building was designed by another of Robert Adam's former draughtsmen, Richard Crichton, whose deft interpretation of the Castle Style was considerably more delicate and balanced than Paterson's. In these and other examples, classical symmetry remained essential to good design but, as the century turned and a 'veritable boom in castle building'[31] gripped rural Scotland, a more boldly towered and increasingly medievalised version of castellar architecture began to develop.

Taymouth Castle
HES Canmore SC371659

The most assured exemplification of this trend took shape at Kenmore in Perthshire where, throughout the eighteenth century, the Campbell Earls of Breadalbane had been transforming their old tower-house of Balloch into the new and grand Taymouth Castle, rival to the Argyllshire Inveraray Castle of their kinsmen. As early as the late 1730s, before he had begun to supervise the building of Roger Morris's design at Inveraray, William Adam had 'regularised' the old Perthshire castle, adding quadrant links and flanking pavilions in the Palladian manner. Several successive proposals for further improvement obtained from John Douglas, Roger Morris, John Paterson and Robert Mylne appear to have removed much of Adam's work but realised little of lasting consequence and it was not until 1801 that the 4th Earl authorised the remodelling of the castle according to a new set of plans drawn up by John Paterson. By 1804, however, Breadalbane declared himself 'determined to remove the New Building now erecting'.[32] This done, he engaged architects Archibald and James Elliot and it is their work which survives as the dominant heart of Taymouth Castle (1806–11). Like Inveraray the plan is square with round corner towers and a central square tower rising

Mousa to Mackintosh | 111

high above the main roof level. But Taymouth is a full storey higher than its predecessor in Argyll and more medievalised. Parapets are machicolated and battlemented and the windows generally Gothic in form and, though not all have pointed arches, those in the central tower providing clearstorey light to the main staircase are tall and traceried. This quasi-ecclesiastical character is intensified by the addition of an arcaded cloister, buttressed and battlemented, surrounding the building in the form of a loggia. All this is, as Macaulay judges, 'a delicate balancing act between Gothic and neo-classicism'.[33] In the Elliots' contemporary castle projects at Loudon, Ayrshire (1804–11), and Stobo, Peeblesshire (1805–11), the same overall symmetries applied, the same towered elements, round and square, appeared, the same castellated parapets etched the skyline, but the introduction of Gothic detail was much more muted. It was at Taymouth, both in the exterior and even more so in the magnificent plasterwork of the interior, that the spirit of medieval architecture seemed to challenge the soberer norms of classicism. And indeed the balancing act was delicate for elsewhere the scales had already been tipped.

That the marriage of the classical and the Gothic had found favour for so long was less than surprising. Adam's Castle Style had been Scottish but, since examples of the style had not been confined to north of the border, not unequivocally so. Similarly, Gothic, ecclesiastical or castellated, might be regarded as English (as indeed it had been at Inveraray) but again this was not the whole story. Add to this the impressment of international classicism to national service and the language of architectural form becomes even more encrypted. In a Britain no more troubled by Jacobite disaffection, settled in its monarchy and parliament, and united in a common patriotism by the challenge of the Napoleonic Wars, such cultural confusions could, for a time at least, be conveniently concealed by an appeal to Britishness.

In terms of their underlying compositional order, Robert Adam's Castle Style mansions were no less rigorous than, and scarcely to be distinguished from,

Scone Palace
Lantern slide of photograph by George Washington Wilson c1890
HES Canmore SC1328504

the many more overtly neo-Palladian country houses which he and his brothers designed. By and large the balancing strictures of classicism applied, with mass and dimension reflected in plan and elevation. A few (a very few) tentative ventures into asymmetry were entertained, as, for example, at Culzean in Ayrshire or Castle Upton in County Antrim, but in the main Adam seemed content to satisfy his romantic inclinations by the introduction of certain allusive details such as machicolated battlements, turrets and bartizans, and by the admission of the picturesque in the 'movement' of castle walls and seemingly irregular turreted skylines. In the early decades of the nineteenth century, however, in parallel with the continuing appeal of the picturesque, the incidence of Gothic forms in country-house architecture increased. So, too, while the desire of every castle-building client to make lineage and heritage architecturally visible led to a preference for indigenous medieval precedent, the growing demand for more convenient plans found in Gothic a more liberating formal language than the symmetrical syntax of classical composition. Thus aesthetic, nostalgic and pragmatic factors combined to effect stylistic change. Castle, hall or priory, a gentleman's home now became attractively asymmetric in form, medievalised in detail and decoration, and better adapted in plan to the practical needs of comfortable living.

In the eighteenth century, as already noted, several Scots architects – Campbell, Gibbs, Chambers and Adam – had been prominent in the development of neo-Palladian classicism south of the border. Now, in the first decade of the nineteenth century, two English architects made significant contributions to the revival of Gothic forms north of the border, bringing Scotland up to speed with the interest in indigenous medieval architecture already underway in the south. In designing what was his first large-scale commission, Scone Palace, Perthshire (1803–12), for the 3rd Earl of Mansfield, William Atkinson introduced the asymmetrical 'picturesque Gothic manner', creating a spread of castellated and turreted ranges whose collegiate nature was 'probably

Tullichewan Castle
Drawing by Robert Lugar 1792
RIBA Collections

intended to evoke the spirit of the vanished Abbey's claustral buildings'.[34] Later, at Rossie Priory, Perthshire (1807–15), Atkinson went further, elaborating the growing fashion for ecclesiastical Gothic in an asymmetrically massed house whose crenellated eaves, spired towers and buttressed church-like gables were alive with crocketted pinnacles. Meanwhile, another Englishman, Robert Lugar, was erecting Tullichewan Castle in Dunbartonshire (from 1808), a battlemented pile with a generous scattering of towers, large and small, round and square, and a high machicolated cylindrical tower with its attached staircase turret, a design claimed to be the 'first asymmetrical Gothic house in Scotland'.[35] Lugar followed this with work at nearby Balloch Castle (1808–9), where a small, towered and turreted, castellated mansion was extended asymmetrically with a concave battlemented wing. A few years later he included both houses in his *Plans and Views of Buildings executed in England and Scotland in the Castellated and Other Styles* (1811), a publication which proved influential in furthering not only the picturesque appeal of the Castellated Gothic style, at once aesthetic and allusive, but also its practical planning advantages. As Lugar wrote, it was a style which 'affords many opportunities of obtaining a number of rooms which are essential to modern habits'.[36] These possibilities, formal, fanciful and functional, were quickly explored.

Scottish architects began to experiment with revived medieval forms, applying neo-Gothic solutions not only to the problem of the country house but gradually also to the design of public buildings and, not surprisingly, churches (see below). A certain reticence persisted, however, for though castellated houses such as Craigend Castle, Stirlingshire (completed 1812) by Alexander Ramsay, Castle Forbes, Aberdeenshire (1814–15) by Archibald Simpson, and Castle Toward, Argyll (1820–1) by David Hamilton all delighted in an irregular disposition of towers and turrets rising from an asymmetrical plan, they remained somewhat severe and robust in detail, eschewing the more delicate and developed forms of ecclesiastical Gothic. The same was true, perhaps fittingly, of Archibald Elliot's County Buildings at Paisley (1818–20) and his County Jail in Jedburgh (1820–3), both of which were battlemented, fortress-like and symmetrical in plan.

In the work of James Gillespie Graham, however, the nascent Gothic Revival in Scotland found more catholic and more convincing expression. Perhaps more committed (if not, by any means, solely so)[37] to exploring the style's full range of possibilities than most of his contemporaries, Gillespie Graham, too, was at first tentative. His first country house, erected at Achnacarry, Invernessshire (1802–3), was in conventional castellated mode, battlemented, with corner turrets and a quatrefoil-pierced parapet, but still symmetrical in plan with no concession to the picturesque. At Culdees Castle, Perthshire (c1810), there were more battlemented eaves and turrets, but also a Gothic porch and Gothic windows, hooded and pointed-arched. More significantly, the overall symmetry was disrupted by a castellated drum tower rising above the battlements at the north-west corner of the plan, a thoroughly picturesque strategy almost certainly drawn from Robert Lugar's Tullichewan. Similar asymmetrically-placed towers appeared in a succession of castellated projects, some engrossing older existing fabric in their design, as seen at Edmonston Castle, Lanarkshire (1813–15), in proposals for Armadale Castle on Skye (1814–22), at Cambusnethan Priory, Lanarkshire (1816–19), and at Dunninald in Angus (1819). Massed in increasingly free groupings, towered and battlemented in varied heights, with hooded often pointedly Gothic fenestration, Gillespie Graham's castle *oeuvre* culminated in a magnificent implosion of towers, square, circular and octagonal, at Duns Castle, Berwickshire (1818–22). Shaped around a pre-existing L-plan tower-house, Duns was a ruggedly picturesque composition 'in which antiquarian correctness was of little interest so long as unrestrained visual effect was achieved'.[38] But it was this visual effect which, in the upward thrust of its multiple towers, mullioned windows and ranked chimneys, ensured the building's essential Scottishness was maintained.

Gillespie Graham's Gothic was not confined to battlemented castles. Commissioned to recase an earlier eighteenth century house at Crawford Priory, Fife (1810–13), he had turned to William Atkinson for inspiration, adopting the more inflected formal language of ecclesiastical Gothic which the

Culdees Castle
Engraving 1822
HES Canmore DP094221

Duns Castle
HES Canmore SC1380577

Rossie Priory
Engraving 1825
HES Canmore DP098222

Englishman had introduced at Rossie Priory. Far from scholarly, the result was a 'confection of assorted flavours'[39] combining Perpendicular windows and a Norman doorway under open parapetted eaves accented by tall crocketted pinnacles. It was, however, in a series of church commissions, both for restoration and new work, that the opportunities presented themselves to increase his knowledge of ecclesiastical detail and exemplify this in his own designs. Yet even before he had been engaged on repair work and 'improvement' to a number of Scotland's most impressive medieval buildings – Dunblane Cathedral, the Church of the Holy Rude at Stirling, St John's in Perth and Glasgow Cathedral – he had already been responsible for the design of two important new Catholic churches both of which would later become cathedrals. St Mary's Chapel in Edinburgh (1813–14) and St Andrew's Chapel in Glasgow (1814–17) were executed in a stiff variant of the *English* Perpendicular style derived in all probability from a study of the views, plans, sections and details of the 'ancient English edifices' illustrated in the early volumes of John Britton's deceptively entitled *Architectural Antiquities of Great Britain*, published between 1807 and 1826. These two projects did much to foster Gillespie Graham's career and led one contemporary Scottish commentator to suggest that the widely acknowledged success of St Mary's Chapel was responsible for 'the general adoption, throughout the country, of the Gothic style in the architecture of churches'.[40] This was, of course, an exaggeration. From the early eighteenth century more than a few Presbyterian centrally-focused churches – oblong, T-plan and octagonal – had pointed-arch doorways and windows. Many of these windows had intersecting tracery, perhaps the earliest being those in the crowstepped gables of the Laigh Kirk in Paisley (1738–40). By the turn of the century, experimentation with quasi-medieval detail had greatly increased with several kirks buttressed and towered. The buttressed walls and curved gables of James Playfair's idiosyncratic Farnell Church, Angus (1788–9) were crenellated and pinnacled.

St Paul's and St George's Episcopal Church, Edinburgh
Engraving c1830
HES Canmore DP095411

Pinnacles rose from the buttresses at each corner of the tower-and-octagon plan of Glenorchy Church (1810) by James Elliot. James Adam's octagonal St George's Episcopal Church in Edinburgh (1792–4) was a quirky castellated hybrid, his Barony Church in Glasgow (1793–1800) an exercise in Castle Style Gothic. At Craig Church in Angus (1799) Richard Crichton adopted a nave-and-aisles plan, until then rare in a Scottish Presbyterian kirk. And it was this more Catholic, more medieval, orientation, adopted in Gillespie Graham's two chapels in Edinburgh and Glasgow, which gave an immediate and more scholarly cast to the developing revival of Gothic in Scotland. Scottish Episcopalians, for whom the nave-and-aisles plan was liturgically appropriate, were quick to follow Catholic example. In Aberdeen, Archibald Simpson built St Andrew's Chapel (1816–17) in the same Perpendicular style that Gillespie Graham had favoured. It, too, became an Episcopal cathedral.

In Edinburgh two large, longitudinal new churches were built at great expense: William Burn's St John's (1815–18) and Archibald Elliot's St Paul's (1816–18) (later St Paul and St George) were both carried out in a still more convincing Perpendicular style, St John's high nave roofed in remarkable fan vaulting. Just as Gillespie Graham had done, Burn and Elliot drew directly on the example of English buildings.

The accessibility of English Gothic architecture, both geographically and through the growing range of publications dealing with the subject, continued to be a powerful factor in determining the direction of the Revival in Scotland. As Lugar and Atkinson had influenced the Scots' grasp of picturesque Gothic in a secular context, so understanding of ecclesiastical Gothic was shaped by a whole range of publications emanating from south of the border. Besides Britton's *Architectural Antiquities*, works such as Thomas Rickman's *An Attempt to discriminate the Styles of English Architecture from the Conquest to the Reformation*, published 1817, and the two-volume *Specimens of Gothic Architecture*, which Augustus Charles Pugin had published between 1821 and 1823, were among the most significant. It was certainly the practical scholarship of Augustus Welby Northmore Pugin, son of Augustus Charles, which mattered most in raising Gillespie Graham's game. Pugin may well have assisted him in the design of the Old Parish Church in Montrose (1832–4) where the steeple with its high pinnacled buttresses, Perpendicular-traceried windows and crocketted needle spire is derived from Louth Parish Church in Lincolnshire. He worked, too, on the Tolbooth Church, Edinburgh (1839–44), a 'galleried auditorium' with a saliently sited steeple closely modelled on 'the ideal parish church of *The True Principles of Pointed or Christian Architecture*'[41] which Pugin published in 1841. And when, from 1838 to 1842, Gillespie Graham was engaged in adding a new west wing to Taymouth Castle,[42] it was Pugin who provided some richly conceived Gothic detail, especially lavish in the magnificent so-called Banner Hall lit by a high Perpendicular-traceried window (a space originally conceived as a chapel).

If the fiasco of the incomplete National Monument had shown international neoclassicism incapable of conveying and honouring national Scottish culture with anything other than an embarrassingly ironic gloss, the revival of Gothic forms, subject as it was in both the secular and the ecclesiastical sphere to English direction, also developed with little or no genuine sense of Scottishness. Both the Greek and Gothic Revivals were, of course, international movements impacting on many differing cultures across Europe and beyond. But while the wellsprings of classical architecture had first surfaced and sparkled in the bright light of a Mediterranean world which, *pace* Cockerell's specious argument, lay far from misty northern climes, the Gothic style could at least claim to have its origins nearer home and (though this did not lead to the same association with national culture as it did in England, France and Germany) to have a considerable indigenous presence in Scotland. That this evidence should have been long ignored testifies to the success of that 'British myth' which was in effect the anglicisation of culture. Power and patronage lay in the south and, whether for economic or social reasons, or both, there were those Scottish architects who chose to train under English architects, some who established offices in England and many who drew on English precedent and scholarship. While none of this necessarily entailed a wholesale surrender to the unionist 'myth',

it inevitably meant a downgrading of national cultural esteem. By the 1830s, the Scottishness of Scottish architecture was all but invisible. But not quite.

It was perhaps significant that some of the first steps in the rehabilitation of Scottish medieval architecture should have been taken by someone who was not an architect. Trained as a carpenter in Peeblesshire, George Meikle Kemp had, from an early age, nurtured an interest in medieval building, drawing and measuring the great Border abbeys. Later, work in Glasgow, Edinburgh and in England enabled him to extend his knowledge of Gothic architecture, experience which culminated in the 1820s in a two-year period spent studying the cathedrals of northern France. On his return home, his familiarity with medieval building now by no means parochial, Kemp focused on recording and preserving the built heritage of his own country. Engaged as a draughtsman by the architect William Burn, he found time to prepare a series of drawings for a publication which, intended to document the legacy of ecclesiastical building in Scotland, would fulfil an equivalent role to John Britton's already influential *Cathedral Antiquities of England*.[43] Undeterred by the abandonment of this project, in 1834 he drew up a folio of suggestions for restoration work at Glasgow Cathedral, unsolicited proposals which were subsequently appropriated by Gillespie Graham with no due acknowledgement given to Kemp. Again, however, the work was aborted. Then, in February 1836, a series of events began to unfold which finally enabled Kemp to secure lasting fame.

An advertisement appeared in 32 newspapers calling for the submission of designs for a monument to honour the memory of Sir Walter Scott, who had died four years before. In their brief, the competition committee envisaged a design 'in which the combination of a Statue and Architecture is indispensable'.[44] No decision on the final location of the monument had been taken and, although the promoters had 'decided – though not unanimously – that this monument should be Gothic rather than Classical',[45] no mandatory requirements in terms of architectural style were laid down. There were fifty-four entries: eleven could be classified as more sculptural than architectural in form; fourteen,

St John's Episcopal Church, Edinburgh
HES Canmore SC1088557

evidently unabashed by the 'ruinous' peristyle on Calton Hill, were Grecian temples; there were five pillars, an obelisk and a fountain; the remaining twenty-two, of which Kemp's entry was one, were Gothic. A willingness to conscript pointed architecture to the challenge of civic building, perhaps because in this particular case the style could be considered more in keeping with the national romanticism of Scott's literary work, appeared to be developing in parallel to the vogue for pediment and portico. At any rate, the designs placed first, second and third were all Gothic and all took the form of a Gothic memorial cross. The winner, an Englishman, Thomas Rickman, was like Kemp a self-taught enthusiast, but already a recognised scholar and authority in matters of medieval architecture. It was Rickman who, in a landmark publication of 1817, had presented a systematic formal analysis of the historical evidence which definitively described the evolution of English Gothic architecture and it was he who had coined the terms used to denominate the stages of the style's development, terms which continue in use today. Kemp, whose knowledge of Gothic if neither as theoretical nor as esteemed as that of Rickman was nevertheless by now 'unrivalled in Scotland',[46] came third.

For some reason, the promoters could not agree to build the winning design and invited new submissions. In March 1838, Kemp, who had again lodged his drawings under the pseudonym 'John Morvo', the name of a fifteenth century mason at Melrose Abbey, was declared the winner of this second competition. Again delays ensued, for a site had still not been determined. Only at the end of the year was it finally decided to locate the monument in Princes Street Gardens at the south end of St David Street. Paradoxically, where the hard elemental forms and precise proportions of the National Monument had been set in a loose picturesque relationship with the landscape of hill and city, now the intricate complexity of Kemp's giant pinnacle was to be located with the axial exactitude of a neoclassical viewpoint. Work began in 1841 and continued until 1844, by which time Kemp, not yet 50, was dead.

The Scott Monument is a 'multi-pinnacled', openwork Gothic spire rising 61 metres over John Steell's white Carrara marble sculpture of the seated novelist. The Monument was designed, according to the minutes of the competition committee, 'in strict conformity with the purity of the taste and style of

Scott Monument, Edinburgh
Photographs from c1850 and 2007
HES Canmore SC1932982, DP039712

Melrose Abbey, from which the author states that it is in all its details derived'.[47] Kemp also asserted that the views of Edinburgh which would be seen from the Monument's seventeen different galleries 'might create an excitement something like one of Scott's own romances'.[48] Apart from offering this experience to those prepared to climb to its topmost gallery, Kemp's pinnacled tower derives certain fortuitous townscape qualities from its location in the city. On the one hand, its axial positioning ties it securely into the neoclassical grid of the eighteenth century New Town while, on the other, the Monument's thrusting daedal steeple resonates with the high jagged skyline of the Old Town rising above the valley to the south.

If this latter relationship seemed to imbue Kemp's 'rather shaggy spire'[49] with a faint flavour of the picturesque, it was far from being the first monument to draw piquancy from the drama of its setting. The siting of several peristylar memorials, not least the National Monument itself, had deliberately invoked this 'anti-urban aesthetic'.[50] A handful of castellated monuments had also been erected in rural or semi-rural locations, such as near Forres (1806), in Glenfinnan (1815, 1834), on Binns Hill, West Lothian (1826), and on Calton Hill in Edinburgh (1807–14) but these were isolated affairs, no more than round or octagonal towers with crenellated parapets, lacking the formal or structural legitimacy to be categorised as Gothic, let alone Scottish Gothic. In designing the Scott Monument, however, Kemp gave native national expression to an international movement, something his contemporaries trailing in the wake of English tutelage had largely failed to do. The design incorporates archaeologically correct ecclesiastical Gothic detail drawn from Melrose Abbey (not without the admixture of certain continental material), but he does not copy, in the sense that there is no attempt to re-create some canonical structure from the medieval past, no parallel for the replication of the Parthenon on Calton Hill. Some may contend, too, that, in contradistinction to that transposed Grecian temple, there is a certain Scottishness in the very verticality of the Monument's form. This may be simplistic and tendentious but there is no disputing the fact that

the building speaks of Scotland in a number of other ways. Its *raison d'être* is to enshrine the memory of one of the country's greatest literary figures; its rich endowment of figurative carvings carried out by a variety of sculptors directly symbolises the wealth of characters brought to life in Scott's historical novels; and, most relevant from the point of view of this study, the Monument's architectural provenance seems to be securely embedded in Scott's own Border country.

That this particular re-assertion of the Scottishness of Scottish architecture should be associated with Sir Walter Scott is significant in a further sense. For it was Scott himself who, in the building of his home at Abbotsford in the Borders some twenty years earlier, had begun a process of cultural rediscovery that would lead Scottish architecture back to its roots by reviving and recasting the Scots Baronial style, the very style William Gordon had seen no reason to reject.

Chapter 6
The Recovery of Scottishness
Abbotsford *Bricolage* to Baronial *Bravura*

'Surely the architecture which grew up among men so nearly allied to us has a preeminent claim upon our attention'
Charles Rennie Mackintosh, Scotch Baronial Architecture lecture

When[1] in 1811 Walter Scott bought the small farm of Clarty Hole (or Cartley Hole) situated beside the Tweed in Roxburghshire not far from Melrose Abbey, his intention seems to have been no more ambitious than to replace the existing one-and-a-half-storey gabled farmhouse with what he called simply 'a beautiful little cottage'.[2] As the years passed, however, and the project developed its stop–start pattern, stimulated variously by the money that came with Scott's literary success, the fancies of his own romantic imagination, the suggestions made by some of his closest friends and the proposals advanced by the architects he employed, this modest aim became less and less appealing. Nothing that was built conformed to convention, to what Scott later called 'the regular shape of a house'; on the contrary, he had, he claimed, achieved 'a picturesque … and entirely new line in architecture'.[3] He called this unprecedented house Abbotsford.

Contemplating building his 'little cottage', Scott first engaged William Stark, an architect regarded by his contemporaries, and not least among them Scott himself, as a man of great ability then 'at the height of his reputation in his profession'.[4] A proposal was duly drawn up for a cottage designed in the style of an 'old English vicarage-house'.[5] But when Stark died in 1813, Scott was cautious, and the project stalled. Perhaps the desire for something identifiably Scottish made Scott hesitate. At any rate, no immediate steps were taken to proceed. Instead, the old farmhouse remained, embellished only with a small pedimented portico of fashionably rustic, tree-trunk columns.

A year or two later, Scott turned for help not to another member of the profession in Edinburgh but to two English architects. In 1816, following a first meeting with Scott, the young Edward Blore, then still more antiquarian draughtsman than practising

Craigends
Watercolour perspective of main elevation by David Bryce c1857
HES Canmore DP061453

architect, presented a set of plans and elevations for accommodation intended to be added to the existing farmhouse. Drawings were also obtained by Scott's actor–architect friend Daniel Terry from William Atkinson whose reputation as a Gothic designer stood high as a consequence of several recent commissions carried out in Scotland. Atkinson's authorship of *Views of Picturesque Cottages* and the fact that both he and Terry had trained under James Wyatt may well also have contributed to his being consulted. Both schemes found favour, Atkinson's because of the more practical arrangement of accommodation, Blore's because its external appearance was, as Scott put it, 'less Gothic and more in the old fashioned Scotch stile [*sic*] which delighted in notch'd Gable ends and all manner of bartizans'. In 1817 building began under Atkinson's control and by summer of the following year a new wing had been added to the south-west gable of the old farmhouse. After all the disruption of building Scott was relieved but wrote that he still had 'half of my house to build when I have the leisure – that is – time and money'.[6]

It was not long before Scott, now Sir Walter, felt able to proceed. In 1822 the farmhouse was demolished to be replaced with new accommodation designed by Atkinson, larger and grander than his earlier work. Throughout the building period relations between architect and client appear to have been under constant strain as Scott's mania for acquiring fragmentary architectural salvage to be incorporated into the fabric and interior of the house necessitated repeated revisions and adjustments. But by 1823 this second phase of building was complete, linked to the earlier wing by a connecting space which served as an armoury. A new porch, similar to that at the approach to Linlithgow Palace, opened to the large walled courtyard that fronted the house to the south-east. The house itself, built in whin stone and ashlar, had a marked Scottish, perhaps Scots Jacobean, character, its plan wholly dismissive of symmetries, its elevations lively with an irregular aggregation of crowstep gables, canted bay windows, turrets, machicolation, corbelling, bartizans and tall chimney shafts. Some have even detected the presence of 'a Fyvie-type arch flanked by crowstepped towers on the river facade'.[7]

It has been suggested that the exterior of Abbotsford 'is secondary to the importance of the internal plan'.[8] This is true, of course, insofar as Le Corbusier's assertion that 'plan is the generator' of architectural form may be conceded. There can be no doubt, too (and perhaps this is more what Gow had in mind), that the eclectic richness of Abbotsford's interiors is exceptional. The house is crowded with fragments and relics evoking Scotland's past, all of them collected by Scott: arms and armour, antique furniture, heraldic devices, plaster-cast Gothic niches and figures of saints from Melrose Abbey, medieval bosses from the vaulting at Rosslyn Chapel, a stone fireplace copied from the cloisters at Melrose, oak panelling from Dunfermline Abbey and, allegedly, Holyrood Palace, and a doorway removed from Edinburgh's Tolbooth on its demolition in 1817. The dense impact of these decontextualised artefacts is provocative, making Abbotsford very much 'a site of memory'.[9] But, in the remembrance of Scottishness which would soon unfold in the evolution of the Scottish Baronial Revival, the significance of the external massing and detail of Scott's home should not be undervalued. Indeed it could be argued that as a consequence of its protracted and intermittent building, the intervention of various amateur and professional advisers, and the constantly changing demands of Scott himself, Abbotsford's interiors and exterior are unified by a common aesthetic strategy, namely that of *bricolage*.[10]

Strictly defined, the word *bricolage* connotes the creation of 'an assemblage of haphazard or incongruous elements'.[11] But the lineaments of the Abbotsford plan, the result of continual debate and discussion between Scott and his several advisers, can hardly be considered a matter of chance. Indeed the various formal elements adduced to the external expression of the plan possess an evident congruence with those same forms repeatedly present in the historical tradition of Scottish architecture. If the term can be justified, its legitimacy can only derive from the seemingly free, almost ad hoc, disposition of rooms and circulation spaces and from the corresponding irregularity in the plan perimeter reflected in the building's three-dimensional form. These aspects of the building's design were later perpetuated by William Burn when he added a large family wing (1853–5) where, although the accommodation is given a certain centripetal cohesion by being gathered around an inner court, the massing remains almost arbitrary with gables of varying height and width advancing on all fronts. There is, then, at Abbotsford an absence of an overarching relational structure or formal discipline such as that afforded by the symmetries of

Abbotsford
HES Canmore SC1058526

plan and elevation which hitherto had governed the architecture of, say, Robert Adam's neo-Palladian or Castle Style country houses. Of course, this essentially picturesque quality is represented in the contemporary castellar country houses of the Gothic Revival. But in such cases the residential conceit is grander, the 'disintegrative' effect is more limited and mitigated by the presence of a dominant symmetrical core (often accented by reflected towers) within the general asymmetrical layout. At the same time, ecclesiastical Gothic forms are preferred to those of more secular, more Scottish provenance. At Abbotsford the scale is different, the *bricolage* intimate, even personal.

Yet there is order in Abbotsford's disorder. The walls defining the building envelope advance and recede in plan and rise and fall in height in a series of what might be termed 'elevational units', the majority of which stand from ground to skyline.

Engrossing architectural elements which are in the main recognisably Scots, these units vary in width and in height. Crowstepped gable, battlemented tower or parapetted stretch of windowed wall, each is generally organised symmetrically. Only occasionally does some off-centre element add a piquant accent. But, though individually symmetrical, the units are packed together in what indeed appears to be a 'haphazard'[12] asymmetrical arrangement conforming to no evident geometrical control, axial or otherwise. In fact, this loose aggregation of form is the direct expression of the building's internal function as determined in plan and section. Overall, Abbotsford exhibits a compositional syntax in which diverse symmetries, or near symmetries, combine in asymmetrical grouping. This would prove to be the fundamental organisational order of Baronial Revival country house design.

But what of Abbotsford's symbolic character, for there is clearly a calculated nationalism in the building's architectural form(s)? Scott, it must be said, has been much criticised for his brand of nationalism, seen by many to be sentimental, cosy and politically emasculated. Nowhere was this more cloyingly evident than in his masterminding of the official visit of George IV to Edinburgh in 1822, the so-called 'King's Jaunt', with all its absurd ceremonial parading of an anachronistic tartan-clad Scotland in an unequivocal, even servile, display of loyalty to the Hanoverian monarch and the British Union. No less for some do his historical novels and poems, with their depiction of an all but vanished rural Scotland (if such a Scotland ever existed), constitute a lifetime's labour which signally failed to come to terms with the harsher realities of modern life. It has been shrewdly observed that 'The contemporary Scottish city does not exist in Scott's novels', an omission made not out of ignorance but rather 'to create a literary *cordon sanitaire*'[13] around intensifying urbanisation and industrialisation. So, too, focused on a collection of historical memorabilia and bric-a-brac, Scott's obsessive antiquarian acquisitiveness turned his home into a kind of folk museum, a metaphor for his own retrospective romantic view of Scotland.

Yet, nostalgic or not, the architecture of Abbotsford did revive a formal language that otherwise might have been disregarded in the assimilating anglicising culture of North Britain. Scott's Scottishness might in many respects be reactionary but, as perhaps the country's most revered literary figure, his espousal of crowsteps, bartizans, towers and turrets ensured that baronial architecture was not to be lightly dismissed. Of course, the revival of 'old Scotch' was only one of several revivalist styles available to the country house architect – writing in mid century, Robert Kerr (see below) would detect as many as ten such styles – but it was one which, in the Scottish context, carried a symbolic charge which could and would empower architecture, from the ancestral affectation of a country seat like Abbotsford to the polemical drama of the Wallace Monument.

While the part played by Abbotsford in influencing what was, it must be stressed, only one of the courses that architecture would take in nineteenth century Scotland is generally acknowledged, opinions differ on the immediacy of its impact. James Macaulay, who regards the house as 'the unsung prototype of Scots-Baronial architecture', nevertheless asserts that, thanks to 'a lack of architectural publicity', Abbotsford's design 'failed to influence contemporary and near contemporary architecture' and had no perceived role in the revival of the Scots Baronial style that took place later in the century.[14] Some, on the other hand, have drawn attention to the published descriptions and illustrations of the house which appeared publicising Scott's achievement and the surely significant fact that from 1833, only a decade after its completion and a year after Scott's death, Abbotsford opened, and remained open, to the public.[15] David Walker, doyen of contemporary architectural historians in Scotland, nevertheless maintains that it was 'quite some time'[16] before Abbotsford's influence began to be felt. Others, however, have noted that 'Abbotsford-inspired' pavilions and mansions were being erected as far afield as Russia and Poland as early as the 1820s[17] and it is difficult to imagine that the house had no comparably prompt resonance within Scotland itself. Contemporary architects must have found Abbotsford provocative. William Burn, for example, a friend of Scott, must surely have been aware of its design, even though he did not visit the house until 1830. Indeed, it has been suggested that it was in response to 'the romantic ideals' which had inspired the design of Scott's home that Burn 'turned his attention to the castellated architecture of his own country.'[18] Yet David Walker is adamant that Burn was 'not in any way influenced by Abbotsford'.[19] Consensus is puzzlingly elusive.

By the time of his visit to Abbotsford, William Burn had established the largest architectural practice in Scotland. He had a number of prestigious public buildings to his credit, while country houses, whether altered, enlarged or new, figured prominently among his many commissions. Like most of his contemporaries he had no difficulty, practical or ethical, in designing in a range of different styles. Many of his public buildings, like his stolidly dignified Custom House in Greenock (1817–18), were carried out in classical style, and while he did at times apply similar disciplines to some of his residential commissions,[20] the majority of his country house projects were designed in a freer, more medievalist, manner. Several of these, particularly those executed in the early years of his career, were in castellated style. By the 1820s, however, following the fashion introduced by the English architect William Wilkins at Dalmeny House, West Lothian (1814–17), he had turned first to Tudor Gothic, as at Carstairs, Lanarkshire (1822–4), and then to a more Jacobethan idiom, employed, for example, in additions made to Riccarton House, Midlothian (1823–7), and Brodie Castle, Moray (1824). Then, just as Scott's architects at Abbotsford had done, Burn adopted more Scottish forms. Faskally House, Perthshire (1829–31), had crowstepped gables, round stair towers and bellcast conic roofs, though the plan was more compact than at Abbotsford, the perimeter walls scarcely modelled and the level of the roof ridges constant. In the additions he made to Tyninghame in East Lothian (1829–30) Burn 'caught something of the grouping of old [Scottish] work'[21] but it was at Milton Lockhart, Lanarkshire (1829–36), ironically for Scott's son-in-law, John Gibson Lockhart,[22] that a bolder Burn became all but Baronial. To be sure, beside the more recognisable Scottish elements, English traits were still evident, notably in the house's elongated mullion-and-transom windows, but the elevations were composed in the same aggregative way as those at Abbotsford. Again, the asymmetries and apparent irregularities were not arbitrary but sprang from the needs of the plan. And in this respect, in solving the increasingly complex social and functional demands of country house living, Burn was a master. It was not surprising that he and others in his wake should find the syntax of the Scots Baronial style congenial to this challenge; it proved indeed remarkably flexible in adapting to need. Still less was it to be wondered at that the semantic charge which the style carried should ignite enthusiasm among those who, following the example set by Walter Scott, wanted to make some architectural confession of Scottishness.

Burn continued to explore Jacobethan and Baronial themes, the latter notably in the turreted additions he made to Pitcaple Castle, Aberdeenshire (c1830), and in the design of Dawyck House, Peeblesshire (1831–2). There, along with the customary crowstepped gables with shaped dormer heads, were stepping string courses and a cone-roofed turnpike tower. Burn's rival, William Henry Playfair, no less a master of stern neoclassical design, had also begun to pursue similar Scottish ends. Though the number of country house commissions he carried out was considerably fewer than Burn's, his was a more literate application of the detail of sixteenth and seventeenth century Scots work based on knowledge drawn from the alterations and

Tyninghame
Elevation of east front 1829
HES Canmore DP087413

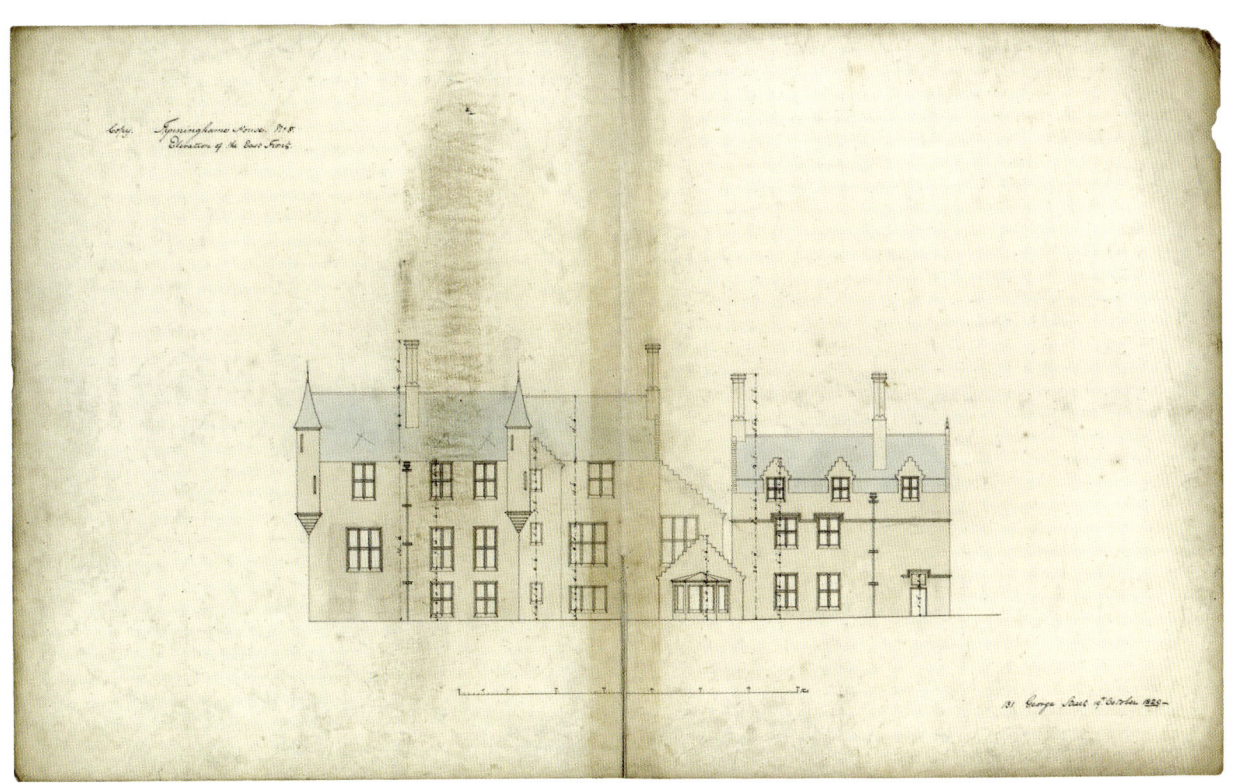

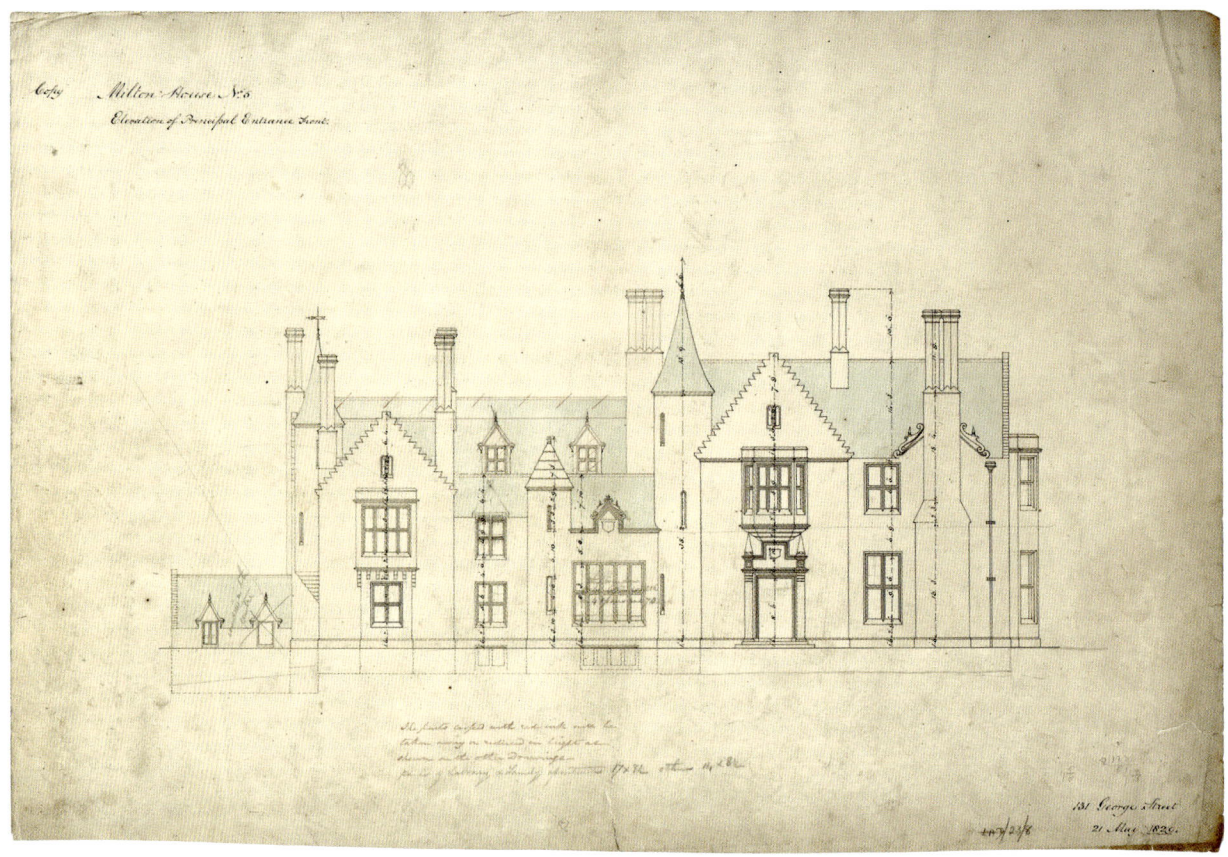

Milton Lockhart
Drawing of principal entrance front 1829
HES Canmore SC954565

additions he made to a number of older buildings. A brief sequence of projects including work at Prestongrange, East Lothian, and Heriot's Hospital in Edinburgh, culminated in the design of Barmore (now Stonefield Castle) in Argyll (1836–40). Magnificently poised above the wooded shore of Loch Fyne, Barmore has been described as 'one of the great landmarks of Scottish architectural history'.[23] Whether such a rhetorical assessment is justified may be questioned. There can be no doubt that Barmore's 'vertical and busily compressed'[24] bulk, unquestionably Scots in its detail and aggregation, is a signpost building. But it does not stand alone. Burn's contemporary Stenhouse (1836) can hardly be considered less convincing in its handling of baronial form, though there it has to be said that he had the advantage of being able to incorporate existing sixteenth century fabric and detail. Still less can the precocious work of Burn's assistant David Bryce be ignored. His somewhat later Seacliff, East Lothian (1841), is the first of a series of country houses, some of gigantic size, which would embody the classic order and ebullience of the Baronial Revival style. Here is the asymmetrical aggregative massing, vigorous and muscular. Here are all the familiar forms: crowstep gables, pediment-gabletted dormers, round towers, bartizans round and square, conic and pyramidal roofs, tall chimneys. Here, too, the characteristic assemblages of forms: the gabled entrance tower flanked by corbelled cone-roofed bartizans; the canted bay windows corbelled back to square under a steep crowstepped gable. Milton Lockhart, Stenhouse, Barmore, Seacliff – these are at once the fulfilment of the Abbotsford dream and the forerunners of a long period of development in which architects would exploit the symbolic potential and compositional flexibility of the Scottish Baronial Revival not only in the design of country houses but in that of virtually every other building type.

Stonefield Castle
HES Canmore SC558838

But before this could happen, before any distinctively national character or composition could be imparted to the increasingly diverse range of building types generated by Victorian society, designers needed to understand the Scottishness of the Scottish architecture they sought to emulate. For those who like Burn, Playfair and Bryce found themselves engaged to alter, extend or replace older buildings in order to meet contemporary needs, opportunities to learn directly from the past readily presented themselves. If Playfair's informed adoption of original details drawn from sixteenth or seventeenth century buildings was more studied than most, Burn's sophisticated planning, devised to resolve the country house's hierarchical social distinctions in a smoothly interlocking sequence of public, private and service spaces without resort to any formal formulae, seemed to fit well with the loose elevational syntax adopted at Abbotsford and its successors. This complementarity would reach its highest expression in the great country houses designed by David Bryce in the 1850s and 60s. Meanwhile, the ability to recognise and deploy historically derived detail with conviction would, for many, increasingly depend not, or not only, on hands-on engagement with the original buildings but on the information conveyed by published studies. Of these printed sources, however, there were few. Unlike the much-documented antiquities of England, the buildings of Scotland's past had received little topographical coverage and no scholarly attention.

By far the earliest published views of the country's towns, colleges, castles and religious buildings were those which appeared in John Slezer's *Theatrum Scotiae*, first printed in 1693.[25] Having risen to the rank of Surveyor of Their Majesties Stores and Magazines in Scotland, Slezer, who was Dutch- or German-born, claimed that the 57 engraved 'prospects' included in his book presented an 'impartial account' of Scotland's urban and architectural wealth. However, his immoderate assertion that 'there is no country in Europe that can brag either of greater piles of buildings, or more regular architecture in its ancient churches and religious fabricks, than Scotland' calls this assumed objectivity into question. By picturing 'many great and remarkable Monuments of Antiquity' at a time when, as the 1814 edition noted, North Britain 'yet remained an independent kingdom', Slezer's work has remained important as the first illustrated record of Scotland's buildings. Its value to nineteenth century architects in search of detailed information about these buildings was, however, limited; Slezer's plates were not measured surveys and the accuracy of their record was not always reliable. Some of the engraved plates by Moses Griffith in Thomas Pennant's *A Tour in Scotland*, first published in 1769, did show buildings but in no greater detail, while those illustrated in Charles Cordiner's *Antiquities and Scenery of the North of Scotland* of 1780 were confined to the north-east of the country. No more useful were the illustrations which appeared in Adam de Cardonell's *Picturesque Antiquities of Scotland* published in London in four parts between 1788 and 1793. Though many of the country's religious houses and castles were depicted, de Cardonell's etchings were small and lacking in detail. More comprehensive and more informative were the drawings which George Henry Hutton collected between 1781 and 1820, more than five hundred views and plans, the majority of which depicted Scotland's religious buildings. Perhaps compiled to form a *Monasticon Scotiae* (though Hutton denied that this was his intention) these remained unpublished and thus essentially inaccessible. More valuable were the engravings contained in *The Antiquities of Scotland* published in two volumes between 1789 and 1791 by the English antiquary and lexicographer Francis Grose, already responsible for the four folio volumes of *The Antiquities of England and Wales* (1773–87). Geographically and typologically his coverage was considerable; his illustrations were accompanied by historical commentary and architectural description, and occasionally dimensional information was given. Grose observed that, during his travels, he had found that North Britain possessed 'every sort of ancient monument usually found in the south, with the addition of some peculiar to itself'.[26] He commented on architectural features which he regarded as distinctively Scottish as, for example, in his note that 'adjoining to the roof, is commonly a triangular gable, the sides diminishing by a number of steps called crow steps'.[27] Nor was Grose alone in providing the evidence for such identifiably Scottish details as crowstepped gables, corbelled battlements, bartizan turrets, turnpike stairs, conic roofs and others. Numerous topographical publications pictured Scotland's historic buildings, though rarely in sufficient detail to be of any value to architects in search of authentic design data. Some were relatively well illustrated anthologies of antiquities and landscape such as Robert Forsyth's five-volume *The Beauties of Scotland* (1805–8) or Walter Scott's two-volume *Provincial Antiquities and Picturesque Scenery of Scotland* (1819–26); some recounted the tours of travellers up and down the country with only the occasional pictorial image. Not until the 1840s, however, nearly two decades after the first tentative attempts had been made at Abbotsford to recover the 'old fashioned Scotch stile [*sic*]', did anyone succeed in producing an archaeologically respectable compendium of Scotland's historic architecture which was at once comprehensive and detailed enough to lie beside the drawing board. Even then, no formal analysis or definition of any such 'stile', ancient or modern, appeared.

But though the historiography of Scottish architecture was as yet underdeveloped, the apprehension of a Scottish Baronial style undoubtedly existed. Indeed it could be said that it was the exploratory practice of such a style by architects such as Burn, Playfair, Bryce and others which provided the impetus to a more scholarly study of the past. As early as the 1830s, David Cousin, a pupil of Playfair, had contributed a model design for 'A Mansion in the Style of a Scotch Baronial House of the Sixteenth Century, with Accommodation and Arrangements suitable to a Villa of the Nineteenth Century' to John Claudius Loudon's *Encyclopaedia of Cottage, Farm and Villa Architecture*. Cousin's mansion had all the familiar baronial forms which he claimed he had derived from certain historical houses, several of which, he noted, could be found illustrated in de Cardonell and Forsyth. He regretted the absence of any authoritative documentation – 'I have been unable to lay my hands on any work treating on the subject' – but, speaking as a designer, he commended the style's adaptability, particularly the ease with which 'it admits of an unlimited extent of additions', contending that it was this quality which made the style 'essentially progressive'.[28] This same argument would appear over a decade later when, in a memorandum of 1848 intended to persuade the Grand Duke Constantine to introduce the style into the Russian empire, James Gillespie Graham advocated the style's 'very great capabilities both of picturesque and commanding external effect, and of easy adaptation for all the conveniences of modern life'.[29] By then, anyone, architect or patron, so persuaded to build in the Baronial Revival style, whether for picturesque or practical reasons, would, unlike David Cousin, have had access to the necessary architectural documentation.

Once again, as with Lugar, Atkinson, Blore, Wilkins and Pugin, it was an Englishman who was instrumental in moving Scottish architecture forward. Thanks to the financial backing of a wide range of subscribers led by William Burn, Robert William Billings, an antiquarian, architect and restorer, succeeded in compiling a four-volume work entitled *The Baronial and Ecclesiastical Antiquities of Scotland*, published in Edinburgh and London between 1845 and 1852. Although Burn had moved to London in 1844 leaving his partner David Bryce in charge in Edinburgh, it was he who, long conscious of the absence of any scholarly documentation of the buildings of Scotland comparable to that available for English architecture, had commissioned Billings,[30] financing the venture with the considerable sum of £1,000. It was an act of significant cultural consequence and a clear measure of the practice's continuing interest in a national, namely Scottish, style.[31] Billings responded to the challenge by producing a work whose 240 engravings of secular and religious buildings illustrated Scotland's architectural heritage as never before, their visual splendour picturesquely presented in often dramatic oblique views. He acknowledged in his introduction that he could not and would not attempt to include all the built evidence but rather 'such a selection as should combine the spirit of the whole, by the features conveyed in those delineated'[32] and although he did not construct any developmental study of the Scottish Baronial style, nor yet a formal analysis – Billings simply presented his examples in alphabetical order, each set of plates described historically and, to some extent, architecturally – he did, significantly, affirm the distinction and originality of Scottish architecture. French and Flemish influences were not to be denied, particularly in the years between 1500 and 1660, but these had been 'so cleverly mingled' with indigenous castellated architecture 'as to produce a Baronial style peculiar to the country'.[33] Such borrowings no more diminished this Scottish style than did those Italian influences at work in the south render the historically parallel Elizabethan style any the less English. But it was not words but images which made Billings' volumes so important.

> His beautifully sharp and vigorous delineations of the nation's architectural heritage surpassed all previous publications in number, size and detail. Consequently their impact was immediate and immense … providing fertile source material, at once tolerably accurate and readily accessible. Now it became possible not only to adduce a more precise imagery to the creation of architectural character, something hitherto generally dependent only on a romantic and vaguely associational notion of what the buildings of Scotland's past actually looked like, but it was also feasible to exploit on a much broader scale than ever before a whole repertoire of clearly specified Baronial elements in attaining the compositional freedom and flexibility which the building demands of the nineteenth century town increasingly sought.[34]

Although the classic forms and formal relationships of the Scottish Baronial Revival style had largely been determined in the country houses which David Bryce built in the 1840s *before* the actual publication of Billings' *Antiquities* – Seacliff (1841), Carradale (1844), Leny (1845), Balfour (1847) and, in grand scale, at Inchdairnie (1845) – it seems that Bryce knew Billings well and 'benefited greatly by having the opportunity to study the book as it progressed'.[35] Clearly he continued to do so after publication for the houses he built in the third quarter of the century assimilate not only many individual baronial forms with identifiable provenance but several larger compositional motifs drawn from the sixteenth and seventeenth century castellar buildings illustrated in Billings. The gable of Maybole Castle with its high-set corbelled bay window appeared at Hartrigge, Roxburghshire (1852), Fothringam, Angus (1859), and The Glen, Peeblesshire (1854–5). Castle Fraser and Castle Huntly provided the model for the drum towers

Mousa to Mackintosh | **133**

at Ballikinrain, Stirlingshire (1864), and Castlemilk, Dumfriesshire (1863–4), while at Craigends, Renfrewshire (1857), and Blair Castle, Perthshire (1862–76), the arched entrance towers were sourced from Fyvie Castle. In many of these houses, most aggressively perhaps at Ballikinrain, such forms were embedded in a compositional strategy of asymmetric concatenation which, introduced at Abbotsford, had in Bryce's hands become quintessentially Baronial.

Historical affinities were certainly meant to be perceived for it was always a part of the style's potency not just to convey a picturesque aesthetic but to inject an affective association with the Scottish past into the present. This Scottishness, the deliberate declaration of national character in architecture, reached its height – literally so – in the third national monument to be erected in nineteenth century Scotland, the Wallace Monument, built on the Abbey Craig near Stirling. As Scottish as the plates in Billings could make it, it did so without explicit allusion to any particular historic building.

The suggestion that a monument might be raised to honour Scotland's national hero, William Wallace, was first made around 1817 but the proposal came to nothing. Repeated attempts to promote building in 1838 and 1846 also failed; evidently 'the proverbial jealousy which had so long existed between Glasgow "folk" and Edinburgh "people"'[36] made it impossible to come to a decision on an appropriate site. Finally, in 1856, agreement was reached when a crowd of 20,000 gathered at King's Park, Stirling, resolved 'by acclamation' to erect 'a National Monument to the Scottish Chief'[37] on the nearby Abbey Craig looking out over the site where Wallace had defeated the English forces at the Battle of Stirling Bridge. A decision was made to launch a competition. In a strange parallel with the sequence of events associated with the Scott Monument, a winning design submitted by Joseph Noel Paton was rejected, its allegorical sculpture regarded as too provocatively anti-English, and in 1859 a second competition instigated. From over a hundred entries received, the design prepared by the architect John T Rochead was chosen, not only by the organising committee but also by the general public who had been asked to record their preference when the entries were exhibited in Glasgow, Edinburgh and Stirling. Construction began in 1862. Rochead, who had worked for seven years in David Bryce's office, created an unequivocally

Ballikinrain
Watercolour view by David Bryce 1865
HES Canmore SC557571

national monument, a Scottish Baronial tower soaring over 60 metres above the wooded crag of Abbey Craig, as commanding in the flat carseland as Stirling Castle itself. At its heavily rusticated battered base the tower is linked to the keeper's house by a high-walled courtyard entered through a huge semi-circular archway ringed by colossal cable-moulding with knotted label stops. An octagonal winding stair, open to the elements, rises at the south-west corner giving access to a series of superimposed barrel-vaulted halls within the tower, these lofty spaces dedicated Walhalla-like not only to Wallace but to the great figures of Scotland's past. At the summit the stair opens onto a windswept parapetted platform over which arch eight pinnacled flying buttresses forming an open crown strongly reminiscent of the High Kirk of St Giles, Edinburgh, pictured in Billings and soon to become again a symbol of revival.

Work was completed in 1869. Billed at the outset by one of its most partisan supporters as 'one of the most remarkable architectural attractions in North Britain',[38] the Monument did not disappoint. Up close it may be unsubtle and intimidating, its details often gargantuan, its knobbly cliffs of rusticated stone implacable and menacing. But viewed from the Hillfoots or the flat haughlands beside the winding Forth, it is a triumph, its scale finely judged in the landscape, its architecture, to invoke Billings' terms, both baronial and ecclesiastical, tower-house and crown-spire steeple. In a way that neither the National Monument on Calton Hill nor the Scott Monument in Princes Street Gardens in Edinburgh had done, the Wallace Monument hypostasised Scottishness.

In Rochead's rocketship-shaped tower, as in the country houses of Burn, Playfair and Bryce already discussed, the Scottish Baronial Revival revived many of the forms of the Scottish Baronial style of the sixteenth and seventeenth centuries. This overt Scottishness was deliberate, the spectrum of intention

Craigends
Watercolour perspective of main elevation by David Bryce c1857
HES Canmore DP061453

Mousa to Mackintosh

stretching from a merely sentimental nostalgia for the past to a more polemical expression of a national consciousness recovering its confidence. What the Revival did not do, of course, was to replicate the planning arrangements of that earlier style; no nineteenth century landowner or new industrialist, however patriotic, wished to live in the relatively primitive domestic conditions that had prevailed some three or four hundred years earlier. In fact, the plans of most of those country houses designed in the Scottish Baronial Revival style were models of functional convenience, at least within the parameters set by Victorian society. Commenting on Bryce's country houses, Colin McWilliam finds 'form always expressing function', a quality he regards as 'the touchstone of the Scottish baronial'.[39] It was this fitness for purpose, the ability to respond to both symbolic *and* practical needs, which, as it proved readily extensible to a broad range of nineteenth century building types, validated David Cousin's assessment of the style's 'essentially progressive' nature.

But the respect in which the legacy of Scottish Baronial architecture was held by the many subscribers to Billings' *Antiquities* and the enthusiasm with which its anticipated reincarnation on the Abbey Craig was greeted by the 80,000 who turned up to witness the laying of the Wallace Monument's foundation stone was not shared by everyone. Especially critical were a number of expatriate Scottish architects who, like many before and since, had been seduced by 'the high road that leads … to England'.[40] James Fergusson, for example, whose historical writings on world architecture were unsurpassed in the nineteenth century in their comprehensiveness and scholarship, gave little attention to the architecture of his own country. More than that, he maintained in the second volume of his *A History of Architecture in all Countries* (1867) that architecture as an art was not indigenous to Scotland, 'a country where the great mass of the people belonged to an art-hating race'.

> No one who knows anything of the ethnography of art would suspect the people who now inhabit the lowlands of Scotland of inventing any form of architecture.[41]

In limited descriptions of the historical architecture of Scotland, which included comment on medieval abbeys, churches and palaces and references to a few

Wallace Monument, Stirling
Engraving 1861
HES Canmore SC959986

'successful adaptations of Classical Architecture', Fergusson stressed an abject submission to foreign influences. French, Irish, Scandinavian, even Spanish ideas were of far greater significance than any native genius. He briefly notes the 'numberless square towers and fortalices scattered over the country' but quickly adds that 'none of these can properly be called objects of architecture'. On the other hand, he does remark that the 'baronial edifices of the succeeding age … are as remarkable as any class of buildings erected after the Middle Ages'. This somewhat surprising concession, which he does not elaborate, seems to have been the result of his recent familiarity with Billings. Fergusson used some of Billings' plates to illustrate his own text; he praised the four-volume work, commenting that had it contained 'the necessary plans and architectural details, [it] would be unrivalled as a monograph of an architectural province'.[42] This admiration for baronial building, the plea for plans and details drawn to scale and the measure of Fergusson's appraisal of Billings' *Antiquities* are perfectly valid but it is the dismissive sting in the tail which reveals the cultural disdain, if not deprecatory then certainly patronising, in which Scottish architecture was held south of the border. Scotland was still provincial North Britain.

Similar if perhaps less supercilious remarks are to be found in *The Gentleman's House, or, How to Plan English* [sic] *Residences from the Parsonage to the Palace*, written by the Aberdonian Robert Kerr and published, like Fergusson's *History of Architecture*, in 1864 while the Wallace Monument was under construction. As its name implies, Kerr's work was not primarily a history, although he did give a short historical survey of the development of domestic planning; he was concerned with practical advice, an approach which entailed not only technical matters but also a review of the stylistic options available to the mid nineteenth century architect. Among these was 'the Scotch Baronial Style', the tenth of ten different styles Kerr identified. He outlined its essential features in a short descriptive chapter. These included

> small turrets on the angles of the building, sometimes carried up from the ground, and sometimes built out on corbelling; crowstepped gables; battlemented parapets; small windows generally; the introduction almost always of a main tower; and over the whole, in one form or another, a severe, heavy, crude, castellated character.[43]

Kerr granted that a number of 'first-rate Mansions' had been built in this manner (even in England) but expressed the view that such buildings could be in harmony only with the Scottish landscape. But he also maintained that the style was in any case 'primarily French of the Tudor period [sic], and Scotch only by modification',[44] the implication being, as with Fergusson, that the style had no inherent indigenous integrity. As if to underline his émigré superiority, he added that it was 'an uncivilized style'.[45]

This so-called 'uncivilised' quality in Baronial, its rude wildness – a quality those of its proponents more orientated toward Ossian than Scott might have called its 'savage nobility' – seemed to alienate some designers in the softer south. Despite the fact that, as Kerr had noted, a number of 'first-rate' houses had been built in the style (among them, Fonthill House in Wiltshire (1856) by William Burn), perhaps this was to be expected. The style had no national legitimacy in England. Yet there were Scots practising in England who could not refrain from criticising what they saw happening back home. J J Stevenson, for example, writing in his *House Architecture*, published in 1880, fulminated over what had been done at Stirling.

> The enthusiasts for Scotch nationality have recently erected, as a monument to Wallace, a tower which alters, and some think destroys, the contour of a beautiful hill near Stirling. Corbelling has run mad in it, making marvelous protuberances where one does not expect them; corners are hacked out of it, and the pieces stuck on somewhere else. The design seems to aim at being wild.

And he continued,

> Such productions are not true expressions of national feeling. National peculiarities and differences have of late become softened down and assimilated by more frequent intercommunication with England and the influence of common culture. We should therefore expect that the architecture of the two countries should become assimilated, as in fact has happened, except in this revival of Scotch 'Baronial' which has exaggerated the peculiarities of the old national style.[46]

Stevenson, in fact, admired the Scots Baronial of the sixteenth and seventeenth centuries, a style whose features, he correctly argued, had 'some reason in necessity or tradition, and were used with a moderation'.[47] Perhaps it was to be expected, then, that he should criticise the nineteenth century revival of the style for its tendency to 'the expression of clumsiness, crude forms, and vulgarity'. It is not difficult to accept something of this view when confronted, as Stevenson was at the time of writing, by the kind of over-indulgence seen in Robert S Ingram's Burns Monument, Kilmarnock (1877–9). To apply such terms to the Wallace Monument is, however, surely excessively pejorative and fails to appreciate Rochead's grasp of architectural scale in the wider landscape. But that Stevenson could see neither 'necessity' in the functional planning of Baronial Revival country houses nor 'tradition' in the symbolism of the architectural elements adduced, seems explicable only in terms of the cultural denial implicit in the imperial and imperious 'British myth'.

Stevenson might have paused to consider why, if indeed 'the architecture of the two countries should become assimilated' in one common British style – whatever that might be – the head of the British state had herself chosen to build in the 'uncivilised' Scots Baronial manner. Stimulated by a succession of trips north in the 1840s, Queen Victoria's love affair with all things Scottish had deepened into a life-long relationship when she obtained the lease of the Balmoral estate in 1848 and bought outright in 1852. Five years later came the laying of the foundation stone of a new Balmoral Castle. Designed by the Aberdeen architect John Smith and his son William, both of whom worked closely with Prince Albert, the Queen's Highland holiday home was completed by 1856.[48] Constructed in grey Aberdeenshire granite and arranged around two linked courtyards linked by a dominating 24-metre-high tower, it was conceived 'so as to appear an organic multi-phase building'[49] as if it had grown over time and might continue to grow. No doubt the agglutinative compositional quality of many nearby sixteenth and seventeenth century Aberdeenshire castles had much to do with this significant and distinctly baronial quality. The queen herself had headed the list of subscribers who had financed Billings' recently published four volumes and certainly all the requisite baronial elements were in evidence: crowstep gables, canted bays, cone-roofed bartizans, round and octagonal turrets, and at the centre the high square tower spiked with tall bartizans at three corners and a higher parapetted round stair tower at the fourth. Impressive as it was, however, the 'castle' was essentially a private home, mingling its 'evocations of "Scottishness"', as architectural historian Simon Green has noted, 'with ideas of comfort, practical planning and recreational escape'.[50] The same description could as easily be applied to Abbotsford for, just as Scott's literary prestige had invested Abbotsford with special architectural significance, so, by building Balmoral, the monarchy set its seal of approval on a specifically Scottish architecture – Baronial by appointment.

It has to be acknowledged that both Abbotsford and Balmoral were built as rural retreats, places of 'recreational escape'. To that extent their architecture might be regarded as the stuff of dreams, fabricated fancy irrelevant to the harder realities of nineteenth century urban life. Equally, it must be admitted that since the function of a monument such as the Wallace Monument is fundamentally symbolic, then the relevance of the stylistic language adopted to questions of 'practical planning', economy and convenience may at best be doubted. Was the Scottish Baronial Revival style, then, no more than the nostalgic indulgence of rich gentry and royalty? The evidence of cleverly conceived functional country-house plans and sections, of a formal syntax flexible in its spatial arrangements and adaptable over time, of a semantic intent understood and embraced by many from the thousands gathered below the Abbey Craig to the queen and her consort on Deeside, suggests otherwise. Perhaps, however, what most exemplifies the 'essentially progressive' quality of the Baronial Revival is its appearance across a range of building types built on the streets of Scotland's booming Victorian towns. In adjusting to the ramifying new demands of activity, process or structure shaping the fabric of the nineteenth century city, the language of form embodied in *The Baronial and Ecclesiastical Antiquities of Scotland* might not always prove as versatile as the gridded grammar of international classicism. But it *would* maintain the persistent evidence of Scottishness in Scottish architecture.

As the title page of Billings' influential work makes clear, it was a study of both the baronial *and* the religious buildings of Scotland's past. It was to be expected then that those architects charged with the design of places of worship might have had recourse to Billings' plates as source material. A church after all was still a church. And churches were needed in nineteenth century Scotland. In 1828, as a result of an enquiry launched by the General Assembly of the Church of Scotland into the adequacy of provision made for public worship, a programme of church building had been instituted. In 1843, following the Disruption, the country-wide needs of the new congregations of the Free Church seceding from the established Church of Scotland created a further boom in construction. But where medieval forms were revived, these tended to be those advocated by the ecclesiological arguments of the English Gothic

Balmoral Castle
HES Canmore SC1201440

Revival. Liturgical compromises were made to suit the predominantly Presbyterian pattern of Scottish worship – the pulpit was often placed behind and above the communion table – but this was done within the nave-and-aisles architectural context of pre-Reformation church design. In most cases, English or Continental Gothic supplied the models for the layout, buttressed walls, traceried windows and crocketted spires of these new churches. As one architectural historian of post-Reformation churches in Scotland has bleakly observed,

> The fully developed mediocrity of the Gothic Revival, which by the time of the Disruption was holding undisputed sway over ecclesiastical and architectural minds alike, dragged its dreary course through the remainder of the century.[51]

Thus, despite Billings, continuity with the particular traditions of Scottish religious building remained very much a minority pursuit. Even David Bryce only occasionally attempted to broaden his interest in a viable national style from the baronial to the ecclesiastical context. His Church of St Nicholas (1847–55), built alongside the medieval collegiate church in Dalkeith, was no more than 'solid and massy with a few well chosen and substantial accents in the manner of many late Scots Gothic kirks'.[52] Tracery in the aisle windows, for example, was based on fifteenth century windows in the collegiate church at Lincluden, Dumfriesshire, a building illustrated in Billings. In shaping the windows and buttresses of his church at Carnwath, Lanarkshire (1865–9), Bryce was again much indebted to the ruined collegiate church nearby. But there was little more. Whatever Scottishness could be identified in mid-Victorian churches was vague and elusive, 'solid and massy' indeed, but generally lacking any precise antiquarian provenance. Crowstepped gables certainly abounded but this was more a matter of survival than revival. Not until the 1880s did interest in Scottish ecclesiastical forms sharpen, a development signalled by a sudden fashion for medieval crown spires. Illustrated by Billings – at St Giles, Edinburgh, and King's College, Aberdeen – this characteristically Scottish form reappeared in parish churches at Buckie (1880), Tarbert (1885–6) and Peebles (1885–7), at Craigmailen Church in Bo'ness (1883–5) and at St Leonard's in the Fields, Perth (1885). More crown spires would follow in the 1890s, by which time scholarly interest in Scotland's historical architecture, castellated, domestic and ecclesiastical, would enter a new phase.

For the moment, however, in mid century, it was not on church buildings but on secular architecture that 'the quest for the "national"'[53] would focus. Now, as the individual elements of baronial form drawn from Bryce and Billings were re-assembled in new relationships in a range of Victorian building types which, unlike churches, were largely without historical precedent, a more robust, hard-edged manifestation of romantic nationalism superseded the soft-centred, Scott-fostered Scottishness of the earlier decades of the century. Nowhere was this street-wise Baronial more in evidence than in the buildings of the law; perhaps more convincingly than any other building types, many of the country's municipal buildings, sheriff courthouses and police courts took on an appearance as distinctively Scottish as the law they administered.

By the middle of the nineteenth century, Scottish towns and cities were developing rapidly under the economic stimulation of industrialisation and imperial trade. As urban populations increased, a range of new civic buildings was required to take the place of the old burgh tolbooths which had hitherto served the administrative, judicial and social needs of local communities. In 1860, responding to this demand, the Sheriff Court Houses (Scotland) Act called for improved accommodation for the dispensation of civil and criminal justice across the country. Costs would be met equally by the Treasury and from the assessment of local lands and heritages, while the buildings were to be 'erected and completed under the supervision of the Commissioners of Supply',[54] the body responsible for overseeing local government in the counties.

Originally a nominated group of local dignitaries, the Commissioners exercised an authority to manage public affairs based on property, superiority or life rent. This link with the land did much to explain not only the choice of architects favoured for the design of these new courthouses (and indeed the administrative offices, halls, jails and police stations often associated with them) but also the very nature of the architectural style adopted for such buildings. Those architects already engaged on Crown commissions or those whose Edinburgh offices put them close to the source of government funding found themselves well placed to benefit from this extensive programme of courthouse building. At the same time it was scarcely a surprise that the Commissioners should endorse the same Baronial manner already invested, or being invested, in the mansions of their own country estates. The baronial administration of justice might be long gone, but 'the old Scotch style' of castle and tower-house would still prove eminently fitted for the courts of Scots law.

Prior to the publication of Billings' *Antiquities* and before the Sheriff Court Houses (Scotland) Act took effect, this national character was not unequivocally in evidence in the buildings of local government. Tudor detailing dominated the design of courthouses at Haddington (1832), Dunblane (1842–4), Tain (1848–9) and Dornoch (1849–50), diminishing any striving – if such it was – for Scottishness. An 'unadventurous Tudorish Baronial display of bartizans and pinnacles'[55] is how John Gifford dismisses Tain. After the passing of the Act, the firm of Brown and Wardrop, who had been responsible for Tain and Dornoch, built courthouses at Alloa (1863–5), Falkirk (1866–8), Forfar (1869–71), Stranraer (1871–4) and Stirling (1874–6) in which they continued to produce a hybrid 'crowstepped Tudor'[56] to which admixtures of French or Flemish Gothic were now and then added.

But in work by David Rhind and Peddie & Kinnear the commitment to Baronial became clearer and more comprehensive. Rhind's courthouses at Dumfries (1863–6) and Selkirk (1868–70) are outstanding, vigorously sculptured, asymmetrical compositions in heavily textured stone, pulsing with cylindrical turrets and bartizans, the skyline peppered with crowsteps, chimneys and cones. Peddie & Kinnear, less full-blown, are more architecturally respectable. At Greenock (1864–7) the composition

Selkirk Courthouse
HES Canmore SC1382607

Lockerbie Town Hall
Greg Balfour Evans / Alamy Stock Photo

is symmetrical, its spiky icing of bartizans, gables and gablets intensified by a tall central tower 'in which these same features are compressed into a steep and agitated pyramid'.[57] A similarly spired tower, gabled on all four faces with tall cone-roofed tourelles corbelled at the corners, recurs in more elevated asymmetrical context in their competition-winning design for the New Town House at Aberdeen (1868–74). Whether these examples should be categorised as French in inspiration or, as one writer has averred, 'self conscious medieval Flemish'[58] may be open to dispute, but such towers became a recurring feature of Scottish town halls, courts and burgh offices. After Greenock and Aberdeen, variations on the theme appeared at Renfrew (1871), Lockerbie (1873), Annan (1875), Huntly (1875), Dunfermline (1875), Crosshill & Govanhill, Glasgow (1879) (now Dixon Halls), Hawick (1884) and Elgin (1885). More would follow. Again, in some instances, it is impossible not to sense Franco-Flemish allusions but, as Colin McWilliam observed, while 'foreign detail enriches the baronial town hall, [this] hardly weakens the case for seeing it as the continuation of a native type'.[59] In townscape terms, these clock towers recall the medieval tolbooth – at Forres, the new town hall of 1838–9 had deliberately reiterated the staged form of the old tolbooth. In architectural terms, foreign flavours might spice the mix but the recipe was essentially Baronial and well rehearsed in the work of David Bryce. The tall crowstepped gable flanked by mirrored bartizans, a formal combination whose historical legitimacy would be homologated in Billings' plates, had already appeared at Seacliff (1841) and Inchdairnie (1845–7). In Bryce's transformation of Kinnaird Castle (1853–8), steep French roof planes rose behind twinned cone-capped tourelles. At

Fettes College, Edinburgh
Stephen Taylor / Alamy Stock Photo

Craigends (1857) a similar arrangement surmounted a Fyvie arch. It was a simple matter to turn these precedents into the town-hall clock tower.

Scottishness also made an appearance in the design of educational buildings, though again, as with courts and town halls, not before mid century. The first of the great foundation schools which were privately or corporately endowed during the early Victorian period were designed with barely a recognisable hint of national affiliation. Begun before 1850, Donaldson's Hospital (School), Edinburgh (1841–51), by William Henry Playfair and Stewart's College (1849–53) by David Rhind were both carried out in a collegiate Tudor or Jacobean style which though much turreted had little to do with indigenous tradition. Playfair, working on his proposals for Donaldson's in 1838, rather gave the game away when he wrote that he was creating a building which 'in the correctness of its parts shall be worthy of comparison with the remains of Old English Architecture'.[60] Not until the 1860s did baronial forms begin to figure in school design. Even then Scottish crowsteps and bartizans found themselves in alliance with steeply pitched French roofs. The most dramatic version of David Bryce's spired tower, for example, enhanced neither town hall nor courthouse but soared above another school – Fettes College in Edinburgh (designed 1862, built 1864–70). Three-storey tourelles and tall chimney stacks stand sentinel around a high, outrageously steep pyramid spire and again, as at Craigends, an arched recess at the centre of the tower shaft hints at Fyvie. The Fettes tower rises axially at the heart of a wide facade lavishly garnished with Scots Baronial and French Gothic detailing, the latter increasingly

Aberdeen Grammar School
HES Canmore SC1266272

fashionable among Edinburgh architects since Bryce had made a Loire château of Kinnaird. Peddie & Kinnear, for example, incorporated Frenchified towers not only in the 1862 competition-winning submission they made for the Town House in Aberdeen but also in their contemporary design of Morgan Academy (1863–6) in Dundee. Despite sharing similar central towers, the Dundee school was, no doubt as a result of budgetary constraint, a modest affair in comparison to the opulent architecture of Fettes. So, too, was the firm's Morrison's Academy, Crieff (1859–60), which, though it did have a turreted three-storey country-house centrepiece, was without the tall tower. But while Morrison's lacked the French sophistication of Fettes, it was determinedly and solidly Baronial. It was as if such stripped-down Frenchness revealed a more rugged Scottish character in the architecture. This was certainly true of James Matthews' design for Aberdeen Grammar School (1860–3), chosen by the Town Council for its unmistakable Scottishness in preference to Italianate and classical schemes he had also submitted. Tudor influences lingered, notably in the provision of generous mullion-and-transom windows made necessary by the need to admit good daylight to school classrooms (not a consideration in a sixteenth century tower-house) but many of the architectural forms adduced to the design of these educational buildings, especially at Aberdeen, could be found in Bryce or Billings. Even so, in all four schools the degree of Baronial commitment was, perhaps inevitably, compromised by symmetrical composition. Again, as with the impact of French ideas, this was at its strongest at Fettes where it was made all the

more implacable by a long axial drive aligned with the school's central high tower.

At Aberdeen things were rather different, for although the main classroom block was symmetrically organised this rigour was subtly but significantly tweaked by the intrusion of a single turret offset beside the central entrance and more blatantly challenged by asymmetrically designed cylindrical and saddleback towers set back on either side of the main facade. But even this retiring acknowledgement of baronial asymmetry was rare; rarer still after the 1872 Act had created local school boards whose building programmes demanded that 'there will be separate entrances and playgrounds, and even separate staircases to enter the classrooms, so that the boys and girls may never associate except while under instruction in the eye of the teacher'.[61] Such symmetrical plans proved best fitted to the disciplines of classical architecture. As a result, the 'old Scotch style' made only sporadic and in the main faint-hearted appearances: for example, at Bellahouston Academy in Glasgow (1874–6), Baronial but barely so with a watered down version of the tourelle-spiked tower; in Alloa where the circular entrance tower of the Burgh School (1875) was capped by a tall cone roof; and in the bartizan-flanked crowstepped gables of Helensburgh's Hermitage Academy (1880). In the hands of Charles Rennie Mackintosh, however, the Baronial school would yet make one last highly polemical contribution to the search for Scottishness in Scottish architecture.

Town halls, courthouses, municipal offices, police stations, schools and colleges were not the only building types to assume something of a nationalist swagger. There were, for example, many Baronial banks. Perhaps the right of the Scottish banks to print and circulate their own currency notes accounted for their readiness to favour a corresponding national assertion in their buildings. In this architectural declaration of Scottishness the National Bank took the lead. In the 1860s, the architect David MacGibbon, who with his partner Thomas Ross would later make a significant literary contribution to the Baronial Revival, was responsible for more than twenty new or altered premises in the style. Peddie & Kinnear also adopted the style for some branches of the Royal Bank and the Bank of Scotland, particularly on difficult corner sites. There were, too, several Baronial hospitals: notable among them, John Burnet's Western Infirmary (1871–4) in Glasgow and, in the capital, David Bryce's huge Royal Infirmary of Edinburgh (1870–9) complete with town-hall clock tower. There were railway stations, built for the Caledonian Railway at Stirling (1855) and at Dundee where the West Station (1888–90) boasted yet another tall town-hall tower. No building type, it seemed, was immune from the Baronial bacillus. In Glasgow it has to be said infection was never virulent. Nevertheless, on the north side of the Trongate, John T Rochead contrived an agitated four-storey office block busy with jagged gables and dormers (1855) which rose on a corner to a bartizan-nipped saddleback tower, while not far away on Ingram Street, Robert Billings had completed a large warehouse (1854) in no less idiosyncratic style. Comparable, if less eccentric, commercial developments began to appear in several Scottish towns. On Edinburgh's narrow Victoria Street, David Cousin completed India Buildings (1864–6), 'a large and highly ornate block of offices'[62] built with Jacobean–Baronial bravado. Nearby, on St Giles Street, David Bryce's buildings for the *Edinburgh Daily Review* (1871–2) and the *Edinburgh Evening Courant* (1872–3) enriched the Old Town skyline with attics sharp with stepped gables and bartizans. In Leith, the Sailors' Home (1883–5), 'a towered Baronial edifice';[63] in Hawick, a Corn Exchange (1864), 'rogue Baronial';[64] in Inverness, the Cameron Barracks (1880–6), a courtyard fortress with machicolated drum towers. Baronial elements even appeared on some industrial buildings: breweries in Edinburgh and Montrose, a calender works in Dundee, and at the Carron Ironworks near Falkirk where crowstepped gables repeatedly punctuated the long two-storey factory facade.

But by far the most ubiquitous presence of Baronial was in urban housing. Its impact on the terraces and tenement ranges so characteristic of the streets of Scotland's cities and towns cannot, of course, be compared to the extent of the influence exerted by classical architecture, whether in terms of organisation, proportion or detail. Nor was its distribution evenly spread across the country; while relatively common in Edinburgh it was rare

Royal Infirmary, Edinburgh
Photograph 1914
HES Canmore DP088698

in Glasgow. But the Baronial did leave its mark on the residential street scene. By the middle of the nineteenth century, environmental conditions in the older quarters of the country's towns and cities had deteriorated to such an extent that slum clearance and redevelopment were desperately needed. In the wake of various reports indicating the scale of the problem, both private developers and municipal authorities began to assume responsibility for the provision of better housing. Several City Improvement Acts were passed (Glasgow, 1866, Edinburgh, 1867, Dundee, 1871). In Edinburgh, a report on the overcrowding of working class housing published in 1860[65] had drawn attention to 'the mean dwellings of the common people' and the need to replace these with housing which both improved the physical and sanitary conditions of urban living and at the same time provided a reasonable financial return on investment. Not only that, but it had gone on to argue that such new housing should 'still bear a general relation to that of the city', by continuing the traditional practice of building tenements and by perpetuating the localised architectural character of the Old Town. There is a certain symmetry in the fact that the writers of the report, imbued as they considered themselves to be with 'all the spirit and patriotism of Lord Cockburn and Sir Walter Scott', should have felt the need to conserve in the city the presence of an architectural idiom which was in effect the urban vernacular dialect of that same architectural language which Scott himself had deliberately revived in the Borders countryside at Abbotsford. A mention of 'pointed gables' in the text of the report evoked the historic skyline of High Street and Canongate and seemed to suggest that the adoption of such an architecture, genuinely romantic and national, might prove more culturally fertile than all the international 'wilderness of square-cut stone'[66] in the eighteenth century New Town across the bridges to the north. In fact, redevelopment had already espoused the Baronial Revival or, at any rate, what *The Builder* called 'the Scottish Domestic style'.

Anxious to capitalise on the opportunity to improve access to the city's new central railway station by clearing the densely built-up slopes below High Street, an Edinburgh company had in 1853 obtained an Act of Parliament authorising the demolitions necessary to permit the laying out of the new curving climbing thoroughfare of Cockburn Street. Shops and flatted housing were to be erected on both sides of the new street. Moreover, Section XXI of the Act stated that

> it is desirable to preserve as far as possible the architectural style and antique Character of the Buildings of that Part of the Old Town[67]

Cockburn Street (1859–64) was the first area of urban redevelopment to be realised in full-blown Scots Baronial Style. Its architects, Peddie & Kinnear, effected a brilliant transition from station to High Street using all the elements of the style in creative combinations adapted to the swinging curve of the street plan and the awkward climbing contours of the slope. Their success may well have led to the incorporation of similar stylistic strictures in the Edinburgh Improvement Act of 1867 which called for the character of the Old Town's townscape to be conserved and required that new housing be 'in harmony with those fine specimens of national architecture in many of the neglected and overcrowded areas'.[68]

In extensive redevelopment which began in 1868 on both sides of High Street this was done. Along St Mary's Street (1868–9), Blackfriars Street (1870–3), Jeffrey Street (1888–92) and elsewhere, plots were feued to private builders who were bound to conform to designs prepared by the Improvement Trust's architects, David Cousin and John Lessels, in a manner which has been alternatively described as 'scholarly Scots Revival' and 'routine baronial'. Whatever the label, these new tenemented streets maintained the visual coherence of Old Edinburgh to such effect that the historical credibility of that part of town is almost as much due to the Baronial redevelopments of Victorian times as it is to the legacy of earlier centuries. These steep crowstepped gables, tall eaves dormers, random bartizans and chimney stacks, modelled on the Lawnmarket roofscapes of multi-storeyed tenement properties like Gladstone's Land and Mylne's Court, are, as *The Builder* noted at the time, 'in keeping with the surroundings, and group well'.[69] Scottishness is here a matter of familiarity, of deliberate urban conservation made possible by the easy syntax of baronial form.

While few towns across Scotland failed to acquire a Baronial tenement or two, in Glasgow, a city whose addiction to classicism was not mitigated,

Cockburn Street, Edinburgh
Drawing c1860
HES Canmore SC793542

as Edinburgh's was, by the counter attraction of a medieval old town, there was little evidence to suggest any strong interest in national architecture. As in Edinburgh, tenements built by the City Improvement Trust on Saltmarket (1880–7) did defer to the crowsteps, chimneys and strapwork of their seventeenth century predecessors but it was not until the turn of the century, with the erection of W J Boston's competition-winning Improvement Trust tenements on High Street north of Duke Street, that any robust Baronial Revival appeared – coincidentally built, like Cockburn Street, on a rising curve to accommodate wheeled traffic. Meanwhile Edinburgh continued to indulge its Old Town-tutored predilection for updated 'old Scotch', its deployment of baronial forms confined neither to social class nor to urban location. While solid Scots tenements continued to be built in the cleared streets around High Street, more elegant middle-class variations on the same theme were going up to the south beyond the Meadows. Nothing excelled the flatted ranges of Marchmont where David Bryce's unrealised 1869 proposals for the residential development of the Warrender Estate were superseded in a *tour de force* of 'emphatically Baronial'[70] fervour. Through the 1870s and 80s, intoxicated by Bryce's elevational ideas, more than a dozen independent architectural practices collaborated in the creation of a four- and even five-storey streetscape full of formal invention, 'as if to assure the prospective buyer that his tenement flat can have as much individuality as a villa'.[71] Here, as nowhere else, the forms of the Baronial country house were brilliantly transposed into the repetitive disciplines of the city tenement.

Warrender Park Road, Edinburgh
HES Canmore SC1828276

Chapter 7
Documentation, Restoration and Revival
Anderson and Lorimer

'a stout protagonist of things Scottish, of the interest and beauty of its national architecture, and the importance to the student of a thorough knowledge of its early examples in relation to the work, however divergent in requirements, of the present day'

A N Paterson on Robert Rowand Anderson, in Sam McKinstry, *Rowand Anderson: The Premier Architect of Scotland*

'He was the first to recognize the charm of unpretentious old Scottish buildings, with their honest plainness and simple, almost rugged massiveness'

Hermann Muthesius on Robert Stodart Lorimer, in *The English House*

In July 1852 *Chambers's Edinburgh Journal* carried an article in praise of 'The Old Castles and Mansions of Scotland'. Enthused by the recent publication of *The Baronial and Ecclesiastical Antiquities of Scotland*, the writer of the piece praised the comprehensiveness of Robert Billings' achievement, noting that the four-volume work contained 'engravings of every thing that is remarkable in the ancient architecture of Scotland' and that 'the remains of antiquity in North Britain were never previously so amply and completely illustrated'.[1] For more than a generation, as Scottish architects plundered the pages of Billings and the forms of the Baronial Revival spread from country houses to the streets and street corners of Scottish towns, this assessment remained valid. By the 1880s, however, architectural scholarship had advanced in scope, detail and, not least, interpretative insight. With the publication in 1887 of the first of the five volumes of David MacGibbon and Thomas Ross' *The Castellated and Domestic Architecture of Scotland*, the search for a contemporary Scottishness in Scottish architecture began to develop in new directions, reinvigorated by a deeper and wider knowledge of the country's built heritage. This intensifying national awareness was not confined to architecture. A much

Scottish National Portrait Gallery, Edinburgh
Photograph c1900
HES Canmore SC684146

broader cultural awakening, extending from the arts to politics, was already in train. In 1886, as the Liberals under Gladstone considered the possibility of devolved government not only for Ireland but for Scotland too, the Scottish Home Rule Association was formed, its aim to establish some form of national assembly. While this stirring of national consciousness was as yet far from being a ubiquitous upsurge of popular feeling, few if any Scots now any longer referred to their country, as the writer to *Chambers's Edinburgh Journal* had done in mid century, as 'North Britain'.

In the preface to volume 1 of *The Castellated and Domestic Architecture of Scotland*, MacGibbon and Ross also acknowledge admiration for the contribution made by Billings: he was, they wrote, 'amongst the very first to recognize and draw attention to the importance of our Scottish Domestic Architecture'.[2] But while they are charmed by the beauty of Billings' plates, they find his failure to include plans and sections drawn to scale 'a serious drawback' to proper study and regret the absence of any systematic analysis of the historical evidence. Accordingly, they declare their aim to be to rectify these omissions. And this they do, filling the pages of their five-volume work with countless measured plans and sections and perspective sketches covering 'almost every building in the land erected before 1650'.[3] For each building they give historical and architectural commentary collating this vast body of evidence in four relatively distinct periods stretching from 1200 to 1700, each characterised by its specific arrangements of architectural form and detail. The result of this enquiry – a task never before attempted and never surpassed since – was to substantiate unequivocally the contention, advanced by several earlier less thorough investigators, 'that Scotland, like every other country in Europe during the period from the thirteenth to the sixteenth century, possessed a Castellated or Domestic Architecture of its own'.[4]

Not that MacGibbon and Ross were arguing for some isolated Scottish architecture cut off from mainstream international culture. On the contrary, they were well aware of the creative dialectic operating between international and national forces. They noted, for example, that the history of Scottish architecture was 'somewhat similar to that of France and England, although … modified by the more unsettled and less prosperous conditions of the country'.[5] Indeed, when in volume 2 they come to introduce these later buildings – those of their designated Fourth Period, 1542–1700 – MacGibbon and Ross are forthright in presenting their case for a specifically Scottish architecture.

> Turrets, steep roofs and gables, corbels, ornamental dormers, and similar features were common to all the Architecture of Western Europe as well as to that of Scotland at the close of the Gothic period and the beginning of the Renaissance, and to the extent of following this general tendency, Scotland may be said to have derived her style from abroad. But when we examine the Scottish buildings carefully and in detail, we discover that the design is of native growth, that it has a national and distinctive character, and forms a style quite as independent as, if not even more so than, any of the Renaissance styles of the other countries of Europe.[6]

How could it have been otherwise? To argue, as, for example, the historian James Fergusson had done,[7] that the architecture of North Britain amounted to no more than a lesser, provincial expression of English or French architecture was as absurd, not to say insulting, in its presumption of cultural superiority, as to suggest any kind of absolute exclusivity or uniqueness in the forms of architecture to be found in Scotland. As always, it was the interplay between international and national forces, between the history of art and the geography of art, which defined cultural specificity.

The significance of the impact made by the publication of *The Castellated and Domestic Architecture of Scotland*, the fifth and final volume of which appeared in 1892, can be gauged both by the creative direction taken by Scottish architecture in the last decade of the nineteenth century and the first two of the twentieth and by the parallel interest in restoration, conservation and heritage which developed over the same period. As a result of their more accurate delineation of architectural form, decorative detail and ornament, and the broadening of their investigation beyond conventionally castellar subject matter to a wide range of humbler urban and rural dwellings, MacGibbon and Ross 'hugely enlarged the repertoire of Scots Renaissance motifs' *and* 'demonstrated the possibilities of a far simpler Scots vernacular than the examples selected by Billings'.[8] Where Billings'

Allermuir, Colinton, Edinburgh
Photograph 1890
HES Canmore SC417126

choice of subject, dramatised by the perspective and *chiaroscuro* of his engraved plates, had stimulated the bold muscular inventiveness of Bryce's Baronial idiom, now a less strident but no less committed Scottishness, at once softer and on the whole more scholarly, began to appear. Two architects, both active in conservation and restoration work, figured prominently in this reorientated search for a national style: one, Robert Rowand Anderson, the advocate of a dignified and correct Scots Renaissance response to the challenge; the other, Anderson's pupil, assistant and, in some sense, successor, Robert Stodart Lorimer, the proponent of a more intimate, crafted reinterpretation of traditional Scottish building. A third designer, Charles Rennie Mackintosh, would, in pondering his self-confessed 'deep and filial affection'[9] for that same Scottish architecture, find a creative way forward, reversing the tide of cultural change back from the edge, from the periphery to the core, from the national to the international.[10]

By the late 1880s, when MacGibbon and Ross began to publish their exhaustively researched work, Anderson had already been in independent practice for almost 20 years. With an impressive list of completed projects which included work on almost 30 churches, the University Medical School and the National Portrait Gallery in Edinburgh, palatial Mount Stuart on Bute, and the huge offices of the Caledonian Railway in Glasgow (later the Central Hotel), he was a well established and much respected architect in Scotland. Scholarly and catholic in stylistic competence, his designs were carried out in differing styles ranging from the conventional classical order of the Italian Renaissance on the one hand to creative interpretations of English and French Gothic on the other, the latter deployed not only in ecclesiastical but, often brilliantly, in secular contexts. But Anderson was also an enthusiast for the architecture of his own country. As early as 1875 he had persuaded the Edinburgh Architectural Association to publish annual collections of measured drawings and sketches of Scotland's historical buildings. He himself contributed drawings to these publications and to the annual exhibitions of the Royal Scottish Academy. In 1879 he began work in the Edinburgh suburb of

Colinton on Allermuir, a relatively modest dwelling designed for himself and his family, which, in the ardent if perhaps exaggerated estimation of Anderson's biographer, embodied 'the essence of Scottishness'.[11] Asymmetrical in disposition, with tall apex chimney stacks, crowstepped gables, canted bays and a square oriel punching through the upper floor eaves, the house was unconventional but hardly remarkable; 'orthodox baronial'[12] is the *Buildings of Scotland*'s brief verdict. But it did prove to be the forerunner of a series of later buildings – among them, the Pearce Institute, Govan (from 1892), the Crum Memorial Library, Thornliebank (1894), and Pollokshaws Burgh Buildings (1897) – in which Anderson revived and permutated Scots Renaissance forms in an effort to arrive at a viable contemporary style. Moreover, Allermuir was perhaps the first built intimation that a Scotsman's house was not necessarily his castle and that the search for a new style was to be pursued in a less castellar, increasingly more domestic, direction.

And yet for all Anderson's good intentions, for all that he seemed to grow 'increasingly concerned with the development of a national style of architecture',[13] Allermuir remained an isolated experiment while no amount of architectural dalliance with shaped and crowstepped gables, pedimented eaves dormers, strapwork, canted bays, oriels, relieving arches and roll mouldings in later larger projects seemed to offer much beyond the reputable precedent of the past, that is to say, historicist respectability. Paradoxically, in an address given in 1889 to the protractedly named Edinburgh Congress of the National Association for the Advancement of Art and its Application to Industry, in which he averred that architects since the Renaissance had been so preoccupied with the 'features, details and proportions of ancient buildings'[14] that they had lost their way, Anderson appeared to acknowledge the hopelessness of the task he had set himself while yet at the same time holding out hope for the future.

> It is impossible that we can ever have a new style of architecture … as all the possible methods of construction are known to us; but although we cannot have that, we can give to our buildings a new and truer expression than they have had since the decline of medieval art.[15]

But what did this mean? In the features and details of Anderson's 'Scottish' buildings, deliberate allusions were still made to historical precedent. Neither functional convenience nor constructional logic may have been sacrificed to form, but yet the liberated three-dimensional excitement of David Bryce's transformations of the Scottish past was lacking. Where the Baronial Revival led by Bryce had translated the 'pictorial values' of Billings' anthology into an inventive architecture, exuberant and unconstrained, Anderson's built attempts to develop a 'national style' could not quite find release from the kind of pale and sober rectitude of the many drawings filling the pages of the published volumes of his friends David MacGibbon and Thomas Ross.

There can be little doubt that the revival of interest in Scottish architecture of the sixteenth and seventeenth centuries which occurred in the years between 1890 and 1920 could not have taken place without the publication of *The Castellated and Domestic Architecture of Scotland*. But it is no less certain that this movement could not have gained momentum without the personal promotion of Robert Rowand Anderson. Anderson's own architecture, that is to say those of his buildings which engrossed certain recognisably 'national' forms, may not have been altogether persuasive but the evident earnestness and intelligence which underpinned their design were compelling enough to command the respect of his contemporaries and would stimulate a similar search for Scottishness in the minds of a new generation of designers, many of whom had served as his apprentices.

These same stern qualities motivated Anderson's significant parallel activities in education and scholarship. Long keen that craftsmen, designers and architects should be educated together, in 1892 Anderson was largely instrumental in setting up a new School of Applied Art in Edinburgh (from 1903, the Edinburgh College of Art). The ethos of the school's curriculum was one of artistic collaboration: 'all who contribute to a building must understand one another'. It is not too far-fetched to recognise in this policy of bringing together the arts and crafts to serve 'the complete conception of the architect'[16] more than a hint of similar radical ideas abroad, for Anderson was well aware of the advances being made in art education on the continent and particularly in the industrial art schools in Germany. In Weimar, for example, the architect Walter Gropius would later establish the

Pearce Institute, Govan, Glasgow
Kenny Williamson / Alamy Stock Photo

Bauhaus as a school of design initially conceived on Arts and Crafts principles where all involved in what was called 'the complete building' collaborated not as teachers and pupils but as masters, journeymen and apprentices. There was, however, no precocious anticipation of the Bauhaus' later revolutionary departure from the past, and the curriculum ensured that the teaching of history figured prominently in students' education. Not only were the principles and examples of the 'Classic, Renaissance and Medieval Arts' to be studied but this programme was to be related to the cultural history of Scotland. As a report by the School's Secretary in 1894 made clear,

> The wish of the Committee is to give the School a national character because there is in Scotland an art of the past with a distinctly local colouring capable of being developed and applied to the wants and necessities of the present day. To enable this to be done the Committee must have an historical collection of examples of the various phases of art left to us from the past.[17]

Thanks to Anderson's endeavours, bursaries were created to further the drawing and study of the country's historical architecture, research which soon led to the foundation of the National Art Survey of Scotland. Begun in 1895, by the end of the century this project, particularly dear to Anderson's heart, had built up the beginnings of a national archive of measured drawings of architecture and the applied arts. Though Anderson had long desired to publish these records, it was not until 1910 that this possibility was first seriously considered. It was not until 1921, the year of his death, that the first of five volumes of drawings finally appeared, the hope being that 'when placed in the hands of architects [the Survey] would enable them to give a distinctly Scottish character to buildings which may be erected during the period of [post-war] reconstruction'.[18] Such quality Anderson had, of course, accorded the many reconstruction and restoration projects, predominantly ecclesiastical commissions, he had carried out during his long professional life – among them, work at Iona, Jedburgh, Dunblane, Paisley and Culross. If his success in imbuing his 'Scottish' new-build projects with comparable character was less convincing, his commitment to the quest for Scottishness in Scottish architecture, as expressed in his teaching and writing, nevertheless ensured that others – colleagues, apprentices and students – would build on his ideas.

Anderson's enthusiasm for the historical architecture of Scotland, his life-long concern that it should be properly documented and his belief that the past remained relevant were founded not on superficial aesthetic delight but rather on moral conviction. Or so he contended. Writing in an appreciative introduction to the 1901 edition of Billings' *Baronial and Ecclesiastical Antiquities of Scotland*, he maintained that it was not the particular forms or arrangements of forms but the inherent 'functional truth' of so much of the castellated and domestic buildings of the country's past which he admired. It was this rather than any 'artificial picturesqueness'[19] which gave to Scots Renaissance architecture that 'national' dignity which rendered it worthy of attention in the present.

> The builders of our Scottish houses and castles … never troubled themselves about picturesqueness or the composition of designs to suit sites. They did what suited their purposes and wants at the time, and the result was … buildings that show an adaptation of means to an end, functional truth, with resulting intelligence, expression, and picturesqueness.[20]

Much as it might have surprised Anderson, this was pure Ruskin.

> The uncultivated mountaineer of Cumberland has no taste, and no idea of what architecture means; he never thinks of what is right, or what is beautiful, but he builds what is most adapted to his purposes, and most easily erected: by suiting the building to the uses of his own life, he gives it humility; and, by raising it with the nearest material, adapts it to his situation.[21]

Written early in Ruskin's life when the simple domestic architecture he had seen on tours in England and Scotland made a powerful impression on him, these observations contrasted sharply with his later view, expressed in his *Lectures on Architecture and Painting* delivered in Edinburgh in 1853, that 'Ornamentation is the principal part of architecture',[22] an assertion that had led Anderson to regard Ruskin, for all his renown as an art critic, as 'a blind guide in regard to architecture'.[23] In fact, while the criticism of Ruskin's elevation of ornament was valid, it failed to take account of what he had gone on to say. Ornament might, in Ruskin's view, be the *highest* quality in architecture, but it was not the fundamental thing: 'the first thing to be required of a building', he wrote 'is that it shall answer its purposes completely, permanently, and at the smallest expense'.[24] It was this belief (though perhaps not always in its extreme economic sense) which lay at the heart of that stream of radical thought which stretched from *The True Principles of Pointed or Christian Architecture* enunciated by Pugin in the 1840s, and with whose writings Anderson was familiar, to the convictions motivating the designers and craftsmen in the workshops of William Morris with whom Anderson had shared a platform in 1889 in Edinburgh at the congress of the National Association for the Advancement of Art and its Application to Industry.

In any event, in addressing the readers of this 1901 re-issue of Billings' *magnum opus*, Anderson was challenging the 'concept of the autonomy of form, pioneered a century earlier in the aesthetic of the Picturesque and the Sublime'[25] and later, to some degree, further elaborated to national effect in the Baronial Revival. He was not denying the '*resulting*' pleasure of the picturesque, only asserting the priority of purpose. This analysis, in which the contemporary relevance of the architecture of the Scottish past was held, on the one hand, to be a matter of moral compulsion derived from functional utility and yet, on the other, to be invested in the aesthetic allure *and* symbolic significance of form as form, identified the parameters of an argument already raging across *fin-de-siècle* Europe. The need to resolve this dialectic was becoming increasingly peremptory. As the adequacy of high-style international historicism to embrace either the functional needs or the technological opportunities of modern life was everywhere more and more called into question, it began to seem that the solution might lie, paradoxically indeed, in low-style national culture with its synthesis of visual charm, crafted

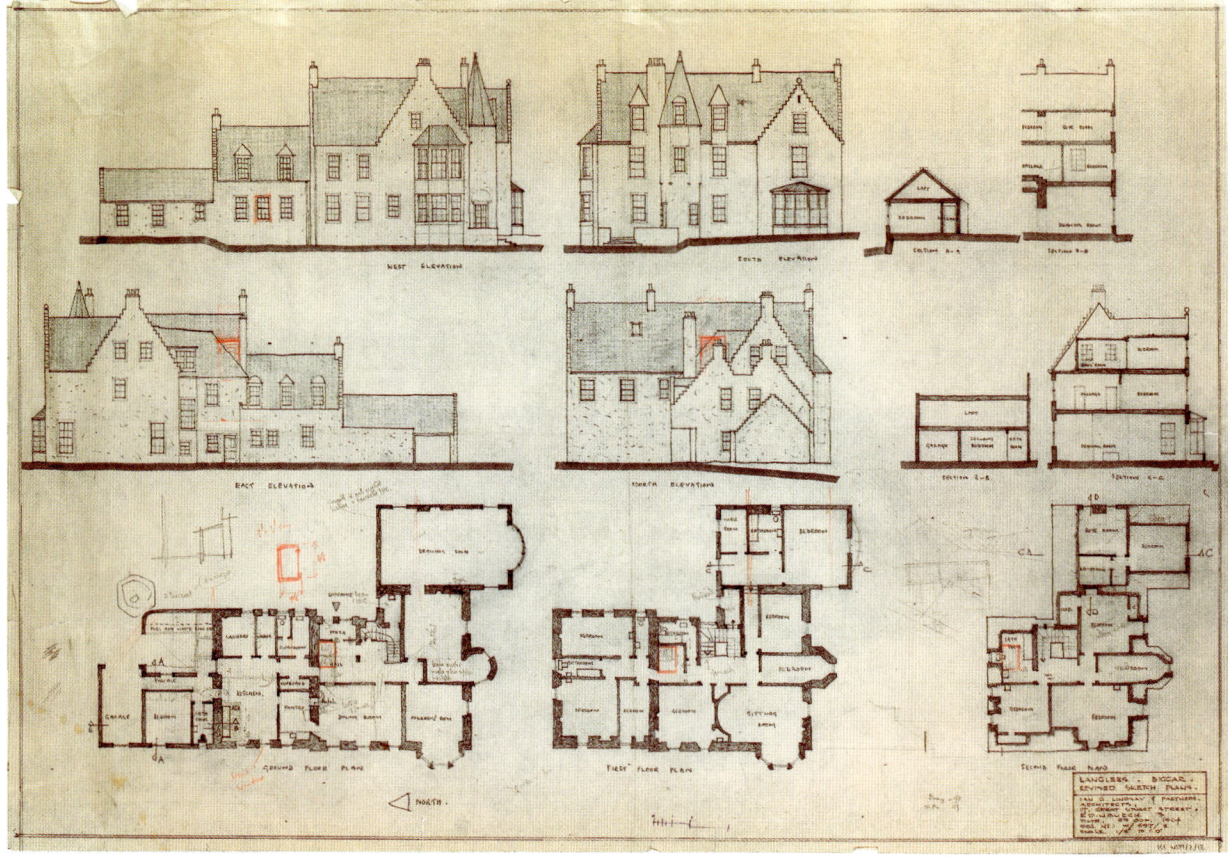

Langlees House, Biggar
Plan and elevations for proposed alterations c1965
HES Canmore SC842378

honesty and symbolic relevance. In Scotland, as elsewhere, attention turned to the vernacular.

In influencing this trend, Anderson's significance was limited: Allermuir did not set the heather on fire. His impact on the architectural profession in Scotland was, of course, considerable and most marked in the east of the country where several of his former assistants and pupils established their own practices. Many of those in the Anderson circle could be counted with him among the most skilled architect–restorers of the time while, in their new-build commissions, they were, like their mentor too, capable of dealing competently with contemporary problems in a broad range of classical and medieval styles. Like Anderson, most found some opportunities to experiment with 'Old Scotch' forms. In 1890–1, for example, George Washington Browne, who had worked as Anderson's principal assistant and for a few years in the early 1880s had been his partner, designed Langlees at Biggar, a compact crowstep-gabled house with a distinct vertical thrust, in which he incorporated early seventeenth century elements drawn from the Argyll Lodging at Stirling. Browne may also have been responsible for the design of Johnsburn at Balerno (c1900), described as a 'cosier mixture of Scots vernacular and Renaissance'.[26] More prolific and more inventive with similar sources, Arthur George Sydney Mitchell, who had worked in Anderson's office from 1879 before leaving to set up his own practice in 1883, showed himself to be a skilled interpreter of 'the seventeenth century genre'[27] in his grouping of flatted housing and social buildings at Well Court in Dean Village, Edinburgh (1883–6). Cone-capped cylindrical towers like those at Falkland and Holyroodhouse appeared in his Students' Union building for Edinburgh

THE GROUND PLAN.

MODERN ARCHITECTURE IN SCOTLAND.
THE WELL COURT, EDINBURGH.
A. BLOCK OF WORKMEN'S HOUSES, FOR J. R. FINDLAY, ESQ.
SYDNEY MITCHELL, ARCHITECT.

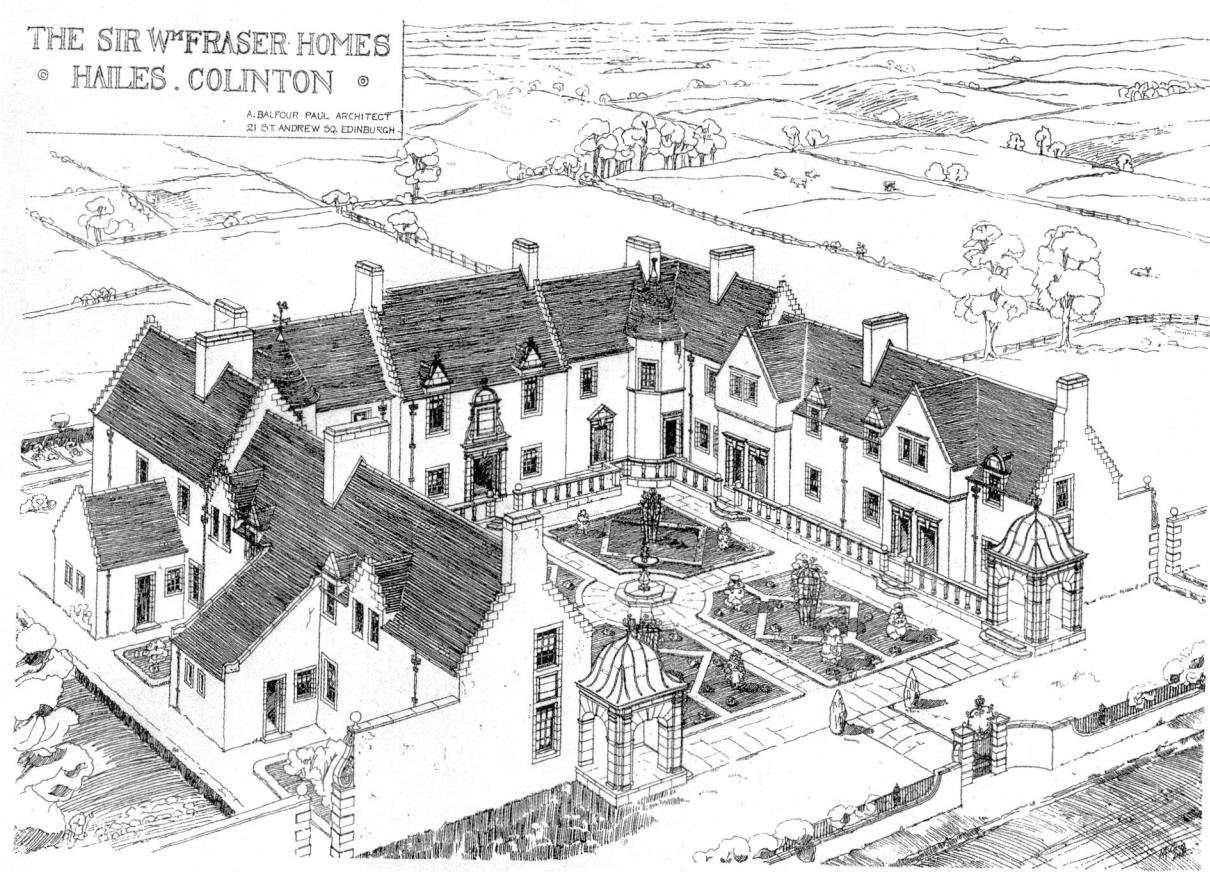

Sir William Fraser Homes, Colinton, Edinburgh
Perspective drawing 1899
HES Canmore SC823509

University (1887). By the beginning of the 1890s, Mitchell was building in castellar style at Duntreath and Sauchieburn, both vast mansions – the former with a Castle Fraser tower, the latter derivative of Tolquhon Castle – designed with a Baronial exuberance still redolent of David Bryce. Decidedly less grandiloquent but still Scottish were the Sir William Fraser Homes built at the close of the century at Colinton, Edinburgh, by A F Balfour Paul, another Anderson protégé later to become a partner in the firm.

Well Court, Dean Village, Edinburgh
'Modern architecture in Scotland' from *British Architect* 1889
HES Canmore SC702531

Scots Jacobean in character with ogee-roofed pavilions, these modest buildings symmetrically arranged around a U-plan courtyard 'might easily be mistaken for Anderson's own work'.[28] No such judgement would be made of the work of Robert Stodart Lorimer, the most talented and most insightful of all Anderson's acolytes, for Lorimer would push 'Old Scotch' beyond anything previously achieved.

Growing up in Fife at Kellie Castle, an ancient mansion of tall crowstep-gabled towers brought back to life by his father's enlightened intervention, Lorimer's introduction to the delights and difficulties of dealing with old buildings had come early. Time spent in Anderson's office, first as an apprentice from 1885 until 1889 and then as an assistant until 1890, brought more of the same with all the added personal, technical and aesthetic challenges of restoration. Perhaps the most formative experience of this early period in his professional life was his work as site architect on the restoration and extension of the Place of Tilliefour in Aberdeenshire, a commission brought to the practice when Hew M Wardrop merged his father's firm of Wardrop and Reid with Anderson's in 1883. Built in rubble masonry, the enlarged two-storey building stretched along the banks of the river Don, its long low extent animated by 'the grouping of its elements into gabled, crowstepped and chimneyed blocks, so that the eye is constantly diverted'.[29] Lorimer may not have had much of a hand in the design of Tilliefour but its free aggregation of traditional forms – crowstepped gables, massive chimney stacks, gabletted eaves dormers, jettied upper floors – taught him much about the handling of materials and the creative possibilities of traditional building. Travel in England and a spell working with G F Bodley in London added to the mix a love of Gothic craftsmanship and brought Lorimer into contact with those developments in the Arts and Crafts movement stimulated by the ideas of William Morris and William Lethaby, exemplified for a time in the 'Old English' country-house work of Richard Norman Shaw and later by Ashbee, Gimson and Voysey, and promoted in the Art Workers' Guild. As a result, the gentler forms of English domestic building would continue to have an appeal. But the stay in England also introduced Lorimer to James MacLaren, a Scottish architect whose simple, white-walled farm buildings on the Glenlyon estate in Perthshire (1889) and nearby cottages in Fortingall (1889) – 'Scots but without self-conscious historicist references'[30] – exerted something of a counter claim reinvigorating Lorimer's allegiance to his native tradition. Back in Scotland in independent practice, he attempted to meld the influences of Tilliefour and Glenlyon in some of the 20 or so houses built from 1893 in what was then the village of Colinton near Edinburgh (from 1895). But the cottagey charm of English domestic design, what Muthesius would call its 'simplicity, homeliness and rural freshness',[31] was difficult to shake off. Lorimer's 'Colinton manner' (his own phrase), though it set an increasingly popular anglophile pattern for the suburban bourgeois villa with its leaded glass lights

Tilliefour
HES Canmore SC1224550

Glenlyon Farmhouse
James Millar JAMM Architects

and red-tiled roof sweeping low over a shaded veranda entrance, failed, for all its white-harled gables and rounded stair towers, to attain any Scottish credibility. Only at Pentland Cottage (1897) in the white abstraction of the west elevation with its asymmetrical chimneyed gable is there a memory of baronial form (a mirror image exists in the high east gable at Earlshall, near Leuchars in Fife) and at the same time perhaps a prescient glimpse of what was to come.

Lorimer spent much of the 1890s at work on the restoration of Earlshall, a building splendidly pictured by Billings and described by MacGibbon and Ross as a 'perfect example of the sixteenth and seventeenth century mansion-house'.[32] The project was prolonged, and Earlshall's attractive massing, its seemingly contingent aggregation of forms, surely intensified the knowledge and love of traditional Scottish building first imbibed at Kellie. Four early houses – the Grange, North Berwick (1893–1904), Ellary (1894)[33] and Stronachulim Lodge (1894) in Argyll and the Manse at West Wemyss, Fife (1897) – all of them illustrated in *The Builder* in 1895, reveal Lorimer's ability to refashion this Baronial experience into the more intimate Arts and Crafts scale he had encountered in England and yet retain, unlike much of his work at Colinton, an unmistakable sense of Scottishness. The familiar forms observed in the castellar contexts of Earshall and Kellie are evident – crowstepped gables, eaves dormers, jettied floors, occasional bowed or bayed projections – but, at more domestic scale, in a white-walled vernacular largely shorn of 'architectural' ornament.

Drawings of Earlshall also appeared in *The Builder* as repair and refurbishment continued. The nature of the commission afforded little opportunity for new work but a charming little gatehouse was built with a rounded turret capped by a bell-shaped roof. Derived from the ogee-domed turrets of Baberton, Heriot's Hospital, Drumlanrig, or several other sources, this feature would become a characteristic motif which Lorimer, doubtless enjoying the sheer three-dimensional geometry of the form, would repeatedly employ in a variety of creative ways – not only the ogival dome, but conic or pyramidal roofs set on the circular, octagonal or square plans of turrets, stairs and small single-cell structures. His earliest lodge

house, for example, built at Balcarres, Fife (c1898), and based on the late sixteenth century garden pavilion at Holyrood known as Queen Mary's Bath House, had a bellcast pyramidal roof. Similar lodges and garden pavilions, some harled, some in random stone, some given bell-shaped domes, some topped with pyramids, appear throughout Lorimer's career, their compact sculptural quality emphasised by jettied upper floors and decoratively gabletted dormers pushing through the eaves of their steeply planed roofs.

The lodge house at Briglands, Kinross-shire, another 'Holyrood gatehouse'[34] with an ogivally hipped roof, was not built until early in the new century, but work on the house itself, a rather plain mid eighteenth century dwelling which Lorimer recast and enlarged in stages, had been begun by 1899. It was the first of a series of progressively larger white houses: freely developed in plan in response to incremental need; its austere harled walls had surrounds, crow-stepped skews, window and dormer heads in dressed stone; a turnpike stair and corner round were capped with bell-shaped roofs. A second white house project, Pitkerro (1902–04), on the edge of Dundee, was again an enlargement of an existing dwelling – in this case a laird's house of sixteenth and seventeenth century date. The choice of materials was the same as at Briglands, making the assemblage of simple vernacular forms equally stark. The completed plan was L-shaped, Lorimer's north-east wing, itself L-shaped, hinged in the re-entrant on a cylindrical turret whose bell-shaped roof echoed the bartizans on the older north-west wing of the house. If the curving surfaces of these roofs added a softer nostalgic quality to the otherwise sharp geometry of peaked dormers and serrated gables, two boxy, flat-roofed projections, one rising high into the north-east gable, the other abutting the adjacent south-east wall, seemed to afford a further hint of an architecture yet to emerge from this white-walled vernacular discipline.

In 1901 Lorimer began work on Rowallan, Ayrshire, his first commission for a wholly new mansion-house. It was located on rising ground to the north of the eponymous sixteenth century castle, a relatively small quadrangular structure distinguished, in a show of 'power without ferocity',[35] by its cone-roofed, twin-drum forework. As originally conceived by Lorimer, the new house, 300 metres to the north, was a vast affair. A congeries of colliding crowstep-gabled blocks of differing heights articulated by buttressed stacks and bell-domed turrets, it was still, even in its curtailed built form, exceptionally large. Gathered around a parapetted tower, gables and roof planes rise and fall in a restless surge; tall window openings, elongated eaves dormers and thrusting chimneys serve to counteract horizontal continuities: 'everything', as Lorimer's first biographer, Christopher Hussey, observed, 'is done to accentuate verticality'.[36] In plan, the building's spreading irregular perimeter seems to give some measure of external expression to almost every room recalling the agglutinative order of Abbotsford. There are decorative touches of carved ornament, but these are kept to a minimum, confined to entrances, high-level windows and dormer heads. The spirit is unequivocally baronial. Had the walls been harled white as Lorimer intended, the prismatic Scottishness of the architecture would have been even further intensified.

Regrettably perhaps, white-walled drama is also missing at Ardkinglas, Argyll (1906–8), a second large residential commission carried out by Lorimer in Baronial style. Located in a romantic Highland landscape near the head of Loch Fyne, Ardkinglas is as grand in its aspiration and as Scottish in its forms as Rowallan. But its composition is tighter. The plan, developed around a small central courtyard, is essentially square, though the perimeter is repeatedly punctuated by projection and recession. The massing of the building is thus more cohesive than at Rowallan. Seen on approach from the east, crowstepped gables, shaped dormer heads and tall chimney stacks point up to a cap-house tower to which a flag-flying cone-roofed bartizan clings. Viewed from the south-west, the impact of the house's tall-windowed, crowstep-gabled corner flanked by a bell-domed drum is again vertical. Yet overall the compacted elements of the composition, the horizontals of receding ridges paralleled by eaves lines, plain or concatenated with dormers, and the long intermittently balustraded terrace walls ground the building in a way which seems, if only barely, to mute its baronial Scottishness.

Pentland Cottage, Colinton, Edinburgh
Photographs from c1975 and c1980
HES Canmore SC548544, photograph by Patricia Macdonald from *Lorimer and The Edinburgh Craft Designers* by Peter Savage

No such criticism, however diffidently expressed, can be levelled at Lorimer's work across the loch from Ardkinglas at Dunderave (1911–12). Here the challenge was to restore an existing late sixteenth century tower-house and add to its accommodation. Four storeys and attic high, Dunderave was built to an L-plan with the square enclosure of a turnpike stair rising in the re-entrant and a round tower on the outer west angle; bellcast cones roofed the tower and the bartizans that flanked the narrowed crowstepped gable of the south-east jamb; a broad chimney stack rose high at the centre of the north-west wall. Lorimer altered none of this. Dunderave kept its gaunt verticality. Nor did he attempt to soften the abrupt way in which its rubble walls erupted from the rough lochside landscape. There are no horizontal terraces here to smooth and civilise the rugged setting, only a snug cobbled court held in the lee of the old tower by the low L-plan buildings Lorimer designed to abut each gable. This respectful strategy not only created an intimate external space, through which entry to the tower-house was subtly contrived, but it also allowed the old structure to retain its robust raw rise from the land. Had Lorimer restored harling to Dunderave's walls, rehabilitation would have been complete.

Commissioned to design what would, after Rowallan and Ardkinglas, be the third of his three grandest houses, Lorimer announced to a close friend that Formakin, near Bishopton in Renfrewshire, would be 'the purest Scotch I've ever done'.[37] Setting aside his restoration work, few would dispute that Lorimer achieved what he set out to do. Set on a rise above a small lake, the mansion-house at Formakin (begun 1911) stands tall, the vertical thrust of gables, tower

Ardkinglas House
HES Canmore DP132198

and elongated mullion-and-transom lights dramatised by the elevated situation. Two three-storey-and-attic crowstep-gabled blocks meet in a right-angled relationship which encloses, as at Dunderave, a square entrance tower in the sheltered north-east re-entrant but is open on the outer south-west side where, beside a round cone-roofed tower, a raised terrace overlooks the lochan. On this exposed but sunnier flank of the house, again as at Dunderave, Lorimer respects the traditionally untempered meeting of stone and earth and 'the park is allowed to reach to the very walls of the house, so that the cattle or hunters may graze underneath the windows'.[38] On the other side of the house extending north and east, service wings, each longer and lower than the dominating L-plan core housing the principal apartments, define the geometries of open courtyards and gardens. In the garden is a small but charming bell-roofed pavilion. This same characteristic form recurs some distance south of the house, at the entrance to the estate, where Lorimer placed two 'Holyrood' gatehouses (1908) in mirrored symmetrical relationship. One on each side of a central gabled archway, each lodge is slightly canted in plan to link into concave walls embracing an open forecourt. Flanking the entrance gate are bell-capped staircase drums, each 'a kind of additional gate pier,'[39] and abutting these, left and right, the higher ogival domes of the lodge roofs. Nearby, the three-storey-and-attic, the so-called bothy block designed to house tack rooms and laundry, takes the form of another crowstep-gabled, L-plan tower, here with a bell-domed octagonal stair tower in the re-entrant. In each of these three estate buildings – mansion-house, gatehouse court and bothy – Lorimer is wholly at ease with the

Dunderave Castle
HES Canmore SC559841

national tradition: rubble walls, though unrendered, are stark and strong, details are severe, forms clean and unequivocal. At Formakin, architecture is indeed distilled to the 'purest Scotch'.

This almost sculptural sensibility is wonderfully indulged in Lorimer's restoration of Balmanno, Perthshire (1916–21). The work entailed stripping away the various accretions made to the late sixteenth century castle and effecting the repair and refurbishment needed to make the L-plan structure habitable. But Lorimer, seizing the opportunity to improve on the legacy of history, did more. Besides building a new gatehouse, adding a low two-storey wing to the north of the castle and creating a walled garden with the by-now-obligatory ogee-domed gazebo, he made a number of interventions in the tower-house itself. Significantly, the most visually critical of these changes were made at wallhead level, perhaps a percipient acknowledgment of the formal polarities inherent in the baronial tradition. On the three-bay south front, the eaves height was lowered, transforming the top-floor windows into eaves dormers, the resultant elevation remarkably similar to that at Formakin. In the north-west re-entrant of the plan where a high square tower-housed the castle's turnpike stair, tower and stair were raised by some five metres to a parapetted platform, while a smaller rounded turret, corbelled from second floor level in the re-entrant between the tower and castle jamb, was also elevated to terminate in another of Lorimer's beloved bell-shaped roofs. The castle's ivory towers and gables soared upwards, walls in white harl, crowstep skews, margins and dormer heads in dressed stone. More than any other building he touched, Balmanno embodied Lorimer's 'early twentieth century vision of Scottishness'.[40]

Residential commissions constituted by far the bulk of Lorimer's work. By the time of the First World War he was known as a skilled restorer of castellated and domestic building and widely regarded as 'Scotland's leading country-house architect'[41] – but he was also responsible for a considerable amount of ecclesiastical work and for the design of many war memorials and cemeteries. These projects in particular make it clear that Lorimer's stylistic capabilities were not confined to the orchestration of forms drawn from the Baronial and vernacular antiquities he so much loved. No less than in his major restoration projects at Dunblane Cathedral (1912–14) and Paisley Abbey (from 1923), his designs for the Thistle Chapel (1909–11) and the Scottish National War Memorial (1924–7), both in Edinburgh, show him competent in Gothic, the Chapel having 'the ruggedness and compact outline characteristic of Scottish Late Gothic'[42] while in the National War Memorial Gothic detail is largely confined to the buttressing and vaulting of the Shrine. And in his domestic work, too, there were occasions, admittedly most associated with the remodelling of existing buildings, where Scottishness was deemed inappropriate: English Tudor at Brackenburgh, near Penrith (from 1901), French and Georgian interiors at Hill of Tarvit, Fife (1905–7), classical reserve at Marchmont, Berwickshire (1914–17), and Midfield, Lasswade (from 1914). But just as Lorimer's workload was predominantly domestic in character, so the majority of the houses he built or altered were designed in what he called his 'Scotch' style. It is through an evaluation of this style that his contribution to the Scottishness of Scottish architecture has to be assessed. How Scottish was it in terms of the national tradition of building? And how relevant was this evolving tradition to the challenges facing architecture in the early years of the twentieth century?

In a postscript to his biography of Lorimer, Peter Savage drew attention to what he believed to be an 'all important distinction between the Baronial and the Scotch styles'.[43] This differentiation seemed to depend upon a socially determined definition of the Scottish Baronial style which had reached its height in the early seventeenth century. Baronial buildings were those erected by the baronial land-owning class while those built by men of lower social status, the so-called 'bonnet lairds', had 'no claim to be considered Baronial even if their buildings lay more or less within the same tradition'! This narrow understanding seems both pedantic and unnecessary, and is in any event compromised by the animadversion to 'the same tradition'. Nor is clarity gained by Savage's denomination of these lesser, less defensive (or less quasi-defensive) buildings as 'Neo-Baronial transitional'. A better appraisal might simply conclude that the forms of the Scottish Baronial style found expression in both up-market and vernacular contexts. Of course, Savage is right to identify a range of formal interest from 'the diagonal shifts of emphasis brought about in the Baronial by corbelling, stepped string courses, or by the irregular addition of turrets' to the 'unpretentious simplicity' of vernacular housing, but is

Formakin House
HES Canmore SC684435

his contention that Lorimer increasingly favoured the latter while turning away from 'the restlessness of the Baronial' a valid view?

In planning his three large country houses – Rowallan, Ardkinglas and Formakin – Lorimer's method is the same as that adopted almost a century earlier at Abbotsford. Each room or group of related rooms finds its own formal expression, the composite plan an aggregation of these individual elements linked together in appropriate functional association with no supervening aesthetic discipline other than that of picturesque form. No less than was the case with the ramifying range of new building types appearing in Victorian Scotland, it is clear that Baronial formal relationships still afford a freedom consonant with the changing functional needs of early twentieth century living. With their irregular perimeters busy with indentations and projections, Lorimer's plans exhibit the ambivalent 'restlessness' characteristic of the baronial tradition, a restlessness which, on the one hand, recognises direct functional contiguities and, on the other, acknowledges the exhilaration of form freed from the strictures of applied order. This picturesqueness is even more apparent in the massing of the elements: crowstep gables, dormered eaves, round turnpikes and turrets, caphouse towers, corbelled bartizans, tall chimneys, which cohere in a vigorous restlessness re-iterating that 'crowding of all architectural features near the roof-line [so] very characteristic of the Scottish castle'.[44]

Balmanno Castle
Perspective view by Walter Fitzgerald Knox Lyon 1890
HES Canmore DP312700

The formal power of Lorimer's houses is intensified by his parsimonious use of external ornament. Unlike Anderson, he largely eschews period detail preferring his own playful invention and then only sparingly at entrances and dormer heads.[45] This ability 'to leave things alone',[46] his rejection, in the main, of correct Scots Renaissance detail, coupled with bare wall-planes of random stonework results in a calculated sense of vernacular simplicity which, escaping stylistic historicism, is the perfect foil to the formal activity animating wallhead and roofscape. Yet, however much all this eschewed the dictates of 'high style' historicism, however committed his abstemious reinterpretation of the national tradition, however much such achievements resonated with similar developments on the international stage, however glowing the appraisals asserted first by Hermann Muthesius and later by Christopher Hussey,[47] Lorimer failed to push Scottish architecture forward.

Chapter 8

'that deep and filial affection'
Charles Rennie Mackintosh and the way ahead

'I remember that steep slope and, turning into Renfrew Street, being "struck" by what I saw ... by the way CRM, on the threshold of the modern movement, yet still within the nineteenth century, had, taking the past with him into the present without doing it again ... pointed to the future.'
Aldo van Eyck, in Murray Grigor and Richard Murphy, *The Architect's Architect: Charles Rennie Mackintosh*

In a fascinating and characteristically erudite essay on 'Victorian and Edwardian High Baronial'[1] David Walker draws a distinction between the 'quite different schools of Scotch Baronial design in Glasgow and the north-east and that of David Bryce and his followers in the Edinburgh mainstream'.[2] That the Baronial Revival was much less in evidence on the streets of Glasgow than it was in the Old Town of Edinburgh and in the capital's expanding suburbs of Bruntsfield and Marchmont is undeniable. It is also true that those few Baronial buildings which did appear in Victorian Glasgow – among them Robert Billings' warehouses on Ingram Street (1854), John T Rochead's City of Glasgow Bank on Trongate (1854) and Rutherglen Town Hall (1861–2) by Charles Wilson – were idiosyncratic in detail and composition, apparently indifferent to any kind of scholarly referential form. That those Baronial country houses designed by architects in the west could be distinguished from the corresponding work of Edinburgh designers is perhaps a less convincing contention – though, again, there is often a freer, less archaeologically constrained deployment of Baronial elements in the work of such architects as David Hamilton, Charles Wilson, John T Rochead, John Burnet and John Honeyman. But that the two cities differed in the 'Scottishness' of their urban fabric is certainly true.

It is important not to forget that the urban form and architecture of Scotland's two largest cities in the late eighteenth and nineteenth centuries were largely shaped by the disciplines of classicism. The gridded streets and lanes of James Craig's plan for Edinburgh's New Town might be more hierarchically ordered and

The Study House and Market Cross, Culross
Photograph by Erskine Beveridge 1896
HES Canmore SC1129170

explicitly deferential to the British Crown than the acquisitive, less inflected, rectilineal network of streets in Glasgow's New Town on Blythswood Hill, which seem indifferent to topography and indeterminate in extent, more egalitarian – it could even be said, American – in its socio-spatial potential. Yet both were governed by the rigour of the right angle. So, too, with architecture. The buildings which lined the streets and squares of both expanding cities were predominantly classical in form – Greek, Roman or Italianate in provenance. But where the urban experience of Glasgow and Edinburgh did differ was not so much in the nature of their New Towns as in that of the Old. Well before the middle of the nineteenth century, the medieval quarters of both cities, strung along the old high streets, were in considerable measure decayed, insanitary and dangerous; packed with overcrowded urban housing, they would become the subject of Victorian improvement acts framed to facilitate demolition and reconstruction. The fabric of Edinburgh's Old Town was, however, much more extensive, intact and architecturally coherent than those fragments which had survived in Glasgow, so that when redevelopment took place in Edinburgh it did so under strict conditions that 'the architectural style and antique character'[3] of the old be reflected in the new.[4] In Glasgow there was no comparable attempt to conserve the character of the late medieval city and, though a few Baronial tenements were built, classical formulae remained dominant into the twentieth century. The attraction of picturesque 'old Scotch' was always more potent in Edinburgh.

Perhaps as much for this visual reason as for that more self-conscious awareness of Scotland's past which the professional and gentrified classes in the nation's politically impotent capital shared with the great landowners in the shires, interest in the historical legacy of Scottish architecture was more explicit in the culture of the east than that of the west. Scott had made the recovery of the past socially acceptable. Billings had made its built expression accessible. Burn and Bryce had made it buildable. MacGibbon and Ross had made it academically respectable.

But in burgeoning Glasgow, soon to become the second city of the British Empire, industrial, mercantile and municipal patronage remained more concerned to draw architectural inspiration from international culture, whether in quasi-Egyptian monumentality, the proportional elegance of Graeco-Roman precedent or the richer language of the Italian or French Renaissance, than from the gabled and turreted forms of the medieval Scottish town house or tower-house. Nowhere was this attitude more entrenched or more creatively exploited than in the work of the greatest Scottish architect of the mid Victorian era. In the texts of eleven lectures delivered to architectural audiences in Glasgow between 1853 and 1874, Alexander Thomson had next to nothing to say about the architecture of Scotland. Despite being 'very well versed in Picturesque theory',[5] he is silent on the castellated and domestic architecture of his own country. In a brief reference in an address on 'The Unsuitableness of Gothic Architecture to Modern Circumstances' given in 1864, he concedes that

> In the very old parts of the city where the houses are tall and narrow, a new erection on Gothic or old Scotch style is at least in keeping with the general aspect of things

only to continue,

> but when we discover it is new, we regard it as an attempt to deceive, and turn away with a mixed feeling of anger and disgust at the miserable forgery that has vitiated to our imagination the integrity of the whole locality.[6]

If this is scorn for abject pastiche, it is to be commended. But Thomson, by all but totally ignoring the built heritage of his own country, *ipso facto* denies any possibility that the architecture of the Scottish past may in some way be transcended and attain a contemporary relevance. Bearing in mind what he himself achieved by a radical reintegration of imported Egyptian, Greek, Romanesque and even Hindu forms, this is at best ironic. Thomson, of course, was exceptional in this as in many other aspects of his work and thought, and his total disregard of the Scottish tradition was not shared by other architects in Glasgow and the west, many of whom had, for example, subscribed to Billings' *Baronial and Ecclesiastical Antiquities of Scotland*. Among the latter was John T Rochead, whose magnificent Wallace Monument, perhaps the most dramatic icon of the whole Baronial movement, has already been discussed.[7] Rochead's post-Billings Baronial houses, like those of John Burnet, James Sellars, William Leiper, J J Burnet, John A Campbell and Alexander Paterson had, however, little interest in fidelity to historical precedent (referring to John Burnet's Baronial residential commissions, David Walker remarks that he had no 'thought of making them resemble original sixteenth century houses'[8]) favouring instead more cavalier permutations of Baronial elements with Romanesque, Gothic, French Renaissance, English Arts and Crafts and even American detail.

Some scholarly and professional interest in the historical development of Scottish architecture paralleling that in Edinburgh did, nevertheless, exist. So, too, the creation of an 'Old Edinburgh' at the exhibition held on the Meadows in the capital in 1886 was echoed in the Glasgow International Exhibition of 1888 where, despite (or perhaps, it could be said, in order to be in tune with) the otherwise rather exotic architectural styles adopted for the various exhibition buildings, the promoters found space for an impressive, if only temporary, reconstruction of that city's long-demolished medieval Bishop's Palace: a gaunt fortified residence with machicolated battlements, bartizans and crowstep-gabled caphouses. It had not, of course, featured in Billings, but was known, in part at least, from engravings. Thus, although Glasgow's architects, when they *were* intent on introducing a measure of Scottishness into their designs, were not much concerned with the strict archaeology of the built past, and though the city did not produce an architect as proficient in Baronial Revival design as David Bryce nor one as committed to the study and recording of the nation's built heritage as Robert Rowand Anderson, there was certainly a growing awareness of Scotland's architectural heritage and, for some, a concern to find a relevance in this legacy for the present. And while there might be no-one in the west to match Lorimer's hands-on creative engagement with 'the Scottish tradition of building',[9] there was one young Glasgow designer who, now travelling the countryside with pencil and sketchbook in hand, now pouring over the pages of MacGibbon and Ross, would discover in the Scottishness of Scottish architecture a way forward from the past not only to the present but, at least potentially, to the future. It was a path that would lead from that national tradition to the International Style.

In February 1891, Charles Rennie Mackintosh was 22. He had built little. That he should, at such a young age, have been invited to deliver a lecture to the Glasgow Architectural Association is no doubt testimony to the brilliance of his student career:

throughout the 1880s he had won several local and national prizes culminating in September 1890 with the award of the Alexander Thomson Memorial Travelling Studentship. If this honour had something to do with the invitation he received to speak to his peers, the Studentship's explicit aim to promote the 'furtherance of the study of Ancient Classic Architecture' lacked any relevance to the subject matter he had chosen for his address. His subject was 'Scotch Baronial Architecture',[10] a topic which was, he owned in the very first sentence of his talk, 'dear to my heart and entwined among my inmost thoughts and affections'.[11]

This 'instinctive affection' for the architecture of his native country was immediately, even poetically, apparent in what the young Mackintosh had to say. Invoking an experience perhaps as familiar to many of his audience as to himself, he referred to

> that deep and filial affection which many a youth untaught in art but gifted by nature with a perception for its beauties, has entertained from his tenderest years towards the old castle of his neighbourhood or that irresistible attraction which compels many of the members of this association to visit the various castles and palaces in this country, not only under the balmy influences of summer, but along muddy roads and snowy path, and with glowing heart but shivering hand to sketch the humble cottage the more pretentious mansion or the mutilated though venerable castle with feelings of the most indescribable delight.

It is this sentiment, he admitted, which is 'so difficult to reason upon, and to which cold investigation seems so uncongenial'. Yet, he continued, how pleasant it is 'to find every new proof that our early feelings have not been misplaced … that those who, strange to say, dislike the archi[tecture] of their forefathers, are now forced to admit some of its beauties: that the style once despised has become generally appreciated'. With this ingenuous acknowledgment, Mackintosh launched on a lecture which, in unfolding the extent of his understanding of indigenous architectural history, would reveal something of the precocious polemic taking shape in his mind.

The talk was illustrated by pencil drawings, watercolour studies and photographs. It is known that Bothwell and Rothesay castles were among the buildings shown but regrettably what other examples were adduced as illustrations remains an intriguing mystery. Mackintosh may well have used his own sketches. But since his early sketchbooks are lost it is impossible to know what exemplars he might have chosen. Sketches made before 1891 at Glasgow, Rowallan and at Elgin and Spynie have survived, and since this indicates a visit to Moray it is not unreasonable to assume that Mackintosh might also have drawn Castle Fraser or Craigievar or Fyvie Castle in nearby Aberdeenshire,[12] and that any of these might have illustrated his lecture. But this is speculation. We cannot know what buildings the audience saw; nor can we know what was actually said. The text alone, which runs to 36 handwritten pages, is the only secure basis on which to assess Mackintosh's knowledge and interpretation of Scottish architecture and thus arrive at an understanding of his evolving credo.

It comes as something of a shock to discover that much of this text – as much as two thirds – is not original. Pages 13 to 35 of the manuscript are taken, more or less verbatim, scissors and paste, without quotation marks and without acknowledgment, from MacGibbon and Ross' *Castellated and Domestic Architecture of Scotland*, the first three volumes of which had been published by the time Mackintosh delivered his talk. He may also have been indebted to MacGibbon's lecture on 'The Characteristics of Scottish National Architecture' given to the 1889 Edinburgh Art Congress and reported in *British Architect*.[13] Such textual theft casts a shadow on the young architect's academic integrity[14] but this tarnish should not obscure the fact that, in drawing on such sources, he proved himself to be impressively up to date with the latest research into the historical development of Scottish architecture. As has been well observed by Stewart Cruden, who first drew attention to this example of Mackintosh's cribbing, 'how much greater would have been the disappointment had he youthfully disdained MacGibbon and Ross'.[15]

In structuring his historical review of 'Scotch Baronial Architecture' in accord with the four-period chronological classification system adopted by his unacknowledged mentors, Mackintosh aggregated extracts from MacGibbon and Ross' text, making reference to almost 40 buildings, the great majority of which are, of course, castles. These exemplify the formal qualities characteristic of each stage of a historical development which culminated in the Aberdeenshire Castles of Mar, the particular qualities of which Mackintosh described in MacGibbon and Ross' words.

> The walls are generally very plain, and the ornamentation is confined to the parapet and upper portions, where it often bursts out with extraordinary profusion and richness, as for instance Castle Fraser and Craigievar …
> The roofs are high pitched broken up and adorned with numerous dormers and have picturesque chimneys and crow stepped gables. Corbelling, both plain and ornamental is one of the chief characteristics of the style. It is used on every possible occasion. The turrets, staircases, parapets etc. are all supported on corbels, and the towers are often changed from a circular base to a square upper part by means of large and elaborate corbels[16]

But it is neither in MacGibbon and Ross' systematic ordering of the historical evidence nor in their descriptions of the formal elements of the Baronial style that the real significance of Mackintosh's lecture lies – though, if not quite hot off the presses, such matters may well have been of topical interest to many in his audience. Rather it is his interpretative take on the past and its relevance to contemporary architectural problems. Mackintosh was not a scholar. He was a designer. And as a designer, albeit as yet with little practical experience, he was well aware of the pluralist nature of architectural style in Victorian Scotland and of the intellectual and visual incongruities this had occasioned. Greek temples, French Gothic churches, Florentine palazzi, Palladian mansions – what cultural locus had these in Scotland? The issue was not, of course, confined to Scotland, nor was it new; indeed, it had festered in European culture for decades, stemming back to the romantic assertion made by the German art historian and archaeologist J J Winckelmann that 'as the circumstances of one people are not applicable to another, concepts of one culture are not valid for another'.[17] What was at stake was the need for a fresh resolution of that recurring creative dialectic between the history of art and the geography of art. It is to Mackintosh's immense credit that he discerned the rudiments of a resolution of this *Dilemma of Style*[18] (as J Mordaunt Crooke would later title his book on the subject) in the specific context of Scotland and – to

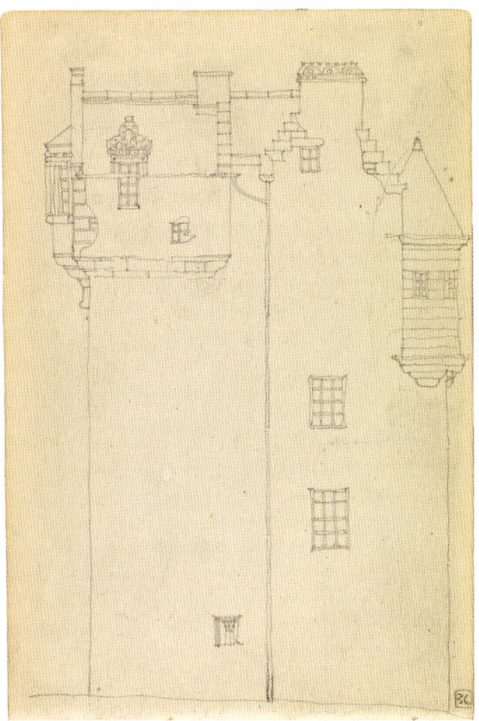

Maybole Castle
Sketch by Charles Rennie Mackintosh 1895
© The Hunterian, University of Glasgow

adopt words used by Colin Rowe in his classic essay on 'Some Vicissitudes of Architectural Vocabulary in the Nineteenth Century'[19] – in the 'character' and 'composition' of Scottish architecture. The tentative nature of his ideas can be sensed in the unplagiarised part of his address, in effect the first dozen or so pages and the last few sentences of the handwritten text.

The importance of cultural *context* is already apparent in the introductory paragraphs of Mackintosh's talk where love of country is seen as a fundamental virtue. If the expression of this affection is perhaps a little too effusive for some, it would be unfair to cast the young architect in the role of Johnson's scoundrel. Among the qualities which make Scottish architecture significant for Scottish architects, so his 'argument' goes, is the fact that it is the architecture of Scottish architects. Naive and tautological perhaps, but the emotion is surely sincere and the message clear. True, there is the suggestion that as Scots 'we have no natural or personal sympathy' with the architecture of such cultures as Egypt, Assyria or Persia, while even for Greek or Roman buildings, whatever Alexander Thomson might have argued, we 'fail to find anything to connect them in any special sense with ourselves'. But these remarks were not so much made in denigration of these styles, rather they were intended as a recall from indiscriminate historicism and eclecticism to an engagement with native culture. Just as more than a century earlier Robert Adam in his castellar mansions had re-orientated classical architecture to respond to the special nature of the rugged Scottish landscape, just as Burn, Bryce and later Rowand Anderson had recast Scots Jacobean, Scots Baronial and Scots Renaissance precedent, so now the architecture of Scotland should once again have 'a preeminent claim upon our attention'. It was Mackintosh's view that Scottish architects were under an obligation to study and understand the architecture of their own country and that such an analysis of the character and composition of 'Scotch Baronial Architecture' – 'the last type of architectural treatment of buildings in this country that was national' – could reveal an answer to the stylistic dilemma that had afflicted the nineteenth century.

Colin Rowe's words describing a 'truly significant building' as 'a structure organized according to *the principles of architectural composition* and infused with a symbolic content which is usually described as *character*'[20] provide a useful definition against which to evaluate Mackintosh's appraisal of the Scottish Baronial style. It is clear from the text of his talk that Mackintosh is opposed to the imposition of *external* principles of composition; any attempt to 'fit on an elevation' is to be deprecated. Such procedures, he contends, inflicted a 'death blow' to architecture, 'subsequent work of the seventeenth century being a mix up between Scottish Baronial and debased Elizabethan Italian Renaissance' since when 'we have had no such thing as a national style'. It appears, then, that he believes it is the honest expression of function which brings certain forms into existence and governs their relational disposition. Whatever 'construction or utility demanded' constitutes the essence of good design. Such principles of formal *composition* as can be inferred from these functional criteria remain perhaps necessarily vague. Baronial architecture exhibits a marked 'boldness, freeness and variety' in the nature of its forms and in the 'grouping of the parts'. This variety is evident in plan and in 'external outline' as the building adjusts its form to 'every accidental [ie contingent] requirement'. There is thus a predisposition

to asymmetry unless the 'conditions of the case' demand symmetrical constraint. And all of this is true as much of 'the humble cottage as and [sic] in the mighty Castle'. Conflating vernacular and Baronial, as Lorimer, too, would do, Mackintosh appears to arrive at the precociously Modernist theoretical stance that 'form ever follows function'.[21] But neither his reading of Scottish architectural history nor the lessons he drew for his own creative activity were quite as simple as the assertion of this familiar Functionalist mantra. Mackintosh is well aware that there is more to satisfactory design than the deceptively straightforward fulfilment of need. 'The character of a style', he writes, is not solely determined by practical considerations; it does not, for example, 'depend upon the mere material from which it has been fabricated, but upon the sentiments and conditions under which it has been developed'. This is a view soundly in tune with Rowe's observation that, in addition to the impression of artistic individuality it may convey, 'character' derives from the expression of functional and symbolic values, 'the expression of the first … the product of pragmatic argument, the expression of the second the product of sentiment'.[22] Clearly functional considerations are fundamental and Mackintosh's perception that, on the one hand, the further back in time one goes 'the more real and necessary' are the forms of the Scottish Baronial style, while, on the other, the later the phase of development the more likely it is that the forms 'are continued and imitated while their true purpose and significance are lost', seems unambiguous enough. But perhaps this apparent judgement relates only to *functional* significance. It is not altogether unreasonable, given the compelling evidence of much in Mackintosh's later career (see below), to suggest he already believed that certain 'old features' might still retain a *symbolic* significance, despite losing their original functional justification.

It is undoubtedly the case, if made explicit only in the very last sentence of the lecture manuscript, that the young Mackintosh was convinced of the continuing relevance of 'Scotch Baronial Architecture'. At the same time he was equally well aware of the need to avoid any stylistic anachronism.

Falkland Palace
Sketch by Charles Rennie Mackintosh c1900
© The Hunterian, University of Glasgow

> From some recent buildings which have been erected it is clearly evident that this style is coming to life again and I only hope that it will not be strangled in its infancy by indiscriminating and unsympathetic people who copy the ancient examples without trying to make the style conform to modern requirements.

Which 'recent buildings' Mackintosh had in mind is a matter for conjecture. Almost certainly he knew of the projects carried out in the late 1880s by James MacLaren at Stirling, Fortingall and Glenlyon, each of which would have an influence on his later design. He might well have admired the Scottish forms of Sydney Mitchell's Well Court (1883–6), built in Edinburgh's Dean Village, particularly perhaps the oriel windows based on those at the Earl's Palace in Kirkwall which he specifically praised in his lecture. The Scots vernacular of Hew Montgomerie Wardrop's Tilliefour in Aberdeenshire (1883), which had had an early influence on Robert Lorimer, could conceivably have come to his attention, perhaps during his sketching trip to Moray in 1889. It is also likely that he was aware of Robert Rowand Anderson's enthusiasm for Scotland's historic buildings, though whether he knew of Anderson's work at Allermuir is more problematic.

Whatever the buildings Mackintosh might have cited as exemplars of a viable modern Scottish architecture, the criteria that would have governed his choice can be convincingly inferred from the text of his talk. Architecture must satisfy all contemporary needs – activity, environment, structure, construction – but in allowing function to find expression in form it need not deny form its symbolic significance. This, as Mackintosh noted in his talk, was as true of 'the humble cottage' as it was of 'the mighty castle'. Vernacular architecture had meaning too.

> A village building in addition to its practical functions has other functions as well, as, for example, aesthetic, magic, regional, social, and so on. A building is not only an object but also a sign. In some regions we can determine, even from a distance, the nationality and social stratification of the household by the outward appearance of the building.[23]

By the last decade of the nineteenth century, the cult of the folk house was well established all across Europe. Nearest to home, of course, the imagery and theoretical writings espoused by the English Arts and Crafts movement had been perhaps the most fundamental force underpinning this revival of interest in vernacular form. In many regions of the continent the folk house served not only as a functional model of fitness and soundness, but also as a sign, a sign which flagged up a more fundamental truth than any equivalent regional variant of high-style revivalism had done. It stood for cultural grassroots which could connote some measure of national political aspiration. Stemming from the ramifying interest in national cultures which romanticism's reaction against the international uniformity of neoclassicism had ushered in a century earlier, such signs were everywhere. In Finland, for example, the Karelian log cabin had been elevated to the status of a national archetype, notably in the work of architects Gesellius, Lindgren and Saarinen. In Zakopane in southern Poland, Stanisław Witkiewicz and a like-minded group of artists and architects had produced new interpretations of the traditional timber architecture of the Tatra mountains which captivated the Polish national consciousness. In Moravia, on the southern Czecho-Slovak side of the same mountain range, Dušan Jurkovič evolved a unique polychromatic reinterpretation of the same vernacular tradition. Shown at the 1891 Jubilee Exhibition in Prague, Jan Koula's re-creation of a 'Czech Cottage' became a model for a number of overtly national villas built in Bohemia. In Hungary, the folk-art Secessionism of Ödön Lechner set in train a search for a modern idiom that would be genuinely Magyar. And in Austria, in 1899, Josef Olbrich, whom Mackintosh would come to know, designed a suburban villa, the Villa Bahr, which was critically praised as 'a real country cottage [looking] as if it had sprung up out of the living soil, like the peasants' houses and the acacia trees'.[24]

In 1891 Mackintosh would have been unaware of any of this, but in a decade's time he, too, would draw on his own indigenous vernacular to create two unequivocally Scottish houses fit for 'modern requirements'. This was to place him securely in the international mainstream of architectural change, but neither this achievement, nor the parallel if less radical work of Mackintosh's contemporary Robert Lorimer, had more than a limited impact on Scottish culture. While many societies in Europe would, in the aftermath of the First World War, see cultural renaissance mature into political independence – in Finland, Poland and Czechoslovakia for the first time in centuries, in Hungary and Austria in a new, non-imperialistic framework – Scotland remained in 'political debility', a regionalised nation with a still provincial culture.

It would be absurd to suggest that Mackintosh's enthusiasm for the baronial and vernacular architecture of Scotland was the sole or even the prime motivating factor in his attempt to find an answer to the *Dilemma of Style*. Other influences were also at work. Although the eclectic high style competence which had brought him so many awards in his student years and continued to feature in a number of early competition submissions was soon rejected, it cannot be said that Mackintosh ever completely broke free from historicism. From time to time, both Gothic and Renaissance references continue to appear in his mature work, though generally in a flirtatious way free from any pedantic respect. Much more significant than such tongue-in-cheek allusions to convention, however, was his addiction to those abstracted, often attenuated, forms of Art Nouveau that sprang from a Ruskinian belief in nature as a well of creative power, and the parallel delight he took, increasingly evident in the latter part of his architectural career, in the gridding and patterning of geometry. These approaches were also strongly developed in his interiors, furniture design and decorative art work. Nevertheless, in Mackintosh's architecture, in the character and composition of almost every building he designed between 1893 when the tower of the *Glasgow Herald* building was conceived and the completion of the west wing of the Glasgow School of Art in 1909, the forms and syntax of the baronial and vernacular architecture of Scotland can, to a greater or lesser degree, be identified.

There is some doubt over the extent of Mackintosh's personal involvement as a young assistant in the firm of Honeyman and Keppie in the design of the *Glasgow Herald* offices (1893–5) but most commentators seem to agree that the upper storeys and tower of the building are substantially his work. These, at any rate, are the features which manifest an engagement with baronial architecture. The octagonal water tower may have vague

Glasgow Herald Building, Mitchell Street, Glasgow
Perspective drawing by Charles Rennie Mackintosh 1894
© The Hunterian, University of Glasgow

THE "HERALD" BUILDING
MITCHELL ST. GLASGOW
JOHN HONEYMAN AND KEPPIE

castellar affinities but its immediate forerunner is the stair tower which James MacLaren had designed for Stirling High School a few years earlier and which Mackintosh had drawn. Parapetted, wide-eaved and capped by an ogee dome (a distinctly Scottish form here markedly depressed), the upper stages of the two structures are remarkably similar, though Mackintosh has infected the *Herald* tower with the germ of Art Nouveau. Much more Scottish is the treatment of the fourth and fifth floors of the West Nile Street elevation for these appear to be jettied forward like 'the flourish atop the old Scottish castles',[25] their irregular wallhead sequence of gabletted eaves dormers recalling that picturesque skyline so typical of sixteenth and early seventeenth century baronial architecture.

An octagonal tower appears again at Queen Margaret College (1894–5). Tucked into the re-entrant entrance of the building, the tower rises to parapet height above which it becomes a belfry capped by a slated ogee dome; 'a Scottish tower', writes Macaulay, suggesting a link to Mackintosh's drawings of Ayrshire castles.[26] Castellar, too, are the building's gables, their skewed triangles rising behind horizontal parapets reminiscent of rooftop caphouses. And perhaps most Scottish of all, the 'unbroken expanses of rough masonry', a daring celebration of tower-house solidity which, as Mackintosh scholar Roger Billcliffe rightly notes,[27] would reach its most dramatic realisation in the Glasgow School of Art.

In January 1897 Honeyman and Keppie were named winners of the architectural competition for the new building that was to house Glasgow School of Art. Designed by Mackintosh, then not yet 30, the completed building (construction took place in two separate main phases, 1896–99 and 1907–10) would come to be regarded as his masterwork, an iconic anticipation of what the twentieth century would call 'Modern Architecture'. Yet, both in its original planning and in its final built form, with the central staircase linked by corridors to stairs in the east and west, the E-plan arrangement which Mackintosh adopted for the school could hardly be described as innovative. Site conditions, of course, had constrained the planning options to what was an essentially symmetrical solution: one that could be found in comparable institutional buildings all over nineteenth century Europe. No doubt conscious of this conventional and, in his eyes perhaps, dangerously banal quality, Mackintosh seems, wherever possible, to have been at pains to make the building 'almost perversely asymmetrical'.[28] Closely linked to functional expression, asymmetry was, of course, a characteristic aspect of the baronial and vernacular tradition. So thirled was Mackintosh to this principle that he applied it here not so much in response to any contingent needs of the plan but as a deliberate anti-historicist ploy, but as a formal strategy intended to counteract the otherwise compelling tendency to symmetry which the brief implied. From the beginning this was true of the principal front with its high, north-lit studios ranged along Renfrew Street. The main entrance was set slightly off-centre, the entrance frontispiece itself asymmetrically organised, the studios to the east lit by three high gridded windows, those to the west by four (two windows identical to those in the east and two similar in height but narrower in width), the whole subtly modulated facade set back from the street behind a sunken area 'like a moat, reinforcing its castle-like appearance'.[29] Asymmetry was even more evident in Mackintosh's design of the school's east gable where one half of the high hillside elevation was entirely without windows, a tall gaunt mass of snecked stone, and the other a composition of varied window shapes and engaged octagonal turret which embodied 'the surging vitality … of a Dunderave or a Craigievar'.[30] This latter, southern half of the east facade was itself divided into two elements: to the right, the octagonal stair turret embedded below parapet height in the massive wall, its thin gunloop openings continued in axial alignment down through the corbelled window of a small teacher's room to lower windows and street doorway; to the left, a second axial arrangement of grander window openings, accented at the skyline by a flattened ogee gable but, again perversely, disrupted by unbalanced window groupings at the lower levels. If, as Alan Crawford, in his concise biography of Mackintosh, has observed, one half of this elevation is 'a matter of function', there being no need for any windows to the studios which lie behind the wall of solid masonry, and the other half decidedly 'a matter of composition',[31] the whole is thus a transformed tower-house – a distillation of the Scottish baronial tradition.

Glasgow School of Art
Elevation of Scott Street and Dalhousie Street, south elevation by Charles Rennie Mackintosh 1910
The Glasgow School of Art

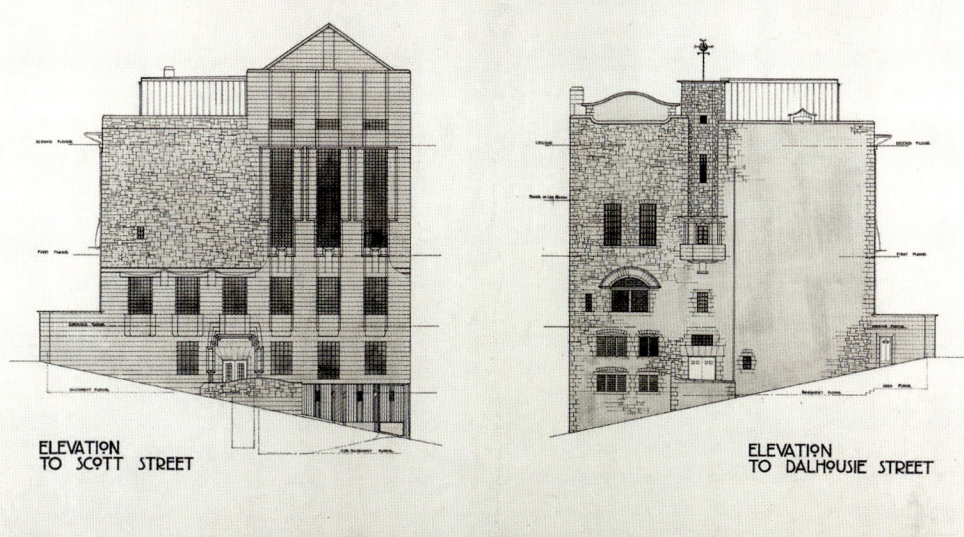
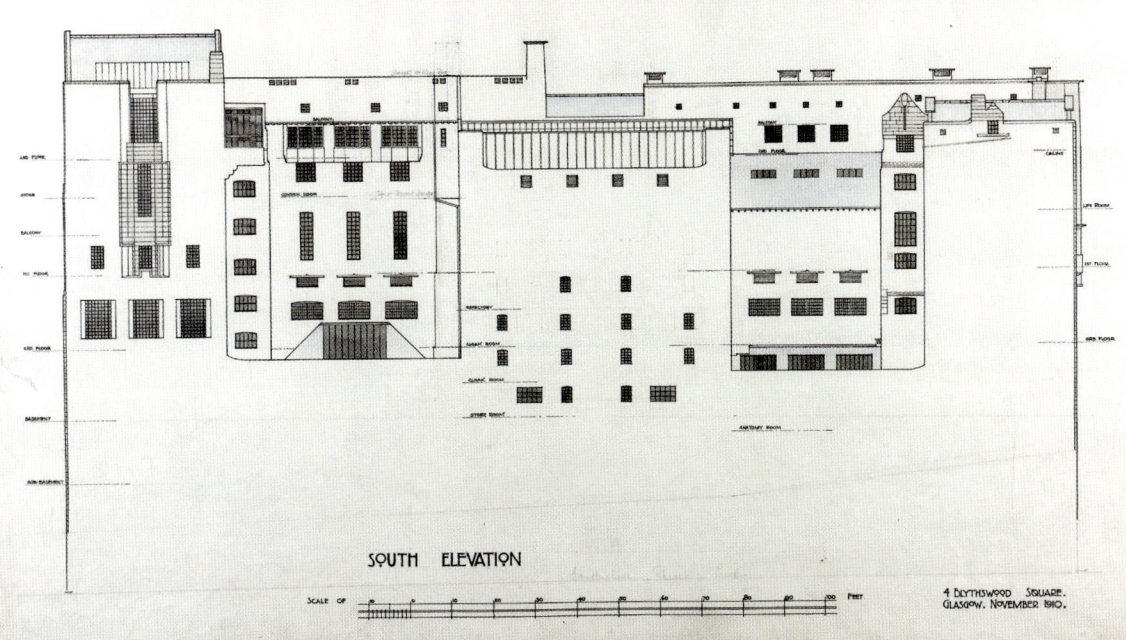

Similar asymmetries were also to be found in the vernacular tradition of Scottish architecture and these, together with the simpler, more limited vocabulary of folk house forms, Mackintosh now freely adduced to the design of a number of dwelling houses as the century turned. Two houses in particular exemplified this transformative skill: Windyhill in Kilmacolm (1899–1901) and the Hill House, Helensburgh (1902–4). Both were austere, patently Scottish buildings, with harled walls and gables and slated roofs: the former farmhouse plain and far from being the 'hillside castle' one commentator has called it,[32] the latter severe, too, but not without distinct castellar affiliation. As Robert Macleod has noted, 'the materials and their constructional assembly are all entirely traditional'.[33] And so, too, are the forms and, in some sense, their compositional assembly. Raking skews, asymmetric gables, gabletted eaves dormers, turnpike stairs,[34] slated cones, vertical window openings with double-hung sashes were all in evidence. Plans were not constrained by any overt formal criteria but seemed to respond to the functional demands of activity, convenience, construction, orientation, prospect, and so on. The massing of the two houses has the scale and casual conviction of vernacular building, raised to baronial aspiration at the south-east corner of the Hill House where a cone-capped turnpike stair articulates the junction of two chimneyed gables. In terms of elevational treatment, however, matters are less straightforward, for both houses exhibit what has long been regarded as an intriguing dichotomy. Seen from the garden side where the houses look towards the view and sun,[35] the elevations have a calculated composure undisturbed by a pleasant asymmetry in the disposition of window openings. Viewed from the opposite side, however, each house presents an agitated aggregation of elements – advancing gables, chimney stacks, apsidal stair enclosures, dormers and 'windows of widely varying shapes and sizes'[36] – the mixture particularly restless in the case of the Hill House. What is happening here? It is as if, having composed the elements of the garden facades in calm coordinated relationship, Mackintosh is troubled by such imposition of his artistic will and decides not to interfere too much on the shaded sides of each house, allowing the internal functional requirements of the plan to find form directly without any applied adjustment of proportion or alignment. The results may appear untidy, even anarchic, but they are not

Windyhill, Kilmacolm
HES Canmore DP211445

random. Windows and dormers are formed as needed, staircases are not subsumed within the building but given their own formal expression, soil and rainwater pipes run as required. This is daring stuff and if there is something of the 'restlessness of the Baronial'[37] in all this, it is perhaps as much related to that style's direct response to need, its 'power of meeting the conditions of purpose'[38] as it is to any aesthetic delight in picturesque complexity. The architecture of Windyhill and the Hill House reveals not so much a dichotomy as a recognition of the ambivalence inherent in design, the need to acknowledge the claims of both function and form, to reconcile practicalities with artistic will. In these two houses, Mackintosh's achievement conforms to the German philosopher Schlegel's dictum that art 'in each of its representations should represent itself too'.[39]

It might also be argued, elaborating the semantic nuances of Schlegel's aphorism, that this *re*presentation is not only a matter of exposing the inner dilemma of the creative process (*both – and*). It might also entail the presentation of new, ie transformed, forms and even a new relational order. Mackintosh takes forms from the Scottish past: some he uses as they had always been used; in other cases he discards the original *raison d'être*. Consider, for example, the boldly shaped staircase units given such sculptural form in both houses. In these cases Mackintosh has, not surprisingly, preferred dog-leg flights to the helical rise of the turnpike, but by retaining the apsidal format at the landing he has kept the symbolic memory of the original without any compromise of function. White-walled, cylindrical, parapetted, to all visual effect flat-roofed, their affinity with the later work of Le Corbusier is impossible to ignore. Consider, too, in more general terms, the harled three-dimensional geometry of Mackintosh's domestic designs: how paradoxical it is that these unequivocally Scottish houses, the latter-day expression of a national vernacular, should vouchsafe intimations of the white-walled abstractions of 1930s International Style villas. It may be exaggerating the case to suggest as James Macaulay has done that there is here 'a determination to try to pin down the future'[40] – to credit Mackintosh with such prescience is carrying national pride too far – but just as this 'interplay of simple geometrical forms … recalls seventeenth century Scottish work',[41] so it anticipates a dehistoricised architecture yet to come.

Windyhill, Kilmacolm
The Glasgow School of Art

184　Chapter 8　'that deep and filial affection' – Charles Rennie Mackintosh and the way ahead

Hill House, Helensburgh
Photographs from 2018 and (above) 1904
HES Canmore DP320453, DP320632, SC677386

This 'precognition' was noted by Thomas Howarth in his ground-breaking biographical study of Mackintosh published in 1952. It was particularly evident in two unbuilt domestic designs drawn in 1901 – one for a Country Cottage, the other for a Town House – to such an extent indeed that Howarth compared the former to a white-walled reinforced concrete house designed by Connel, Ward and Lucas at Platt in Kent in 1933! Perhaps because there was little likelihood of their being built, the two houses are more startling and less derivative in form than either Windyhill or the Hill House, but this does not mean that they were entirely without precedent. A predilection for architectural mass rather than the frame-and-fill of trabeated construction, the consequential dominance of solid over void, the asymmetric scatter of windows, these are surely the recast legacy of the baronial tradition. Not only that but 'the artful imbalance' of window placement[42] – axial groupings wilfully disturbed by offset secondary axes – is a strategy which can also be sourced in baronial building. This Janus-like quality in Mackintosh's design approach, which permits critical interpretation to be *both* retrospective *and* prospective, is again to be found in the drawings he prepared for the Haus eines Kunstfreundes (House for an Art Lover) competition run by the Darmstadt publication *Zeitschrift für Innendekoration* in 1901. Once more the solidity of white-harled walls, skew gables and massive chimney stacks which characterise Mackintosh's award-winning design evokes a measure of baronial provenance, and while this scarcely results in a building 'as sternly, austerely functional as … a hundred Highland fortress dwellings' – these are Howarth's words[43] – it does impart the unmistakable flavour of Scottishness to the design. But here, too, are the intimations of the International Style. The flat-roofed, round-ended slab of the staircase tower, the stark white cube of the porch and the no less gaunt, no

House for an Art Lover

Designs for the Haus eines Kunstfreundes competition by Charles Rennie Mackintosh 1901–2

© The Hunterian, University of Glasgow

less cubic, mass of the high north-west corner of the building, all anticipate the formal language that would be spoken by Adolf Loos, Le Corbusier and many others a generation later.

Whether consciously or unconsciously elicited, evidence of Mackintosh's 'instinctive affection' for the baronial and vernacular architecture of his own country continued to appear in his work. In his treatment of the *Daily Record* offices in Glasgow (1901) – a building whose framed structure and four-bay, six-storeyed elevations, predominantly built in glazed brick and generously glazed, ought surely to have been devoid of any castellar evocation – he contrived to enliven the wallhead storeys with canted oriels, decorative dormers linked by an undulating parapet, and the muted form of a tower rising over canted bays tiered above the street entrance. Might these three wallhead oriels with their superimposed dormers be a reference to the three great oriels added to Huntly Castle at the beginning of the seventeenth century? Mackintosh had specifically mentioned them in his Baronial address. Certainly the 'delight in [the] sheer height of a block of building'[44] coupled with this architectural elaboration of the wallhead, both qualities seen already in the design for the *Glasgow Herald* offices, can be regarded as characteristically Scottish.

So, too, can the astonishing staircase towers Mackintosh devised for Scotland Street School (1903–06). Here again the nature of the building seems far removed from any possible association with castellar architecture: responding to the requirement for separate boys' and girls' entrances, the plan and massing of the design are necessarily symmetrical, while in terms of elevational patterning Mackintosh is clearly 'in geometric mode'.[45] And yet these twin cone-capped, cylindrical towers are reminders of tower-

house turnpikes, perhaps of the coupled drum towers seen at Falkland, Holyrood, Tolquhon and Rowallan. There is, of course, no functional reason why the stairs in a school should take this semi-circular plan form; it would be absurd to expect rushing children to negotiate winding turnpike flights. Indeed, Mackintosh's stairs are straight flights returning at *rectangular* landings, a strategy which entails no such formal consequences. Even so, the tower form is deliberately retained, its cylinder-and-cone form still symbolic, if no longer functional. But more than this, the form is *transformed* into something new. It is at once old and new. Rather than the solid tower-house drum penetrated by occasional small openings, each tower is glazed from top to bottom with closely gridded astragals through which light floods across a dramatic three-storey void onto landing and stairs. But provenance remains clear. And even on the flat south elevation, where allusion is confined to the almost graphic limitations of ornament, there is a stylised thistle motif at the very centre of the facade. This is, after all, *Scotland* Street.

A study of the plan arrangement of Scotland Street School reveals further evidence of Mackintosh's engagement with baronial precedent. The school's symmetrical plan comprises two rectangular ranges of classrooms lying in contiguous parallel, one longer, one shorter. This geometry creates two re-entrant angles into which the staircases are placed. Imagine now that this plan of the school is cut along its main axis: the result, the reflected forms of an L-plan tower-house, each with its staircase (historically a turnpike) in the re-entrant angle. The necessary modification of the tower-house's helical circulation to straight flights is not, in Mackintosh's hands, permitted to impair the original baronial form any more than the clever mirroring of the L-plan can wholly conceal the same provenance.

Not long after the contract for Scotland Street School came to an end, Mackintosh's last major project began. It is ironic and, in the general context of national culture, shameful that the end of his creative architectural career in Scotland should follow hard on the heels of his completion of the Glasgow

Scotland Street School, Glasgow
Perspective drawing by Charles Rennie Mackintosh 1904
© The Hunterian, University of Glasgow

School of Art (1907–10), for no building more fully attested his genius or, in the long term, secured his fame. By then a partner in the firm of Honeyman and Keppie, barely 40, but buoyed by the confidence of practical experience and foreign recognition, he completed the western half of the building, and in particular its attenuated south-west corner, with a sophisticated abstraction devoid of all historicism that must have belied expectation and was to ensure his international reputation. And irony upon irony, even in this achievement, which would bring him a place in Nikolaus Pevsner's pantheon of European *Pioneers of Modern Design*, Mackintosh found ways of 'admitting national tradition'.[46] Here again, in the west elevation, as in the east, the contrast of stark masonry wall-plane and formal complexity; here again, in the soaring oriel windows, that Scottish exultation in sheer verticality; here again the tall, closely gridded glazing of the Scotland Street stair towers; and here again, in the gaunt, grey-harled bastions of the south elevation, the castellar cliffs of the baronial past. More specific references are not lacking in the completed building, for this same south elevation with its advancing and receding wall planes has been persuasively likened to the towered front of Fyvie Castle. And is the 'compulsive restlessness'[47] which agitates part of the south wallhead not the result of the addition of the corbelled and cantilevered conservatory and the three Huntly oriels which light the arcuated loggia?

Few critical appraisals are more epigrammatic than Robert Macleod's assessment that Mackintosh had 'demonstrated the capacity to accept architectural precedent, form and tradition, and to transform it'.[48] In his 1968 biographical study of the architect he was concerned with balancing Thomas Howarth's earlier, all but canonical, view of Mackintosh as a percipient forerunner of the twentieth century Modern Movement. Macleod reasserted the significance of cultural context, stressing Mackintosh's indebtedness to the writers and Arts and Crafts designers of the nineteenth century and evaluating his work as the fulfilment of that Victorian tradition, not limiting such precedent to the baronial and vernacular architecture of Scotland. But he would not have denied its importance. Indeed, his study devoted considerable attention to Mackintosh's interest in the Scottishness of Scottish architecture: 'to understand his work', Macleod wrote, 'it is necessary to look carefully at his view of the native tradition which he treasured so highly'.[49]

Such scrutiny, applied both to Mackintosh's writings and in turn to his designed buildings, makes it clear that he knew and understood the baronial and vernacular architecture of his native land, that he acknowledged its forms to be both functional and beautiful, and that he engaged with these forms and their relationships in his own creative work. More importantly, however, he recognised not only that such forms might give direct expression to function but that, should their original function be eliminated or superseded in some way, they might yet be employed to symbolize a broader cultural or national provenance. More important still, the same forms might be further *transformed* to reach a new level of deracinated abstraction capable of international exchange. In a relatively short career of little more than two decades, Mackintosh explored all three of these approaches. It was a journey which, had he been able to sustain his architectural career in Glasgow, might have brought him – and perhaps others – to the brink of real architectural change. Instead, he left the country. Living in London, he attempted to establish a practice in England but, as war intervened, failed to find more than a handful of small commissions. Only exile remained and from 1923 Mackintosh spent the last five years of his life painting in and around the little town of Port Vendres in the far south of France.

Back in Glasgow, Mackintosh's name was, for the moment, all but forgotten, the significance of his built oeuvre remarked by only a few. For a time during his brief 20-year career, it had seemed that some aspects of his work – particularly his decorative art and interior design – might become the creative focus for what later came to be known as the Glasgow Style, that Art Nouveau fusion of tendril, leaf and flower forms with melting classical detail. Loosely associated by friendship and a common interest in the organic and esoteric, Mackintosh and a small group of artists, designers and architects attained a measure of national and international celebrity, even notoriety, based on the enthusiastic commendation which exhibitions of their work both at home and abroad had drawn from *The Studio* magazine and a number of continental art journals. This somewhat precious and predominantly graphic trend, however influential it proved in terms of furniture design and interior design in general, had limited impact on architecture in Glasgow and even less elsewhere in Scotland. But then again it could not be said that Mackintosh's more inherently architectural journey from the castellated and domestic buildings of Scotland's past to the threshold of European Modernism found more than a few fellow travellers in the city. Almost the only architect to declare himself sympathetic, both in his writings and his buildings, was Mackintosh's friend James Salmon.

Salmon's admiration for the Glasgow School of Art building was unequivocal and grounded in his recognition that the quality of its architecture had much to do with its designer's creative grasp of tradition. He spoke out against those who had criticised Mackintosh.

> It amuses me, knowing the architect of the School of Art as I do and appreciating his work with constant delight, to find that some people think him an outrageous innovator. Why? I think he shows in this building more reverence and inward feeling for Tradition than all the Scottish Antiquarians added together.[50]

Enthusiasm for Scottish building had not led Mackintosh to any mere copying of the past but rather to a judicious selection and at times transformation of forms and formal relationships to meet the needs of the present. As for Mackintosh, so for Salmon, there was something in the 'distinctive character' and composition of baronial and vernacular building which could continue to be relevant. But it was Salmon's particular perception to sense a creative relationship between the old baronial castle and the new high-rise office building. In a lecture outlining the potential of steel and concrete structures, given to the Glasgow Institute of Architects in 1908, he maintained that certain formal aspects of 'the Scottish style, I mean especially that of the old rough-cast castle'[51] had a coincidental affinity with reinforced concrete construction. But while Mackintosh clung to the idea of architecture as mass embodied in the baronial and vernacular tradition and deprecated the 'rosetinted hallucinations' of frame-and-fill structures like the Crystal Palace, Salmon and his partner John Gaff Gillespie, though no less admiring of the 'vast and enormous plain masses' made possible by the new materials, nevertheless recognised the structural and formal potential of steel and reinforced concrete frame construction. In their Lion Chambers building, erected on Hope Street, Glasgow (1904–06) using the Hennebique reinforced concrete system of

The Lion Chambers, Glasgow
HES Canmore DP166477

190　Chapter 8　'that deep and filial affection' – Charles Rennie Mackintosh and the way ahead

construction, tower-house and high-rise were uniquely conflated. On the one hand, the grey-rendered concrete walls might almost be harled; upper zones of the building are jettied and corbelled forward; an engaged octagon topped by an ogee dome (a favourite motif of the practice) marks the north-west corner with castle-like conviction; steep pediment gables and tall chimneystacks rise at the skyline. On the other, as befits a framed structure, window openings are disposed regularly, especially on the north elevation where three bays of shallow canted bay windows soar uninterrupted for almost the full height of the building. Yet even here, at the elongated attic storey of this dramatically glazed north wall (the refinement of an elevational strategy introduced in the rear wall of their Mercantile Chambers building in Glasgow almost a decade earlier), it is impossible not to be reminded once again of the oriel windows at Huntly.

In 1908, Salmon's partner Gillespie won the architectural competition for new Municipal Buildings in Stirling. Another octagonal corner tower, more steep pediment gables and, in addition, two 'Holyrood-like drums'[52] with conical roofs were incorporated into the design. No more than orthodox Baronial Revival with a heavy admixture of Scots Renaissance, the building had a solid civic assurance but lacked the structural bravura of Lion Chambers. A few years after construction was complete – building took place during the war years 1915–18 – Salmon himself submitted an entry in a much more prestigious international competition held to determine the design of the offices of the *Chicago Tribune* newspaper. It was 1922, Salmon was suffering from cancer and knew he had not long to live. Raymond O'Donnell, in his meticulously researched biography of the architect, speculates that Salmon's knowledge of his mortality coupled with his wry sense of humour may account for the 'outrageous Scots Baronial style'[53] proposal which he produced. It is difficult to take Salmon's submission seriously for the design comprised a multi-storey office tower, relatively plain though profiled with canted bays, on which, high in the sky, perched a fairy-tale baronial castle peppered with turrets! The competition certainly attracted a number of idiosyncratic entries; amongst the best known that of Adolf Loos, who proposed a high-rise tower in the form of a single Doric pillar, no doubt intended as a visual pun on the idea of the newspaper column. It is tempting to conjecture that Salmon, recalling that newspaper proprietors are often known as press 'barons', might have perpetrated a comparable pun. Whatever was in his mind, the absurdity of the conceit is best dismissed by laughter, for surely this was not to be the bathetic finale to all that had begun at Abbotsford a hundred years before?

Design for the *Chicago Tribune* Tower competition 1922 by James Salmon
HES Canmore

Chapter 9
National Tradition and the International Style
The Scottish Thirties

'Alas, poor country, –
Almost afraid to know itself!'
William Shakespeare, *Macbeth*, Act iv, Scene iii

James Salmon's castle-topped *Chicago Tribune* skyscraper proposal was hardly to be taken seriously, but the very absurdity of a baronial castle perched on a multi-storey office building may nevertheless serve to symbolise that failure to find a satisfactory way to fuse tradition with modernity which plagued Scottish and world architecture between the wars. Just as political independence post-First World War proved a step too far – a succession of post-war bills and motions brought before the House of Commons in the hope of realising 'Scottish national self-determination'[1] repeatedly failing when put to the vote – so attempts to realise a contemporary architectural Scottishness were compromised by unresolved conflicting allegiances. On the one hand, a few individuals, sensing, as Mackintosh had done, the abstract potential inherent in baronial and vernacular building, sought to find formal affinities between this national tradition and what came to be known as the International Style: in effect, an attempt to integrate a specifically Scottish expression of the geography of art with those wider anti-historicist changes in the history of art then sweeping Europe. On the other hand, there were those who regarded the white walls, strip windows and flat roofs of this New Architecture as unacceptably foreign, cosmopolitan, crude and socialist International Style. For such, conservative convention prevailed: for many public buildings 'a flat-faced monumental classicism'[2] found favour, while new much-needed housing schemes were built not as parallel rows of balconied continental flats but couthy crescents of four-in-a-block roughcast cottages. Looking back in 1938 at the built legacy of two decades of this unresolved conflict, one writer claimed to see only 'an unceasing stream of shoddy, denationalised and uninspiring building'.[3] Thus wrote George Scott-Moncrieff in an introduction to *The*

Commercial Bank, Bothwell Street, Glasgow
Elevation drawing 1934
HES Canmore DP061450

Stones of Scotland, a collection of essays which traced the historical development of the Scottish tradition of building. His somewhat severe opinion on this latter-day fall from grace was that 'the main blame lies with the indifference of the Scottish people'. A year earlier Sir James Stirling Maxwell, in his *Shrines and Homes of Scotland*, had lamented the same 'present indifference'.[4] No doubt this inculpation, albeit that the charge was one of quiescent disinterest rather than outright hostility to change, was as justified in matters of culture as it was in political terms. But how had it come to this?

For Scott-Moncrieff, Mackintosh had been the last to engage creatively with the forms and formal order of baronial and vernacular building and though he had 'never fully consummated' that relationship he had done enough to lay bare the possibilities for future encounters. But that was 30–40 years ago. Even Lorimer, who 'had a genuine sense of the values that inspired the native traditions'[5] and who, unlike Mackintosh, had remained in Scotland and continued to practise there until his death, failed to achieve consistent progress towards the goal much of his earlier work had seemed to presage. Perhaps this was inevitable, for Lorimer's decade of post-war work was dominated by memorial and ecclesiastical commissions – countless cemeteries and monuments to the fallen at home and abroad, restoration projects at St John's Kirk, Perth and Paisley Abbey, and the most important project of his entire career, the Scottish National War Memorial.

In every way, the commission for the National Memorial was intensely prestigious. The client was the nation itself, represented in committee by members of the armed services, the aristocracy, parliament, the Church, the press, educational establishments and the provosts of Edinburgh, Glasgow, Aberdeen, Dundee and Perth. The brief called for a building, neither church nor chapel, which would serve as a national shrine dedicated to the memory of the 150,000 Scottish servicemen and women who had died in the Great War. The cost was prodigious; the realisation of the original proposal estimated to reach £250,000. The site chosen lay at the heart of the nation on the heights of Edinburgh Castle. It is difficult to imagine a building more architecturally challenging, or one so imbued with national expectation. That Lorimer should have been appointed to design the Memorial is surely a measure of the widely shared esteem in which he was held, an esteem which judged him to be at once a 'modern architect' and one 'who [had] thoroughly absorbed the old building traditions of his country'.[6] But, perhaps not surprisingly, things did not go smoothly. Appointed in 1919, Lorimer produced a first proposal only to have it rejected. The project dragged on, dogged by controversy, and it was not until 1923 that a final design was agreed and work started. Four years later the Memorial was finally opened with much solemn ceremony.

Lorimer housed the Memorial's great Hall of Honour in the rubble-built shell of a disused three-storey barracks building on the north side of Edinburgh Castle's Crown Square.[7] The walls were recast and the floors of the old building removed to create an impressively tall inner space. Short wings advanced from the Hall on the south side to form an E-plan, the shorter wing at the centre dramatised by a high round-arched recess over the entrance. On this central axis, the buttressed apsidal Shrine, rising higher than the Hall behind a crowstepped gable, projected to the north; at its base, exposed rock. Implacably symmetrical, its height humbling, the Memorial had all the gravitas to be expected of a national monument. Stylistically it was historicist and eclectic, but not without specifically Scottish allusion. The tall rubble walls, 'very vertical and very strong'[8] had an unmistakable castellar character. The high-arched niche over the entrance, set at the centre of a five-part facade, recalled Fyvie. There were architectural motifs drawn from Falkland Palace and Stirling Palace. Inside, the barrel-vaulted Hall of Honour, its nine bays marked by octagonal columns, was 'a sumptuous nave-like space … of Scots Renaissance character'.[9] Over the Shrine, Gothic rib vaulting.

A mixture of styles and sources, the building was as retrospectively referential in form and detail as it necessarily was in function, yet it contrived to be noble, erect and erudite, an impressive, even inspirational, achievement and for this Lorimer was justly fêted. Among the many honours he received was Edinburgh University's Doctor of Laws degree, the citation for which praised his 'revival of the best traditions of Scottish building'.[10] Revival, however, was one thing – renewal another. The National War Memorial failed to transform or transcend the past. Despite the uniquely symbolic nature of the commission, Lorimer was ultimately unable to

Scottish National War Memorial, Edinburgh
North elevation drawing c1924
HES Canmore SC741958

capitalise on the opportunity it might have afforded to take Scottish architecture forward. Two years after the completion of the Memorial, he died. Mackintosh, who for more than a decade had had no opportunity to build anything, had died the year before.

While Mackintosh painted in exile and Lorimer was preoccupied with eclectic if reverent revival, others responded in differing ways to the more secular building needs of post-war society. The long-established disciplines of international classicism, now re-interpreted by a number of leading Scottish architects through their experience of Beaux Arts historicist training in Paris and, in some cases, influenced by developments in contemporary American architecture, took on new life. Just as in the nineteenth century the elevational proportions of the terraced Georgian town house had been distorted to fit the flatted street front of the ubiquitous urban tenement, so the columned, pilastered and corniced grid of the Renaissance palazzo facade, much in vogue in the mercantile heart of the Victorian city, was now further elaborated to conform to the demands of the steel or concrete frame structures of post-war civic and commercial building. Deferring as much perhaps to the diminishing availability of skilled craftsmanship in the straitened economic conditions of the time as to any more essentially architectural preference for an austerity of form, this 'versatile modernized classicism',[11] acquired an increasingly severe stripped-down quality. Whereas Victorian and Edwardian civic buildings, banks and commercial chambers had displayed their wealth, often in a heavily modelled profusion of ornament and facade sculpture, now these same building types, though still stolidly monumental and symmetrical, seemed in their decorative reserve to proclaim the virtues of sound economy and thrift.

This new classicism was particularly in evidence in a series of bank and office buildings designed by James Miller and completed in Glasgow in the

St Andrew's House, Edinburgh
David MacDonald / Alamy Stock Photo

1920s and 30s. Beginning in 1924 with the Union Bank on St Vincent Street, strongly stereometric but still patently classical with giant-order columns and pilasters and bold cornicing, continuing with the Commercial Bank, West George Street (1930–1), where the same elevational formula was refined to flat white facades barely modelled by bas relief detail, and ending with a second building for the Commercial Bank in Bothwell Street (1934–5) in which the tall block-like attic storey was without a cornice, Miller pushed classicism toward its ascetic limits.[12] None of this had, of course, anything to do with 'Scottishness' yet. Paradoxically, just as Mackintosh's exploration and transformation of Scottish forms and formal relationships had some 20 years earlier led to a precocious anticipation of the International Style, so now this later progressive reduction of classical ornament and detail produced an almost cubic simplicity of form. This was evident, for example, in J J Burnet's office building at 200 St Vincent Street, Glasgow (1925–7), which bore comparable if not altogether convincing affinity to the new white-walled European architecture. In their 1937 competition-winning design for Kirkcaldy Town House, the architectural practice Carr and Howard carried this cubic, stripped-down classicism further. All too often, however, any resonance with emergent Modernism was compromised by persistent symmetry and a massy monumentality, qualities nowhere more evident than in the two most important buildings commissioned for the nation in the early 1930s. Both projects were built in the capital: Reginald Fairlie's National Library of Scotland on George IV Bridge (designed 1934–6, but not realised until 1950–5) and Thomas Tait's St Andrew's House, accommodation for the Scottish Office on the lower slopes below Calton Hill (1936–9). Both were relentlessly symmetrical. But while the Library presented a bleakly institutional face to the street, the tiered offices of Tait's building, splendidly detailed with here and there references to the work of the Dutch architect Willem Marinus Dudok and the American Frank Lloyd Wright, spilled south down the Edinburgh hillside, Potala-like, 'a work of real imagination and grandeur'.[13]

Commercial Bank, West George Street, Glasgow
Photograph c1930
© Newsquest (Herald & Times). Licensor Scran

However ill-disposed Scott-Moncrieff may have been toward such 'modernized classicism', it is impossible to regard Tait's work or indeed the inter-war commercial buildings of Miller, Burnet, Keppie and Henderson, Wylie Wright and Wylie, and other architects as 'shoddy' or even 'uninspiring'. But 'denationalized' – no doubt. And while this was something for which these architects would have made no apology, there were also those designers who on occasion chose to work within the national tradition. Paisley architect T G Abercrombie, for example, built the Victory Baths in Renfrew (1921) in a symmetrical Scots Renaissance style incorporating crowstepped gables, eaves dormers with broken pediments clasping thistle motifs and a central entrance drum crowned with a wide-eaved bell-shaped dome. Lorimer's extension to the Burgh Chambers in Galashiels (1923–7), a square whinstone tower with a corbelled upper stage and bellcast pyramid roof, was similarly Scottish in derivation: part Renaissance, part Gothic. Many designers, however, especially those engaged in less civic projects, made no more than minimal, less overt, references to the forms and materials of baronial and vernacular architecture. This modest Scottishness was early evident in the houses built (1919–20) by Stewart and Paterson for the Scottish Veterans Garden Settlement in Callander. These 'homes fit for heroes' formed a 'beautifully composed baronial crescent'[14] of piended slated roofs, gabletted eaves dormers and cone-capped cylindrical towers. Rather grander but less subtle were the Cottage Homes which Mears and Carus-Wilson designed for retired mill workers at Galashiels (1930–3). Here a gabled community hall, lit by tall windows breaking through the eaves as pedimented dormers, was dramatised by an octagonal tower capped by a characteristically Scottish ogee dome. Both projects were built in stone: random rubble in one case, whinstone with sandstone dressings in

Lucy Sanderson Cottage Homes, Galashiels
HES Canmore SC1378458

Scottish Veterans Garden Settlement, Callander
© Mr J Gerrard, Scottish Civic Trust

Broughton Place, Biggar
Photograph c1938
HES Canmore SC1030655

the other. Harling – no less Scottish – was more common in many of the inter-war local authority housing schemes built as two-storey cottages and terraces or, later, three-storey tenements. Here, too, muted references to the traditional forms of Scottish domestic building were sometimes made. Throughout the 1930s Ebenezer MacRae in Edinburgh, Joseph Weekes in Dunbartonshire, Basil Spence at Dunbar and James Steel Maitland in Renfrew all made significant contributions to such 'neo-Scots housing',[15] though only Maitland's work betrayed a complementary awareness of architectural events in Europe. No such allusions appeared in private speculative housing schemes where, although some modish Art Deco villas were built in a few more progressive developments such as Broom Estate at Whitecraigs, Renfrewshire, a fixation on bungalow living all but dominated the market.

While public and private housing estates proliferated, commissions for individual private houses in the country or suburbs were increasingly rare. But the fashion for Scottishness persisted. Following in Lorimer's footsteps, the young William Kininmonth and Basil Spence designed a number of houses in Colinton in the early 1930s in what might be called a Scottish Arts and Crafts idiom. As late as 1936–7 Spence was building Broughton Place in Peeblesshire, a tall, three-storey-and-attic, L-plan house, white-harled with steep crowstepped gables, pedimented eaves dormers and three towers circular in plan with bellcast conic roofs. So complete was Spence's mastery of early seventeenth century precedent, that from some

The Broom Estate, Whitecraigs
Detail of advertisment 1935, tinted photograph c1938
Mactaggart and Mickel Ltd, HES Canmore SC421773

The Lane House, Dick Place, Edinburgh
HES Canmore SC684028

angles this unequivocally Scottish house may easily be mistaken for the real thing. Meanwhile, alongside this revivalism the same architects also designed several houses in classical style and some in a surprisingly mature modern manner. Of the latter, Kininmonth's own house in Edinburgh, the Lane House, was for its time – 1933 – 'a remarkably assured essay in white cubic architecture'.[16] Spence, too, could be current. Compromised perhaps by an ungainly quasi-classical flirtation with symmetry, his Gribloch House near Kippen (1937–9) had the white parapetted walls, flat (at any rate, seemingly so) roof, curving planes of glass and porthole windows of contemporary avant garde fashion: if not quite convincingly Modern it had at least that flavour of Art Deco implicit in the more modish term 'Moderne'. Neither of these houses could be adjudged in any derivative sense Scottish. Overall,

Gribloch House, Kippen
Photographs c1940, 1984
HES Canmore SC684960, SC1057306

however, the evidence suggests that there was in Spence's work at this time 'an innate tension between the universal values of "Internationalism", whether international classicism or international Modernism, and the need to respond to regional patterns of building'.[17] Spence's position was shared by those architects, not content with revival, for whom the need to develop and maintain some link between the national tradition and the international Modern Movement continued to be the *sine qua non* of any valid architecture.

But what were these 'universal values of "Internationalism"'? The principles of international classicism were, of course, well understood – symmetry, tripartition, rectangular gridding, order 'applied hierarchically from the whole to the part',[18] – while the elements of classical architecture could in their purest state, denuded of decoration, be reduced to the fundamental forms of three-dimensional geometry. International Modernism, however, was less clearly apprehended – at least in visual, stylistic terms. All were agreed that modern buildings must function rationally, responding to need. But what should they look like? For extreme Functionalists this was a redundant question; form would, with ineluctable logic, follow the satisfactory resolution of all 'scientific' functional criteria. Others, however, took a less materialistic view, contending that aesthetic criteria had a life of their own. Among those who espoused such a view was the French-Swiss architect Le Corbusier, whose buildings and, not least, his polemical writings would have a profound influence on the course of twentieth century architecture. For him, the formal nature of the New Architecture had much in common with naked classicism: cylinder, pyramid, cube, rectangular prism and sphere, these were, indeed, the ultimate building blocks, basic and beautiful. 'Architecture', he declaimed, 'is the skilful, accurate and magnificent play of masses seen in light'.[19] The more Platonic these masses, the more beautiful.

A decade later, however, the Americans Henry-Russell Hitchcock and Philip Johnson, in their canonical exposition of the formal principles, *The International Style*, contrarily claimed that 'The effect of mass, of static solidity, hitherto the prime quality of architecture, has all but disappeared.'[20] For them modern architecture was first not about mass but about space, perceptible volume, frame construction clad in enclosing screens, solid or glazed, like 'a skin tightly stretched over the supporting skeleton'.[21] A second principle they described as 'regularity', the need for standardisation invoked by new methods of construction, new product manufacture and new patterns of urban living. While linked to the economy of form and means implicit in the first two principles, a third entailed 'the avoidance of applied decoration'. Having prefaced their discussion of style with the caveat that 'Architecture is always a set of actual monuments, not a vague corpus of theory',[22] Hitchcock and Johnson, historian and architect, wisely illustrated the text of their book with photographs and plans of a range of recently completed building projects drawn mainly from several countries in Europe but also from the United States and Japan. These illustrations revealed a crisp, clean-cut architecture of generally asymmetrical compositions of white stucco planes, glazed walls, *fenêtres en longueur*, standardised repetitive elements and the occasional appearance of 'non-rectangular shapes'. Here was a formal order no longer in thrall to symmetry, non-hierarchical, a still gridded order based not on the subdivided whole but the repeated and aggregated part. But how well was this understood in Scotland?

The evidence presented by Charles McKean in his indispensable study *The Scottish Thirties* makes it clear that architects in Scotland were in fact relatively well informed about this New Architecture and not a few committed to design in the International Style, or at least a watered-down Art Deco version of that style. He counts almost 200 houses built in Scotland in the new modern idiom during the 1930s and suggests a figure of approximately 780 in England over the same period, a comparison which, on the basis of population, indicates a greater willingness to embrace stylistic change north of the border.

While some Scottish architects had travelled to see for themselves what was happening in Scandinavia, the Netherlands, France, Germany and, not least, Central Europe, notably in the new state of Czechoslovakia, and some were familiar with the writings of Le Corbusier, Gropius and other influential figures in the Modern movement, in their original languages or later translation, the majority relied on the architectural journals, particularly those which were well illustrated, to keep abreast of events. Of these, the *Architectural Review* was particularly influential, not least because of a series of articles, written by P Morton Shand between 1933 and 1935, documenting architectural developments on the continent. Under a succession of progressive editors which included John Summerson, R Mervyn Noad and Ian G Lindsay, the *Quarterly* journal of the Royal Incorporation of Architects in Scotland, far from being the turgid organ of a provincial professional institute, also carried 'articles on modern continental work and architectural theory'[23] and served as a Scottish forum in which the latest ideas could be presented and discussed. From time to time the *RIBA Journal* provided a similar platform for new ideas: in May 1934, for example, it published a long article on 'The Formal and Technical Problems of Modern Architecture and Planning', the text of a lecture Walter Gropius had delivered to the Design and Industries Association in London. In this, though he referred to the various individuals and artistic groups who had contributed to the development of Modernism, the forms of the New Architecture were seen, somewhat deterministically, to be the 'consequential product of the intellectual, social and technical conditions of our age'.[24] The following year these thoughts were more fully elaborated when Gropius' book, *The New Architecture and the Bauhaus*, appeared in English for the first time.

Ravelston Gardens, Edinburgh
Perspective view 1935
HES Canmore SC453895

In 1936 Nikolaus Pevsner's *Pioneers of the Modern Movement*[25] was published, the first comprehensive, English language, historical survey of the ideas and imagery of modern art, design and architecture, 'from William Morris to Walter Gropius',[26] and, significantly, the first serious study to rehabilitate Charles Rennie Mackintosh, if decidedly in the mould of an international (cosmopolitan) Modernist.

Scottish architects were informed, but it would be wrong to suggest that enthusiasm for the new was universal. There were still those who regarded Modernism as little more than a passing fashion, a bag of aesthetic tricks, constructionally and environmentally flawed, even an international socialist conspiracy. Nevertheless, many Scottish designers were thirled enough to attempt to emulate what they had seen in the journals and build in what they believed to be the International Style. McKean's researches have not only revealed a surprisingly high number of 'modern' houses but have also shown how broadly based is the legacy of building from *The Scottish Thirties*. The characteristic architectural motifs – white walls, flat roofs, bands of horizontal glazing, corner windows, semi-circular glazed bays, nautical railings and so on – appear across the full range of building types. Much, of course, was of indifferent quality. Sometimes symmetry might persist, often in the form of a central tower, without any compelling functional justification or, where the plan demanded it, it might be oppressively overblown. Sometimes, particularly in cinema and shop design, a self-conscious Art Deco decorativism obtruded on form. Sometimes, indeed often, it was simply heavy-handedness or half-heartedness which compromised austere elegance. But there were also buildings – though perhaps not many – which could stand comparison with contemporary architecture in Europe. Amongst the best were Thomas Tait's council housing on Howwood Road, Johnstone (1935), and Neil and Hurd's private flats at Ravelston Gardens, Edinburgh (1935), both built with something of the crisp balconied chic of continental flats. Some of the housing commissioned in the late 1930s by the Scottish Special Housing Association from Kininmonth and Spence, Sam Bunton, Carr and Howard and others, was still more uncompromising

Rothesay Pavilion
HES Canmore DP101594

in its cubic austerity. A cylindrical glazed bow window appeared in Kininmonth's precocious house at Dick Place, Edinburgh (1933), perhaps the first use of a motif that would prove popular in a variety of contexts. Semi-circular bows appeared in Thomas Tait's Infectious Diseases Hospital in Paisley (1932–5), where the long marine-like wards had terraces and balconies cantilevered and canopied. In James Carrick's competition-winning Rothesay Pavilion (1936), the same form made a dramatic impact, its curved roof terrace and glazed restaurant boldly cantilevered over a smaller glazed half-cylinder at ground level – though here Mendelsohn and Chermayeff's nearly contemporary De La Warr Pavilion at Bexhill-on-Sea is the more likely precedent. The influence of Marinus Dudok's brick box Dutch Modernism was widespread, most elegantly exemplified perhaps in the pithead baths built at Cardowan Colliery near Stepps (1934) and in McKissack and Anderson's Cosmo Cinema, Glasgow (1939). Glass walls were rare but for the Luma electric light bulb company, Shieldhall, Glasgow (1936), Cornelius Armour raised 'a bulbous, entirely glazed, conning tower',[27] two-storeys high over the factory roof. In Edinburgh, a three-storey curtain wall of gridded glass formed the street facade to the St Cuthbert's Co-operative Store on Bread Street (1937), a *tour de force* by T P Marwick and Son, bearing a remarkable likeness to the better-known Bílá Labuť store in Prague, completed by Kittrich and Hruby (1937–9). Whether there was any direct influence at work in this particular case, the similarity is testimony to the International Style design skills attained by some Scottish architects in the inter-war period.

This awareness of both the buildings and the principles of the international Modern Movement coincided with a renewed interest in Mackintosh and a growing consciousness of the contribution he had made to architectural change. Mackintosh's death in 1928 had prompted some favourable obituaries, while, after the death of his wife, the artist and designer Margaret Macdonald, in 1933, his work received

St Cuthbert's Co-operative Association, Edinburgh
Photograph 1979
HES Canmore SC710121

public recognition in a Memorial Exhibition held in Glasgow. Architectural drawings, paintings and several items of furniture went on show. The RIAS *Quarterly* took note, recommending its readers to visit the exhibition, the editor, Mervyn Noad, describing Mackintosh as a Scottish artist whom 'many regard as one of the founders of modern architecture'.[28] Reviewing the exhibition in *The Spectator*, Robert Hurd regretted the unfortunate fact 'that even the educated Scotsman does not seem to realize the international importance of MacKintosh [sic] as an architect',[29] before going on to praise Mackintosh's achievement in producing a body of work which, despite the occasional 'distasteful stamp' of Art Nouveau, gave clear proof of the 'affinity that exists between the native tradition of Scots architecture … and the "functional" building of today'.[30]

Hurd's admiration for Mackintosh's work sprang from a burning interest in traditional Scottish building and the belief that that national tradition had the potential, both functional and formal, to coalesce with international Modernism. This conviction, in his view vindicated if not fully fulfilled by the achievements of Mackintosh, stemmed from his experience at Cambridge where he had come under the influence of Mansfield Duval Forbes, an English Studies don, Fellow of Clare College and fellow Scot.[31] A coterie of young intellectuals, among them architects Raymond McGrath, Ian G Lindsay, with whom Hurd had been at school, and Oliver Hill, had gathered around Forbes, attracted by his interest in architecture, particularly Scottish architecture. In Cambridge, Forbes 'was widely regarded to know more about Scotland than anyone else, its archaeology and architecture, history and folklore'[32] and though he wrote little on the subject his knowledge and enthusiasm, regularly topped up by visits to the great castles of Angus and Aberdeenshire, stimulated his admiring circle. What Forbes saw in the Castles of Mar – Midmar, Craigievar and Castle Fraser – were architectural forms with 'distinct aesthetic values'. Studying these baronial buildings, he, and through him his young acolytes,

> warmed to the blend of functional aptness with the beauty which is due to the expression of an aesthetic idea by means of forms placed in relation to one another. In Scotland as nowhere else was there the rich variety of shapes, cylinders, cubes, cones, oblongs, pyramids, and the various cupola shapes[33]

These were forms which might, Forbes thought (for he was also intrigued by the possibilities of new materials and technologies), be reborn in the modern medium of reinforced concrete – an interesting parallel to James Salmon's speculations.

These ideas embracing the differing but inseparable values of functional fitness and formal relationships resonate with the contemporary words of Le Corbusier. His stress on the importance of the plan as 'generator' (admittedly understood not so much at the practical level of 'functional aptness' as in a more mystical sense) and the necessary delight of 'volumes disposed in precise relationships'[34] advanced a similar thesis – though without the nuance of national pride. It is tempting to speculate that had Le Corbusier's route *Towards a New Architecture* (*Vers une Architecture*) taken him on a journey to view the castles, towerhouses, cottages and brochs at the north-west edge of Europe rather than on his *Voyage d'Orient* to the classical monuments and white-walled vernacular of the Aegean, he might well have written these same words. At any rate, this belief in the relevance of the Scottish architectural tradition to the predicament of the twentieth century Scottish designer, so to say a precocious Critical Regionalism, was the view ardently advanced by Mansfield Forbes and his circle. Regrettably no-one developed the thesis at length – an offer of a two-year fellowship at Clare College given to Mervyn Noad to study how the Scottish vernacular might 'form the basis of a modern Scottish idiom'[35] was turned down, though Noad remained an 'outlying member' of the Forbes group. But Lindsay and Hurd, returning from Cambridge to work and write in Scotland, would play a prominent role in ensuring that the Scottish architectural tradition continued to receive sympathetic understanding and cultural respect.

In the years before the Second World War, both Lindsay and Hurd seized opportunities to campaign and publish on Scottish architecture while seeking to establish themselves professionally. Ian G Lindsay, who had already published his first book, on the *Cathedrals of Scotland*, in 1926 while still a student at Cambridge School of Architecture, became editor of the RIAS *Quarterly* in the early thirties at much the same time as he set up in practice. Through a professional link with Reginald Fairlie, whom he assisted on the early stages of the National Library project, Lindsay also found himself recommended to the Marquess of Bute as the most appropriate person to continue the listing of buildings of architectural quality and historical association which had been begun by the recently formed National Trust for Scotland. Bute, assisted by George Scott-Moncrieff, a tireless campaigner for the Trust, had already identified 15 towns worthy of attention. By 1936 Lindsay had expanded this to 103; two years later 1,168 buildings had been listed and categorised A, B or C. The completion of these lists led to statutory protection for the nation's architectural heritage and to Lindsay's appointment in 1945 as Chief Inspector of Historic Buildings under the Town and Country (Planning) Act. Lindsay's own design portfolio in the 1930s, relatively undeveloped compared to what it was to become after the war, focused largely on conservation. Amongst his commissions were St Finnan's Church, Invergarry (1938) 'a couthy crowstepped Scots kirk',[36] the renovation of the monastic buildings at Iona Abbey (begun 1938), and the restoration of Stenhouse (1937–9), 'a typical seventeenth-century Scottish town house' which – significantly – Thomas Howarth, in his biography of Mackintosh, would later illustrate alongside the Hill House.[37]

Robert Hurd's early career followed a similar pattern. After working for Mears and Carus-Wilson, he went into independent practice with Norman A G Neil, who had been his senior in the Mears office. Neil was largely responsible for the design of the firm's remarkably up-to-the-minute Ravelston flats in 1935. At that time, Hurd's work was probably more concerned with the firm's conservation and restoration commissions, among them work on Acheson House, Edinburgh (1936–7), and Lamb's House, Leith (1937–9), both of which dated from the early seventeenth century. This interest in the past brought him into the orbit of the National Trust for Scotland and in 1936 he was a member of the group delegated by the Trust to persuade the Secretary of State for Scotland of the need to preserve the nation's architectural heritage. Three years later he wrote *Scotland under Trust*, the first extended account of the National Trust's holdings. Throughout the 1930s Hurd appeared regularly in print not only documenting the country's heritage but arguing that traditional Scottish buildings, reduced to their essential solid geometrical forms, could provide the basis for a modern Scottish architecture. In perceiving this truth, Mackintosh had, in Hurd's view, been unique and still remained the paradigm for progress.

At once intellectual and practical, the challenge to resolve the tension between a Scottish architectural tradition, with its own specific qualities of character and composition, and an International Style escaping from the past through its espousal of functional rationalism and ahistorical form was not something universally embraced. Some architects, eschewing Modernism, were content to continue to practise in what they regarded as an ongoing tradition. Many more, seeing that same tradition as anachronistic and provincial, sought to emulate continental precedent, believing the New Architecture to have an objective cross-border cosmopolitan legitimacy. While for conservative designers there was always the pitfall of a parochial 'kailyard' historicism blind to new ideas, Modernists might be seduced by a spurious internationalism which spurned the very word's inherent and necessary concept of constituent national cultures. For those who acknowledged the claims of both national *and* international culture, the creation of a viable modern Scottishness, reformed rather than merely revived, proved something of a chimera. In the inter-war years no building of any size or social significance merited such categorisation, not the Scottish National War Memorial, not the National Library (designed but still to be built), not the Scottish Office. Indeed, it is difficult to identify *any* building erected in Scotland in the inter-war years which might be said to advance the programme adumbrated by Mackintosh or satisfy the criteria advocated so earnestly by Hurd and Lindsay.

An obvious location in which evidence of such an architecture might be expected to have appeared was the Empire Exhibition held in Bellahouston Park, Glasgow, in 1938. The exhibition was, of course, multi-national in nature – at any rate within the imperial context – but it was also explicitly intended 'to stimulate Scottish work and production and to direct attention to Scotland's historical and scenic attractions'.[38] In terms of its architecture, however, this exhibition was far from being a hotch-potch of diverse cultural traditions and building styles. On the contrary, thanks to the overall control exerted by Thomas Tait and his team of like-minded

Scottish Pavilions, Empire Exhibition, Glasgow
Photograph 1938
© Stanley K Hunter, Scottish Exhibitions Study Group. Licensor Scran

young designers, including Basil Spence, Jack Coia and Margaret Brodie, an uncompromising cubic Modernism characterised almost every one of more than a hundred structures. 'Not since the great Exhibition of 1851,' said a review in the *Manchester Guardian*, 'has an exhibition in this country shown such unity of style in its building.'[39] A strictly limited range of materials was permitted: steel, timber and asbestos cladding panels. The familiar features of the International Style abounded: plain parapetted walls, flat roofs, the simple geometries of apsidal, concave and convex forms, colonnades, fins, glazed grids curved and planar, and towers, the most dramatic of which was the exhibition's showpiece,

Tower of Empire, Empire Exhibition, Glasgow
Photograph 1938
Bryan & Norman Westwood / RIBA Collections

the Tower of Empire, set on Bellahouston Hill. 'Tait's Tower', as it was known, rose to a height of more than 90 metres in parallel planes of silvered steel soaring to four superimposed balconies from which visitors could look down on the exhibition site. Above the balconies, sandwiched between vertical planes, a single vertical vane 'served to counteract wind torque'.[40] Not only did this tower become the signature image of the event but in simplified form and smaller scale it 'was repeated elsewhere in the Exhibition, notably in the towers of the Scottish Pavilions'.[41]

There were, in fact, two Scottish Pavilions, mirror images of each other on opposite sides of the site's Scottish Avenue. The designer of the pavilions, Basil Spence, working under Tait, 'drew directly from progressive European practice'.[42] Each building was an asymmetrical composition of cubic, Dudok-like forms in dark and light blue, diminishing in height from a tall, glazed entrance hall flanked by a 36.5-metre-high tower. While the asymmetry of each individual pavilion was relatively unusual – most pavilions were to a greater or lesser degree symmetrical in their organisation – the reflected location of the two buildings nevertheless submitted to a grander

Mousa to Mackintosh 211

symmetry in the site layout: Scottish Avenue was a broad axial boulevard terminated by viewpoints, at one end by the Palace of Art and at the other by the exhibition's Concert Hall. This deference to symmetry, and thus by implication to classicism, evident in much of the site layout and in individual buildings where colonnades, porticos and towers dramatised axial entrances, compromised the radical nature of the architectural language which otherwise unified the exhibition. Comparisons with similarly 'unified' exhibitions in Brno in Czechoslovakia, 1927–8, or Stockholm, 1930, confirm the somewhat cautious Modernism adopted at Glasgow. No doubt the asymmetrical composition of the individual Scottish Pavilions – though this was, of course, compromised by their mirrored relationship – qualifies them to be counted among those exhibition structures whose design was more in tune with the principles of the International Style.

On the other hand, looked at from the perspective of national culture, there was no evident allusion to indigenous tradition in the architecture of the Scottish Pavilions. It might be argued that the specific employment of half-cylinder forms wrapped in gridded glazing was a reference to Mackintosh's staircases at Scotland Street School. Certainly, the overall simplification of form to boxy austerity evinced something of that process of reduction which, when applied to traditional Scottish architecture, would, in the opinion of Robert Hurd and others among the Mansfield Forbes circle, have led to a Scottish architecture for the twentieth century. But, whatever the validity of the thesis, the evidence of Spence's pavilions scarcely amounts to convincing corroboration, for the simplification of form he achieved was drawn not from any purging of tradition but from recent continental (notably Dutch) precedent. Even so, in the infinitely more modest context of his design for a potentially prototypical 'Cottage or Country House', commissioned for the exhibition by the Council for Art and Industry – a smart, white-walled, middle-class, two-storey dwelling with a pitched roof and a tall chimney tower – Spence did attain an integrity of form and material, a cool reserved Scottishness, that was both vernacular and contemporary.

Another kind of 'Scottishness' was, however, much in evidence at Bellahouston. Following the example of the 1911 exhibition, the promoters constructed An Clachan, a Highland village complete with its 'Castle of the Glen', black house, smithy, and pre-Reformation 'cill' or chapel, all clustered around a small loch beyond which painted backdrops provided views of Scottish scenery. Designed by Colin Sinclair, this stage-set fabrication, though 'its historical accuracy was irrefutable'[43] and its declared aim to promote development and modernisation in the Highlands wholly admirable, seemed to consign architectural 'Scottishness' to Potemkin parody and Brigadoon nostalgia. It was perhaps a fitting irony that An Clachan was located in a part of the exhibition park close to Tait's Tower. Dreaming in sentimental reverie by the side of the lochan, the exhibition visitor could still see, rising above the trees enclosing the *ersatz* village, the iconic form of a different world. Though the relationship of the images was reversed – here high-rise over castle rather than castle over office tower – the absurdity of the contrast was as great, the irony of a missed opportunity as visible, as it had been in James Salmon's design for the *Chicago Tribune* tower.

The extreme contrast between the International Style of the exhibition buildings, even if that style was not expressed in its most radical form, and the retrospective faux-folk buildings of An Clachan, coupled with the elusiveness of any identifiable 'Scottish architecture of the twentieth century', inevitably points to the possibility that perhaps any kind of creative alignment between the national and the international was a naive expectation. After all, there were distinct differences between the two. The Scottish tradition of building, for centuries fundamentally conditioned by the country's geography and geology, was one of stone construction – an architecture of mass in which solid dominated void. The New Architecture, on the other hand, freed from solid, earth-bound load-bearing mass by advances in steel and concrete technology, was a more volumetrically liberated architecture of frame and fill in which walls of glass might vitiate any solidity of form. Moreover, the native tradition was one in which verticality of form was frequently preferred, whether in the baronial castle and tower-house or in the compositional elements of the Baronial Revival mansion.

An Clachan, Empire Exhibition, Glasgow
Photographs 1938
© Stanley K Hunter, Scottish Exhibitions Study Group. Licensor Scran

Mousa to Mackintosh 213

The ubiquitous International Style, by contrast, seemed to favour the horizontal. Much indigenous historical Scottish building had a formal restlessness and irregularity, springing either from a direct response to contingent need or from an aesthetic delight in the formal consequences that need had created. Contrastingly the socio-economic changes of the nineteenth and twentieth centuries, introducing industrial mass production and new demands for denser urban living, had resulted in the regularised, standardised forms of International Style architecture. Yet there were also evident similarities. Modern architecture's stress on function, its rejection of supervening historicist formulae, was echoed, as Mackintosh had observed, in much of baronial and vernacular building. Both shared an inclination to asymmetry, in part the simple consequence of such functional design. Both espoused an austere aesthetic, decoratively abstemious, geometrical, white.

And it was doubtless the potential inherent in these affinities which persisted in the minds of those architects who continued to believe that there could be a fusion between the old and the new – among them Robert Hurd, Ian G Lindsay, Basil Spence and Alan Reiach. In 1941, frustrated by the previous decade's failure to produce what they would have regarded as a viable modern Scottish architecture and conscious of the reconstruction challenge which would face the country when the war ended, Reiach and Hurd wrote *Building Scotland*. Published and promoted by the recently founded Saltire Society whose broadly based championing of Scottish culture was expressed as a concern 'with the past, because it is the basis of the present [and] with the present, because from it must grow the future',[44] it was a slim booklet, short on words but tersely polemical and generously illustrated with black and white photographs of what the authors considered good and bad building. This juxtaposition of these examples recalled the method of presentation adopted in Pugin's *Contrasts* published a century earlier but lacked that seminal document's theoretical exposition. There was, too, in the clipped text something of the manifesto-like quality of Le Corbusier's *Vers une Architecture* but without its sustained rhetoric and poetry. Nevertheless, the book's message was clear: 'Love of good traditions should combine with desire for experiment'. Though no mention was made or illustration given of castle or tower-house (perhaps because as a building type such structures were deemed irrelevant to post-war needs), the 'sturdiness, simplicity and charm' of Scotland's urban and rural vernacular was commended and the confused stylistic historicism of the past condemned. The 'lightness, freshness and good planning' of recent European work – housing, churches, civic buildings, schools, libraries, hospitals, industrial buildings, commercial buildings, buildings for transport, buildings for recreation – was repeatedly illustrated and praised; architecture's lustration presented in the clean white forms of the International Style. As the authors explained in the preface to the book's second edition in 1944, they were presenting their case through contrasts and comparisons 'with older Scottish buildings and modern architecture from our own and other lands'. The fact that they could find only one contemporary Scottish building – a pithead baths in Lanarkshire – worthy of inclusion alongside their continental examples was a measure of the inter-war design deficit in Scotland. But for all their enthusiasm for the new international architecture, Reiach and Hurd were not prepared to sacrifice tradition, still less to give up on its relevance to contemporary national culture.

> Tradition is the pool of a nation's continuous experience from which we can draw both inspiration and warning. Slavish copying of period styles in buildings for modern needs produces dreary archaisms, but plan, form, proportion and colour of building in one country differ from those in another, and it would be foolish to ignore the social, physical and psychological reasons behind these national differences. The pioneer architect Charles Rennie Mackintosh, whose influence on modern European design was considerable, himself drew inspiration from basic Scottish traditions … but he was a prophet in his own country.

This sting in the tail, appropriately biblical for a still religious Scotland – 'a prophet is not without honour, save in his own country'[45] – is revealing. Half a century had passed since Mackintosh had seen signs of what he took to be a new Scottish style 'coming to life again', yet here were Reiach and Hurd admitting, if guardedly, that little had been done to nurture this promise. Looking back over the inter-war years, they found, as George Scott-Moncrieff had done a year or two before, little to enthuse over. The New Architecture, coming from Europe as it always did, was welcome. But while it had made a considerable though muted impact, no satisfactory resolution of the inevitable dialectical tension between imported international ideas and indigenous culture had emerged. It was a judgement with which the longer perspective of hindsight would, at least in broad terms, agree. Fifty years after the publication of *Building Scotland*, on the occasion of the 150th anniversary convention of the Royal Incorporation of Architects in Scotland, Professor Isi Metzstein of Edinburgh University delivered an address which, in acknowledgment of the fundamental changes in building materials and methods which architecture had undergone, he entitled 'After the Stone Age'. Reviewing the aspirations and achievements of Scottish architecture post-Mackintosh, his tone was critical. He praised the invaluable work done by Charles McKean in recording the quantity of built evidence of the International Style in his book *The Scottish Thirties* but was considerably less sanguine as to its quality. With characteristically mordant wit, he referred to McKean's architectural anthology as an 'ornithology', damning the buildings documented with the remark that 'most are lame ducks, and quite a few are dead ducks'. 'The truth is', he went on to say, 'that the period between the wars, and particularly the thirties, was a very thin time for Scottish architecture.'[46] Not everyone would take such a harsh view of the evidence. But whether, as with Metzstein, the judgement based on a more general evaluation of the quality of the architecture of the Scottish inter-war period in the wider European context is dismissive and pessimistic, or as with Reiach and Hall, despite some disappointment, it is more optimistic on the degree to which architecture had succeeded in embodying some resonance of Scottishness, it is difficult to avoid the conclusion that expectations remained to be fulfilled.

Chapter 10
Scottishness at the Millennium
From Modern to Post-Modern

'New architecture in Scotland ... is not yet the new architecture of Scotland: until it is grafted into the Scottish mind and spirit it will not mature. But the national tradition embodied in an old building is alive, to enrich, expand, and deepen our understanding ... If we in Scotland are to continue to make our distinctive contribution as a nation to the sum of human well-being – surely the object of internationalism as opposed to aggressive nationalism – then we must maintain our national identity, individuality, and tradition.'
Moultrie R Kelsall and Stuart Harris, *A Future for the Past*

'It is not behind us but ahead.'
Ian Begg, 'Filling the Gap' in *Prospect*, No 39

The wartime publication of Reiach and Hurd's *Building Scotland*, first in 1941 and again in 1944, was motivated both by a consciousness of the impending demand to construct a new and better living environment once hostilities ended and by the desire to incorporate into that built future the same 'sturdiness, simplicity and charm'[1] evident in what

Hutchesontown Area C, Gorbals, Glasgow
Photograph by Henk Snoek 1964
© Courtesy of HES (Spence, Glover and Ferguson Collection)

the authors believed to be the best of the buildings of the Scottish past. In his introduction to the second edition of the book, the then Secretary of State for Scotland, Thomas Johnston, endorsed this ambition with a plea that the buildings of the new post-war Scotland – by which he implied, as the book's illustrations did, housing, schools, hospitals, offices and factories – should be constructed 'not for utility only, but for utility plus beauty'.[2]

But, in the post-war climate of comprehensive social reconstruction, such aesthetic considerations seemed barely to animate the extensive state- and municipal-led programmes which, 'more so than in any other

Moss Height Flats, Glasgow
Photograph c1955
© CSG CIC Glasgow Museums Collection

developed country',[3] began to rebuild and reshape the nation's cities and towns. If the prevailing ethos in a now-socialist Scotland was not quite the outright 'militant utilitarianism'[4] that some have suggested, the practical and moral imperatives of a new, more equitable society were paramount. As the economy slowly recovered from the strains and sacrifices of the war years, vast housing schemes designed to improved living standards were commissioned by both municipal and national authorities (such as the Scottish Special Housing Association, founded in 1937), schools were constructed, factories, collieries, health centres and hospitals built. In meeting these challenges, which were perceived to be not merely national but pan-European, most architects espoused a design approach which was correspondingly international, and, as they believed, Modernist and objective. In high-rise, high-density housing projects like Moss Heights flats in Glasgow (1950–4), in new schools like Cranhill Secondary in Glasgow (1961–6), in municipal offices like Lanark County Buildings in Hamilton (1959–64), in hospitals like Vale of Leven Hospital in Alexandria (1952–5), rectilineal geometries established an economy of form in which the repetitive aggregation of standardised components prevailed. While this commitment was never explicitly avowed or articulated in the extreme philosophical terms of pre-war continental Functionalism, throughout the 1950s and into the early 1960s most Scottish designers nevertheless found the rational, scientific, technological and social aspects of Modernism more congenial to the material needs of the moment than any consideration of 'form' as form. Still less did they consider the assimilation of the imagery and symbolism of a 'national' architecture – transformed or not – in any sense pertinent. For most architects, whatever their particular personal perspective might be, the architecture of the past had no relevance to their contemporary task.

For most – but not all. For two quite dissimilar architectural approaches emerged which, while radically different in derivation, would prove complementary in their assertion of architectural

Vale of Leven Hospital, Alexandria
Architectural Press Archive / RIBA Collections

values beyond those of strictly functional performance. These attitudes, in their successive and latterly overlapping impact, would effect a restitution of respect for the aesthetic qualities of architecture, both plastic and iconic, and, for some designers at least, occasion a renewed and interrogative interest in the traditional materials, methods and forms of Scottish building.

Maintaining their thirties' affection and concern for Scotland's architectural heritage, a handful of like-minded designers continued to believe that a creative resolution of the national/international dialectic could be achieved. Among such were Robert Hurd, Alan Reiach, Ian G Lindsay, and, for a time, Basil Spence. Hurd and Reiach were active in the Saltire Society, Hurd as president from 1943 to 1948 and secretary until 1956. Founded in 1936 not only to promote excellence in Scottish housing but 'to restore the country to its proper place as a creative force in European civilization' the Society had financed Reiach and Hurd's 'cautionary guide' to *Building Scotland*.

Ian G Lindsay, too, continued to write, though less polemically, publishing books on *Georgian Edinburgh* (1948) and *The Scottish Parish Kirk* (1960). Returning from active service, he had been appointed chief investigator of historic buildings under the provisions of the Town and Country Planning (Scotland) Act of 1945, a direct consequence of his pre-war involvement with the Marquess of Bute and the National Trust for Scotland. In this capacity he engaged a number of part-time inspectors who began the process of statutory listing which would secure the long-term protection of the country's wealth of buildings of architectural and historical importance. Such activities stimulated architectural scholarship and nurtured an increasingly influential heritage lobby. In their architectural practices, Hurd and Lindsay carried out a considerable amount of sensitive and informed restoration of historic buildings, but it was in their new-build projects that they found themselves obliged to confront the issue of rendering the past relevant to the present and the new respectful of the old.

Circumscribed in scope by the nature of these projects – for the most part housing developments, many of them set in contexts of restoration or infill

Little Houses, Dunkeld
HES Canmore SC985632

– their success in doing so may be adjudged modest. Yet this in itself must be considered an apposite and positive measure of their re-interpretation of a vernacular tradition which had preserved some 'Scottish essence'.[5] Indeed, through the 1950s and early 1960s, such projects as Basil Spence's housing at Dunbar and Newhaven, Ian G Lindsay's restored streetscape for the National Trust for Scotland's Little Houses Scheme in Dunkeld, Robert Hurd's flatted infill on the Canongate, Edinburgh, as well as similar residential developments, equally respectful and unassertive, by Wheeler and Sproson, Moira and Moira and the in-house architects of the New Towns of East Kilbride, Glenrothes and later Cumbernauld, were all given Saltire Society awards for that very reason. Running in parallel to the growing concern to restore and conserve the best of the past (see below), this 'persistent strand of smaller-scale interventions in small-town or historic contexts'[6] made a tangential but significant impact on the evolving course of Scottish architecture. It could certainly be argued that none of these projects achieved what might be termed a *radical* synthesis of the national tradition with international Modernism, but by responding to place, by acknowledging the claims of the *genius loci* to be in creative tension with those of the *Zeitgeist*, they kept alive that recurring conviction that through the manipulation of form and material there could be an identifiable Scottishness in contemporary Scottish architecture.

Seen in the context of mainstream design where the clamant demands of social need, the economies of technical standardisation and the scientific pretensions of design method and building performance found abstract form in a 'brave new world' of flat roofs and gridded curtain walls, such

Canongate Flats, Edinburgh
Photograph 1995
HES Canmore SC955156

a prospect seemed to many at best a peripheral indulgence, at worst an effete irrelevance. By the 1960s, however, international Modernism itself had already begun to undergo internal change. Thanks largely to the impact of Le Corbusier's work at Ronchamp, La Tourette and Chandigarh, a reassertion of the importance of sculptural and tactile values, coupled with a corresponding enthusiasm for the textural qualities of *matières brutes* – grainy off-the-shutter concrete, roughly rendered wall surfaces, exposed aggregates, rubble masonry, and that historically most un-Scottish of materials, brick – became increasingly evident in the work of some architects. Form, always essentially the abstract relational structure implicit in architectural composition and detail, now recovered a fuller architectural significance as these designers acknowledged its role as the medium of aesthetic delight as well as organisational order. Nowhere was this development more clearly or more contiguously seen than in Glasgow in the contrasting approach to high-rise housing taken by two of the country's leading post-war designers, Robert Matthew and Basil Spence.

Throughout the third quarter of the century, Scotland's largest city prepared successive reports and proposals geared to drive residential and commercial regeneration. In parallel with a policy of population overspill to the New Towns of East Kilbride and Cumbernauld, plans entailed extensive slum clearance, new housing in the suburbs and in the inner city, and new transport infrastructure. Already in the 1950s, no less than 29 Comprehensive Development Areas (CDAs) were designated based on these ideas. Of these, Hutchesontown/Gorbals, where almost every existing building was scheduled for demolition,

presented perhaps the greatest challenge and the most prestigious possibilities. Four redevelopment zones were identified within the boundaries of the CDA and commissions allocated; Area B went to Matthew, Area C to Spence.

Both architects were based in Edinburgh. Matthew, after a number of years as Architect to London County Council, during which time he had been engaged in building schools, health centres, housing and, not least, the Royal Festival Hall, had returned to the capital in 1953 to take up the university's Chair of Architecture and found his own practice, Robert Matthew, Johnson-Marshall.[7] Coincidentally, in that same year, Spence had moved his family and his principal office to London, though he continued to practise in Edinburgh as Sir Basil Spence, Glover and Ferguson.

While both offices' proposals for the new Gorbals featured high-rise housing, their respective[8] designs differed markedly. Of the two, Matthew conformed more closely to the acknowledged principles of the international Modern Movement. His four, eighteen-storey, flatted towers (1958–64) were aligned to achieve the ideal functional orientation, a decision resulting in a dramatic oblique departure from the prevailing gridded matrix of streets which for a century and a half had determined Glasgow's urban form both north and south of the river. Derived from the more formal tradition of the International Style, the patterning of the towers' west and east facades remained rigorously rectilinear and repetitive. Spence, on the other hand, who chose to set his two parallel, twenty-storey, slab blocks (1960–6, demolished 1993) in alignment with the historic street grid, invested his composition of '400 crossover maisonettes' with a more expressive quality distilled from the experience of a visit he had made to Le Corbusier's Unité d'Habitation in Marseilles. The main structural piers of shuttered concrete rose from the ground in tapering buttresses, the long facades were deeply indented with double-height 'hanging gardens', the walls clad in exposed aggregate panels, the end elevations boldly modelled with wide cantilevered balconies. Where Matthew's building appeared to be assembled, as it were, from a kit of standardised parts, Spence's seemed cast, monolithic and monumental.

Hutchesontown Areas B & C, Gorbals, Glasgow
Photographs c1964
HES Canmore SC1150404, SC1052311

As at Hutchesontown/Gorbals, so in the increasingly prolific output of their respective offices, Matthew and Spence remained unequivocally committed to the theory and practice of international Modernism. There were, of course, as is evident at Gorbals, distinct differences of design emphasis. Matthew, much in the manner of Walter Gropius, concerned to achieve a rational impersonal resolution of the social, structural and technical problems of architecture through research and teamwork. Spence, moved by the poetics of Le Corbusier's architecture, was ever anxious to endow his buildings with some degree of formal zest, though too gentlemanly a designer to commit himself wholeheartedly to what soon came to be known as the New Brutalism. Yet both Scots still owned a measure of innate affection for their native tradition.

As a young architect, Matthew had spoken of the 'strong and almost unique character' of what he called 'Braid Scots in architecture'.[9] If this betrayed an admiration for the national architecture of centuries past, it did not necessarily imply any desire to emulate the formal legacy of Scotland's castellar tradition but rather the functional integrity of its vernacular building. The two were, of course, as Mackintosh had observed, often intimately connected, but for Matthew it was particularly in the functional 'honesty' of humbler buildings that lessons were to be learned and tradition fused with the ethos of the international Modern Movement. Besides this intellectualised relationship between the past and the present, he was attracted by the tactile quality of traditional local materials. Rubble stonework, for example, appeared in several designs, not only in low-density, low-scale housing but in larger projects such as power stations and university buildings. Commenting on Matthew's Turnhouse Airport buildings (1954–6), where stone was also incorporated, the Edinburgh architect Michael Laird claimed to detect what he believed to be 'the matrix of a new Scottish vernacular in the modern movement'.[10] This observation had, however, as much, if not more, to do with the austere ('chaste' was Laird's word) formal quality of the building's cubic geometry as its use of materials. Whether Matthew ever seriously envisaged his developing career as a 'crusade for Scottish Modernism', as some have suggested,[11] is open to doubt. In any event, as his practice was increasingly commissioned for major planning investigations and ever larger building complexes, drawing-board considerations of 'Scottishness' were pushed into the background. On the other hand, even while his expanding practice acquired international status and he set out to pursue the role of architectural diplomat on the international stage, Matthew was committing himself to the cause of conservation. Throughout the 1960s and into the 70s, openly acknowledging the debt the burgeoning heritage movement owed to Hurd, Lindsay and others in the 1950s and, indeed, to Lorimer long before, he was active in the Saltire Society, served on the Historic Buildings Council and Royal Fine Arts Commission, campaigned for the conservation of the New Town of Edinburgh, helped found the Scottish Civic Trust and advised the Secretary of State for Scotland on conservation policy.

The impact of Scotland's historical architecture on Spence was rather different in nature and development. At first as much a matter of formal pleasure as functional persuasion, it diminished as his career developed. In the 1930s, as he was establishing himself in private practice in a series of commissions carried out in a variant of the International Style tinged with Art Deco – for example, 11 Easter Belmont Road, Edinburgh (1934–5), Gribloch at Kippen (1937–9) and the pavilions he designed for the Empire Exhibition of 1938 – he was at the same time restoring Quothquhan in Lanarkshire (1938) in a plain Scottish Georgian idiom and building a new Broughton Place, Peeblesshire (1936–7) in a bravura Scottish Baronial style so Lorimer-like as to be almost the genuine article. Allusions to traditional forms and materials continued to appear in the post-war work of Spence's Edinburgh practice but in a much more muted way as, for example, in small housing enclaves at Dunbar (1949–52), praised by the Secretary of the Saltire Society, Robert Hurd, as setting 'an inspiring lead' to other burghs, and Newhaven, Edinburgh (1955–6), where the overall redevelopment plan had been devised by Ian G Lindsay. In the heart of Edinburgh, the practice built infill flats at 79–121 Canongate (1966–8) using traditional harling, rough-faced stonework and arched concrete canopies recalling the arcades of the Old Town. This long stretch of four-storeyed streetscape has been controversially

Canongate Flats, Edinburgh
Photograph c1968, elevation drawing c1965
HES Canmore SC684956, SC792276

described as 'one of the most curious manifestations of Scottish revivalism' *and*, perhaps for that very reason, 'some of the most stimulating (if aggressive) modern architecture in Edinburgh'.[12] But such projects formed only a small part of Spence's output. Like Matthew, Spence was inundated with more and more commissions – housing, schools, hospitals, offices and, especially, university buildings, including three completely new campuses – a workload of large projects which, particularly after he had decided to live and work in England, afforded little opportunity or context in which to pursue those design possibilities which some of his earlier Scottish-orientated work seemed to presage. Moreover, unlike Matthew, Spence, feted and honoured in England, played no personal part in the growing awareness of, and concern for, Scotland's architectural heritage.

Heritage has its history. As Charles McKean observed in 1990, 'the notion of a Scottish architecture, in a self-conscious way, goes back to c1845'[13] when Robert Billings published the first volume of his *The Baronial and Ecclesiastical Antiquities of Scotland*. No doubt, too, the lectures which John Ruskin gave in Edinburgh in 1853, the year following the publication of Billings' final volume, added to this awareness. Ruskin's main message might have been to commend the beauties of Gothic to his audience but his collateral rubbishing of classicism, his view that the much vaunted New Town of Edinburgh was 'nothing but square-cut stone – square-cut stone – a wilderness of square-cut stone for ever and ever',[14] and, not least perhaps, his occasional asides acknowledging the qualities of 'the ruins of Melrose Abbey or Linlithgow Palace or Lochleven Castle'[15] or 'the massy keeps of your Crichtoun and Borthwick and other border towers'[16] must have added the commendation of celebrity to the reviving interest in Scotland's own architectural tradition. Or was Ruskin simply advocating what was in part at least a somewhat anglicised view of the north – romantic, castellar, a wild land of mountain and flood? Certainly he failed to acknowledge the genuinely urban architectural tradition of Edinburgh's Old Town.

It might well be argued, of course, that awareness of the national tradition of building, if not its serious study, antedates these events. But it is with Robert Billings and even more with the later work of David MacGibbon and Thomas Ross that consciousness of Scotland's architectural heritage first acquired both its academic validation and that provocative creative edge which keened the work of Burn, Bryce, Anderson, Lorimer and particularly of Mackintosh. The Baronial Revival might sometimes run to excess but, across a wide range of building types, it was responsible for some of Victorian Scotland's finest and most distinctly Scottish architecture. And yet, despite the Revival's culmination in the informed and inventive efforts of Mackintosh to hone some kind of incisive consequence for contemporary design, the early decades of the twentieth century saw a dulling of this national edge.

As the new century progressed, the balance in the recurring dialectic between local and global cultural forces had shifted once more and by mid century the triumph of international Modernism was complete, the formal lineaments of architectural design in Scotland little, if at all, distinguished from what might be seen across the border, elsewhere in Europe, or beyond. On the other hand, perhaps not altogether paradoxically, awareness of the richness of the country's architectural heritage now intensified as the breadth and depth of academic knowledge and criticism developed and a concern for proper preservation, restoration and conservation expressed itself more confidently in organised institutional advocacy.

The Scottish architectural profession in its local and national manifestations had, of course, always been active (to varying degree) in the study and care of the built environment as well as its creation. And the existence of lay bodies dedicated to the stewardship of different aspects of the environment was not something new. As early as 1875 the Cockburn Association had been founded, becoming, in its support of the Edinburgh Old Town renewal movement, a forerunner in the determination of 'guidelines for conservation'.[17] In 1926 the Association for the Protection of Rural Scotland began to articulate concern for Scotland's countryside and for buildings in the natural landscape. The origins and objectives of the National Trust for Scotland (1931) and the Saltire Society (1936) have already been referred to above. Later, particularly from the mid 1960s, such amenity bodies proliferated. Among them were the Scottish Georgian Society (1959), which would transform itself into the more culturally catholic Architectural Heritage Society of Scotland (1984), the New Glasgow Society (1965), the Scottish Civic Trust (1967), self-styled 'champion of Scotland's places', the Edinburgh New Town Conservation Committee (1970) and the Charles Rennie Mackintosh Society (1973).

Parallel legislative developments at national and local government level empowered the increasingly visible and vociferous heritage movement. By far the most important statutory support came with the passing of the Civic Amenities Act in 1967 which afforded protection to listed buildings and made possible the designation and conservation of areas of architectural or historic interest. While central government continued to list significant buildings, local planning authorities, often under pressure from amenity associations, began to identify those buildings and groups of buildings to be given the protection of Conservation Area status. In Glasgow, for example, a few small city-centre Conservation Areas were quickly designated under the act. Then in 1971, following the recommendations of the Esher Report commissioned by the city of Glasgow, nine suburban areas were added and a much larger Central Conservation Area provisionally identified. In 1975, the boundaries of this downtown area were first defined in a major report prepared by the city's planning officer. Up and down the country, similar step-by-step developments, stimulated by committed local authority architects and planners, by the research of a small number of historians (most of whom were based in the Royal Commission on the Ancient and Historic Monuments of Scotland, the Scottish Office or in the architecture schools), and, by no means least, by the work of heritage group enthusiasts, gradually secured the long-term protection of Scotland's architectural heritage.

The success of the heritage lobby in winning statutory powers and raising both public and professional awareness was reflected in an increase in the number of architectural commissions related to the regeneration of existing buildings or groups of buildings. Such projects could entail the restoration of virtually every building type from cottage to castle – through the 1970s the Saltire Society awarded over 40 housing design commendations for this kind of creative reinstatement. More often, less rigorous but still sympathetic conservation was effected through rehabilitation, alteration and, perhaps, augmentation. Alongside the continuing practices of Hurd, Lindsay and Reiach, others began to specialise in this work whether in the highly academic and scientific field of painstaking faithful restoration or in more creative adaptation of existing buildings. The range of activity was all-inclusive, from tower-house and country house to the internal and external revitalisation of tenemented streets. Coincidentally, as national heritage impinged in these various ways on the workload of Scottish architects, the number of state- or local authority-led commissions had begun to diminish. Moreover, as architects in Scotland once more began to ponder the possible relevance of the national tradition to contemporary problems, at the level of international culture the very credo of mainstream Modernism was being called into question.

By the 1970s it was clear that, after a generation of more or less ubiquitous application to the building needs of the post-war welfare state, the Modern Movement, though hardly in decline, had lost some of its early assurance. In part, this was due to technical and social failures: flat roofs leaked, the physical and environmental sustainability of some buildings was suspect, regular building maintenance was poor, vandalism and alienation blighted many of the vast housing schemes and multi-storey flatted blocks built with little thought for community, amenity or landscape. But these problems, important as they were, were not the essential issue for architectural design: as one commentator observed, such '"problems" don't produce architecture. They produce instead "rational" solutions to oversimplified questions.'[18] This realisation, that architectural design was a much more nuanced activity than the mere 'problem-solving' of matters of function and building performance, and that architecture had more to offer than the univalent form and content of mainstream Modernism, was best articulated by the American architect Robert Venturi whose book *Complexity and Contradiction in Architecture* – 'the most important writing on the making of architecture since Le Corbusier's *Vers une Architecture*' – was first published in Britain in 1977. Venturi's message, his 'gentle manifesto' as he called it, was not that 'Less is more', as one of the high priests of Modernism, Mies van der Rohe, had declared, but rather that 'More is not less': architects should not be 'intimidated by the puritanically moral language of orthodox Modern architecture'[19] but should acknowledge the compelling historical evidence that architecture can afford a richness of form and content full of ambivalent delights. Architecture need not be confined by the forms of Modernist abstraction, nor by the single-minded 'puritanical' ethos these forms connoted.

To some extent, a less rigid adherence to the flat roof, flat facade forms of 'orthodox Modern architecture' was already evident in Scotland in the 1960s, as it was elsewhere. Mention has already been made of Basil Spence's almost Brutalist flats in the Gorbals, Glasgow (1960–6), but a similar attraction to more inventive spatial modelling and the use of strongly textured surfaces appeared, for example, in the remarkable work of Gillespie, Kidd and Coia, notably in St Peter's College at Cardross (1959–66) and St Bride's Church, East Kilbride (1963–4), in the megastructural sculpture of Geoffrey Copcutt's Cumbernauld Town Centre (1963–7) and in some more intimate projects realised in the later 1960s in the Borders by Peter Womersley. As designers were liberated from the formal straightjacket of Modernism's cubic massing and rectilineal facades, so, correspondingly, the full, Post-Modern, symbolic potential of architectural form began to be revealed. Instead of an architecture univalent in terms of form and content, polyvalent possibilities emerged with all the complexities, contradictions and ambiguities that entailed.

By the end of the 1970s, however, despite Robert Venturi's adjuration and Charles Jencks's headline-seeking proclamation of 'The Death of Architecture'[20] Modernism was by no means moribund. Nevertheless, having exchanged the patronage of the centralised socialist or social democratic state for the competitive market-place of multi-national capitalism, several alternative design options were evolving. These trends, indicative of a new pluralistic Post-Modern culture, were not always clearly distinguishable. Perhaps most convincing, though not without controversy, were the attempts at classification first articulated in 1982 by the architect, critic and historian Kenneth Frampton. Included in his putative canon was 'Populism', which embraced Venturi's 'cardboard scenography' of Main Street, adducing a free-wheeling radical eclecticism to architectural design which was, in Frampton's view, as superficial metaphorically as it was literally. 'Productivism', on the other hand, in its overt reification of the structural and environmental processes of architecture, appeared to perpetuate the technological allegiances of Modernism – if now in fetishistic form. A third approach, 'Rationalism', which also had affinities with Modernism, was, however, in Frampton's analysis, more in thrall to a

St Bride's Church, East Kilbride
HES Canmore SC856780

reinterpreted classicism. It would be possible to detect faint intimations of these changes in the work of some Scottish architects but this would be without relevance to the question of the Scottishness of Scottish architecture. For all of these tendencies, in terms of their respective form and content, could be regarded as global in their impact, each in its own way implying a world in which everything everywhere was the same. But Frampton identified a further trend in which the forms of 'orthodox Modern architecture' were variously modified according to contingent cultural context.

Given the contemporaneous impact of the heritage movement, it was not surprising that this 'Critical Regionalism'[21], even if not explicitly acknowledged, should find a sympathetic audience in Scotland. In 1986 a short paper entitled 'Local Roots and the Revival Cycle' appeared in *Prospect*, the quarterly journal of the Royal Incorporation of Architects in Scotland. In it, the ever-polemical Charles McKean, having attempted first to identify the 'essence' of Scottish architecture, relating this national quality to a series of familiar influences – materials, climate, location, the law, economics and politics, and a certain Calvinistic spirituality – went on to argue that, from the eighteenth century to the present, there had been four distinct architectural revivals of this Scottishness. These revivals he broadly dated to the 1780s and 90s, the 1850s and 60s, the 1890s and 1900s, and the 1930s. One may take issue with McKean on some aspects of his thesis (why, for example, is there no mention of Mackintosh? Can the tentative efforts of the 1930s be seriously compared to the achievements of the earlier periods?) but he was right to identify a recurring historical phenomenon which is not so much a matter of 'revival' in the sense of faithful reproduction as the recurring clash of international culture with local context, that cyclical dialectic between the history of art and the geography of art. He was surely also right to end his paper with a plea to contemporary Scottish architects to 'return to their roots for invigoration'.[22]

Cumbernauld Town Centre
Photograph c1990
HES Canmore SC702557

Mousa to Mackintosh

This question – 'how to be modern and return to sources', how to express both the spirit of the times and the spirit of the place – had been repeatedly asked and answered by such Scottish architects as Robert Adam, David Bryce, Robert Rowand Anderson, Robert Lorimer, Charles Rennie Mackintosh and those designers nurtured and stimulated by the extended influence of Mansfield Forbes' Cambridge coterie. It was, indeed, a question of more than architectural import, its immediate intellectual provenance traceable to the writings of the French philosopher Paul Ricoeur. Ricoeur's 1965 essay 'Universal Civilisation and National Culture' had addressed the fundamental dilemma of accelerating civilisation (a dilemma more keenly and potentially more tragically evident in the twentieth century than ever before), of how to promote liberating global access to material progress while still responding to 'the exigency of safeguarding our [regional] heritage'.[23] In short, how to reconcile the universal with the local. Posing this question in the context of architecture, it was Kenneth Frampton's insight to remind architects that such oppositions are 'mediated through form'.[24] But what forms?

For some it seemed that it was enough that the recovery of Scottishness be mediated, as it were indirectly, through reiteration of the formal vocabulary employed by Charles Rennie Mackintosh. At the most superficial level this entailed the decorative use of repetitive rectilineal grids as, for example, in the interior of Keppie Henderson & Partners' Sheriff Court in Glasgow (1980–6). A more architectural deployment of the same motif was, however, evident in the gridded glazing of the staircase towers of Andrew Merrylees' National Library of Scotland Causewayside Building in Edinburgh (1985–7), a design assimilation at once bolder and, in its distanced allusion to the glazing of the stair drums at Scotland Street School, more subtle. A more literal, and thus less convincing, reincarnation of these same Scotland Street stair towers was made in student housing on Collins Street, Glasgow (1983–90), designed by G R M Kennedy & Partners. There is nothing new, of course, in the incorporation of architectural quotation, that is to say the deliberate reference to a specific detail of a particular building or architect. It can be erudite and witty. But it can also be banal. Emulation of Mackintosh, however, failing to reach the deeper tradition underpinning much of his work, produced in the main only second-hand, ersatz goods. Condemned, on the one hand, to degenerate into cliché, on the other (when in 1988 Professor Andrew MacMillan was commissioned to build Mackintosh's partially designed Haus eines Kunstfreundes), it was prepared to settle for outright 'restoration'.

National Library of Scotland, Causewayside Building, Edinburgh
HES Canmore SC883876

If not Mackintosh, what then for those in search of a Scottish take on Modernism? In an essay entitled 'A Garden of Delights', published in the 1986 edition of *Prospect*,[25] Roger Emmerson presented what in his subtitle he described as 'preliminary notes for a developing theory of Scottish architecture'. Couched in these cautious terms – 'preliminary', 'notes', 'developing' – his argument nonetheless touched on several complex and contradictory theoretical issues affecting any critical appraisal of the history of architecture: he questioned the idea of any Golden Age or Ages, contended that opposite trends are simultaneously at work, observed the recurring cycle of growth and decay, and so took the view that any kind of equilibrium could only be temporary and impermanent. By addressing the question of a 'theory of *Scottish* architecture' he was, in effect, declaring himself a Critical Regionalist. Accordingly, while he was less than enthusiastic about what he saw around him, attributing the indifferent quality of late twentieth century Scottish architecture to (among other factors) 'intellectual timidity' and 'gung-ho philistinism', he was obliged to declare what forms, drawn from 'traditional Scottish architecture', architects might best espouse. In a last, less than optimistic paragraph he confessed that these were

> the old faithfulls: seemingly functional planning, mass construction, verticality, asymmetric elevations, bare walls, punched-out windows and elaborated upper levels. The facility with which [we] reel them off convinces us we know whereof we speak, but, at root, our seeming inability to effect satisfactory transformations of these elements … suggests that the cultural base for such a conceit as a Scottish architecture may no longer exist.[26]

John Jamieson Close, Lerwick
Photograph c1982
© Charles McKean. Licensor Scran

Looking back now with the benefit of hindsight, Emmerson's suggestion of a disappearing 'cultural base' seems unaccountably strange. As the 1980s came to a prestigious end with the designation of Glasgow as European City of Culture and the approaching millennium induced the nation to feel itself on the edge of an era as well as a continent, a sense of Scottish consciousness intensified and with it the feeling that a new beginning might be possible both in the arts and in the political arena. But Emmerson was writing in the mid 1980s and, as he reviewed the immediate past, his depressing assessment of the Scottishness of Scottish architecture is perhaps not so difficult to understand. Except in restoration and conservation projects and in some low-scale, new-build housing – modest developments at Tweedbank, Galashiels (1975), Commercial Street, Perth (1978), Harbourlea, Anstruther (1981), John Jamieson Close, Lerwick (1982), and in the New Towns of Cumbernauld and Irvine all won awards and commendations from the Saltire Society, Scottish Civic Trust and RIBA – there was little substantial evidence of any architectural desire to infuse contemporary problems with the spirit of traditional building. Perhaps the only truly successful marriage of the new and the old was that achieved by Nicoll Russell Studios at the Grianan Building, Dundee (1985–7) where a quadripartite glass box of two-storey offices, rigorously geometrical and urbane, was embraced and penetrated by a rolling wall of rural random rubble. It was a simple but potent relationship.

Writing in the mid 1990s,[27] Emmerson was more explicit about the need for 'a conscious attitude to Scottish culture' in order to 'free us from the threat that universal civilisation and its offshoot, mass culture, presents to authentic cultural tradition, its symbols and their meanings', but he remained unable to furnish his reader with any contemporary creative exemplars of such an attitude – except his own 'curved

Grianan Building, Dundee
Photograph 1988
Architectural Press Archive / RIBA Collections

Scots cubism'![28] As a practising architect, Emmerson, of course, had his own view on what such an attitude should entail. It was clearly his contempt for 'pastiche, reproduction, eclecticism and misplaced tradition' that precluded any discussion of the work of Ian Begg. Yet, in the context of considering the Scottishness of Scottish architecture, three major new-build projects carried out by Begg in the late 1980s and early 1990s, each unambiguously Scottish in its intent and content, demand critical evaluation.

Begg's Scottophile lineage was impeccable. In 1951 he joined the office of Robert Hurd, becoming a partner in 1963, the year in which Hurd died. Through the 1960s, 70s and 80s the practice's work was much concerned not only with the restoration of individual buildings – castles, churches and country houses – but with the restoration and revitalisation of historic townscape, particularly in the Old and New Towns of Edinburgh where Begg campaigned vigorously in defence of the city's exceptional urban heritage. As early as 1964, for example, the completion of Chessels Court on the Canongate, enlivened by street arcades and coloured harling, made a major contribution to the conservation of a streetscape which Begg regarded as 'the most important intense example of Scottish building existing'.[29] But it was not until the late 1980s that the opportunity to make a major new-build intervention on Edinburgh's Royal Mile presented itself. For an empty High Street site bounded by Blackfriars Street and Niddry Street, long an embarrassing gap in the fabric of the Old Town described by the Cockburn Association as 'one of the most important undeveloped urban sites in Europe',[30] Begg proposed a high-rise residential development which, taking into account the slope of the land, provided accommodation on ten levels – a clear evocation of the city's long established tenement tradition. Originally intended as flatted

Scandic Crown Hotel, Edinburgh
Photograph 1992
HES Canmore SC426694

housing augmented by shops, food market, workshops and others, the project was in fact finally realised as the four-star Scandic Crown Hotel (1988–90). The design responded brilliantly to its context not only in terms of street scale but, by respecting the through circulation routes of the old closes and wynds that had crossed the site, the building's facade was broken down into several vertically proportioned elements, an aggregative elevational strategy familiar in Baronial Revival design. Though the structure of the building was reinforced concrete, the exposed materials were traditional: rubble stonework, coloured harling and timber. So, too, were the forms: stilted chimneyed

Ravens' Craig, Plockton
Photograph 1992
HES Canmore DP236331

gables, attic dormers, jettied upper storeys and a cone-capped, cylindrical 'Holyrood-style' corner tower.[31] Begg described his design as a serious attempt 'to re-connect … with our earlier tradition'.[32]

At the same time as he was working on Edinburgh's High Street, Begg was engaged on another large new-build project on the High Street of Glasgow. Located off Cathedral Square, this was to be a visitors' centre for the Friends of Glasgow Cathedral but, as in Edinburgh, original intentions were aborted and the building became the St Mungo Museum of Religious Life and Art (1989–93). Essentially a tall, rubble-clad, L-plan tower-house, said to emulate in some respects the design of the former Bishop's Palace which had once stood on the site until its demolition in the eighteenth century, the museum was not embedded in a dense existing streetscape as was the case with the Edinburgh hotel but stood alone, albeit in relationship to some adjacent new buildings and spaces planned 'to show the Cathedral to better advantage'.[33] The museum's isolation, its unrelenting random rubble masonry, its recourse to 'old faithful' traditional forms (including even Gothic windows) dramatised its unapologetic, if somewhat sentimentally nostalgic, Scottishness. The design proved controversial, to some its architectural 'pretence' unacceptable.

Harled and much more intimate in scale, the home which Ian Begg built for himself, Ravens' Craig near Plockton in Ross and Cromarty (1987–9), offers a third piece of evidence with which to evaluate the architect's engagement with the idea of Scottishness in contemporary Scottish architecture. Seen externally, the building's tower-house form, its material and details, undoubtedly connect with 'our earlier tradition'. But the structure is of concrete blocks with reinforced concrete beams, there is underfloor electric heating and (besides a generous turnpike stair) a lift links the different levels; the building is a comfortable modern home. Between the outer perimeter wall and an inner wall, spaces are provided to accommodate stairs, stores, toilets, sitting and viewing neuks, a strategy taken perhaps from earlier tower-houses such as the demolished fifteenth-century Elphinstone Tower or even, as Mary Miers has suggested, 'borrowed from ancient brochs'.[34] Visitors speak of Ravens' Craig's intriguing spaces as confusing but delighting. While the building's exterior manifests a pleasant if relatively unmodified historicism, the experience of these internal ambiguities, both environmental and spatial –

what is old and what is new? – though modest enough, seems to bring a richer more piquant architectural reward. As Begg has written, 'The surprises and sequences of spaces experienced burst through the simple logic of it all, I like to think, like life.'[35]

Perhaps it is the very absence of such lively ambiguity in Begg's two larger buildings which limits and which, for all their sincere and sensitive Scottishness, to some extent impoverishes his architecture. Of course, there is the same contrast between the interior comfort and functional efficiency of a modern hotel or modern museum and the knowledge that this is being experienced within a historicist shell. And this may well afford a certain touch of ironical pleasure. But it is the lack of any ambivalence (*ambi*-valence[36]) of *external* architectural form which is the essential problem. One looks in vain for a creative engagement with the forms or formal relationships of Modernism, whether in their assimilation or transformation. This is especially true of the St Mungo Museum which makes no external concession to 'orthodox Modern architecture' and remains, for all its command of traditional forms, yet not quite convincing enough. The hotel, on the other hand, is more successful. Its traditional forms and materials are street-wise and contextual, a consequence perhaps of Begg's stated view that the tenemented streets of Edinburgh's Old Town are 'packed with tower-houses, cheek by jowl'.[37] On the other hand, the hotel's high walls of repetitive fenestration are inevitably a departure in scale and disposition from tower-house precedent, though this repetition of window size and alignment is hardly a conscious demonstration of the second principle – concerning

St Mungo Museum of Religious Life and Art, Glasgow
Peter Chisholm / Alamy Stock Photo

regularity – of Hitchcock and Johnson's International Style. Neither the museum nor the hotel exhibits that creative dialectic, that kind of formal conflict or aesthetic ambivalence which Robert Hurd, Begg's mentor, must have had in mind when, dreaming of *Building Scotland*, he and Alan Reiach filled the pages of their slim wartime publication with pictures of the crisp white architecture of international Modernism set provocatively alongside those of their own national tradition of building.

Ian Begg's life's-work endeavour 'to re-connect … with our earlier tradition', not only through the restoration of the country's damaged or derelict heritage but in the creation of new buildings capable of providing all the amenities of twentieth century living, must be held, in these terms, an unquestionable success. That he did not embrace the national *and* the international, that he was not prepared to challenge his allegiance to the forms and formal relationships of the indigenous tradition with those of Modernism, that he was unable, to use Emmerson's words, 'to effect satisfactory transformations', does not mean that he should be dismissed, as some have done, as a stubborn reactionary or mere purveyor of pastiche. In its mastery of the tradition, Begg's work is salutary, for while his revivalist aesthetic is *ipso facto* static, it is also fortuitously didactic, a timely declaratory display, a reminder – provocatively restated in the present – of the depth and range of Scottish building forms and materials that might, in other designers' hands, be deployed to contextualise Modernism.

It was surely this convincing display of Scottishness that, late in the 1990s, prompted the Canadian architect Moshe Safdie to seek Ian Begg's collaboration in a project of almost fairy-tale nature which most architects can only conjure in their most romantic imaginings. Commissioned to design a large (a very large) shooting lodge in a spectacular location on the shore of remote Loch Ossian, Safdie engaged Begg's practice, then known as né Begg, to act as executant architects on site. Begg himself had no part in the design, but the building, built between 1999 and 2004, unashamedly modern in its daring forms and much of its structure, did exhibit Safdie's quasi-Baronial take on the Scottish country-house tradition. The house rises to five storeys between low crowstep-gabled outbuildings which have survived from the original Corrour Lodge, completed in 1897 but later destroyed by fire in 1942. The accommodation is arranged as an assemblage of individual units, some rectangular in plan, some circular or semi-circular, each given its own three-dimensional expression

Corrour Lodge, Loch Ossian
Architectural model
Moshe Safdie Architects / Morris and Steedman Associates

and separated from its neighbour by a clear gap. Though the scale, elevational treatment and detail are wholly different, this asymmetrical aggregation of the plan elements is not dissimilar in principle to that adopted at Abbotsford. Three forms dominate the composition: the great hall, with its glazed quadrant roof leaning against a battlemented parapet, and two higher granite-clad masses, one cuboid, the other cylindrical, each punctured by randomly disposed 'hole-in-the-wall' windows. The masonry solidity of these two forms is dramatically slashed by elongated glass structures, one conical, the other pyramidal. There is nothing pedantically revivalist or historicist in all this, but, as Mary Miers has observed, while Safdie's design is conceived as a 'hard-edged, geometrical composition in an idiom daringly alien to the Highlands, it nonetheless expresses something of the stark grandeur of its surrounds [with] a suggestion, too, of tower and broch-like forms in the principal blocks'.[38] Safdie is not in the business of sacrifice or compromise, and Corrour Lodge is an attempt to bring time and place together, to create an architecture which is both contemporary and contextual. Whether he succeeds, whether this interplay of the now and the here, which is also an interplay of the new and the old, is satisfactorily resolved or not may be debated – the Royal Fine Art Commission for Scotland's view that the building was 'destined to become one of the few examples of world class twentieth century architecture in Scotland'[39] seems wildly overblown – but what is significant is that the game of synthesis is being played.

It was ironic that Safdie, someone with an altogether different cultural background, should have alluded, however subtly, to the Scottish tradition. Not many architects in Scotland were prepared to play the same game. Other than those rare cases where the client's brief might demand it, or in the context of restoration and conservation projects, where, should rehabilitation entail a measure of alteration or addition, the new and the old might co-exist (if not necessarily in any conflated form), or in certain relatively small-scale housing developments, where the parsimony and severity of traditional materials and forms might readily be re-presented in an austere modern idiom, there were few occasions where the nature of the problem suggested a design response bearing, at the very least, some kind of regionalist gloss. In the two decades overlapping the turn of the millennium there were several examples of historic

Pier Arts Centre, Stromness
HES Canmore DP114238

buildings brought back into use by a deft combination of careful restoration and added new-build. In such cases, success depended on preserving the distinct identities of the old and the new rather than any formal fusion. Notable in this respect was the work of Reiach and Hall at Loudoun Hall, Ayr (1995–7), and the Pier Arts Centre, Stromness (2005–7) and that of Elder and Cannon at Castlemilk Stables, Glasgow (2005–7). Over the same period, however, a number of practices involved in the design of housing did attempt to integrate the materials, forms and formal relationships of traditional building into the context of modern living. While speculative builders continued the numbing of middle-class taste with facing brick, concrete tiles and Tudor timbering, architects like Richard Gibson in Shetland, Dualchas in Skye and the Highlands, Malcolm Fraser in Bo'ness, Roan Rutherford in Irvine and Kilwinning, Page and Park in Newmilns, Studio KAP at Fintry, and several others experimented with a hard-edged, often white-walled, gable-ended domestic architecture that bore the austere inherited stamp of a viable vernacular. But, as already implied, this engagement with the national tradition was largely confined to individual houses and suburban or rural residential enclaves. One of the few successful urban examples, a project which by virtue of its conservation of historic streetscape character might as easily fall into the category of restoration, was the completion in 2004 of Tron Square housing on Old Fishmarket Close off the Royal Mile in Edinburgh by Richard Murphy. Detailed in the architect's instantly recognisable and uncompromisingly modern manner, the two flatted buildings are equally identifiable with those tall tower-houses which Ian Begg found 'cheek by jowl' along the streets of the capital's Old Town. In its plan the development maintains the dimensions of the medieval plots adding a new narrow close to the pattern. Harled walls with 'hole-in-the-wall' windows rise to the upper levels where, castle-wise, under pitched roofs, the formal activity intensifies with the introduction of timber cladding echoing the

Tigh na Drochaide, Duisdale Beag, Skye
© Dualchas Building Design, Licensor Scran

Mousa to Mackintosh

Tron Square Housing, Edinburgh

woolver / Alamy Stock Photo

National Museum of Scotland, Edinburgh
HES Canmore SC1377173

timber top storeys of earlier centuries. Responsive to location and tradition and without the least suggestion of pastiche or revivalism, Murphy achieves a wholly convincing contemporary Scottishness.

As much because of the quality of its designer as the demands of its embedded site, Tron Square is an exception. Faced with larger less circumscribed projects, most Scottish architects felt no inclination to modify or compromise what they regarded as the up-to-the-minute, internationally respectable quality of their designs with any concern for an indigenous tradition they saw as provincial and passé – and particularly not in projects above domestic scale. No more than a handful of designers seemed prepared to bring tradition into 'big league' open play. Of the few who did play the game, however, two practices scored notable successes.

In 1991, the firm of Benson and Forsyth was named winner of the international competition for the design of a new Museum of Scotland on Chambers Street in Edinburgh. To be sure, this was no greenfield site, requiring, as it did, both the re-creation of urban streetscape and a harmonious 'fit' to an existing related building, the Royal Museum of Scotland, an 'elegant Italianate palace'[40] designed by Francis Fowke in 1861. But the site was large and the brief no less so, the designation 'Museum of Scotland' succinctly describing the proposed merging of the extensive collections of the adjacent Royal Museum with those of the National Museum of Antiquities of Scotland then located across the city on Queen Street.[41] The design problem presented competitors with a task far from that of mere gap-site infill or modest 'keeping in keeping' enlargement. This was

National Museum of Rural Life, East Kilbride
John Peter Photography / Alamy Stock Photo

'big league' architecture: from the outset, the Museum of Scotland was intended to be a 'major new building [with] displays focusing on the history and culture of Scotland'.[42] As such, it was hoped it would become, in the enthusiastic words of Lord Bute, 'a sanctuary of national pride'.[43] Faced with this call to create a building which 'will be seen as a symbol of national identity'[44] – a Walhalla rather than a black box – Benson and Forsyth's design engrossed both past and present in a subtle and sophisticated Scottishness not seen since Charles Rennie Mackintosh.

It was not until 1996 that building began and two more years before the museum was opened to the public. Even so, the level of Scottish inspiration, so evident in the competition drawings, remained relatively undiminished. Around a tower of stacked galleries rising at the heart of the plan, the designers of the new museum wrapped an 'inhabited wall' of side galleries, staircases, circulation and orientation spaces, a conceit that was perhaps a magnified reinterpretation of the Elphinstone tower-house plan or, as Charles McKean has suggested, a version of 'a Gaeltachd medieval curtain-walled stronghold'[45]

such as Dunstaffnage. A tall, stone-clad, drum tower, its solidity penetrated by a number of shadowed openings with deep reveals, marked the junction of Chambers Street and Candlemaker Wynd with castellar drama. So, too, high on the skyline, jettied out over the central tower, a rooftop promenade and garden evoked a memory of the parapet walks and viewing platforms of Scottish castles. All this was accomplished not by revivalist repetition of traditional forms but by *trans*formation, by translation into an uncompromisingly modern language that owed much to Le Corbusier. Other Scottish architects had already shown themselves similarly indebted, notably Basil Spence and the Glasgow practice of Gillespie, Kidd and Coia, but, as the former failed to ally an otherwise evident respect for the Scottish tradition with post-Ronchamp form and the latter evinced no more than diffident intimations of Scottishness in their Corbusier-influenced work, no-one had achieved anything approaching the level of Post-Modern *ambivalence* so successfully embedded in the architecture of the Museum of Scotland.

The second practice to adopt a Critical Regionalist stance, Page and Park, did so in two major projects designed and built around the turn of the millennium. On a rural lochside site near Balloch, their Lomond Shores visitors' centre (1998–2002) soars to a height of 26m, a bold unexpected broch of a building wrapped in a drum of black whin rubble; in every sense, literal and metaphorical, a *tour de force*.

> Emerging unwrapped from this embrace is a second, inner drum, its implicit vulnerability toughened by white-harled solidity. This, too, has its provenance as, for example, in the gatehouse gables and turret that rise tentatively behind the great masonry of Dunstaffnage Castle … Between the two drums, a slow staircase ramp fills the circumferential gap. As the stair descends, so too does the dark immuring hug of whinstone, falling from its parapeted summit under a helical helter-skelter of glazing and stepping roof. So this is broch and castle too'[46]

But again, this is no pastiche. Again, past allusion and present need are provocatively fused. Taking advantage of the prospect north to Loch Lomond, a high wall of glass slices across the face of the broch. Laid above this and partially cantilevered beyond the curving wall of the drum is a wide glazed 'bridge', a high-level deck offering spectacular views intended no doubt to steer visitors' thoughts to dreams of Highland history and myth.

Much more reserved in its formal expression and thus less romantic in insinuation, Page and Park's Museum of Scottish Country Life, East Kilbride (1999–2001), now the National Museum of Rural Life, nevertheless also succeeds in conveying an appropriate and convincing Scottishness. Here there is no evocation of brochs, castles or tower-houses beyond, that is, the white walls, slated roofs and blocky massiveness of the building. But this is enough. Despite its 'unprecedented' scale for a building set in open countryside (the perimeter walls enclose a series of successive displays in a rectilinear spiral plan), a vernacular simplicity of material and form imparts an undeniable dignity. Yet besides this farm-like modesty there is, in the building's austere materials and its hard, foursquare massing in the landscape, something almost fortress-like.

The image of gaunt walls rising abruptly from the land is one repeatedly reflected in castle, cottage and broch back through the centuries. This relationship with the hard landscape is unequivocally Scottish: 'there is a deliberate, even brutal, detachment of stone from soil: architecture confronts nature'.[47] As the millennium came to an end, it seemed that the Catalan architect Enric Miralles, designer of the competition-winning Scottish Parliament Building (1999–2004), under construction at the same time as Page and Park's Museum of Scottish Country Life, had grasped something of this truth when he wrote that 'the parliament should be able to reflect the land it represents', adding by way of democratic validation his belief 'that individual identification with the land carries collective consciousness and sentiments'.[48] The Parliament Building's location at the lower eastern end of the Royal Mile, much criticised as it was, afforded Miralles the opportunity to respond not only to the city but also to the land, specifically to the landscape of Holyrood Park rising above Salisbury Crags to Arthur's Seat. While on the northern side of the site he contrived to heal the damaged urban fabric by the restoration of the late seventeenth century Queensberry House and the termination of Canongate in a strong street wall stretching to the corner with Horse Wynd, to the south of the new building he extended a spray of radial turf roofs and 'profiled earthworks'[49] intended to merge seamlessly into the open landscape of Holyrood Park. In this Miralles was, as the critic Dejan Sudjić has observed, 'suggesting that he wanted to build a parliament that felt like a natural part of the site, *rather than an imposition on it*'(my italics).[50] But it is – in part – in this very intention, with all its designed consequences, that doubts arise as to the degree to which the landscaping of the Parliament Building succeeds in evoking in Scots any recognition of national identity.

Moreover, it cannot seriously be argued that the building itself engages in any formal sense, whether explicitly or subtly engrossed, with the idea of Scottishness. The plan is wonderfully imaginative, a compressed fan of vesica shapes creating 'a "dense urban fabric"', which may imitate, if the Scottish writer Neal Ascherson is to be believed, 'the sort of built jumble which coagulates organically over centuries' and which, in turn, as if in desperate search for some indigenous comparison, he likens to 'a close-packed Fife fishing village'.[51] But this comparison is surely to push things too far. In fact, the plan is like nothing so much as the scatter of leaves and stems Miralles is said to have cast on the table when asked to describe his concept for the building. These leaves and the upturned boats which appeared on his competition drawings are the sources of his vision, *not* the past or present buildings of the Scottish towns and countryside. These simple sources are transformed by Miralles' genius into an architecture whose dispositions are open, non-hierarchical and thus appropriately democratic, whose external forms and formal relationships are complex and, if often overworked, nonetheless endlessly intriguing, and whose internal spaces, notably the garden lobby and debating chamber, offer experiences of rare delight. That the Scottish Parliament Building is an outstanding work of architecture is not in doubt – at least not in the estimation of architects and professional critics. Disagreements may exist as to the measure its greatness: Ascherson sees 'the most marvellous and imaginative public structure to rise in Europe for a decade';[52] for Sudjić it is 'one of the most remarkable pieces of new architecture in Britain for 30 years';[53] while, still more fulsome, Charles Jencks rates the Parliament 'without parallel in the last 100 years of British architecture'.[54] But the consensus is clear. Even if this enthusiasm is not universally shared it is not because the building lacks engagement with the forms or spirit of traditional

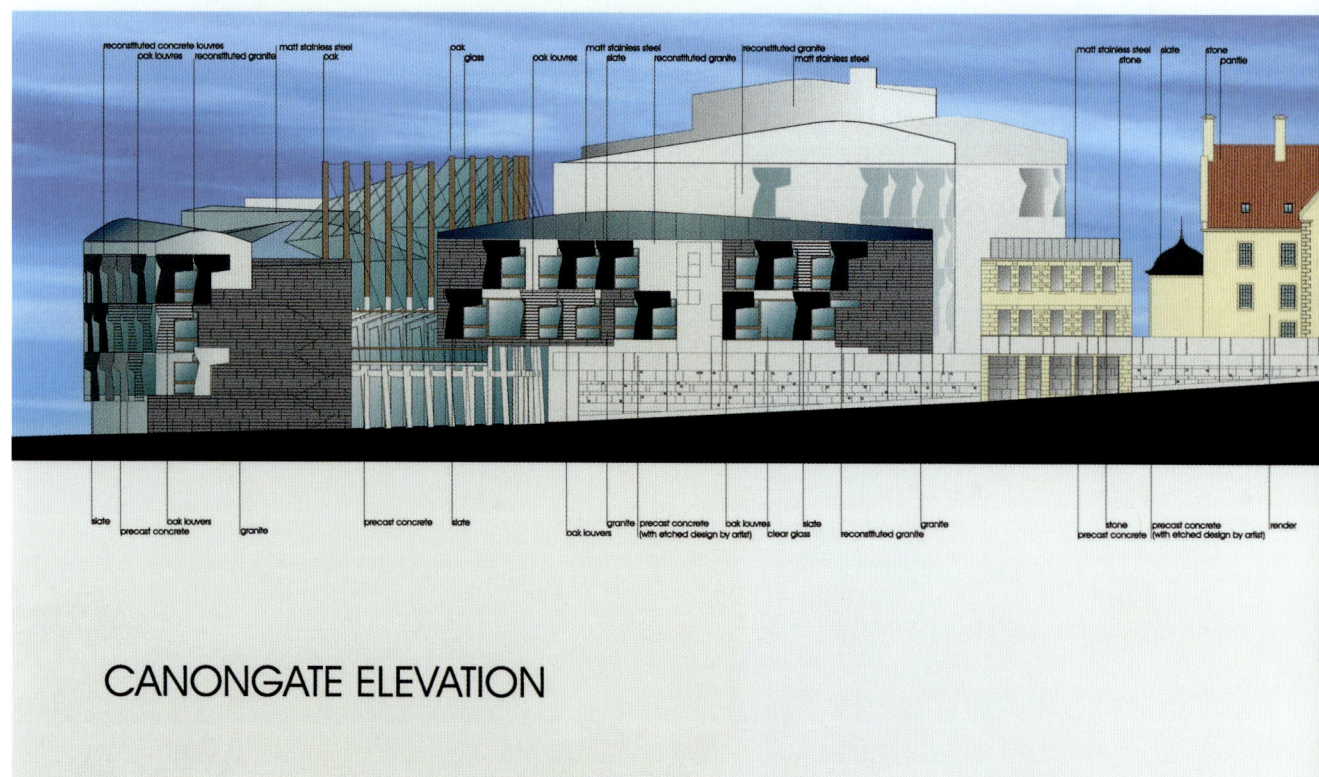

Scottish architecture but because Miralles has created something wholly without precedent and with only the most mystical of allusions.

Writing at the turn of the millennium in *Building a Nation: The Story of Scotland's Architecture*, in the very year that, following a national referendum and the passing of the Scotland Act 1998, the Scottish Parliament had been re-established, Ranald MacInnes maintained that hope for the future 'will undoubtedly focus on a building: Scotland's new parliament'.[55] It is perhaps both paradoxical and salutary then, at the end of this investigation into the Scottishness of Scottish architecture, to acknowledge, on the one hand, that this hope was not disappointed and, on the other, to remind ourselves that good architecture takes many forms.

Scottish Parliament, Canongate, Edinburgh
Planning elevation 2000
EMBT / RMJM / Scottish Parliament

Chapter 11
Envoi

'Yesterday returneth not'
carved on a garden wall at Formakin estate, Renfrewshire

In his work at Formakin, in the years before the First World War, Robert Lorimer was bound to the past through the nostalgia of the Arts and Crafts movement and love of the traditional forms of Scottish architecture. Yet there is a foreboding tone in this lithic inscription which merits reflection. And this is especially so at the end of a chronological review which has sought to identify and define the *recurring* presence of a particular architectural quality in a particular cultural context, namely 'the Scottishness of Scottish Architecture'. Does Scottishness return or doesn't it? In this survey of the historical development of architecture in Scotland, I have argued that this quality of Scottishness, a quality which time and again we recognise and identify in certain forms and formal relationships, *does* recur. I make no apology for discussing or evaluating architecture in terms of *form*, for form, it seems to me, is the revelatory essence of architecture not only in its creative realisation but in its ultimately aesthetic apperception. From time to time forms and formal relationships recur. *To some extent*, they are familiar, recognisable as yesterday's forms. And yet they are not. Except in the most slavish revivalism, the past is not simply repeated but rather, as a consequence of creative engagement, *trans*formed. It is as if, looking at a faded sepia photograph of our great-grandparents, we see something of ourselves in a fleeting impression, in the look of the eyes, in the tilt of the head. The genes betray us. In architecture, too, an elusive common identity can persist in the differing identities of successive generations.

But it is not so simple. In his book *The Undivided Past*, the historian David Cannadine reminds us

Formakin House
Photograph 1910
Country Life, Future Publishing Ltd

that 'Both individually and collectively, we are all creatures of multiple rather than single identities.'[1] In broad terms, 'beyond our differences', it is clear that we are – and here is the paradox – 'identical': we share a generational gene-pool; ultimately we share a common humanity. Yet, at the same time, we still remain individuals, each with his or her own unique identity. Moreover, identities change. We may remain individuals but the composite interactive nature of our individual identity is constantly in flux, challenged by new experiences both perceptual and intellectual. Again, there is a parallel with architecture.

In writing this book one of my intentions has been to try to rescue particular architectural identity not so much from neglect (for there is more than enough contemporary evidence of scholarly research, respectful restoration and condign conservation of Scottish building) but rather from the indifference and even denigration of those whose dismissal of *national* culture, affirmed with every good intention to eschew narrow provincialism, nevertheless renders the ostensibly progressive *inter*-nationalism they claim to espouse if not altogether void then certainly emasculated. And since, as Cannadine affirms, it is 'the primary job of the historian … not to assist in constructing the artifice of discrete, self-contained, self-regarding, and mutually exclusive groups',[2] but rather to seek and celebrate that which lies in the resolution of seemingly contrary forces, so it seems to me that there is always the need to recognise, interrogate and, in an open dialectic, synthesise in some way those cultural identities, local and global, which impact on architecture. There is always an engagement with the geography of art *and* the history of art, with the *genius loci* and the zeitgeist, with place *and* time. In such engagement a healthy indigenous culture, albeit as a reinterpreted tradition, continually strives to assert its relevance in the face of challenging and compelling new ideas. Intermittently it succeeds.

But only intermittently. To propose an ever-present Scottishness in Scottish architecture would be to ignore the historical evidence. Deceptively naive as it may have appeared, the cautionary reminder with which the last chapter of this book ended is important. Good architecture takes many forms. These forms (and formal relationships) may be apprehended, at one extreme, as predominantly those of international provenance and exchange, or they may, at the other, be distinctly national in their cultural legibility. Whatever the emphasis in the resolution of this creative dialectic, the degree to which the presentation of such forms may be evaluated as 'good architecture' will, of course, depend not only on the aesthetic delight they afford. Architecture is about commodity and firmness as well as delight; buildings need to provide shelter and convenience, they need to stand and not fall. But judgements will vary – person to person, era to era; there may be consensus, there may be disagreement. It is not my principal purpose to make such judgements (though no doubt my own preferences have been here and there apparent) but rather to bring into sharper focus the recurrent historical presence of a recognisable Scottishness in the architecture of Scotland. I have not been describing mere revivalism, still less pastiche; on the contrary, what seems to me from time to time properly present in the architecture of Scotland is a creative endeavour that is persistent, radical (that is to say, 'rooted') and transformative. Some may, however, regret and perhaps criticise my failure to bring into focus all that has been designed and built in Scotland over the very recent past. My response is twofold. In the first place, for the historian it is a dangerous venture to make precipitate judgements of the contemporary scene. Secondly, my cautious aversion, whether understood or criticised, may serve to stir the reader's own thoughts on just what is – or might yet be – the Scottishness of Scottish Architecture. I have chosen not to essay any prescriptive indication of what this Scottishness might be. That is not the historian's job. Still less have I wished to suggest that this Scottishness is always necessary, desirable or necessarily admirable. Only that it may be.

Writings on Scottish Architecture

Much has been written about the architecture of Scotland. For anyone, academic or amateur, stimulated to discover more about buildings seen and admired in town or country, there is no lack of descriptive or critical commentary. The bibliography is extensive. In a wide variety of ways the literary documentation of Scotland's built environment, an activity comprehensively pursued particularly from the mid twentieth century to the present, has been impressive.[1] Configured, more often than not, in historical perspective, these studies have been developed along three frequently intersecting but clearly distinguishable paths – the locational, the typological and the biographical.

No published survey of the country's built heritage has been more ambitious than that carried out by the Royal Commission on the Ancient and Historical Monuments of Scotland (RCAHMS), the government-funded body charged with the task of recording and interpreting information related to the built environment. Organised within a *locational* framework (county by county), the Commission's published Inventories deal in detail with the country's architecture (and archaeology) and though, because of the limitations imposed by their statutory brief, they have had little to say about buildings later than the first quarter of the nineteenth century, their coverage of earlier years is exemplary in its scholarship.

Beginning in 1909 with *Berwick*, some 30 volumes appeared throughout the twentieth century. By the 1990s, however, so demanding had been the academic standard of work called for that only half the country had been covered, while the task had become so financially burdensome that, following the publication of the last of the seven volumes dealing with *Argyll* (1971–92), the whole project was abandoned. That such a decision should – ironically – have been made at a time when, with a new devolved government in Edinburgh, Scotland was recovering much of its cultural and political self-respect, remains a loss to academic studies.

But, while the abandonment of the publication of these Inventories is regrettable, the Royal Commission's introduction of the Canmore database has created an unparalleled online resource. Canmore provides a comprehensive catalogue not only to Scotland's architecture but also to the country's archaeological, industrial and marine heritage; up-to-date detailed information, drawings, photographs and references have been made readily accessible to all. Assimilated into this database has been the work of a second governmental body, Historic Scotland (the two bodies merged in 2014 as Historic Environment Scotland), part of whose responsibility has been to compile 'lists of buildings of special architectural or historic interest'.[2] Successive legislation has elaborated this statutory obligation, the lists acting as a basis on which both national and local conservation policies have been developed and, by exerting a measure of planning control, protecting the country's architectural heritage. The lists are organised on a locational basis, each local authority district divided by parish and burgh. The decision to list a particular building or group of buildings is governed by published criteria, with each listing given one of three categories – A, B or C – according to its assessed importance or state of conservation. Each entry is accompanied by an architectural description recording map reference, address, the building's date(s), the name of the architect(s) involved, stylistic information (if appropriate), bibliographical references, and, of course, category. The elaboration and refinement of these descriptive lists is an ongoing process; the number of buildings designated to date is approaching 75,000.

Two commercially orientated publishing ventures, each in its own way as ambitious as the work of RCAHMS and Historic Scotland, have, in the last quarter of the twentieth century, been concerned with their own detailed locational coverage of the country's buildings. If these projects do not aspire to be as academically definitive in their studies of the architecture (and certainly not the archaeology) dealt with in the Inventories, they do, on the other hand, set out to be more comprehensive by covering the buildings of the nineteenth, twentieth and twenty-first centuries as well as those of earlier times. In *The Buildings of Scotland* series, published from 1978 by Penguin and from 2002 until the completion of the series in 2016 by Yale University Press, 15 weighty volumes have appeared, each polished, prestigious and as thorough as the moment will allow. In each area, detailed gazetteers describe and discuss a wide range of buildings regarded as architecturally distinguished, historically significant, idiosyncratically endearing and, not the least important in conveying the spirit of a particular place, unspectacularly characteristic. Less scholarly perhaps, but written and illustrated to be accessible to a wide readership, a parallel programme of publication undertaken by the Royal Incorporation of Architects in Scotland has, since 1982, produced a library of pocket-book architectural guides, their appearance averaging roughly one a year until 2008. Some 30 or so of these guides have been published, covering almost all the shires and administrative districts of the country. These two series, each framing factual information and measured critical comment in a locational context, represent a major cultural achievement and, while it would be dangerous to assert that this coverage is without precedent elsewhere, it is beyond question an invaluable and enviable resource. Several other more focused place-specific studies, notably a number of admirably researched books dealing with the architecture of Scotland's largest cities, Edinburgh, Glasgow, Aberdeen and Dundee, have deepened this knowledge and evaluation, while many other publications both scholarly and academically less rigorous have thrown light on the built development of smaller towns across the country.

The number and scope of *typological* studies is no less wide-ranging. Almost every important building type has found its willing apologist, and frequently more than one. A wealth of detailed research and comment has appeared on castles, churches and country houses, though until more recently rather less on those urban, industrial and rural buildings that have shaped the physical environment of the vast majority of the population. Such attention to building type is not, of course, a phenomenon of more recent scholarship. The works of Grose (1789–91), Billings (1845–52) and MacGibbon and Ross (1887–92 and 1896–7) constitute a long and respectable tradition in which the description and illustration of Scotland's architectural 'antiquities', both castellated and ecclesiastical, advanced from the picturesque to the scholarly. Probably often as much a matter of patriotic celebration as disinterested academic investigation, this documentation of castles[3] and churches,[4] augmented by an interest in the decoratively fortified and unfortified 'châteaux'[5] of the nobility, continued into the twentieth century. Studies of the *Shrines and Homes of Scotland*,[6] as one 1930s publication was entitled, proliferated as numerous writers, both amateur and professional historians, added a growing body of knowledge and appraisal.

As the recorded evidence accumulated and intensified so, from time to time, did each new commentary glint with a new interpretative gloss. Over time, however, and as church buildings emptied and religion found itself side-lined in an increasingly secular Scotland, as the aristocracy and the landed classes, no longer identified with national dignity, found themselves impoverished and redundant in a less subservient, more confident, egalitarian society, so some architectural writers began to turn their attention from the past to the present, from castle, church and country house to the humbler buildings of the Scottish burgh and those of the more modern world. Since no building type was more ubiquitous and none more directly experienced, the Scottish tenement became the focus of studies. This led not only to a number of documentary and analytical publications[7] but, through the work of ASSIST[8] and others, effected a radical revalorisation of the urban housing stock leading in turn to a redemptive transformation of the Victorian and Edwardian flatted streets and terraces of Scotland's cities and towns. It was a measure of both the academic and popular success of these achievements that the Tenement House in Buccleuch Street, Glasgow,[9] was adopted into the canon of the National Trust for Scotland, an organisation otherwise largely orientated towards the grander, predominantly castellar buildings of the past. More recently, notably in the published research of Historic Scotland and RCAHMS, the study of house types has moved on from the tenement to look in detail at later speculative suburban housing[10] and multi-storey flats,[11] though as yet there appears to be little comparable nostalgia, whether architectural or social, for high-rise living.

Besides housing, other building types have received scholarly attention. Industrial archaeologists have recorded the forms, structures and materials of mills, foundries, factories, docks, bridges, railway stations and more, often remarking their continuing cultural significance as much as the economic role they originally played in shaping our modern environment.[12] Others have applied similar analytical and classificatory methods to the buildings of the countryside,[13] a field of architectural study for too long disregarded. In the towns, tolbooths, town houses, schools, hospitals, cinemas and warehouses have been scrutinised. Perhaps the most ambitious coverage so far attempted has been the comprehensive commentary on *Scotland's Buildings*[14] prepared as Volume 3 of the 14-volume Scottish Life and Society series. At one end of the typological spectrum, the city itself has been viewed from an architectural perspective with several studies of the urban form of Scottish cities, towns and villages appearing; royal burgh plans of the twelfth century; planned communities of the eighteenth century; neoclassical expansion in Edinburgh, Glasgow and Aberdeen; New Towns of the 1950s and 1960s:[15] all these have been studied. At the other end of the typological range, there is both the garden,[16] more often than not the garden of the castle or mansion-house, and also, where researchers have returned to look at the country house in yet more intimate detail, the interior.[17]

Many *biographical* studies of Scottish architects have also added to the corpus of information and interpretation. Among important monographs, all, of course, by their very nature set within a historical framework, are those dealing with William Adam, Robert Adam, Alexander Thomson, Robert Rowand Anderson, Charles Rennie Mackintosh, Robert Lorimer, James Salmon and Basil Spence. Of these, figures of acknowledged international status such as Robert Adam, 'Greek' Thomson and Charles Rennie Mackintosh have naturally drawn the attention of numerous scholars worldwide who, while in some cases compiling an exhaustive list of works, have also extended the spectrum of study well beyond the purely 'archaeological' to the critical and theoretical. The Mackintosh architecture website, Mackintosh Architecture, Context Making and Meaning, hosted by the University of Glasgow, is a remarkably comprehensive critical catalogue of Mackintosh's architectural design projects, both built and unrealised. Many other lesser-known individual designers, as well as a number of influential architectural practices, have also been the subject of research. Much, though not all of this has, has been and continues to be absorbed into the Dictionary of Scottish Architects 1840–1980, probably the most exhaustive online architectural archive in the world. Drawing on the life-long researches of the doyen of Scottish architectural historians, David Walker, this astonishing resource, begun in 2002 and ongoing, attempts to document the life and work of every architect active in Scotland in a span of time covering most of the nineteenth and twentieth centuries. Personal details of family, education and architectural practice are included. Individual buildings are identified by type, place and date. In effect, locational, typological and biographical (and indeed bibliographical) data are concentrated in a freely available single archive. In this respect, no country has been better served.

And yet in all this endeavour, in all the surveys, catalogues and monographs, in all that has been accomplished, inclusive and informative as it aims to be, and admirable as it undoubtedly is, there is a danger that bigger issues are set aside. It is one thing to study the trees, quite another to grasp the nature of the wood, let alone acknowledge that the wood itself is but part of a larger landscape. Of course, it would be grossly unfair to criticise the compilers of regional inventories, building type studies or biographical research for taking the narrow view; it is the very purpose of such work to exercise a sharp and circumscribed focus. On the other hand, while it is understandable that the broader supervening matter of what it might be that characterises and identifies the *Scottishness* of those Scottish places, buildings and architects should be regarded as taken for granted, it is surely reasonable to expect this issue to be confronted when the area under investigation is the whole country. Put more succinctly, as the level of context is raised, different questions arise: what, one must ask, distinguishes Scottish architecture in the context of international culture?

While the detailed study of Scotland's built heritage and the architects who created it has been and continues to be academically thorough and the consequent literature extensive, there have been remarkable few attempts to deal with Scottish architecture *as a whole*. In the past, discussion of Scottish architecture in wider British or European contexts has all too often been ill-informed and patronising, consigning built events on the Atlantic edge to little more than a dismissive footnote. In the last half century or so, however, a number of architectural historians based in Scotland have attempted to set the record straight. In the 1990s, Edinburgh University Press embarked on a publishing programme intended to cover the subject in a series of volumes each dealing with a carefully defined historical period. Richard Fawcett's *Scottish Architecture: From the Accession of the Stewarts to the Reformation, 1371–1560* appeared in 1994 and in the following year Deborah Howard's *Scottish Architecture from the Reformation to the Restoration, 1560–1660*.[18] But the planned coverage has never been completed and the individual published volumes remain limited to their particular historical context rather than part of a longer narrative. Only a few books have attempted the broader view.

One of the earliest of these, appearing in 1938, was the simply but significantly named *The Stones of Scotland*,[19] written perhaps in reaction to the inter-war 'cosmopolitanism' of the international Modern Movement. Edited by George Scott-Moncrieff, whose introduction scourged the romantic sentimentality of much Scottish history, the abrogation of 'those who should be responsible custodians' of the built environment and the regrettable 'indifference of the Scottish people', the book describes several aspects of the development of the country's architecture from prehistoric times until the early nineteenth century. The scope was broad, though not exhaustive, and included some serious attention to the humbler dwellings of the Scottish burgh. Judged from today's perspective, however, the book's success is compromised by a failure (understandable in its historical context) to deal with the Victorian period[20] and by the absence of any linking thread of Scottishness that might have been abstracted from its various authors' contributions.

In *The Historic Architecture of Scotland* (1966), still an authoritative and highly respected text, John Dunbar begins his examination with the evidence of the twelfth century (a date which those with an archaeological perspective might regard as much too late) and ends (many would say prematurely) with the late Georgian period. Once again the rich built legacy of more modern times is ignored. Commendably, however, besides dealing with the grander architecture of castle, church and country house, Dunbar also gives generous space to industrial buildings, bridges and farms, though only within the restricted time frame. A year later, in the preface to his *A History of Architecture in Scotland* (1967), T W West observed that no concise survey of 'the entire field of architecture in Scotland from the prehistoric and Celtic periods to the work of the public authority housing departments of our own time' yet existed. Eschewing any scholarly pretension, his attempt to fill the vacuum provided an introductory account of the country's long built history, straightforward and informative, but no more detailed than his own clear if somewhat naive sketches with which the book was generously illustrated. It remained the only such survey for more than a quarter of a century.

In 1996 a much more ambitious and scholarly text appeared. The chronological span of *A History of Scottish Architecture* (1996) by Miles Glendinning, Ranald MacInnes and Aonghus MacKechnie was, however, still curtailed. Beginning, even later than Dunbar, with the impact of Renaissance ideas towards the end of the fifteenth century (as the book's subtitle, *From the Renaissance to the Present Day*, makes clear), the authors did, nevertheless, carry their study to the last quarter of the twentieth century. The book is a majestic work, intensely informative, scholarly yet accessible: if it disappoints a little by largely ignoring industrial and rural buildings, the breadth and detail of its description and discussion of both nineteenth century and twentieth century architecture (the first publication ever to present a comprehensive account of the latter) are unsurpassed.

Here and there these books touch on what Dunbar refers to as 'the distinctive characteristics of [a] national style',[21] though Glendinning, MacInnes and MacKechnie are particularly cautious on this question, content to define their working understanding of the term 'Scottish architecture' as 'all architecture in Scotland, or built elsewhere by architects based in Scotland'[22] and leave it at that. Both books do, however, note a number of specific traits in Scottish building and both recognise wider contexts by acknowledging the influence of various European precedents, but in neither study is there an attempt to distil a distinctly Scottish spirit in Scottish architecture. Nor is this achieved by Glendinning and MacKechnie's *Scottish Architecture* (2004), though this concise compendium, if restricted in its text, is, like West's earlier survey, more ambitious in its historical scope. Covering the subject in a succinct chronological account that stretches from Neolithic times until the present day, it makes the rather grand claim that 'Scotland is almost unique among smaller European nations in the distinctiveness and richness of its architectural heritage'.[23] Yet in a brief concluding commentary the authors are tentative in identifying common themes bound up in this distinctiveness. The relatively unchanging influences of climate and geology, the use of stone as a building material, these are seen as unbroken threads. The importance of the castle, as building type and image, and the strength of classical architecture are suggested as subordinate recurring themes. Perhaps most intriguing is their perception of a persistent openness to 'radical change and discontinuity ... unmatched by any other small country',[24] though this Parthian shot is scarcely substantiated. And there is no extended analysis, nor any attempt to define or even adumbrate what might be the characteristic formal attributes of this so distinctive Scottish architecture. In *Building a Nation: The Story of Scotland's Architecture* (1999), MacInnes, Glendinning and MacKechnie set out to tell 'the whole story', examining the evidence for 'a Scottish architecture'.[25] But once again the story opens late (1500), again the narrative continues to the present, and again the investigation reveals little to distinguish the nation's architecture beyond the fact that Scottish buildings have generally been 'more monumental, more solid than their European counterparts'.[26]

It is in the belief that more can be said that this book has been written.

Glossary

A

aedicule
an architectural frame comprising two columns or pilasters supporting a pediment

Antique
'the Antique' – ancient Greek or Roman culture

apse
semi-circular or polygonal end to an apartment, especially the chancel of a church

arcade
a row or series of arches carried on columns

architrave
the lintel-like lowest element of an entablature

Art Deco
a style of design in architecture and the decorative arts current in the 1920s and 30s. Using bold colours, strong geometrical forms and at times streamlining, it was often jazzy and decadent in character. The name derives from the Exposition Internationale des Arts Décoratifs et Industriels Modernes, held in Paris in 1925.

Art Nouveau
a style of design in architecture and the decorative arts prevalent in the 1890–1910 period. In breaking free from established historical styles it employed sinuous and attenuated forms drawn from nature.

Arts and Crafts
a late nineteenth century movement in design advocating truth to materials, high levels of craftsmanship and the integration and collaboration of the fine arts, decorative arts and architecture

Ashlar
masonry of stone blocks with dressed faces and square-cut edges

astragal
a glazing bar between glass panes

astylar
lacking any clear style; in a Classical building, having no columns

attic
in a Classical building, the storey above the main entablature

B

balustrade
a run of short pillars or balusters, often bellied in form, supporting a coping ledge or rail

barbican
defensive outwork at the entrance to a castle

baroque
a style strongly developed in Europe between the late sixteenth and early eighteenth century. In architecture it broke away from the stricter disciplines of the Renaissance, favouring greater drama, extravagance and inventiveness, often entailing the interplay of concave and convex shapes.

bartizan
a round or square corbelled turret

bastion
a defensive structure, circular or polygonal in plan, projecting from the main wall of a castle, fortress or city

bay
a division of a wall or space regularly defined by arches, columns, windows, etc

bay window
a window one or more storeys high which projects from the wall face

bellcast
that part of a sloping roof which reduces in angle over the eaves

billet
a moulding of small rectangular or half-cylindrical blocks set in line

boss
a knob or projection, eg at the intersection of vaulting ribs

bow window
a curved window, projecting from the wall face

brattishing
ornamental wallhead cresting, often of miniature battlements

broch
a tower-like structure of double-wall drystone construction, its circular plan diminishing slightly towards the wallhead. Thought to have been places of security in time of danger, brochs date from between 100 BC and AD 100 and are found in west and north Scotland.

Brutalism
a trend in architectural design during the 1960s and 70s which favoured bold forms and rough materials such as unfinished concrete

Byzantine
a style originating in Byzantium (Constantinople) in the fifth century AD. The round arches, vaults and domes of Roman architecture were adopted, though decorative ornament of symbolic significance was preferred to more orthodox strictly classical detail.

C

cable
a moulding shaped like the twisted strands of a rope

cairn
a heap of stones forming a mound over one or more burials

canted bay window
a bay window with a straight front and angled sides

caphouse
a small chamber at the head of a turnpike stair opening to a parapet walk

capital
the head or crowning element of a column

cashel
a ring-fort of drystone walling

castellation
battlemented parapet

chevron
a moulding of successive V-shapes

choir
that part of a cathedral or church where services are sung; located beyond the crossing of the plan

Classical
a term used to describe the architecture of Ancient Greece and Rome and its revival in Renaissance and later times

clearstorey
the uppermost storey of a church where windows provide light to the interior

close
a court, yard or vennel allowing access to a number of buildings. Also used to describe the passage leading to the common stair in a tenement.

colonnade
a range of columns supporting a continuous entablature (not arches)

corbel
a brick or stone projecting from the wall to support something above; often in the form of a continuous corbel course carrying a parapet or wall-plate

Corinthian
the third and most slender of the three Classical orders; the capital is ornamented with acanthus leaf

cornice
a projection at the top of a wall, flat-topped with the underside decoratively moulded; the uppermost element in a Classical entablature

crannog
a small man-made island constructed in timber, earth and stones, built to support a dwelling

crenellation
a battlemented parapet; the name derived from the crenels or regular openings formed

Critical Regionalism
an approach to architecture evolved in the late twentieth century which, in rejecting both the austere 'placelessness' of much Modern architecture and the caprice and ornamentation of Post-Modern architecture, reasserted the value of localised cultural context

crocket
in Gothic architecture, a leafy hook or knob of stone formed on a capital or along the edge of gablets, pinnacles, etc

crown spire
a church steeple in which curved flying buttresses create the shape of an open crown

crowstep
a squared stone step in a series of such steps along the skew of a gable

cupola
a small dome on a larger dome. Also a small lit dome over an internal space such as a stairwell

curtain wall
a glazed wall facade independent of a building's structure. Also a masonry wall between castle towers

D
Diocletian window
a semi-circular window with two mullions, also known as a thermal window

Doric
the first and plainest of the three Classical orders; the capital is plain but the column fluted

drum
a masonry structure circular or polygonal in plan, sometimes supporting a dome or cupola

dun
a small stone-walled fort

E
embrasure
a splayed recess or opening in a masonry wall

engaged (portico/column)
partially merged into the wall

entablature
in Classical architecture the collective term for cornice, frieze and architrave carried by columns or wall

F
fenêtres en longueur
horizontal bands of glazing appearing in International Style architecture

finial
a spikey ornamental feature on a cupola, gable or spire

fluting
vertical concave grooves on a (Doric) column

forework
a structure protecting an entrance

Functionalism
the theory that the form buildings take should derive solely from their function or purpose

G

garderobe
a privy built into the thickness of the external masonry wall of a castle or tower-house

gatehouse
a building incorporated into the gated entrance to a castle

giant order
in Classical architecture an order carried through two or more storeys; also known as 'colossal order'

Glasgow Style
an approach to design evident in the art, decorative arts and architecture of Glasgow in the period from 1890 until the First World War; in its sinuous natural shapes and often elegantly attenuated forms essentially a manifestation of Art Nouveau

Gothic
the style of the medieval period characterised by the structural and decorative use of the pointed arch

Gothick
a somewhat romantic and less than scholarly eighteenth century revival of medieval architecture preceding the more archaeologically correct Gothic Revival of the nineteenth century

gunloop
an opening in a wall for a firearm

H

harling
wet dash rendering to a stone wall

historicism
in architecture the revival of historical style(s) whether in a strict scholarly way or a more eclectic manner; characteristic of much nineteenth century design

hood moulding
a profiled moulding projecting over a lintel or arch intended to throw off water

I

International Style
a cosmopolitan style of architecture current in the 1920s and 30s, it rejected historicism in favour of forms held to be abstract, rational and derived from the building's function. It was characterised by an emphasis on volume rather than mass, planar surfaces, repetitive mass-produced elements and a rejection of ornament

Ionic
the second of the three Classical orders; the capital is distinguished by volutes (inward curving spirals)

J

Jacobean
an architectural style originating in the seventeenth century characterised by shaped gables, strapwork, emblematic ornament

jamb
the vertical side of an opening in a wall; also a wing or extension abutting a rectangular block, eg in a tower-house

jetty
the projection of an upper storey over the wall below, usually in timber-framed structures

L

label stop
an ornamental projection or boss at the end of a hood moulding

M

machicolation
a series of openings between corbels carrying a parapet; used decoratively in post-medieval castles and country houses

Mannerism
a style in the painting, sculpture and architecture originating in later sixteenth century Italy in which elongation, distortion and a general disregard for conventional Classical methods and motifs prevailed

Modern Movement/Modernism
in architecture, broadly the style of the twentieth century which rejected historicism and revivalism in favour of a more analytical and rational approach expressed through unadorned geometry

modillions
small brackets on the underside of a cornice, often an eaves cornice

mullion-and-transom window
a window the glazed lights of which are divided by vertical (mullion) and horizontal (transom) members usually of stone

N

nave
the body of a cathedral or church west of the crossing of the plan

neoclassicism
an eighteenth century approach to the revival of Classical art and architecture emphasising a purity of form and composition, especially that of Greek sculpture and architecture

New Architecture
a catch-all term used in the early days of Modernism

Norman
the term used in English architecture to describe the Romanesque architecture of the eleventh and twelfth centuries; it is characterised by the use of the round-headed arch both structurally and decoratively

O

oculus
a circular opening

ogee
a curve bending one way and then the other; an ogee or ogival arch or roof is pointed at its apex

orders
the versions of the post-and-lintel system of construction adopted in Classical architecture. There are three principal orders – Doric, Ionic and Corinthian – Greek in origin but appearing also in Roman versions.

oriel window
a bay window on corbels or brackets above ground level

P

Palladian
relating to the built work and writings of the sixteenth century Italian architect Andrea Palladio, knowledge of which was introduced to Britain first in the seventeenth century and in the following century had a widespread impact, particularly on country-house design

pediment
a formalised gable above the frontal and rear colonnades of a Classical Greek or Roman temple; the form was later adapted to surmount aedicules, windows and doors

peripteral
of a Greek or Roman temple having a perimeter colonnade or peristyle

peristyle
a colonnade all round a Greek or Roman temple

Perpendicular
the last phase of English Gothic architecture characterised by the use of four-centred arches and fan vaulting

perron staircase
a central stairway rising in a double curve plan to a doorway

piended roof
a roof with hipped ends rather than gables

pilaster
flat low-relief representation of a Classical column

pinnacle
a spike or turret-like termination to a buttress, parapet, etc

portico
a columned pedimented porch

Post-Modernism
a controversial term generally used to describe the late twentieth century reaction to Modernism, a reaction which reintroduced historical forms and decorative elements often in an ironic way

Q

quadrant
a range of buildings, often service wings, following a quarter-circle concave plan; appearing in flanking pairs symmetrically abutting a country house

quoin
a stone block at the corner angles of buildings distinguished in some way from the stonework of the wall surfaces

R

range
a stretch of building

re-entrant
an L-shaped angle of plan, eg that formed between a tower-house and its abutting jamb

relieving arch
an arch built into a wall to relieve superimposed load, often constructed above a lintel

Renaissance
in architecture the rediscovery and re-interpretation of the forms and ornament of Classical Greek and Roman building occurring first in fifteenth century Italy

Rococo
an eighteenth century European style developing from baroque but more intimate than dramatic; characterised by asymmetry, shell-like shapes and almost organic forms, it was essentially concerned with interior design

roll moulding
a moulding of semi-circular or more than semi-circular section

Romanesque
a European style of the eleventh and twelfth centuries based on the use of the round-headed arch both in structure and ornament. The British equivalent term is Norman.

round
a rounded turret, usually roofless

roundel
a circular plate or a small decorative circular window

roundhouse
a prehistoric dwelling built to a circular plan

rustication
a variety of textured treatments of masonry to give emphasis or suggest strength; usually on base courses or quoins

S

saddleback roof
a pitched gabled roof on a tower

skew
plain or shaped stones forming the sloping edge of a gable upstanding from the roof surface

snecked
of stonework where regular courses are broken by smaller stones

socle
a plinth without ornamentation

strapwork
stone ornament in the form of interlaced leather straps

string course
a horizontal band or moulding projecting from the wall surface

stylobate
the top of the stepped platform acting as a base for a Classical temple

T

tetrastyle
describing a portico with four frontal columns

tourelle
turret

trabeation
a system of building based on post-and-lintel construction

tracery
openwork masonry or timber in an opening, especially the upper part of the opening; generally arcuated in form

triforium
the middle storey of a church interior

triumphal arch
originally a free-standing Roman monument of a single archway or a central main arch flanked by minor arches; the motif adopted in later architecture

turnpike stair
a helical staircase ascending round a central newel; also known as a spiral stair

V

vallum
ramped earthwork around a Roman camp

Z

ziggurat
a massive masonry structure of stepped pyramidal form

Notes

Introduction

1. This is how Scotland's leaders described their geographical situation to Pope John XXII in the 'Declaration of Arbroath' of 1320 (*RPS* 1320/4/1. Date accessed 16 December 2022).
2. The earliest legislation regarding woods was in 1425 (*RPS* 1425/3/11 and 12. Date accessed 22 December 2022), but it was certainly not the last time.
3. It was reputedly Pope Martin V who said: 'In truth, the Scotch are the only antidote to the English' on hearing of the victory of a French army led by the Scottish earl of Buchan against the English Duke of Clarence at Baugé in 1421 (see, for example, Beale, 1859, 76).
4. NatureScot, 'Managing the Land', updated 27 January 2023, www.nature.scot/professional-advice/land-and-sea-management/managing-land; Scottish Government, 'Scottish Agricultural Census', June 2018, www.gov.scot/publications/results-june-2018-scottish-agricultural-census/pages/2/; Scotland's Environment, 'Land Use and Management', November 2011, www.environment.gov.scot/media/1211/land-land-use-and-management.pdf
5. Ditchburn and Macdonald, 2001, 97; National Records Scotland, 'Mid-2021 Population Estimates Scotland', last updated 13 July 2022, www.nrscotland.gov.uk/statistics-and-data/statistics/statistics-by-theme/population/population-estimates/mid-year-population-estimates/mid-2021; UK Population Data, 'Population of England 2022', populationdata.org.uk/population-of-england. England's population had reached Scotland's current one by 1700. By 1800 it was nearly 8 million; by 1900 it had ballooned to 30 million and was nearly 50 million in 2000. While other factors must be taken into account to explain economic development and urban expansion, geography clearly plays a crucial role.
6. See Watson and Dixon, 2018, Introduction and elsewhere for a more detailed exploration of Scotland's early history and the relationship between topography and human activity.
7. See Clancy and Crawford, 2001, 44 onwards for an analysis of the impact on the coming of Christianity to Scotland.
8. Armit, 1998, 130–2; Annals of Ulster 658.2; Canmore, 'Dunsinane Hill', canmore.org.uk/event/698083; Canmore, 'Dunadd', canmore.org.uk/site/39564; Aitchison, 2006; Jones, Evans, Martínez Cortizas, Mighall and Noble, 2021, 897–914
9. Annals of Ulster 538.3; Woolf, 2006, 182–201
10. See, for example, Lowe 1999, 47
11. Note that until well into the nineteenth century the word 'architecture' conveyed Classicism and the correct disposition of the Classical orders
12. Brochs were a uniquely Scottish form of drystone, hollow-walled building style that flourished between 100 BC and AD 100.
13. Woolf, 2007, Part One, Chapters 1, 3 and 4, 41–176; Clancy and Crawford, 2001, 28–90
14. Watson and Dixon, 2018, 86–7. For the most up-to-date biography of the important reign of David I see Oram, 2020.
15. Stevenson, 1870, 393–8
16. Ditchburn and Macdonald, 2001, 97, 115
17. See Watson, 2022; Penman, 2014, 106, 124, 127, 130–3, 137–8, 210, 243, 260–1
18. Ditchburn and Macdonald, 2001, 97–101 and 114–118. Also Ditchburn, 2000
19. The chronicler Abbot Bower records that one-third of Scots died, though the impact of the disease may not have been evenly spread across the country (Bower, 1998, 230–1).
20. *RPS*, 1430/12; 1430/13
21. See for example Historic Environment Scotland, 'Visit a Place: Doune Castle', www.historicenvironment.scot/visit-a-place/places/doune-castle/history
22. Ditchburn and Macdonald, 2001, 116
23. See Broun, 2009, 49–82; *RPS*, 1369/3/5-7. Date accessed 22 December 2022.
24. Edington, 1998, 69–78; Lindsay, 1728, 146–7
25. It should be noted that Scottish kings made international marriages in the thirteenth century, so the intervening period of domestic unions might be seen as a sign of the insecurity certainly on the part of the Stewart dynasty, when it was new on the throne after 1371.
26. A staple port was one through which a ruler had stipulated that all his kingdom's overseas trade should be conducted. Ditchburn and Macdonald, 2001, 113, 117, 165, 174
27. See Brown, 2001, 182–5
28. Lynch, 1998, 208–12; 282, 458 n9
29. Brown, 2001, 188–93, 226–8; Lynch, 1998, 198–200. Robert Burns refers to the 'cutty stool' where those accused of immoral behaviour had to sit at church to encourage repentance, but his poem 'The Fornicator' deals explicitly with his own experience of it.
30. Lynch, 1998, 228–9; Brown, 2001, 195–9
31. Brown, 2001, 205–6, 234–6; Lynch, 1998, 237; Brown, 2004, Chapters 3 and 4
32. Smout, Macdonald and Watson, 2007, Chapters 6, 7 and 12
33. Brown, 2001, 241–253
34. Lee R A, Government and Politics in Scotland, 1661–1681, unpublished PhD thesis, University of Glasgow, 1995, theses.gla.ac.uk/74927
35. Brown, 2001, 205–8, 259–66; Lynch, 1998, Chapter 18; Pittock, 2003, 194–202
36. Pittock, 2003, 190–2, 204–6, 209–13; Lynch, 1998, 329–39. The term Jacobite comes from the Latin name for the exiled King James – Jacobus.
37. Devine, 1990
38. Devine, 2015; *The Herald*, 'Sir Tom Devine: Scotland's role in slavery must be acknowledged', 14 June 2020, www.heraldscotland.com/news/18516148.sir-tom-devine-scotlands-role-slavery-must-acknowledged
39. Watson and Dixon, 2018, 100–1; Devine, 2010
40. Watson and Dixon, 2018, 179, 139–42
41. Sinclair, 1793, 296–7
42. Watson and Dixon, 2018, 104, 106, 116–17, 101, 227, 70, 20, 57
43. Ibid, 190–1, 179–81
44. Lynch, 1998, 411

45 See, for example, Hunter, 2015, though the literature of the Highland clearances is copious.
46 Cameron, 1996
47 Morton and Morris, 2001, 363–9
48 Ibid, 357–60
49 W W Knox, 'A History of the Scottish People: Health in Scotland, 1840–1940', 4 (www.docsity.com/en/a-history-of-the-scottish-people-health-in-scotland-1840-1940-lecture-notes-united-kingdom-history-w-w-knox/41249)
50 Foster, 2001, 417–22
51 Ibid, 423
52 Ibid, 424–30; Lynch, 1998, 424–8, 433–7; The Churchill Project, Gordon J Barclay, 'Glasgow, 1919: "Churchill Rolled the Tanks"', 20 May 2019, winstonchurchill.hillsdale.edu/glasgow-tanks-george-square
53 Foster, 2001, 464–5; Watson and Dixon, 2018, 169–70; NHS Highland, Directorate of Public Health, 'Paper 1 of a population needs assessment for Skye and Lochalsh', April 2019, nhshighland.publichealth.scot.nhs.uk/wp-content/uploads/2019/08/SkyeAndLochalsh-PopulationAndDemography.pdf, 32
54 Watson and Dixon, 2018, 71–2, 166–7

Preface

1 MacInnes, Glendinning and Mackechnie, 1999, 120
2 Morris, 1978, 470
3 Wölfflin, 1950, 235

Chapter 1

1 Quoted in Robertson, 1990, 180. The words, unacknowledged by Mackintosh, are from Ruskin's *The Stones of Venice*, Vol 1, Chapter 21.
2 Wölfflin, 1950, 235
3 Glendinning and MacKechnie, 2004, 33
4 Dunbar, 1966; Glendinning, MacInnes and MacKechnie, 1996; MacInnes, Glendinning and MacKechnie, 1999; Glendinning and MacKechnie, 2004
5 Rowe, 1976, 59–87
6 Fenwick, 1974, 16
7 Glendinning, MacInnes and MacKechnie, 1996, xiii
8 Dunbar, 1966, 15
9 Quoted in Scott, 1993, 232
10 MacInnes in a note to the author.
11 Glendinning, MacInnes and MacKechnie, 1996, xiii
12 De Botton, 2007, 228
13 Ibid, 229
14 Robertson, 1995, 9
15 Quoted in Robertson, 1990, 49
16 Quoted in Watkin, 1977, 5n
17 Watkin, 1977, 5
18 Barth quoted in Heather, 2010, 25
19 Craig, 1996, 206
20 Ibid, 205
21 Pevsner, 1976, 15–25
22 Masson, 1852, quoted in Davie, 1982, 317
23 Lynch, 1972
24 Craig, 1996, 117
25 Quoted in Davie, 1982, 323
26 Dunbar, 1966, 16
27 Wölfflin, 1950, 235

Chapter 2

1 Pevsner, 1976, 15
2 Ibid, 15
3 To avoid any negative connotation the word might have (see OED), I have introduced the hyphen.
4 Oakshott in Ferguson, 2010, 8
5 The ambivalent meaning of 'forging', ie both 'shaping/creating' and 'counterfeiting', seems wholly appropriate.
6 The provenance is arguably as Irish as it is Scottish.
7 Herder in Berlin, 1980, 172
8 Jefferson in a letter to Charles MacPherson, Albemarle, Virginia, 25 February 1773, 'The Letters of Thomas Jefferson 1743–1826'; see American History: From Revolution to Reconstruction and Beyond, www.let.rug.nl/usa/presidents/thomas-jefferson/letters-of-thomas-jefferson, accessed 17 February 2021
9 Burns in a letter to Agnes McLehose, 18 March 1788
10 Scott in *Edinburgh Review*, 1805, quoted in Gaskill, 2004, 31
11 Saunders, 1894, 81
12 Quoted in Berlin, 1980, 163
13 MacQueen, 1971
14 Winckelmann quoted in Irwin, 1972
15 Rykwert, 1972
16 Quoted in Berlin, 1980, 172
17 See Rykwert, 1972, 82–8, for a discussion of Sir James Hall's thoughts on the origins of Gothic.
18 Fingal, Book 1, in MacQueen, 1971, 21
19 Croma in MacQueen, 1971, 547
20 Ibid, 547
21 Trevor-Roper, 2009, 107
22 Ritchie, 1989, 44
23 Coulath and Cuthona in MacQueen, 1971, 305
24 Carric-Thura in MacQueen, 1971
25 Carthon in MacQueen, 1971
26 Martin, 1999
27 Trevor-Roper, 2009, 123
28 Martin, 1999, 17
29 Ibid, 216
30 Ibid, 217
31 Ibid, 99
32 Calthon and Colmal in MacQueen, 1971, 473
33 Rykwert, 1972, 82
34 Martin, 1999, 64
35 Ibid, 164–5
36 Ibid, 17
37 Ibid, 18
38 Ibid, 217
39 Ritchie and Ritchie, 1991, 62
40 Ashmore, undated, 16
41 Ritchie and Ritchie, 1991, 32
42 Martin, 1999, 17
43 Ibid, 156
44 Ritchie, 1988, 17–19
45 Martin, 1999, 17
46 Ibid, 99

47 Ibid, 66
48 Ritchie, 1988, 44
49 Barrett, 1981, 212
50 Wacher, 1978, 140
51 Stukeley, 1720. See also Brown and Vasey, 1989
52 See Rykwert, 1972, 41–71
53 Wacher, 1978, 140
54 Ritchie, 1989, 44
55 Sharples, 2005
56 Cruden, 1986, 4
57 Glendinning and MacKechnie, 2004, 24
58 Bede quoted in ibid, 27

Chapter 3

1 Cruden, 1981, 17
2 Ibid, 63
3 Kildrummy's gateway has been described as 'of characteristic Edwardian style', modelled perhaps on harled. See Stell in Dakin, Glendinning and MacKechnie, 2011, 16
4 Cruden, 1981, 104
5 Stell in Dakin, Glendinning and MacKechnie, 2011, 21
6 An exception is the cylindrical fifteenth century Orchardton Tower, Kirkcudbrightshire.
7 Cruden, 1981, 105
8 Glendinning, MacInnes and MacKechnie, 1996, 2
9 Boece, 1527
10 See Campbell, 1995a
11 Cruden, 1986, 183
12 Campbell, 1995a, 302
13 Cruden, 1986, 183
14 Cant, 1976, 6
15 Glendinning and MacKechnie, 2004, 52
16 Campbell, 1995a, 1
17 Ibid, 3
18 McWilliam, 1978, 293
19 Fawcett in Gifford and Walker, 2002, 674
20 McKean, 2001, 56
21 Fawcett in Gifford and Walker, 2002, 680
22 MacInnes, Glendinning and MacKechnie, 1999, 21
23 Gifford, McWilliam and Walker, 1984, 143
24 MacKechnie in Dakin, Glendinning and MacKechnie, 2011, 53
25 Gifford, 1988, 215
26 Dunbar, 1966, 51
27 McKean, 2001, 168
28 Ibid, 15
29 Ibid, 9. See also Simpson, 1975, 3, for an early use of the term.
30 McKean, 2001, 3
31 Stell in Dakin, Glendinning and MacKechnie, 2011, 8
32 Pevsner, 1976, 145
33 Ibid, 47. See also, however, 143–4 where Pevsner suggests that in the case of Robert Adam 'no distinction can be made between Scottish and English qualities' – a contention with which some might disagree.
34 Ibid, 145
35 Simpson, 1975, 13
36 Glendinning, MacInnes and MacKechnie, 1996, 43
37 McKean, 1990, 6
38 McKean, 2001, 224
39 Ibid, 195

40 Ibid, 205
41 Pride, 1990, 8
42 West, 1967, 105
43 Glendinning and MacKechnie, 2004, 88
44 MacKechnie in Dakin, Glendinning and MacKechnie, 2011, 47
45 Ibid, 53
46 McKean, 2001, 264
47 Gifford, 1996, 223
48 West, 1967, 115
49 McKean, 2001, 247
50 Colvin, 1978, 219
51 Fleming, 1962, 331 (n)
52 See Wemyss, 2013, 117–32
53 Ibid, 123
54 Ibid, 121. Wemyss applies the phrase to Bruce's 'early clients', but it is equally valid in relation to Bruce himself.
55 MacKechnie, 2013, 13
56 Glendinning, MacInnes and MacKechnie, 1996, 96

Chapter 4

1 Colvin, 1978, 182
2 Campbell, 2007, 3
3 Macaulay, 1987, 55
4 Ibid, 21
5 Stewart, 1987, 23
6 Fleming, 1962, 35
7 Ibid, 36
8 Glendinning, MacInnes and MacKechnie, 1996, 104
9 Floors Castle was later (1837–47) heightened by W H Playfair and given its busy skyline of parapets, chimneys and ogee-capped square bartizans so reminiscent of George Heriot's Hospital.
10 Macaulay, 1987, 42
11 See Adam, 1980
12 See Di Mambro, 2012, 111–43
13 See Macaulay, 1987, 38 and Stewart, 1998, 25–8
14 See Wemyss, 2013, 128–9, for an argument which relates the Scottishness of Duff House to the desire of William Duff, 1st Earl of Fife and later Lord Braco, to proclaim in architectural terms his descent from the medieval earls of Fife. Wemyss suggests that it was 'this ambition that determined the distinctive corner turrets at Duff House'.
15 Macaulay, 1987, 76
16 Gow and Clifford, 1995, 35
17 Ibid, 36
18 Lindsay and Cosh, 1973, 26
19 Ibid, 43
20 Slated cones were added to the towers by Anthony Salvin in 1878.
21 Quoted in Sanderson, 1992, 29
22 Fleming, 1962, 65
23 Lindsay and Cosh, 1973, 40
24 Ibid, 37
25 Ibid, 35
26 Colvin, 1978, 560
27 Lindsay and Cosh, 1973, 38–41
28 Macaulay, 1975, 46
29 Ibid, 46
30 Ibid, 33

31 MacKechnie in Dakin, Glendinning and MacKechnie, 2011, 228
32 Murdoch and Sher in Devine and Mitchison, 1988, 129
33 Keay and Keay, 1994, 407
34 Sanderson, 1992, 17
35 McWilliam, 1978, 213–14
36 Lindsay and Cosh, 1973, 140
37 King, 1991, 1
38 Sanderson, 1992, 40
39 Quoted in Fleming, 1962, 135
40 Sanderson, 1992, 35
41 Quoted in Fleming, 1962, 152
42 Ibid, 165
43 Quoted in Scott, 1975, 228
44 Colvin, 1978, 47
45 Quoted in Fleming, 1962, 244
46 Scott, 'The Lay of the Last Minstrel', 1805
47 King, 1991, 14
48 Adam and Adam, 2006, 1
49 Kay, 1993, 32
50 Adam was responsible for the Castle Style design of Castle Upton, Co. Antrim, Northern Ireland (1783–8), 'the only notable facade in which Adam made no attempt at symmetry' (King, 1991, 223). A design was also prepared by the office for Wenvoe Castle, South Glamorgan, Wales; similar in style to Wedderburn Castle, it was built in 1776–7, but demolished in 1910.
51 Astley, 2000, 15
52 Irony upon irony, Adam had produced a proposal for a Castle Style mansion for Macpherson at Putney Heath!
53 Adam and Adam, 2006, 1
54 Glendinning and MacKechnie, 2004, 113
55 Quoted in Close and Riches, 2012, 247
56 Macaulay, 1987, 99
57 Ibid, 57
58 Close and Riches, 2012, 247

Chapter 5

1 For example, the Barony Church, Glasgow (1793–4) by James Adam, and the Bridewell Jail, Edinburgh (1791–4), Robert Adam's 'only secular building done in the castle style' (King, 1991, 56)
2 The inclusion of Allan Dreghorn (1706–64) may be challenged as the number of buildings of any type known to have been designed by him is very small. The design of Greenbank House, Clarkston, Renfrewshire, has, however, reasonably been attributed to him.
3 Wiebenson in Cohen, 1985, 83
4 Campbell, 2007, para 3 of introduction
5 Cruft, Dunbar and Fawcett, 2006, 58
6 Colvin, 1978, 338
7 Glendinning, MacInnes and MacKechnie, 1996, 157
8 At Pitfour House the so-called Temple of Theseus bath-house was built c1835. A hexastyle Doric temple, its 34 granite columns supported a timber entablature.
9 William Stark's Justiciary Court House in Glasgow (1809–14) was the first building in Scotland to have a portico of giant Doric columns and 'probably the second largest in Britain' (Gomme and Walker, 1968, 70).
10 Glendinning, MacInnes and MacKechnie, 1996, 189
11 *The Times*, 29 April 1817; see National Library of Scotland MS 638
12 Davie, 1982, 128
13 Le Corbusier, 1976, 203
14 *Scots Magazine*, February 1820, see National Library of Scotland MS 638
15 Ibid
16 Statement by sub-committee of the General Committee of Subscribers to the National Monument, 24 January 1822, National Library of Scotland MS 638
17 Ibid
18 Letter from W H Playfair to C R Cockerell, 30 June 1829; see National Library of Scotland MS 638
19 *Quarterly Review*, 26 (1822), 330
20 McWilliam, 1975, 79
21 It was the intention of James Craig, whose plan for Edinburgh's First New Town was implemented, to name the square at the west end of George Street St George's Square. It was, however, called Charlotte Square after Queen Charlotte.
22 Stevenson, 1889, 123
23 Shakespeare, *Macbeth*, act IV, sc. iii
24 Emmerson, 1985, 16
25 MacGibbon and Ross, Vol 2, 1977, 354–55
26 See Walker, 1996, 33–40
27 Emmerson, 1985, 17
28 Simpson and Simpson, 1973, 50
29 Ibid, 50
30 McKean, 1987b, 115
31 Glendinning, MacInnes and MacKechnie, 1996, 227
32 Quoted in Macaulay, 1975, 195
33 Ibid, 198
34 Gifford, 2007, 691
35 Dunbar, 1966, 127, gives 1792 as the date of construction. Recent research favours 1808–9 as a more likely date.
36 Quoted in Macaulay, 1975, 203
37 Like many of his contemporaries, Gillespie Graham was competent in a variety of architectural styles.
38 Cruft, Dunbar and Fawcett, 2006, 240
39 Pride, 1990, 91
40 Quoted in Macaulay, 1975, 236
41 Gifford, McWilliam and Walker, 1984, 170
42 By 1822 William Atkinson had built a new east wing replacing William Adam's work.
43 Britton would later write to Kemp praising Kemp's Gothic design for the Scott Monument: 'What pyramid, obelisk, Greek or Roman temple is comparable in adaptation to the florid cenotaph you have designed?' Burn, too, would compliment Kemp on his design's 'purity as a Gothic composition, and more particularly the constructive skill exhibited'. See Holmes and Stubbs, 1979, 8–9
44 Quoted in Walker in Gordon, 1985, 130
45 Ibid, 130
46 Colvin, 1978, 485
47 Quoted in Walker in Gordon, 1985, 131
48 Ibid, 133
49 Gifford, McWilliam and Walker, 1984, 316
50 Curl, 1999, 498

Chapter 6

1. Much of this chapter draws on Walker in Gordon, 1985, 125–59
2. Macaulay, 1975, 224
3. Ibid, 227
4. Buck and Garside, 2014, 44
5. Quoted in Cruft, Dunbar and Fawcett, 2006, 92
6. Quoted in Macaulay, 1975, 225–6
7. Glendinning, MacInnes and MacKechnie, 1996, 238
8. Cruft, Dunbar and Fawcett, 2006, 91
9. Rigney in Hendrix, 2008, 77
10. The word is used by MacInnes, Glendinning and MacKechnie, 1999, 87, but only in relation to Abbotsford's assemblage of miscellaneous historical artefacts and not in the context of architectural composition as is argued here.
11. See *Shorter Oxford English Dictionary*, Vol 1, 2002
12. Cruft in Stell, 2003, 58
13. Noble in Markus, 1982, 264–5
14. Macaulay, 1975, 227–8
15. Gow and MacKechnie in Dakin, Glendinning and MacKechnie, 2011, 91
16. Walker in Dakin, Glendinning and MacKechnie, 2011, 94
17. Glendinning, MacInnes and MacKechnie, 1996, 240
18. Maxwell, 1937, 202
19. Walker in Dakin, Glendinning and MacKechnie, 2011, 95
20. For example, Camperdown House, Dundee (1820–6)
21. Walker in Fiddes and Rowan, 1976, 28
22. The remains of Milton Lockhart were transported to Japan in 1987 where they were re-erected on the island of Hokkaido and renamed Lockheart Castle.
23. Walker in Dakin, Glendinning and MacKechnie, 2011, 95
24. Walker, 2000, 60
25. Slezer, 1814
26. Grose, 1797, i. See also MacInnes, 2014, 1–20
27. Ibid, xviii
28. Loudon, 1846, 885–890
29. Graham, Memo on Baronial Style to Grand Duke Constantine (SRO GD121/67/1/409). Information from Professor Charles McKean
30. Billings had been a pupil of John Britton, author of *Architectural Antiquities of Great Britain*, 1807–26
31. Burn, whose name had appeared as co-author with Billings when the work was first published, withdrew his capital in 1850.
32. Billings, 2008, Vol 1, 1
33. Ibid, 6
34. Walker in Gordon, 1985, 135
35. Fiddes and Rowan, 1976, 30
36. *Some Records of the Origin and Progress of the National Wallace Monument*, London, 1880 (for private circulation), 6
37. Rogers, 1860, 3
38. Ibid, 12
39. McWilliam, 1978, 61
40. Boswell, 1830, 129
41. Fergusson, 1867, Vol 2, 79
42. Ibid, 81
43. Kerr, 1864, 376
44. Ibid, 377
45. Ibid, 377
46. Stevenson, 1880, 377–8
47. Ibid, 377
48. For a discussion of Balmoral and some of the architectural experiences and influences of German Romanticism which Prince Albert brought to its realisation, see MacKechnie and Urban, 2015, 159–96. Confronting the question of how it was possible in nineteenth century Britain 'to absorb Scottish baronial with similar ease into a national discourse as English neo-Gothic or Tudor revival', MacKechnie and Urban argue that such 'a variety of regional styles could metonymically stand for England, Scotland or the whole of Britain, as long as they were convincingly tied to the glory of the state and monarch'. While this argument clearly holds good in relation to Balmoral Castle, it can hardly be extended to cover the style's ubiquitous incidence across a wide range of building types. Indeed, even if the absence of any overt, socio-political intention in the application of the Scottish Baronial style is conceded (and this could certainly be regarded as problematical), it may still be contended that, over time, however inadvertently, the style has a formally subversive, and thus progressive, impact on architectural design.
49. Glendinning and MacKechnie in Dakin, Glendinning and MacKechnie, 2011, xvii
50. Green in Dakin, Glendinning and MacKechnie, 2011, 255
51. Hay, 1957, 142
52. Fiddes and Rowan, 1976, 66
53. Glendinning, MacInnes and MacKechnie, 1996, 237
54. The Sheriff Court Houses (Scotland) Act, 1860; see Richards, 1860, 753–757
55. Gifford, 1992, 460
56. Gifford, 1996, 533
57. Walker, 1986, 129
58. Brogden, 1986, 8
59. McWilliam, 1975, 145
60. Quoted in Gifford, McWilliam and Walker, 1984, 367
61. *The Builder*, 27 March 1875, 274
62. *The Builder*, 25 January 1868, 57
63. Walker in Stell, 2003, 158
64. Walker in Stell, 2003, 644
65. *Report of a Committee of the Working Classes on the Present Overcrowding and Uncomfortable State of Their Dwelling Houses*, Edinburgh, 1860
66. Ruskin, 1907b, 61
67. Quoted in McWilliam, 1975, 195
68. Ibid, 196
69. *The Builder*, 7 August 1869, 623
70. Fiddes and Rowan, 1976, 101
71. Gifford, McWilliam and Walker, 1984, 499

Chapter 7

1. *Chambers's Edinburgh Journal*, Vol 18, 10 July 1852
2. MacGibbon and Ross, 1977, Vol 1, v
3. Dakin, Glendinning and MacKechnie, 2011, 130
4. MacGibbon and Ross, 1977, Vol 1, vii
5. Ibid, 61
6. Ibid, Vol 2, 4
7. See Chapter 6
8. Dakin, Glendinning and MacKechnie, 2011, 130
9. Quoted in Robertson, 1990, 49
10. See Chapter 8

11 McKinstry, 1991, 88
12 Gifford, McWilliam and Walker, 1984, 520
13 McKinstry, 1991, 150
14 Quoted in ibid, 129
15 Quoted in ibid, 129
16 Quoted in ibid, 142
17 Quoted in Gow, 1984, 543
18 Ibid, 551
19 Quoted in Glendinning, MacInnes and MacKechnie, 1996, 336
20 Anderson in Billings, 2008, Vol 1
21 Ruskin, 1907a, 59
22 Ruskin, 1907b, 88
23 Quoted in McKinstry, 1991, 131
24 Ruskin, 1907b, 88
25 Glendinning, MacInnes and MacKechnie, 1996, 334
26 McWilliam, 1978, 87
27 Dictionary of Scottish Architects 1840–1980, 'Arthur George Sydney Mitchell', www.scottisharchitects.org.uk, accessed 4 February 2021
28 McKinstry, 1991, 165
29 Shepherd, 2006, 148
30 Gifford, 2007, 404
31 Muthesius, 1987, 4
32 MacGibbon and Ross, 1977, Vol 2, 282–3
33 The original house of 1870, by David Bryce, was recast by Lorimer, 1894–8, following a fire.
34 Savage, 2005, 41
35 McKean, 2001, 168
36 Hussey, 1931, 65
37 Savage, 2005, 115
38 Hussey, 1931, 72
39 Ibid, 75
40 Gifford, 2007, 182
41 Savage, 2005, 116
42 Gifford, McWilliam and Walker, 1984, 109
43 Savage, 2005, 153
44 Summerson, 1953, 330
45 Lorimer's interiors are not discussed here.
46 Glendinning, MacInnes and MacKechnie, 1996, 338
47 See Muthesius, 1987, 62 and Savage, 1953, 6

Chapter 8

1 Walker in Dakin, Glendinning and MacKechnie, 2011, 93–142
2 Ibid, 93
3 Quoted in McKean, 1992, 24
4 See Chapter 6
5 Stamp, 1999, 4
6 Quoted in ibid, 58
7 See Chapter 6
8 Walker in Dakin, Glendinning and MacKechnie, 2011, 119
9 Hussey, 1931, v
10 For the full text of Mackintosh's 1891 lecture and commentary, see Walker in Robertson, 1990, 29–63.
11 Ibid, 49. Unless otherwise noted, subsequent quotations from Mackintosh are taken from his lecture text. Note that Mackintosh's idiosyncratic spelling and punctuation have been corrected in the quotations given.
12 See Crawford in Robertson, 1999, 12
13 Robertson, 1990, 18 and 24 n4
14 Ibid, 18. As Robertson notes, 'the catalogue of Mackintosh's largely unacknowledged sources is lengthy'. Ruskin, Fergusson and Lethaby were all plundered.
15 Quoted in Robertson, 1990, 31
16 Quoted in Robertson, 1990, 32
17 Quoted in Irwin, 1972, 51
18 Crook, 1987
19 Rowe, 1976, 59–87
20 Ibid, 62
21 Sullivan in Benton and Benton, 1975, 13
22 Rowe, 1976, 69
23 Bogatyrev quoted in Walker in Frew and Jones, 1991, 56
24 Hevesi in Vergo, 1975, 125
25 Macaulay, 2010, 20
26 Ibid, 135
27 Billcliffe, 2012, 20
28 Macleod, 1968, 50
29 Billcliffe, 2012, 39
30 Howarth, 1977, 81
31 Crawford, 1995, 36
32 Billcliffe, 2012, 90
33 Macleod,1983, 79
34 In fact, only the south-east service stair is a true turnpike; the other staircases are all straight flights returning at apsidal landings.
35 The principal rooms at Windyhill look west – or, to be more accurate, west-south-west. Howarth wrongly suggested the view was to the south, an error perpetuated by others.
36 Howarth, 1977, 101
37 Savage, 2005, 154
38 Quoted in Robertson, 1990, 52
39 Quoted in Furst, 1979, 25
40 Macaulay, 2010, 230
41 Howarth, 1977, 103
42 Macleod, 1983, 87
43 Howarth, 1977, 158
44 Pevsner, 1976, 145
45 Billcliffe, 2012, 70
46 Pevsner, 1960, 170
47 Macleod, 1983, 122
48 Macleod in Robertson, 1990, 214
49 Macleod, 1983, 26
50 Quoted in O'Donnell, 2003, 116
51 Ibid, 115
52 Gifford and Walker, 2002, 710
53 O'Donnell, 2003, 61

Chapter 9

1 Quoted in McKean, 1987a, 15
2 Glendinning, MacInnes and MacKechnie, 1996, 410
3 Scott-Moncrieff, 1938, 5
4 Maxwell, 1937, 9
5 Scott-Moncrieff, 1938, 5
6 Maxwell, 1937, 206
7 Built in 1755, the North Barracks Block was altered and upgraded by Robert Billings in 1863.
8 Gifford, McWilliam and Walker, 1984, 100
9 Glendinning, MacInnes and MacKechnie, 1996, 388

10 Quoted in Savage, 2005, 151
11 Glendinning, MacInnes and MacKechnie, 1996, 387
12 Much of the credit for these designs must go to Richard Gunn (1889–1933), who worked as Miller's chief assistant from 1918 until his death in 1933. As a young man, Gunn had worked in the United States and in Miller's office became 'a master of American commercial classicism' (Dictionary of Scottish Architects 1840–1980, 'Richard McLeod Morrison Gunn', www.scottisharchitects.org.uk, accessed 17 February 2021).
13 Glendinning, MacInnes and MacKechnie, 1996, 442
14 McKean, 1994, 99
15 McKean, 1992, 76
16 Edwards, 1995, 19
17 Ibid, 10
18 Tzonis and Lefaivre, 1988, 18
19 Le Corbusier, 1976, 202
20 Hitchcock and Johnson, 1966, 41
21 Ibid, 45
22 Ibid, 21
23 Quoted in McKean, 1987a, 32
24 Gropius, 1934, 679
25 Later published with the title *Pioneers of Modern Design*.
26 Pevsner, 1960
27 McKean, 1987a, 113
28 Information from Professor Charles McKean
29 *The Spectator*, 25 May 1933, 17
30 Ibid
31 Though not himself born in Scotland, Mansfield Forbes' forbears came from Aberdeenshire, an ancestry of which he was proud.
32 Carey, 2010, 52
33 Ibid, 60
34 Le Corbusier, 1976, 203
35 Dictionary of Scottish Architects 1840–1980, 'R Mervyn Noad', www.scottisharchitects.org.uk, accessed 17 February 2021
36 Gifford, 1992, 40
37 Howarth, 1977, Plates 37A and 37B
38 Quoted in Crampsey, 1988, 12
39 Ibid, 128
40 Kinchin and Kinchin, undated, 158
41 Ibid, 158
42 Edwards, 1995, 34
43 Kinchin and Kinchin, undated, 156
44 Reiach and Hurd, 1944, preface. Note that this publication has no page numbers. The quotations which follow without endnote references are from this publication unless otherwise stated.
45 Gospel of St Matthew, 13:57
46 Metzstein, 1990, 6

Chapter 10

1 Reiach and Hurd, 1944, unnumbered pages
2 Ibid, foreword
3 Chambers, 2004, 18
4 Glendinning and MacKechnie, 2004, 196
5 Glendinning, MacInnes and MacKechnie, 1996, 434
6 Glendinning and MacKechnie, 2004, 207
7 Later Robert Matthew Johnson-Marshall and Partners.
8 Young and Doak, 1971, nos 198 and 199
9 Glendinning, MacInnes and MacKechnie, 1996, 440
10 Ibid, 441
11 Dictionary of Scottish Architects 1840–1980, 'Robert Hogg Matthew', www.scottisharchitects.org.uk, accessed 16 February 2021
12 McKean, 1992, 37
13 McKean, 1990, 24
14 Ruskin, 1907b, 61
15 Ibid, 48
16 Ibid, 40
17 The Cockburn Association, www.cockburnassociation.org.uk, accessed 16 February 2021
18 Jencks, 1977, 13
19 Venturi, 1985, 16
20 Jencks, 1977, 9–37
21 The term appears to date from 1981: Tzonis, Lefaivre and Alofsin, 'Die Frage des Regionalismus' in Andritzky, Burckhardt and Hoffman, 1981
22 McKean, 1986, 13
23 Ricoeur, 1965, 27
24 Frampton quoted in Thakara, 1988, 56
25 Emmerson, 1986, 8–10
26 Ibid, 10
27 Emmerson, 1996, 83–96
28 Ibid, 90
29 Begg, unpublished text for *EAA Review*, 1987, 4
30 Ibid, 5
31 Glendinning, MacInnes and MacKechnie, 1996, 485
32 Begg, unpublished text for *EAA Review*, 1987, 7
33 Williamson, Riches and Higgs, 1990, 107
34 Miers, 2008, 192
35 Begg, 1995, 11
36 The prefix 'ambi' implies 'both, on both sides, both ways' (OED). Here the intention is to suggest a valid architecture can be strong (valent) both in its relationship to the past and its relevance to the present.
37 Begg in Dakin, Glendinning and MacKechnie, 2011, 307
38 Miers, 2008, 46–7
39 The Moshe Safdie Archive, McGill University Library, cac.mcgill.ca/moshesafdie/index.php, accessed 26 April
40 McKean, 1992, 65
41 McKean in Fladmark, 2000, 125–6
42 Ibid, 126 (see also 142, n10)
43 Ibid, 125
44 Ibid, 126 (see also 142, n13)
45 Ibid, 135
46 Gifford and Walker, 2002, 197
47 Walker, 2000, 3
48 Quoted in Sudjić in MacDonald, 2004, 9
49 Lewis, 2004, 12
50 Quoted in Sudjić in MacDonald, 2004, 9
51 Ascherson, 2004, 22
52 Ibid, 22
53 Quoted in Sudjić in MacDonald, 2004, 8
54 Quoted in *Sunday Herald*, 23 January 2005
55 MacInnes, Glendinning and MacKechnie, 1999, 9

Envoi

1. Cannadine, 2014, 260
2. Ibid, 263

Writings on Scottish Architecture

1. For an overview of publication dealing with Scottish architecture, see McKean, 2006, 89–114. For a bibliography covering the period 'from the renaissance to the present day', see Glendinning, MacInnes and MacKechnie, 1996, 535–42.
2. See *Scotland's Listed Buildings* booklet, Historic Scotland, 2000, *passim*
3. Cruden, 1981; Dakin, Glendinning and MacKechnie, 2011; McKean, 2001; Mackenzie, 1927
4. Cruden, 1986; Fawcett, 2011; Hay, 1957
5. Gow and Rowan, 1995; Macaulay, 1975, 1987; McKean, 2001
6. Maxwell, 1937
7. Gomme and Walker, 1968; Horsey, 1990; Worsdall, 1979; also Robinson, P, 1991, Aspects of a Scottish Flat Tradition, unpublished doctoral dissertation, University of Strathclyde
8. Young, 2011. Begun as a research unit in the Department of Architecture and Building Science in the University of Strathclyde, ASSIST spearheaded a programme of tenement rehabilitation and refurbishment. Now an independent architectural practice, their work continues to embrace conservation, sustainability and community engagement.
9. The Tenement House, 145 Buccleuch Street, Glasgow, was acquired by the National Trust for Scotland in 1982 and is open to the public. It is a museum 'time capsule' of home life in a city flat, the interior of which has remained largely unaltered since the last decade of the nineteenth century.
10. Glendinning and Watters, 1999
11. Horsey, 1990
12. Hume, 1976
13. Glendinning and Martins, 2008; Naismith, 1985
14. Stell, 2003
15. Brogden, 1996; Naismith, 1989; McWilliam, 1975
16. Brown, 2015; Buxbaum, 1989; Gow, 2007
17. Gow, 1992
18. Fawcett, 1994; Howard, 1995
19. Scott-Moncrieff, 1938
20. Brief mention is, however, made of Robert Lorimer who 'had a genuine sense of the values that inspired the native traditions' and of Charles Rennie Mackintosh 'who to our shame worked too little in Scotland, was essentially indebted to the vital, and never fully consummated, tradition of pre-1700 Scottish architecture'.
21. Dunbar, 1966, 15
22. Glendinning, MacInnes and MacKechnie, 1996, xiii
23. Glendinning and MacKechnie, 1999, cover
24. Ibid, 217
25. MacInnes, Glendinning and MacKechnie, 1999, 9
26. Ibid, 11

Bibliography

Introduction

Aitchison, N 2006
 Forteviot: A Pictish and Scottish Royal Centre, Stroud: Tempus

Annals of Ulster
 celt.ucc.ie

Armit, I 1998
 Scotland's Hidden History, Stroud: Tempus

Beale, D 1859
 The Student's Text-book of English and General History from BC 100 to the Present Day, London: Bell and Daldy

Bower, W 1998
 A History Book for Scots: Selections from Scotichronicon, ed Watt D E R, Edinburgh: John Donald

Broun, D 2009
 Attitudes of Gall to Gaedhil in Scotland before John of Fordun, in Broun, D and MacGregor, M D (eds), *Miorun Mòr Nan Gall, 'The Great Ill-Will of the Lowlander?' Lowland Perceptions of the Highlands, Medieval and Modern,* Glasgow: Centre for Scottish and Celtic Studies, University of Glasgow

Brown, K 2001
 Reformation to Union, 1560–1707, in Houston, R A and Knox, W W J (eds), *The New Penguin History of Scotland*, London: Penguin

Brown, K 2004
 Noble Society in Scotland: Wealth, Family and Culture from Reformation to Revolution, Edinburgh; Edinburgh University Press

Cameron, E 1996
 Land for the People? The British Government and the Scottish Highlands, c1880–1930, East Linton: Tuckwell Press

Clancy, T O and Crawford, B E 2001
 The Formation of the Scottish Kingdom, in Houston, R A and Knox, W W J (eds), *The New Penguin History of Scotland*, London: Penguin

Devine, T M 1990 (1975)
 The Tobacco Lords: A Study of the Tobacco Merchants of Glasgow and Their Trading Activities, c1740–90, Edinburgh: Edinburgh University Press

Devine, T M 2010
 Clearance and Improvement: Land, Power and People in Scotland, 1700–1900, Edinburgh: John Donald

Devine, T M (ed) 2015
 Recovering Scotland's Slavery Past: The Caribbean Connection, Edinburgh: Edinburgh University Press

Ditchburn, D 2000
 Scotland and Europe: The Medieval Kingdom and its Contacts with Christendom c1215–1545 Vol 1: Religion, Culture and Commerce East Linton: Tuckwell

Ditchburn, D and Macdonald, A J 2001
 Medieval Scotland, 1100–1560, in Houston, R A and Knox, W W J, (eds), *The New Penguin History of Scotland*, London: Penguin

Edington, C 1998
 Paragons and Patriots: National Identity and the Chivalric Ideal in Late-medieval Scotland, in Broun, D, Finlay, R and Lynch, M (eds), *Image and Identity*, Edinburgh: John Donald

Foster, J 2001
 The Twentieth Century 1914–1979, in Houston, R A and Knox, W W J (eds), *The New Penguin History of Scotland*, London: Penguin

Hunter, J 2015
 Set Adrift upon the World: The Sutherland Clearances, Edinburgh: Birlinn

Jones, S, Evans, N, Martínez Cortizas, A, Mighall, T and Noble, G 2021
 Settlement, Landscape and Land-use Change at a Pictish Elite Centre: Assessing the Palaeoecological Record for Economic Continuity and Social Change at Rhynie in N.E. Scotland, *The Holocene*, 31 (6), 897–914

Lindsay, R 1728
 History of Scotland, Edinburgh

Lowe, C 1999
 Angels, Fools and Tyrants, Edinburgh: Canongate with Historic Scotland

Lynch, M 1998 (1991)
 Scotland: A New History, London: Pimlico

Morton, G and Morris, R J 2001
 Civil society, governance and nation, 1832–1914, in Houston, R A and Knox, W W J, (eds), *The New Penguin History of Scotland*, London: Penguin

Oram, R 2020
 David I, King of Scots, 1124–1153, Edinburgh: John Donald

Penman, M 2014
 Robert the Bruce: King of Scots, New Haven, CT: Yale University Press

Pittock, M 2003
 A New History of Scotland, Stroud: Sutton

RPS
The Records of the Parliaments of Scotland to 1707, ed Brown, K M *et al,* St Andrews (2007–2017), rps.ac.uk

Sinclair, J 1793
Old Statistical Account, Vol 5 Edinburgh: William Creech

Smout, T C, Macdonald, A R and Watson, F 2007
A History of the Native Woodlands of Scotland, 1500–1920, Edinburgh: Edinburgh University Press

Stevenson, J 1870
Documents Illustrative of the History of Scotland 1286–1306, Vol 2, Edinburgh: H M Register House

Watson, F 2022 (1998)
Under the Hammer, Edinburgh, Birlinn

Watson, F and Dixon, P 2018
A History of Scotland's Landscapes, Edinburgh: Historic Environment Scotland

Woolf, A 2006
Dun Nechtain, Fortriu and the Geography of the Picts, *Scottish Historical Review* 85, 182–201

Woolf, A 2007
From Pictland to Alba 789–1070, Edinburgh: Edinburgh University Press

Mousa to Mackintosh – The Scottishness of Scottish Architecture

Adam, R and Adam, J 2006 (1788–1822)
The Works in Architecture of Robert and James Adam, New York: Dover

Adam, W 1980 (1812)
Vitruvius Scoticus, New York: Dover

Andritzky, M, Burckhardt, I and Hoffmann, O (eds) 1981
Für eine andere Architektur 1, Frankfurt am Main: Fischer Taschenbuch

Ascherson, N 2002
Stone Voices, London: Granta

Ascherson, N 2004
Shock and Awe, *The Herald Magazine,* 28 August 2004

Ashmore, P undated
Maes Howe, guide, Edinburgh: HMSO

Astley, S 2000
Robert Adam's Castles, exhibition catalogue, London: Soane Gallery

Barrett, J C 1981
Aspects of the Iron Age in Atlantic Scotland, *Proceedings of the Society of Antiquaries of Scotland* 111, 205–19

Baxter, N 2008
Glasgow Institute of Architects Review of 2007–8, Glasgow: RIAS

Beaton, E 1997
Scotland's Traditional Houses, Edinburgh: HMSO

Begg, I 1995
Towers in Scotland, *Prospect* 54, 11

Benton, T and C with Sharp, D 1975
Form and Function, London: Crosby Lockwood Staples / Open University

Berlin, I 1980 (1976)
Vico and Herder, London: Chatto and Windus

Beveridge, C and Turnbull, R 1989
The Eclipse of Scottish Culture, Edinburgh: Polygon

Beveridge, C and Turnbull, R 1997
Scotland after the Enlightenment, Edinburgh: Polygon

Billcliffe, R 2012
Visiting Charles Rennie Mackintosh, London: Frances Lincoln

Billings, R W 2008 (1845–52)
The Baronial and Ecclesiastical Antiquities of Scotland, Edinburgh: Birlinn

Boece, H 1527
Historia Gentis Scotorum, Paris

Bonnar, T 1892
Biographical Sketch of George Meikle Kemp, Edinburgh: Blackwood

Boswell, J 1830 (1791)
The Life of Samuel Johnson, LLD, London / New York: Sharpe / Jackson

Brogden, W A 1986
Aberdeen, Edinburgh: Scottish Academic Press

Brogden, W A (ed) 1996
The Neo-Classical Town, Edinburgh: Rutland Press

Brown, I G and Vasey, P G 1989
Arthur's O'on again: newly discovered drawings by John Adair, and their context, *Proceedings of the Society of Antiquaries of Scotland* 119, 353–60

Brown, H 1978
Early Travellers in Scotland, Edinburgh: James Thin

Brown, M 2015 (2012)
Scotland's Lost Gardens, Edinburgh: RCAHMS

Buck, M and Garside, P 2014
Early Planning at Abbotsford, 1811–12, *Architectural Heritage* 24, 41–65

Buckle, H T 1970
On Scotland and the Scotch Intellect, Chicago, IL / London: University of Chicago Press

Buxbaum, T 1989
Scottish Garden Buildings, Edinburgh: Mainstream

Campbell, C 2007 (1715–25)
Vitruvius Britannicus, New York: Dover

Campbell, I 1995a
A Romanesque Revival and the Early Renaissance in Scotland c1380–1573, *Journal of the Society of Architectural Historians* 54, 302–25

Campbell, I 1995b
Linlithgow's 'Princely Palace' and its influence in Europe, *Architectural Heritage* 5, 1–20

Cannadine, D 2014 (2013)
The Undivided Past, London: Penguin

Cant, R G 1976
The Building of St Machar's Cathedral, Aberdeen, occasional paper 4, Aberdeen: Friends of St Machar's

Carey, H 2010
Mansfield Forbes and his Cambridge, Cambridge: Cambridge University Press

Chambers, A 2004
Retrospective, *Prospect* 100, i–xv

Chambers, 1852
The Old Castles and Mansions of Scotland, *Chambers Edinburgh Journal* 18 (445)

Clark, R W 1981
Balmoral, Queen Victoria's Highland Home, London: Thames and Hudson

Close, R and Riches, A 2012
Ayrshire and Arran, New Haven, CT / London: Yale University Press

Close, R, Gifford, J and Walker, F A 2016
Lanarkshire and Renfrewshire, New Haven, CT / London: Yale University Press

Cohen, R (ed) 1985
Studies in Eighteenth Century British Art, Berkeley: University of California Press

Colvin, H 1978 (1954)
A Biographical Dictionary of British Architects 1600–1840, London: John Murray

Coupe, L 1997
Myth, London: Routledge

Craig, C 1996
Out of History, Edinburgh: Polygon

Craig, C 2011 (2003)
The Scots' Crisis of Confidence, Edinburgh: Polygon

Crampsey, B 1988
The Empire Exhibition of 1938, Edinburgh: Mainstream

Crawford, A 1995
Charles Rennie Mackintosh, London: Thames and Hudson

Crook, J M 1987
The Dilemma of Style, Chicago, IL: University of Chicago Press

Cruden, S 1986
Scottish Medieval Churches, Edinburgh: John Donald

Cruden, S 1981 (1960)
The Scottish Castle, Edinburgh: Spurbooks

Cruft, K, Dunbar, J and Fawcett, R 2006
Borders, New Haven, CT / London: Yale University Press

Curl, J S 1999
Dictionary of Architecture, Oxford: Oxford University Press

Dakin, A, Glendinning, M and MacKechnie, A (eds) 2011
Scotland's Castle Culture, Edinburgh: John Donald

Davie, G 1982 (1961)
The Democratic Intellect, Edinburgh: Edinburgh University Press

Davie, G 1986
The Crisis of the Democratic Intellect, Edinburgh: Polygon

Davis, M C 1996
Scots Baronial, Ardrishaig: Spindrift

Devine, T M 1999
The Scottish Nation, 1700–2000, London: Allen Lane / Penguin

Devine, T and Mitchison, R (eds) 1988
People and Society in Scotland, 1, Edinburgh: John Donald

De Botton, A 2007 (2006)
The Architecture of Happiness, London: Penguin

Di Mambro, R 2012
James Smith at Hamilton: a Study in Scottish Classicism, *Architectural History* 55, 111–143

Donaldson, G 1980 (1974)
Scotland: The Shaping of a Nation, Newton Abbot: David and Charles

Dunbar, J G 1966
The Historic Architecture of Scotland, London: Batsford

Edwards, B 1995
Basil Spence 1907–1976, Edinburgh: Rutland Press

Emmerson, R 1985
The Building of Fyvie Castle, *Treasures of Fyvie*, exhibition catalogue, Edinburgh: HMSO

Emmerson, R 1986
A Garden of Delights, *Prospect* 26, 8–10

Emmerson, R 1996
　The Emperor's New Clothes: Pastiche and Reproduction, *Architectural Heritage* 6, 83–96

Fawcett, R 1994
　Scottish Architecture from the Accession of the Stewarts to the Reformation, 1371–1560, Edinburgh: Edinburgh University Press

Fawcett, R 2011
　The Architecture of the Scottish Medieval Church, New Haven, CT / London: Yale University Press

Fenwick, H 1974
　Scotland's Historic Buildings, London: Hale

Fenwick, H 1986
　Scottish Baronial Houses, London: Hale

Ferguson, R 2010 (2009)
　The Hammer and the Cross, London: Penguin

Ferguson, W 1998
　The Identity of the Scottish Nation, Edinburgh: Edinburgh University Press

Fergusson, J 1867
　A History of Architecture in all Countries, Vol 2, London: John Murray

Fiddes, A and Rowan, A 1976
　David Bryce 1803–1876, exhibition catalogue, Edinburgh: Edinburgh University Press

Fladmark, J M (ed) 2000
　Heritage and Museums, Shaping National Heritage, Shaftesbury: Donhead

Fleming, J 1962
　Robert Adam and his Circle, London: John Murray

Frew, J and Jones, D (eds) 1991
　Scotland and Europe, St Andrews: University of St Andrews Press

Furst, L R 1979
　The Contours of European Romanticism, London: Macmillan

Gaskill, H (ed) 2004
　The Reception of Ossian in Europe, New York / London: Continuum

Gifford, J 1988
　Fife, Harmondsworth: Penguin

Gifford, J 1989
　William Adam 1689–1748, Edinburgh: Mainstream

Gifford, J 1992
　Highlands and Islands, Harmondsworth: Penguin

Gifford, J 1996
　Dumfries and Galloway, Harmondsworth: Penguin

Gifford, J 2007
　Perth and Kinross, New Haven, CT / London: Yale University Press

Gifford, J 2012
　Dundee and Angus, New Haven, CT / London: Yale University Press

Gifford, J and Walker, F A 2002
　Stirling and Central Scotland, New Haven, CT / London: Yale University Press

Gifford, J, McWilliam, C and Walker, D 1984
　Edinburgh, Harmondsworth: Penguin

Glendinning, M and MacKechnie, A 2004
　Scottish Architecture, London: Thames and Hudson

Glendinning, M and MacKechnie, A 2019
　Scotch Baronial, London: Bloomsbury Visual Arts

Glendinning, M and Martins, S W (eds) 2008
　Buildings of the Land, Edinburgh: RCAHMS

Glendinning, M, MacInnes, R and MacKechnie, A 1996
　A History of Scottish Architecture, Edinburgh: Edinburgh University Press

Glendinning, M and Watters, D (eds) 1999
　Home Builders, Edinburgh: RCAHMS

Gomme, A and Walker, D 1968
　Architecture of Glasgow, London: Lund Humphries

Gordon, G (ed) 1985
　Perspectives of the Scottish City, Aberdeen: Aberdeen University Press

Gow, I 1984
　Sir Rowand Anderson's National Art Survey of Scotland, *Architectural History* 27, 543–54

Gow, I 1992
　The Scottish Interior, Edinburgh: Edinburgh University Press

Gow, I 2007 (1997)
　Scottish Houses and Gardens, London: Aurum

Gow, I and Clifford, T 1995
　Duff House, exhibition catalogue, Edinburgh: National Galleries of Scotland

Gow, I and Rowan, A (eds) 1995
　Scottish Country Houses 1600–1914, Edinburgh: Edinburgh University Press

Grigor, M and Murphy, R 1993
　The Architect's Architect, London: Bellew

Gropius, W 1934
　The Formal and Technical Problems of Modern Architecture and Planning, *RIBA Journal* vol 14 issue 13

Grose, F 1797
　The Antiquities of Scotland 1 and 2, London: Hooper and Wigstead

Hay, G 1957
　The Architecture of Scottish Post-Reformation Churches 1560–1843, Oxford: Clarendon Press

Hay, G 1977
Architecture in Scotland, London: Oriel Press

Heather, P 2010 (2009)
Empires and Barbarians, London: Pan

Hendrix, H (ed) 2008
Writers' Houses and the Making of Them, New York: Abingdon

Herman, A 2003 (2001)
The Scottish Enlightenment, London: Fourth Estate

Hitchcock, H-R 1954
Early Victorian Architecture in Britain 1, New Haven, CT / London: Yale University Press

Hitchcock, H-R and Johnson, P 1966 (1932)
The International Style, New York: Norton

Holmes, N M McQ and Stubbs, I M 1979
The Scott Monument, A History and Architectural Guide, Edinburgh: City of Edinburgh Museums and Art Galleries

Horsey, M 1990
Tenements Towers, Edinburgh: RCAHMS

Howard, D 1995
Scottish Architecture from the Reformation to the Restoration, Edinburgh: Edinburgh University Press

Howarth, T 1977 (1952)
Charles Rennie Mackintosh and the Modern Movement, London: Routledge and Kegan Paul

Hume, J, 1976
The Industrial Archaeology of Scotland 1, London: Batsford

Hurd, R 1939
Scotland under Trust, London: Adam and Charles Black

Hussey, C 1931
The Work of Sir Robert Lorimer, London: Country Life

Irwin, D (ed) 1972
Winckelmann – Writings on Art, London: Phaidon

Jencks, C 1977
The Language of Post-Modern Architecture, London: Academy

Kay, W 1993
Robert Adam: Some Responses to a Scottish Background, *Architectural Heritage* 4, 23–38

Keay, J and Keay, J 1994
Collins Encyclopaedia of Scotland, London: HarperCollins

Kelsall, M R and Harris, S 1961
A Future for the Past, Edinburgh: Oliver and Boyd

Kerr, R 1864
The Gentleman's House, London: John Murray

Kinchin, P and Kinchin, J undated
Glasgow's Great Exhibitions, Wendlebury: White Cockade

King, D 1991
The Complete Works of Robert and James Adam, Oxford: Butterworth-Heinemann

Koch, J T (ed) 2006
Celtic Culture: A Historical Encyclopaedia, Santa Barbara, CA: ABC-CLIO

Le Corbusier 1976 (1927)
Towards a New Architecture, London: Architectural Press

Lewis, P 2004
Holyrood Landscape, *Prospect* 99, 12–13

Lindsay, I G 1947
Old Edinburgh, Edinburgh: Oliver and Boyd

Lindsay, I G 1948
Architecture in Scotland, exhibition catalogue, London / Edinburgh: Arts Council of Great Britain

Lindsay, I G 1960
The Scottish Parish Kirk, Edinburgh: Saint Andrew Press

Lindsay, I and Cosh, M 1973
Inveraray and the Dukes of Argyll, Edinburgh: Edinburgh University Press

Lindsay, M 1986
The Castles of Scotland, London: Constable

Loudon, J C 1846 (1833)
An Encyclopedia of Cottage, Farm and Villa Architecture and Furniture, London: Longman, Brown, Green and Longmans

Lugar, R, 1836 (1811)
Plans and Views of Buildings, Executed in England and Scotland, in the Castellated and Other Styles, London: Taylor

Lynch, K 1972 (1960)
The Image of the City, Cambridge, MA / London: MIT

Lynch, M 1998 (1991)
Scotland, A New History, London: Pimlico

Macaulay, J 1975
The Gothic Revival 1745–1845, Glasgow / London: Blackie

Macaulay, J 1987
The Classical Country House in Scotland 1600–1800, London: Faber and Faber

Macaulay, J, 2010
Charles Rennie Mackintosh, New York / London: Norton

McCrone, D, Morris, A and Kiely, R 1995
Scotland – the Brand, Edinburgh: Edinburgh University Press

MacDonald, S (ed) 2004
Architecture in Scotland 2002–2004, Glasgow: The Lighthouse

MacInnes, R, Glendinning, M and MacKechnie, A 1999
Building a Nation, The Story of Scotland's Architecture, Edinburgh: Canongate

MacInnes, R 2014
Robert Burns, Antiquarianism and Alloway Kirk, *Architectural Heritage* 24, 1–20

MacGibbon, D and Ross, R 1977 (1887–92)
The Castellated and Domestic Architecture of Scotland, Edinburgh: James Thin

McKean, C 1986
Local Roots and the Revival Cycle, Prospect 27, 12–13

McKean, C 1987a
The District of Moray, Edinburgh: Scottish Academic Press

McKean, C 1987b
The Scottish Thirties, Edinburgh: Scottish Academic Press

McKean, C 1990a
Banff and Buchan, Edinburgh: Rutland Press

McKean, C 1990b
The Scottishness of Scottish Architecture, *RIAS Jubilee Souvenir 1840–1990*, Edinburgh: RIAS

McKean, C 1992 (1982)
Edinburgh, Edinburgh: RIAS

McKean, C 1994 (1985)
Stirling and the Trossachs, Edinburgh: Rutland Press

McKean, C 2001
The Scottish Chateau, Stroud: Sutton

McKean, C 2006
From Castles to Calvinists: Scottish Architectural Publishing over the last 50 Years, *Architectural Heritage* 17, 89–114

MacKechnie, A 2013
Introduction: Sir William Bruce and Architecture in Early Modern Scotland, *Architectural Heritage* 23, 1–14

MacKechnie, A and Urban, F 2015
Balmoral Castle: National Architecture in a European Context, *Architectural History* 58, 159–96

Mackenzie, W M 1927
The Medieval Castle in Scotland, London: Methuen

McKinstry, S 1991
Rowand Anderson, The Premier Architect of Scotland, Edinburgh: Edinburgh University Press

Macleod, R 1983
Charles Rennie Mackintosh, Architect and Artist, London / Glasgow: Collins

MacQueen, J, [Macpherson, J] 1971
Poems of Ossian, Edinburgh: James Thin

McWilliam, C 1975
The Scottish Townscape, London: Collins

McWilliam, C 1978
Lothian, Harmondsworth: Penguin

Markus, T A 1982
Order in Space and Society, Edinburgh: Mainstream

Martin, M 1999 (1703)
A Description of the Western Isles of Scotland, Edinburgh: Birlinn

Maxwell, J S 1937
Shrines and Homes of Scotland, London: Maclehose

Metzstein, I 1990
After the Stone Age, The Royal Bank Playfair Lecture, *Prospect* 40, supplement, 6

Miers, M 2008
The Western Seaboard, Edinburgh: Rutland Press

Morris, J 1978
Farewell the Trumpets, London, Faber and Faber

Muthesius, H 1987 (1904–5)
The English House, Oxford: BSP

Naismith, R J 1985
Buildings of the Scottish Countryside, London: Gollancz

Nicoll, J B 1908
Domestic Architecture in Scotland, Aberdeen: Daily Journal

O'Donnell, R 2003
James Salmon 1873–1924, Edinburgh: Rutland Press

Petzsch, H 1971
Architecture in Scotland, Upper Saddle River, NJ: Prentice-Hall Press

Pevsner, N 1960 (1936)
Pioneers of Modern Design from William Morris to Walter Gropius, Harmondsworth: Penguin

Pevsner, N 1976 (1964)
The Englishness of English Art, Harmondsworth: Penguin

Phillipson, N T and Mitchison, R 1996 (1970)
Scotland in the Age of Improvement, Edinburgh: Edinburgh University Press

Pride, G 1990
The Kingdom of Fife, Edinburgh: RIAS

Pringle, D 1989
Linlithgow Palace, guide, Edinburgh: HMSO

Reed, P (ed) 1999
Glasgow, The Forming of a City, Edinburgh: Edinburgh University Press

Reiach, A and Hurd, R 1944 (1941)
Building Scotland, Edinburgh: Saltire Society

Richards, G K (ed) 1860
The Statutes of the United Kingdom of Great Britain and Ireland, London

Ricoeur, P 1965
History and Truth, Louisville, KY: Evanston

Ritchie, A 1989
Picts, Edinburgh: HMSO

Ritchie, G and Ritchie, A 1991
Scotland, Archaeology and Early History, Edinburgh: Edinburgh University Press

Ritchie, J N G 1988
Brochs of Scotland, Aylesbury: Shire

Robertson, G 1995
Raising a Challenge, *Prospect* 54, 9

Robertson, P (ed) 1990
Charles Rennie Mackintosh: The Architectural Papers, Wendlebury: White Cockade

Robertson, P (ed) 1999
Charles Rennie Mackintosh: Architectural Sketches, Glasgow: Hunterian Gallery

Rogers, C 1860
The National Wallace Monument … , Edinburgh: Menzies

Rowan, A 1985
Designs for Castles and Country Villas by Robert & James Adam, Oxford, Phaidon

Rowe, C 1976
The Mathematics of the Ideal Villa and Other Essays, Cambridge, MA / London: MIT

Ruskin, J 1907a (1837–8)
The Poetry of Architecture, London: Blackfriars

Ruskin, J 1907b (1847)
Lectures on Architecture and Painting, London: Blackfriars

Rykwert, J 1972
On Adam's House in Paradise, New York: MOMA

Rykwert, J and Rykwert, A 1985
The Brothers Adam, The Men and the Style, London: Collins

Sanderson, M H B 1992
Robert Adam and Scotland, Edinburgh: SRO

Saunders, B 1894
The Life and Letters of James Macpherson, London: Sonnenschein

Savage, P 2005 (1980)
Lorimer and the Edinburgh Craft Designers, London: Steve Savage

Scott, J 1975
Piranesi, London: Academy / St Martin's Press

Scott, P H (ed) 1993
Scotland: A Concise Cultural History, Edinburgh: Mainstream

Scott-Moncrieff, G (ed) 1938
The Stones of Scotland, London: Batsford

Sharples, J, Walker, D W and Woodworth, M 2015
Aberdeenshire: South and Aberdeen, New Haven, CT / London: Yale University Press

Sharples, N 2005
The End of a Round House, paper delivered at 'Circular Arguments, the Archaeology of Roundhouses' conference, Scottish Archaeological Forum, Glasgow

Shepherd, I 2006
Aberdeenshire: Donside and Strathbogie, Edinburgh: Rutland Press

Simpson, A and Simpson, J 1973
John Baxter, Architect, and the Patronage of the Fourth Duke of Gordon, *Bulletin of the Scottish Georgian Society* 2, 47–57

Simpson, W D 1965
The Ancient Stones of Scotland, London: Hale

Simpson, W D 1975
Craigievar Castle, guide, Edinburgh: National Trust for Scotland

Slezer, J 1814 (1693)
Theatrum Scotiae … , London: Leake

Stamp, G (ed) 1999
The Light of Truth and Beauty: The Lectures of Alexander 'Greek' Thomson, Glasgow: Alexander Thomson Society

Stell, G (ed) 2003
Scotland's Buildings, East Linton: Tuckwell

Stevenson, J J 1880
House Architecture 1 and 2, London: Macmillan

Stevenson, R L 1889
Edinburgh: Picturesque Notes, Edinburgh: Seeley

Stewart, M C H 1987
An Exiled Jacobite's Architectural Activities … , *Journal of the Architectural Heritage Society of Scotland* 14, 10–28

Stukeley, W 1720
An Account of a Roman Temple, and other Antiquities near Graham's Dike in Scotland, London

Summerson, J 1953
Architecture in Britain 1530–1830, Harmondsworth: Penguin

Thakara, J 1988
Design after Modernism, New York: Thames and Hudson

Trevor-Roper, H 2009 (2008)
The Invention of Scotland, New Haven, CT / London: Yale University Press

Tzonis, A and Lefaivre, L 1988 (1986)
Classical Architecture: The Poetics of Order, Cambridge, MA / London: MIT

Venturi, R 1985 (1966)
Complexity and Contradiction in Architecture, London: Architectural Press

Vergo, P 1975
Art in Vienna 1898–1918, London: Phaidon

Wacher, J 1978
Roman Britain, London: Book Club Association

Walker, D W and Woodworth, M 2015
Aberdeenshire: North and Moray, New Haven, CT / London: Yale University Press

Walker, F A 1986
The South Clyde Estuary, Edinburgh: Scottish Academic Press

Walker, F A 1996
Nobel Savage and Savage Noble, alt'ing. *The Scottish Journal of Architectural Research*, 1 (1) 33–40

Walker, F A 2000
Argyll and Bute, London: Penguin

Watkin, D 1977
Morality in Architecture, Oxford: Clarendon Press

Watkin, D 2001
Morality and Architecture Revisited, London: John Murray

Wemyss, C 2013
Image and Architecture: A Fresh Approach to Sir William Bruce and the Scottish Country House, *Architectural Heritage* 23, 117–132

West, T W 1967
A History of Architecture in Scotland, London: University of London Press

West, T W 1985
Discovering Scottish Architecture, Aylesbury: Shire

Williamson, E, Riches, A and Higgs, M 1990
Glasgow, London: Penguin

Wölfflin, H 1950 (1932)
The Principles of Art History, New York: Dover

Worsdall, F 1979
The Tenement – a Way of Life, Edinburgh: Chambers

Wrinch, A M 1971
George Kemp and the Scott Monument, *Country Life*, 5 August 1971

Young, A M and Doak, A (eds) 1971 (1965)
Glasgow at a Glance, Glasgow: Collins

Young, R 2011
ASSIST in Govan, *Architectural Heritage* 21, 93–108

Youngson, A J 1966
The Making of Classical Edinburgh, 1750–1840, Edinburgh: Edinburgh University Press

Journals

AHSS (The Magazine of the Architectural Heritage Society of Scotland)
ARCA
Architectural Heritage
Architectural History (Journal of the Society of Architectural Historians of Great Britain)
Building Design
Bulletin of the Scottish Georgian Society
Country Life
Journal – Charles Rennie Mackintosh Society
Journal of the Society of Architectural Historians (United States)
Newsletter – Charles Rennie Mackintosh Society
Proceedings of the Society of Antiquaries of Scotland
Prospect (Architecture and Design in Scotland)
RIAS Quarterly
RIBA Journal
The Builder
The Building Chronicle
The Scots Magazine
Urban Realm

Acknowledgements

I owe a personal debt of gratitude to Charles McKean whose wide-ranging and enthusiastic research into the architecture of Scotland long ago captured my allegiance and affection. His death robbed Scottish architecture of one of its most informed and articulate advocates.

Thanks are due too to Neil Baxter, then secretary and treasurer of the RIAS, who first believed in the viability of this book and completed some early editing.

I am more than grateful to Ranald MacInnes of Historic Environment Scotland who committed to publication and drove things forward. I thank him too for his patience when my own was ebbing. Gestation was sometimes slow – an experience many authors would no doubt share – but it proved sure. At HES I also benefited greatly from the skills and suggestions of Christine Wilson and Alasdair Burns. Christine's editorial care was precise, her critical comments always pertinent, polite and frequently most helpful. Alasdair's design of the book's format, his layout of text and illustrations, has contributed immensely to the project. I watched with awe his mastery of computer graphics. I am also grateful for the expert assistance of the HES Archives Team, especially Veronica Fraser, Mindy Lynch, Joe McAllister, Lynn Teggart, Kristina Watson, Kevin MacLean and Derek Smart, and their help with archive material, photography and scanning.

Thanks also to Mairi Sutherland for proofreading and Zoe Ross for the index.

Finally, of course, I want to acknowledge the impact and influence of all those architects, historians, enthusiasts and students who, throughout my life, have increased my knowledge and 'deep and filial affection' for the architecture of Scotland.

Index

Page numbers in *italics* refer to images.

abbeys 13, *48*, 49–50
Abbotsford (Roxburghshire) 125–9, 131, 138
Abercrombie, T G 198
Aberdeen:
    Grammar School 143, 145
    New Town House 141
    St Andrew's Chapel 117
    St Machar's Cathedral 54
    university 89
Acheson House (Edinburgh) 209
Achnacarry (Invernessshire) 114
Adam, James 90, 91, 117
Adam, John 87, 89, 90, 102
Adam, Robert 27, 83, 87, 89–94, 96–7, 99, 108–13
Adam, William 81, 82, 84–6, 87, 91, 111
administrative buildings 140–1, 145
agriculture 10, 12, 15, 16
Airthrey House (Stirlingshire) 93, 97
Alasdair, Alasdair Mac Mhaighstir 89
Alba 11
Albani, Cardinal 90
Allermuir (Colinton) 153–4, 157, 177
Alloa:
    Burgh School 145
    Courthouse 140
Alnwick Castle (England) 90
An Clachan (Glasgow) 212, *213*, 214
Anderson, Robert Rowand 153–7, 159–60, 173, 177
Anglo-Saxons 11, 13
Annan 141
Antique style 90–1
Antiquities of Athens (Stuart and Revett) 102
Antonine Wall 44–5
Ardkinglas (Argyll) 163, *164*, 167
Argyll, 3rd Duke of 86, 87, 88–9
Argyll's Lodging (Stirling) 68, *69*
Armadale Castle (Skye) 114
Armour, Cornelius 206
Art Deco 203, 205
Art Nouveau 178, 180, 189
Arthur's O'on (Stenhouse) 44
Arts and Crafts movement 160, 161, 178

Atkinson, William 114, 117, 126
Auchinleck House (Ayrshire) 84
Austria 178

Baberton House (Kilbaberton) 67–8, 70
Balbridie (Aberdeenshire) 34, 43
Balcarres (Fife) 163
Balcaskie (Fife) 70, 72–3
Balfour Paul, A F 133, 159
Ballikinrain (Stirlingshire) 134, *135*
Balloch Castle (Dunbartonshire) 114
Balmanno Castle (Perthshire) 166, *168*
Balmoral Castle (Aberdeenshire) 16, 138, *139*
banks 145
Barmore *see* Stonefield Castle (Argyll)
Baronial Revival style 62–5, *66*, 67, 108–9, 126–31, 132–4, 136–43, 145–8, 171
    and Lorimer 159–61, 163–7, 169
    and Mackintosh 173–5, 177–8
    and Rochead 172–3
Barony Church (Glasgow) 117
Barrie, J M 17
Batoni, Pompeo 90
Bauhaus movement 154–5
Baxter, John 101, 109–10
Beaux Arts 195
Begg, Ian 233, 235–8
Bellahouston Academy (Glasgow) 145
Benson and Forsyth 241–3
Billcliffe, Roger 180
Billings, Robert William 145, 171
    The Baronial and Ecclesiastical Antiquities of Scotland 133, 134, 136–7, 138, 140, 151, 152–3, 156
Black Death 12
Blackness Castle (Linlithgow) 91
Blair Adam (Kinross) 91
Blair Castle (Perthshire) 134
Blairdrummond (Stirlingshire) 82
Blenheim Palace (England) 86, 87
Blore, Edward 125–6
Bodley, G F 160

Boece, Hector: *Historia Gentis Scotorum* 53
Bothwell Castle (Lanarkshire) 12, 50, *51*
Bower, Walter: *Scotichonicon* 53
Boyne Palace (Banffshire) 60
Braco, Lord 84, 85, 86
Braemar Castle (Aberdeenshire) 91
Breadalbane, Earls of 111
Brechin 81–2
bricolage 126–7
Bridewell Prison (Edinburgh) *100*
bridges 12
Briglands (Kinross-shire) 163
Britton, John:
    Architectural Antiquities of Great Britain 116
    Cathedral Antiquities of England 118
brochs 34, 35, 38, *39*, 40–1
Brodie, Margaret 211
Brodie Castle (Moray) 128
Bronze Age 43
Broom Estate, Whitecraigs (Renfrewshire) *200*, 201
Broughton Place, Biggar (Peeblesshire) 201, 203
Brown and Wardrop 140
Browne, George Washington 157
Bruce, Sir William 72–5, 77, 79, 81, 82, 83
Bryce, David 130, 131, 133–4, 136, 139, 171
    and Edinburgh 148
    and Kinnaird Castle 141–2, *143*
    and Royal Infirmary 145
Buchan, John 17
Buchanan, Dugald 89
Buckie (Moray) 140
Bunton, Sam 205
Burgh Chambers (Galashiels) 198
burial cairns 34, 35, *37*, 38
Burlington, Lord 87, 91, 102
Burn, Robert 110
Burn, William 104, 117, 118, 133
    and styles 128–9, 130, 131
Burnet, J J 172, 197
Burnet, John 145, 171, 172
Burns, Robert 13–14, 32
    Poems Chiefly in the Scottish Dialect 89

Burns Monument (Ayr) 104, *105*
Bute, Marquess of 209, 219

Caerlaverock Castle (Dumfriesshire) 12, 50, *52*
Cairness House (Aberdeenshire) 102, *103*
cairns 34, 35, 36, *37*, 38
Calanais (Isle of Lewis) *35*, 36
Caldwell House (Renfrewshire) 93
Caledonian Railway (Glasgow) 153
Cally House (Kirkcudbrightshire) 102
Calton Hill (Edinburgh) 104, *106*, 107–8
Cambusnethan Priory (Lanarkshire) 114
Cameron, Charles 102
Cameron Barracks (Inverness) 145
Campbell, Colen 79, 87, 101–2, 113
Campbell, Dugal 86, 87
Campbell, John A 172
Canmore dynasty 49, 54
Cannandine, David: *The Undivided Past* 247–8
Canongate Flats (Edinburgh) 220, *221*, 224, *225*, 226
Cardonell, Adam de: *Picturesque Antiquities of*
    Scotland 132
Careston (Angus) 70
Carnwath (Lanarkshire) 139
Carr and Howard 197, 205
Carrick, James 206
Carron Ironworks (Falkirk) 145
Carstairs (Lanarkshire) 128
Castle Forbes (Aberdeenshire) 114
Castle Fraser (Aberdeenshire) 62, 64, 133–4
Castle Howard (England) 87
Castle Huntly (Aberdeenshire) 62, 64, 133–4, 141
Castle Style 92–4, 96–7, 99, 101, 108–13
Castle Sween (Argyll) 50
Castle Toward (Argyll) 114
Castle Upton (Co Antrim) 113
Castlemilk (Dumfriesshire) 134
Castlemilk Stables (Glasgow) 238
castles 11, 12, 34, 50, *51*–*2*, 53, 56–8
    and castellar style 86–94, *95*, 96–7, *98*, 99
    Kisimul 35
    Scots Baronial 62–5, *66*, 67

cathedrals 12, 13, 54, 116, 166
Catholicism 13, 14
caves 34
Ceolfrid, Abbot 45
Chambers, William 90, 102, 113
chapels 34, 46, 116–17
Charles I, King 14
Charles II, King 14
Charles Edward Stewart, Prince 88
Château de Marly (France) 81
Chessels Court (Edinburgh) 233
Chicago Tribune Tower competition 191, 193
Chiswick House (London) 87
Christianity 10–12, 13–14, 16, 45
Church of Scotland 16, 138–9
Church of St Nicholas (Dalkeith) 139
Church of the Holy Rude (Stirling) 54, 116
churches 116–18, 138–40
Cineád mac Alpin (Kenneth MacAlpin) 46
circular settlements 41, *42*, 43, 45
Civic Amenities Act (1967) 227
Claish (Callander) 34, 43
Clarty Hole *see* Abbotsford
classicism 101–2, 104, 107–13, 171–2, 195, 197–8
Clearances 15, 89
Clérisseau, Charles-Louis 90, 91
Clerk of Penicuik, Sir John 44, 75, 101
Cockburn, Henry 107
Cockburn Street (Edinburgh) 146, *147*
Cockerell, C R 107
Coia, Jack 211
Colinton (Edinburgh) 153–4, 159, 160–1
Collins Street (Glasgow) 230
Columba, St 45
Commercial Bank (Glasgow) *192*, *196*, 197
Commercial Street (Perth) 232
Constantine, Grand Duke 133
Copcutt, Geoffrey 228
Cordiner, Charles: *Antiquities and Scenery of the North of Scotland* 132
Corgarff Castle (Aberdeenshire) 91
Corn Exhange (Hawick) 145
Corrour Lodge (Loch Ossian) 237–8
Cottage Homes (Galashiels) 198, *199*
County Buildings, Paisley 114
County Jail, Jedburgh 114
courthouses 140–1
Cousin, David 132–3, 136, 145, 146
Craig, Cairns 27, 28

Craig, James 107
Craig Church (Angus) 117
Craigend Castle (Renfrewshire) 114, *124*, 134, *135*
Craigievar Castle (Aberdeenshire) 62, 64, *66*
Craigmailen Church (Bo'ness) 140
Craigston Castle (Aberdeenshire) 67
Cranhill Secondary (Glasgow) 218
crannogs 11
Crathes (Aberdeenshire) 62
Crawford Priory (Fife) 114, 116
Crichton, Richard 111, 117
Critical Regionalism 208, 228, 230, 232, 243
Crofting Act (1886) 16
Cromwell, Oliver 13, 14
crosses 34, 45
Crosshill & Govan (Glasgow) 141
Cruden, Stewart 53, 174
Crum Memorial Library (Thornliebank) 154
Culdees Castle (Perthshire) 114, *115*
Culzean Castle (Ayrshire) 93–4, 96–7, *98*, 99, 113
Cumbernauld 220, 221, 228, *229*, 232
Custom House, Greenock 128
Czechoslovakia 178

Daily Record offices (Glasgow) 186
Dal Riata 11, 45
Dalkeith House (Midlothian) 83
Dalmeny House (West Lothian) 128
Dalquharran House (Ayrshire) 93
David I, King 11
David II, King 53
Dawyck House (Peeblesshire) 129
Dick Place (Edinburgh) 206
Dirleton Castle (East Lothian) 50
Disruption of 1843 16, 138
Donaldson's Hospital (School) (Edinburgh) 142
Donibristle House (Fife) 82
Donn, Rob 89
Dornoch Courthouse (Sutherland) 140
Douglas, John 101, 111
Doune Castle (Stirlingshire) 53
Dreghorn, Allan 101
Drumlanrig Castle (Dumfriesshire) 73–4, 77, 88
Dualchas (Skye) 238
Duart Castle (Argyll and Bute) 91
Duddingston House (Edinburgh) 102, *103*
Dudok, Willem Marinus 197
Duff House (Aberdeenshire) 82, 83, 84–6
Dugald Stewart Monument (Edinburgh) 104

Dumbarton Castle 91
Dumfries Courthouse 140
Dumfries House 84, *85*, 90
Dun Beag (Skye) 40, *41*
Dun, Lord 81
Dun Telve (Glenelg) 38, *39*, 40–1
Dun Troddan (Glenelg) 38, *39*, 40
Dunadd (Argyll) 10
Dunbar, John 58
    The Historic Architecture of Scotland 28
Dunblane Cathedral 116, 166
Dunblane Courthouse 140
Dundee 143, 145, 146, 232, *233*
Dunderave (Argyll) 164, *165*
Dundurn (Strathearn) 10
Dunfermline 13, 49, 141
Dunkeld Cathedral 54
Dunninald (Angus) 114
duns 34, 35, 38, *39*, 40–1
Duns Castle (Berwickshire) 114, *115*
Dunstaffnage Castle (Argyll and Bute) 50
Dunvegan Castle (Skye) 50
Dutch East India Company 14
Dwarfie Stone (Hoy) 34

Earl's Palace, Birsay (Orkney) 58, 177
Earlshall (Fife) 161
East India Company 14
East Kilbride 220, 221, 228, *242*, 243
Eastbury Park (England) 87
Edinburgh 12–13, 14, 146–8, 171–2
    Bridewell Prison *100*
    Calton Hill 104, *106*, 107–8
    Canongate Flats 220, *221*, 224, *225*, 226
    Castle 53, 91
    churches 116, 117, 118
    George Heriot's Hospital 70, *71*
    Hermitage of Braid 110
    Holyrood Palace 58, *59*, 70, 73
    hospitals *144*, 145
    and Lorimer 166
    and Modernism 205, 206
    National Library of Scotland 197, 230, *231*
    National Museum of Scotland *18*, 19, 241–3
    National Portrait Gallery (Edinburgh) *150*, 153
    National War Memorial (Edinburgh) 166, 194–5
    Royal Mile 233, *234*, 235, *236–7*, 238, *240*, 241
    St Giles Cathedral 54, *55*
    schools 142–3, 145

    Scott Monument 118, 120, *121*, 122
    Scottish Parliament Building 243–5
    University 89, 157, 159
    Wrychtishousis 68
Edinburgh Daily Review (newspaper) 145
Edinburgh Evening Courant (newspaper) 145
Edinburgh Improvement Act (1867) 146
Edmonston Castle (Lanarkshire) 114
educational buildings 142–3, 145
Edward I, King 12, 50
Eglinton (Ayrshire) 110–11
Eileach an Naoimh (Firth of Lorne) 45, *46*
Elder and Cannon 238
Elgin (Moray) 141
Elgin, Lord 107
Elizabeth I, Queen 13, 14
Elliot, Archibald 111–12
Elliot, James 111–12, 117
Emmerson, Roger 230, 232–3
Empire Exhibition (Glasgow) 209, *210*, 211–12, *213*, 214
England 9, 10, 11, 12, 14, 27
    and castellar style 87–9
Enlightenment 89

Fairlie, Reginald 197, 209
Falkirk Courthouse 140
Falkland Palace (Fife) 58, 60, *176*
Farnell Church (Angus) 116
Faskally House (Perthshire) 129
Fawcett, Richard 57
Fergusson, J D 17
Fergusson, James: *A History of Architecture in all Countries* 136–7
Fergusson, Robert 89
Fettes College (Edinburgh) 142–3, 145
Fingal, An Ancient Epic Poem (Ossian) 32
Finland 178
First World War 17
Floors Castle (Roxburghshire) 82, *83*, 84
Fontana, Carlo 102
Forbes, Mansfield Duval 208
forecourts 82–3
Forfar Courthouse 140
Formakin (Renfrewshire) 164–6, 167, *246*, 247
Forsyth, Robert: *The Beauties of Scotland* 132
Fort Augustus (Highland) 91
Fort George (Invernessshire) 91
Fort William (Highland) 91

Forteviot (Perthshire) 10
Fortingall (Perthshire) 160
Fortriu kings 11
forts 34, 38; *see also* hill forts
Fothringham (Angus) 133
Frampton, Kenneth 228, 230
France 9, 12, 13, 81
Fraser, Malcolm 238
Functionalism 218
Fyvie Castle 60, 62, *63*, 64–5, 67, 70
    and Adam 108–9

George IV, King 16, 128
George Heriot's Hospital (Edinburgh) 70, *71*, 130
Germany 154–5
Gibbs, James 101–2, 113
Gibson, Richard 238
Gifford, John 140
Gillespie, John Gaff 189, 191
Gillespie Graham, James 114, 116, 117–18, 133
Glasgow 15, 17, 54, 146–7, 171–2, 173
    Barony Church 117
    Cathedral 116
    conservation areas 227
    Empire Exhibition 209, *210*, 211–12, *213*, 214
    high-rise flats 218, 221, 223–4, 228
    High Street 235, 236
    hospitals 145
    Mackintosh 178, 180, 186–8, 189
    Miller 195, 197
    Pearce Institute 154, *155*
    St Andrew's Chapel 116
    schools 145
    university 89
Glasgow Herald Building 178, *179*, 180
Glasgow School of Art *22*, 180, *181*, 187–8, 189
Glen, The (Peeblesshire) 133
Glenelg (Highland) 38, *39*, 40–1
Glenlyon (Perthshire) 160, *161*
Glenorchy Church (Argyll) 117
Glenrothes 220
Goethe, Johann Wolfgang von 32
Gombrich, E H 26
Gorbals (Glasgow) *216*, 221, *222*, 223–4, 228
Gordon, Alexander, 4th Duke of 109–10
Gordon, William 108–9
Gordon Castle (Fochabers) 109–10
Gosford (England) 91
Gothic Revival style 114, 116–18, 120, 122, 138–9

Gothic style 113–14
Gothick style 86, 87, 88, 89–90
Greek Revival style 102, 104, 107–8, 118
Greenock Courthouse 140–1
Grianan Building (Dundee) 232, *233*
Gribloch House (Kippen) *202*, 203
Griffith, Moses 40, 132
Gropius, Walter 154–5, 205, 224
    The New Architecture and the Bauhaus 204
Grose, Francis: *The Antiquities of Scotland* 132

Haddington Courthouse 140
Haddo House (Aberdeenshire) 82, 108
Hamilton, David 104, 114, 171
Hamilton, Thomas 104
Hamilton Palace (Lanarkshire) 15, 81, 83
Harbourlea (Anstruther) 232
Hardouin-Mansart, Jules 81
Hawick 141
Henry VIII, King 13
Herder, Johann Gottfried 32, 33
heritage movement 226–7, 228
Hermitage Academy (Helensburgh) 145
Hermitage of Braid (Edinburgh) 110
high-rise housing 218, 221, 223–4
Highlands 15–16
hill forts *8*, 10, 11
Hill House (Helensburgh) 182–3, *184*, 185
Hill, Oliver 208
Hitchcock, Henry-Russell: *The International Style* 204
Holyrood Palace (Holyroodhouse) (Edinburgh) 58, *59*, 70, 73
Honeyman, John 171, 180
Hope, Charles 90
Hopetoun House (West Lothian) *78*, *79*, *80*, 81, 82, 83, 84, 90
hospitals 145, 218, *219*
House for an Art Lover (Haus eines Kunstfreundes) 185–6, *187*
houses 34, 67–8, *69*, 70, *71*, *72*–5, *76*, 77
    and castellar style 86–94, *95*, 96–7, *98*, 99
    and estates 198, 201, 203
    and folk 178
    and Lorimer 160–1, 163–7, 169
    and Modernism 205–6
    and Palladian 79, 81–6
    and post-war 220–1
    prehistoric 43
    and tenements 146–7

see also high-rise housing
Howarth, Thomas 185, 188
Howwood Road (Johnstone) 205
Hoy 34
Hume, David 89
Hungary 178
Hurd, Robert 208, 209, 219, 227, 233, 237
   Building Scotland 214–15, 217
Hussey, Christopher 163, 169
Hutchesontown, Gorbals (Glasgow) 216, 221, *222*, 223–4
Hutton, George Henry: *Monasticon Scotiae* 132

I quattro libri dell'architettura (*The Four Books of Architecture*) (Palladio) 79
Inchdairnie (Perthshire) 133, 141
India Buildings (Edinburgh) 145
Infectious Diseases Hospital (Paisley) 206
infrastructure 15
Ingrams, Robert S 137
International Style 185–6, 193, 203–4, 211–12, 214–15
Inveraray Castle (Argyll) 15, 86–9
Inverness 145
Iona 45, 54, 209
Ireland 45
Iron Age 43
Irvine 232
Italy 79, 81, 90–1, 102

Jacobethan style 128, 129
Jacobite Rebellion 14–15, 89
James I, King 56
James III, King 13
James IV, King 56, 57, 58
James V, King 13, 53, 56, 57, 58
James VI and I, King 14
James VII and II, King 14
Jedburgh 49
Jefferson, Thomas 32
Jeffery, Francis 107
John Jamieson Close (Lerwick) 232
John of Fordun: *Chronica Gentis Scotorum* 53
Johnsburn (Balerno) 157
Johnson, Philip: *The International Style* 204
Johnston, Thomas 217
Jones, Inigo 102
Jurkovič, Dušan 178

Kedleston (England) 91
Kellie Castle (Fife) 159, 161
Kelso Abbey *48*, 49
Kemp, George Meikle 118, 120
Kenmore (Perthshire) 111
Kent, William 87, 91
Keppie Henderson & Partners 230
Kerr, Robert: *The Gentleman's House, or, How to Plan English Residences from the Parsonage to the Palace* 137–8
Kildrummy (Aberdeenshire) 12, 50
kingdoms 10–11, 13
King's College Chapel (Aberdeen) 54
Kininmonth, William 201, 203, 205
Kinnaird Castle (Angus) 141–2, 143
Kinross House 74–5, *76*, 77
Kirkcaldy Town House 197
Kirkwall 49
Kisimul Castle (Barra) 35, 50
Koula, Jan 178

Laigh Kirk 116
Laird, Michael 224
Lamb's House (Leith) 209
Lanark County Buildings (Hamilton) 218
Lane House, Dick Place (Edinburgh) *203*
Langlees (Biggar) 157
Langley, Batty: *Ancient Architecture, Restored, and Improved, by a Great variety of Grand and Usefull Designs, Entirely New in the Gothick Mode for the Ornamenting of Buildings and Gardens* 88
Lanrick (Perthshire) 110
Le Corbusier 126, 183, 186, 204, 221, 223
   Towards a New Architecture (*Vers une Architecture*) 208, 214
Lechner, Ödön 178
Leiper, William 172
Leith 145
Lessels, John 146
Lethaby, William 160
Lewis *35*, 36, 38
Lindsay, Ian G 204, 208–9, 214, 219, 220, 227
Linlithgow 54, 56–7, 70
Lion Chambers (Glasgow) 189, *190*, 191
Little Houses (Dunkeld) 220
Lloyd Wright, Frank 197
Lochleven Castle *76*, 77
Lockerbie 141
Lockhart, John Gibson 129

Lomond Shores (Balloch) 243
Loos, Adolf 186, 191
Lorimer, Robert Stodart 153, 159–61, 163–7, 169, 173
   and Formakin 247
   and National War Memorial 194–5
Lorraine, Claude 96
Loudon, John Claudius: *Encyclopaedia of Cottage, Farm and Villa Architecture* 132
Loudoun Hall (Ayrshire) 112, 238
Low Countries 9, 12, 13
Lugar, Robert 114, 117
Lulworth Castle (England) 88
Luther, Martin 13
Luton Park (England) 91

Macaulay, James 88, 128
MacColla, Alasdair 14
MacDiarmid, Hugh 74
Macdonald, Margaret 206
MacGibbon, David 145
   The Castellated and Domestic Architecture of Scotland 151, 152–3, 154, 174
McGrath, Raymond 208
McKean, Charles 20, 24, 61, 74, 228
   The Scottish Thirties 204, 205, 215
MacKechnie, Aonghus 77, 88
Mackintosh, Charles Rennie 17, 20, 23, 25, 153, 194
   and buildings 178, 180, 182–3, 185–9
   and emulation 230
   and lecture 173–5, 177–8
   and memorials 206, 208
   and Pevsner 205
   and schools 145
MacLaren, James 160, 177, 180
Macleod, Robert 182, 188
Macpherson, James 16, 38
   Fragments of Ancient Poetry, collected in the Highlands of Scotland, and translated from the Gaelic, or Erse Language 32, 33, 34–5, 89
MacRae, Ebenezer 201
McWilliam, Colin 56, 136, 141
Maeshowe (Orkney) *37*, 38
Maitland, James Steel 201
Malcolm III, King 49
Mansfield, William Atkinson, 3rd Earl of 113–14
Mar, John Erskine, Earl of 81–2
Marie de Guise 13

Mar's Wark (Stirling) 60, *61*
Martin, Martin: *A Description of the Western Isles of Scotland* 34, 35–6, 38
Mary, Queen of Scots 13, 14, 77
Matthew, Robert 221, 223–4
Matthews, James 143
Mauldslie Castle (South Lanarkshire) 93, 96
Mavisbank (Midlothian) 82
Maxwell, Sir James Stirling: *Shrines and Homes of Scotland* 194
Maybole Castle (Roxburghshire) 133, *175*
Mellerstain House (Berwickshire) *92*, 93, 96
Melrose Abbey 120
Melville Castle (Midlothian) 110
Mengs, Raphael 90
Merrylees, Andrew 230
Methven Castle (Perthshire) 70
Metzstein, Isi 215
Michelgrove (England) 88
Midmar (Aberdeenshire) 62
Miers, Mary 235, 238
Mies van der Rohe 227
Miller, James 195, 197
Milton Lockhart (Lanarkshire) 129, 130
Mingary Castle (Kilchoan) 50
Miralles, Enric 243–5
Modernism 203–6, 208, 209, 211
   and post-war 218, 220–1, 224, 227–8
monasteries 11–12, 45
Montrose, Marquis of 14
Monzie Castle (Perthshire) 110–11
Morgan Academy (Dundee) 143
Morris, Roger 86, 87, 88, 89, 111
Morris, William 156, 160, 205
Morrison's Academy (Crieff) 143
Moss Height Flats (Glasgow) 218
Mount Stuart (Bute) 153
Mousa Broch (Shetland) *18*, 19, 38
Mull 38
Municipal Buildings (Stirling) 191
Murphy, Richard 238, 241
Museum of Scotland *see* National Museum of Scotland
Muthesius, Hermann 160, 169
Mylne, Robert 102, 111

National Library of Scotland (Edinburgh) 197, 230, *231*
National Monument (Edinburgh) 104, *106*, 107–8

National Museum of Rural Life (East Kilbride) *242*, 243
National Museum of Scotland (Edinburgh) *18*, 19, 241–3
National Portrait Gallery (Edinburgh) *150*, 153
National Trust for Scotland 219, 226
National War Memorial (Edinburgh) 166, 194–5
Nechtan, King 45
Neil, Norman A G 209
Neolithic structures 33–6, *37*, 38
New Architecture 204–5, 209, 214–15
New Town House (Aberdeen) 141
New Towns 17, 220, 232
Nicoll Russell Studios 232
Noad, R Mervyn 204, 208
Normans 11
Norsemen 11

O'Donnell, Raymond 191
Olbrich, Josef 178
Old Parish Church (Montrose) 118
Orkney 13, 36, *37*, 38, 58
   Skara Brae 41, *42*, 43
Ossian 32–5, 94, 96
Ossian's Stone, Sma' Glen *30*, 33
Oxenfoord House (Midlothian) 93

Page and Park 238, 243
Paisley Abbey 166, 194
palaces 12, 54, 56–8, *59*, 60–2
Palladian style 79, 81–6, 101–2
Palladio, Andrea 79, 87
Panmure (Angus) 70, *72*
Parthenon (Greece) 104, 107
Paterson, Alexander 172–3
Paterson, John 110–11
Paton, Joseph Noel 134
Paxton Brown, Helen 17
Paxton House (Berwickshire) 102
Pearce Institute, Govan (Glasgow) 154, *155*
Peddie & Kinnear 140, 145. 146
Peebles 140
Pennant, Thomas: *A Tour in Scotland and Voyage to the Hebrides* 40, 132
Pentland Cottage (Colinton) 161, *162*
Peploe, Samuel 17
Pevsner, Nikolaus 20, 62–3
   The Englishness of English Art 31
   Pioneers of Modern Design 188, 205

Philipstoun 70
Picts 11, 45–6
Pier Arts Centre (Stromness) 238, *239*
Piranesi, Giovanni Battista 90, 91, 92
Pitcaple Castle (Aberdeenshire) 129
Pitkerro (Dundee) 163
Pitreavie (Fife) 68, *69*, 70
Playfair, James 102, 116
Playfair, William Henry 104, 107, 129–30, 131, 142
Poland 178
Pollokshaws Burgh Buildings (Glasgow) 154
Presbyterianism 13, 14
Prestongrange (East Lothian) 130
Protestantism 13–14
Pugin, Augustus Charles: *Specimens of Gothic Architecture* 117
Pugin, Augustus Welby Northmore 118

Queen Margaret College (Glasgow) 180

railway stations 145, 146
Ramsay, Alexander 114
Ramsay, Allan 90
Ravelston Gardens (Edinburgh) 205
Ravens' Craig (Plockton) 235–6
Reformation 13
Reiach, Alan 219, 227
   Building Scotland 214–15, 217, 237
Reid, Robert 104
Renaissance style 57–8, 60–2, 70
Renfrew 141
Rhind, David 140, 142
Rhynie (Aberdeenshire) 10
Riccarton House (Midlothian) 128
Rickman, Thomas: *An Attempt to discriminate the Styles of English Architecture from the Conquest to the Reformation* 117
Ricoeur, Paul 230
Ring of Brodgar (Orkney) 36
Ritchie, Anna 33–4
Ritchie, Graham 38
Robert Bruce, King 12
Rochead, John T 134, 145, 171, 172–3
Roman Empire 10, 43–5
Romanesque style 46, 49–50, 53–4
Romanticism 101
Ross, Thomas 145
   The Castellated and Domestic Architecture of Scotland 151, 152–3, 154, 174

Rossie (Angus) 111, 114, 116
Rothesay Castle (Bute) 50, *51*
Rothesay Pavilion (Bute) 206
Rowallan Castle (Ayrshire) 60, *62*, 163, 167
Rowe, Colin 175, 177
Royal Infirmary (Edinburgh) *144*, 145
Royal Mile (Edinburgh) 233, *234*, 235, 236–7, 238, *240*, 241
Ruperra (Wales) 88
Ruskin, John 156, 226
Russia 133
Rutherford, Roan 238
Rykwert, Joseph 45

Safdie, Moshe 237–8
Sailors' Home (Leith) 145
St Andrews 13, 49, 89
St Andrew's Chapel (Glasgow) 116, 117
St Andrew's House (Edinburgh) 197–8
St Bride's Church (East Kilbride) 228
St Cuthbert's Co-operative Store (Edinburgh) 206, *207*
St Finnan's Church (Invergarry) 209
St George's Episcopal Church 117
St Giles Cathedral (Edinburgh) 54, *55*
St John's Episcopal Church (Edinburgh) 117, *119*
St John's Kirk (Perth) 194
St Leonard's in the Fields (Perth) 140
St Machar's Cathedral (Abereen) 54
St Magnus Abbey (Kirkwall) 49
St Mary's Chapel (Edinburgh) 116
St Mary's, Haddington 54
St Michael's Cathedral (Linlithgow) 54
St Mungo Museum of Religious Life and Art (Glasgow) 235, 236
St Paul's Church (Edinburgh) 117
St Peter's College (Cardross) 228
Salmon, James 189, 191, 193
Saltire Society 219, 220, 224, 226, 227
Sandby, Paul 91
Savage, Peter 166
Scandic Crown Hotel (Edinburgh) *234*, 235, 236–7
Schiller, Friedrich 32
School of Applied Art (Edinburgh) 154
Scone Palace (Perthshire) 15, *112*, 113–14
Scotland Street School (Glasgow) 186–7, *188*
Scots Baronial style *see* Baronial Revival style
Scott, Sir Walter 16, 32, 107, 125–9, 138, 146
  Provincial Antiquities and Picturesque Scenery of Scotland 132

Scott Monument (Edinburgh) 118, 120, *121*, 122
Scott-Moncrieff, George 209
  The Stones of Scotland 193–4, 198
Scottish National Party 17
Scottish Parliament Building (Edinburgh) 243–5
Scottish Pavilions (Glasgow) 211–12
Scottish Veterans Garden Settlement (Callander) 198
Seacliff (East Lothian) 130, 133, 141
Second World War 17
Selkirk Courthouse 140, *141*
Sellars, James 172
Serlio, Sebastiano 65, 87
Seton House (East Lothian) 93, *95*, 96, 97
Shand, P Morton 204
Shaw, Richard Norman 160
Sheriff Court (Glasgow) 230
Sheriff Court Houses (Scotland) Act (1860) 140
Shetland 13
Simpson, Archibald 104, 114, 117
Sinclair, Colin 212
Sir William Fraser Homes (Colinton) 159
Skara Brae (Orkney) 41, *42*, 43
Skipness Castle (Argyll) 50
Skye 36, 38, 40, *41*
slave trade 15
Slezer, John: *Theatrum Scotiae* 131–2
Smith, James 73, 79, 81
Smith, John 138
Smith, William 138
Spence, Basil 201, 203, 205, 211, 214
  and post-war 219, 220, 221, 223–4, 226
standing stones 34, *35*, 36, 45
Stark, William 104, 125
Stenhouse (Edinburgh) 130, 209
Stevenson, J J: *House Architecture* 137
Stevenson, Robert Louis 108
Stewart's College (Edinburgh) 142
Stirling:
  Argyll's Lodging 68, *69*
  Castle 56–8, 91
  Church of the Holy Rude 54, 116
  courthouse 140
  Mar's Wark 60, *61*
  Municipal Buildings 191
  railway station 145
  Wallace Monument 134, 136, 137–8, 172
Stobo (Peeblesshire) 112
Stobs House (Roxburghshire) 93, 97

stone 9, 12, 24
stone circles 34, 35–6
Stonefield Castle (Argyll) 130, *131*
Stranraer Courthouse (Dumfriesshire) 140
Stuart dynasty 54, 56–8, 60
Study House and Market Cross (Culross) *170*
Stukeley, William 44
Summerson, John 204
Sydney Mitchell, Arthur George 157, 159, 177

Tain (Ross-shire) 13, 140
Tait, Thomas 197–8, 205, 206, 209, 211
Tantallon Castle (Berwickshire) 53
Tarbert (Argyll) 140
Taymouth Castle (Perthshire) 82, 111–12
Temora (Ossian) 32
temples 102, 104
Terry, Daniel 126
Thirlestane (Selkirkshire) 73, 77
Thistle Chapel (Edinburgh) 166
Thomson, Alexander 172
Tigh na Drochaide, Duisdale Beag (Skye) *239*
Tilliefour (Aberdeenshire) 160, 177
timber 9, 43
Tioram Castle (Lochaber) 50
tobacco trade 15
Tolbooth Church (Edinburgh) 118
Tolquhon (Aberdeenshire) 58, 159
Town and Country Planning (Scotland) Act (1945) 219
Tron Square Housing (Edinburgh) 238, *240*
Tudor Gothic style 128
Tullichewan Castle (Dunbartonshire) *113*, 114
Turnhouse Airport 224
Tweedbank (Galashiels) 232
Tyninghame (East Lothian) 129

Ugbrooke (England) 93, 96
University Medical School (Edinburgh) 153
urbanisation 16

Vale of Leven Hospital (Alexandria) 218, *219*
Vanbrugh, John 86–7, 88, 91–2
Venturi, Robert: *Complexity and Contradiction in Architecture* 227, 228
Victoria, Queen 16, 138
Victory Baths (Renfrew) 198
Vitruvius Britannicus (Campbell) *80*, 87, 102

Walker, David 128, 171
Wallace, William 134
Wallace Monument (Stirling) 134, 136, 137–8, 172
Wardrop, Hew M 160, 177
Warrender Park Road (Edinburgh) *148*
Weekes, Joseph 201
Well Court, Dean Village (Edinburgh) 157, *158*, 177
Wemyss, Charles 75
Western Infirmary (Glasgow) 145
Whitehaven (England) 93
Whithorn (Dumfriesshire) 13
Whitton Palace (England) 88
Wilkins, William 128
William III and II, King 14
Wilson, Charles 171
Winckelmann, J J 174
Windyhill (Kilmacolm) 182–3, 185
Winton House (East Lothian) 68
Witkiewicz, Stanisław 178
Wölfflin, Henrich 28–9
Wollaton Hall (England) 88
Womersley, Peter 228
Wood, Robert 90
wool trade 12
Works in Architecture of Robert and James Adam, The (Adam) 94
Works of Ossian, The (Ossian) 32
Wren, Christopher 102
Wrychtishousis (Edinburgh) 68
Wyatt, James 126

Yester House (East Lothian) 83, 89